DEVELOPMENTAL
DISABILITIES

DEVELOPMENTAL DISABILITIES

Etiologies, Manifestations, Diagnoses, and Treatments

ROBERT J. THOMPSON, JR.
DUKE UNIVERSITY MEDICAL CENTER

AGLAIA N. O'QUINN
DUKE UNIVERSITY MEDICAL CENTER

New York / Oxford
OXFORD UNIVERSITY PRESS
1979

Copyright © 1979 by Oxford University Press, Inc.

Library of Congress Cataloging in Publication Data

Thompson, Robert Joseph, 1945–
Developmental disabilities: Etiologies, manifestations, diagnoses, and treatments.

Includes bibliographical references and index.
1.   Child development deviations.
2.   Developmentally disabled children.
I.   O'Quinn, Aglaia N., joint author.   II.   Title.
RJ135.T48   618.9′2   78-5515
ISBN 0-19-502421-4
ISBN 0-19-502422-2 pbk.

Printed in the United States of America

To
Shirley and Christopher
and Will

Preface

Our goal in this book is threefold: to examine in detail the concept of developmental disabilities; to summarize the etiologies and manifestations of recognized developmental disabilities; and to understand the management issues they present and the interdisciplinary approaches they permit. Throughout, we include case materials to portray more fully developmental disabilities and their assessment and handling through an interdisciplinary approach.

The first chapter, which deals with the evolution of the concept of developmental disabilities, focuses on the interaction of professional and lay input through the legislative process, not only in the initial formulation of this concept but also in its continual redefinition and expansion. A schema for conceptualizing developmental disabilities—their various causes and multiple manifestations—is presented.

The next six chapters present facts—current, general, and significant—about the etiology and manifestation of the following specific developmental disabilities: mental subnormality, autism, cerebral palsy, seizure disorders (epilepsy), disorders associated with cerebral dysfunction (including minimal brain dysfunction and dyslexia), and sensory disorders. We make no attempt to study each disability exhaustively but rather to provide serious learners with current knowledge of each disability and with a schema for perusing more detailed specialized knowledge if they so wish.

The final chapter examines issues involved in managing developmental disabilities and shows how these have led to the development of an interdisciplinary approach to screening, intervention, diagnosis, and treatment.

We express our grateful appreciation to Dr. Samuel Katz and Dr. Keith Brodie for their support and encouragement and for establishing a stimulating atmosphere in which our endeavors could come to fruition. We also wish to acknowledge the invaluable support by the Developmental Disabilities Branch of the North Carolina Department of Human Resources. We are indebted to Louise Johnson for her patience and attention to detail in the preparation of the manuscript and to Marcus Boggs and Martin Stanford for their editorial assistance. Finally, we would like to express our appreciation to our teachers, students, and patients and their families from whom we have learned much and to our colleagues at the Duke Developmental Evaluation Center for their support and for the opportunity to learn from them.

Durham, N.C.   Robert J. Thompson, Jr.
March 1979   Aglaia N. O'Quinn

Contents

    History   156
    Types of Epilepsy   160
    Transient Forms of Epilepsy   162
    Primarily Generalized Epilepsy   166
    Secondarily Generalized Epilepsy   170
    Partial Seizures with Elementary Symptomatology   172
    Partial Seizures with Complex Symptomatology   174
    General Considerations: Manifestations and Treatment   178

6. DISORDERS ASSOCIATED
    WITH CEREBRAL DYSFUNCTION   195

    Minimal Brain Dysfunction and Hyperactive Child Syndrome   195
    Neurologically Based Learning Disabilities   222
    Dyslexia   227
    Concluding Remarks   236

7. SENSORY DISORDERS   244
    Definition   245
    Incidence   247
    Etiology   248
    Manifestations   252

8. INTERDISCIPLINARY DIAGNOSTIC
    AND TREATMENT APPROACHES   266

    The Multidisciplinary versus the Interdisciplinary
    Approach in Principle   268
    The Interdisciplinary Approach in Practice   273
    Conclusion   300

DEVELOPMENTAL DISABILITIES

1

Evolution of the Concept
of Developmental Disabilities

PRESIDENT'S PANEL ON MENTAL RETARDATION

The starting point for the evolution of the concept of developmental disabilities can reasonably be considered to be the appointment of the President's Panel on Mental Retardation by John F. Kennedy on October 17, 1961. The panel consisted of 28 outstanding physicians, lawyers, psychologists, social scientists, and educators. In pursuit of its mandate to prepare a national plan to combat mental retardation, the panel was charged to make a broad study of mental retardation and to explore treatment and prevention methods.

The panel was specifically requested (Hormuth, 1963) to make recommendations with regard to:

1. The personnel necessary to develop and apply the new knowledge.
2. The major areas of concern that offer the most hope.
3. The present programs of treatment, education, and rehabilitation.
4. The relationships between the federal government, the states, and private resources in efforts to eliminate mental retardation.

To accomplish its mandate, the panel used (Mayo, 1963) four main methods of study and inquiry:

1. Task forces were established for specific subjects.
2. Seven major cities were chosen as sites for public hearings at which public officials, teachers, professionals, parents, and others reported on the effec-

3

tiveness of local and state programs and made recommendations for improving them.

3. Investigators were sent to England, Sweden, Denmark, Holland, and the Soviet Union to study methods of care and education of the retarded and to become acquainted with current research in those countries.
4. Published findings were reviewed on mental retardation and on selective facilities and programs devoted to care of the mentally retarded.

One year later on October 16, 1962, the panel presented its report to President Kennedy. It reflected what was then known about the etiology of mental retardation as well as views then current regarding services and training. Mental retardation was presented as a major national health, social, and economic problem, and 90 recommendations were made. The number of children affected was estimated at 5.4 million and the annual cost of care at $550 million, plus several billions of dollars lost in national economic output. The proposed program of action was based on the panel's well-documented conclusion that "mental retardation is a complex phenomenon stemming from multiple causes (many of which are known and can be prevented or the results treated). However, in the majority of cases a specific cause cannot be identified yet." The report pointed out the

remarkably heavy correlation between the incidence of mental retardation, particularly in its milder manifestations, and the adverse social, economic, and cultural status of groups of our population. This is especially true for low income groups where the mother and the children receive inadequate medical care, where family breakdown is common, and where individuals lack opportunity and adequate education. . . . therefore, the panel has concluded that "to be successful in preventing mental retardation on a large scale, a broad attack on the fundamental adverse conditions will be necessary." (Hormuth, 1963, p. 29).

The panel's recommendations were grouped under eight categories: research, prevention, clinical and social services, education and training, residential care, law, organization of services, and public awareness. For a detailed presentation of the recommendations, the interested reader is directed to a concise review by Hormuth (1963).

Central to the panel's recommendations are several concepts and findings. First, throughout the report, the panel emphasized prevention and the need for sustained and mutual stimulation of mother and child. The panel concluded that mentally retarded infants can be cared for at home, provided mothers are given skilled advice and encouragement. In fact, the panel's report rests "on a strong conviction that the mentally retarded person should be served with as little dislocation from his normal environment as is consistent with the special character of his needs and that these needs should be met as close to his home as possible and in such a way as to maintain his relationship with his family and peers" (*Report of the Task Force on Coordination*, August 1963).

Second, the panel anticipated the eventual evolution of the concept of developmental disabilities. It called for additional federal funding of the crippled children's program so that children who are physically handicapped and also mentally retarded can be served more fully.

Third, the panel endorsed what is perhaps its most critical finding and concept in developing services for the mentally retarded: the concept of the "continuum of care." This concept stresses "the selection, blending, and use, in proper sequence and relationship, of the medical, educational, and social services required by a retarded person to minimize his disability at every point in his life span" (Hormuth, 1963, p.30).

Fourth, because effective care is a continuum, the panel asserted that the problems of the mentally retarded cannot be the sole domain or responsibility of any one discipline or agency. A coordinated approach is thus required. The panel recommended not only that federal grants be made to states for comprehensive planning but also that priority for grants be given to joint endeavors coordinating research, training, and service programs. In addition, programs for interdisciplinary training were specifically recommended. Because of the focus on a continuum of care and on interdisciplinary and multiagency approaches, a premium was placed on careful planning and coordination of diagnostic and therapeutic services (Hormuth, 1963, p.30).

Fifth, the panel urged that a national campaign to combat mental retardation be staged largely at the state level. It was pointed out that the states provide two basic types of services to the mentally retarded— residential institutions and special education through the public schools. However, these services provided for less than 10% of the mentally handicapped. To minimize the dependency and disability of all the mentally handicapped, the panel favored setting up—and maintaining for decades to come—"comprehensive and diversified programs of community-based services accessible to the retarded and their families according to need." As examples of the services needed, the panel singled out "diagnostic clinics;

nursery classes for preschoolers; parent education and guidance for groups and individuals; suitable recreation for all ages; vocational training and experience, job placement and follow-up; half-way houses or group homes and short-stay provisions; special medical and dental services; legal aid and protection, to name only a few" (*Report . . . Task Force*, 1963, p.2).

Finally, the panel addressed directly the need for additional interaction and coordination between universities and state service agencies. While acknowledging the fundamental differences in the objectives and functions of these institutions, it stressed the interdependence of service, training, and research in the area of mental retardation. It perceived the states as responsible for including training and research in their missions of ongoing service. "Services cannot exist without a steady influx of trained personnel and new knowledge. Nor can professional training and research flourish in isolation from service. Coordination of these three activities must be given high priority in State Planning" (*Report . . . Task Force*, 1963, p.24). The panel recommended that academic and service agencies cooperate in supporting university-sponsored training and research as a means of furthering the primary commitment of agencies to direct services.

PRESIDENTIAL LEADERSHIP

On October 16, 1962, the panel presented its report, *A Proposed Program for National Action to Combat Mental Retardation*, to President Kennedy. Shortly thereafter, the U.S. Department of Health, Education and Welfare analyzed the report to ascertain which recommendations involving the federal government could be carried out under existing authority, which would require new authority, and what actions would be necessary to implement these recommendations.

It is often alleged that a politically expedient way of managing a problem is to create, with considerable fanfare, a panel or committee and have it report a year or so later when interest in the problem has cooled. Then, the panel or committee's report is quietly accepted and placed on a shelf alongside other erudite endeavors of the past. There, with the others, it collects dust and endures benign neglect.

Such was not the fate of the panel's report on mental retardation. President Kennedy had experienced at firsthand in his family the mental retardation of a sister and felt keenly about improving care for the mentally retarded and mentally ill. The degree of President Kennedy's commitment and his exercise of national leadership was stimulating. His spokesmanship for programs to combat mental retardation and mental illness is most eloquently reflected in his message accompanying the proposed legislation he based on the panel's report and sent to Congress. Because his message demonstrates the capacity of a president to lead and act, because it is unusually insightful and sensitive, and because it is moving, we shall quote it at length.

SPECIAL MESSAGE TO THE CONGRESS ON MENTAL ILLNESS AND
MENTAL RETARDATION. FEBRUARY 5, 1963

To the Congress of the United States:

It is my intention to send shortly to the Congress a message pertaining to this Nation's most urgent needs in the area of health improvement. But two health problems—because they are of such critical size and tragic impact, and because their suceptibility to public action is so much greater than the attention they have received—are deserving of a wholly new national approach and a separate message to the Congress. These twin problems are mental illness and mental retardation.

From the earliest days of the Public Health Service to the latest research of the National Institute of Health, the Federal Government has recognized its responsibilities to assist, stimulate and channel public energies in attacking health problems. Infectious epidemics are now largely under control. Most of the major diseases of the body are beginning to give ground in man's increasing struggle to find their cause and cure. But the public understanding, treatment, and prevention of mental disabilities have not made comparable progress since the earliest days of modern history.

Yet mental illness and mental retardation are among our most critical health problems. They occur more frequently, effect more people, require more prolonged treatment, cause more suffering by the families of the afflicted, waste more of our human resources, and constitute more financial drain upon both the public treasury and the personal finances of the individual families than any other single condition.

There are now about 800,000 such patients in this Nation's institutions—600,000 for mental illness and over 200,000 for mental retardation. Every year nearly 1,500,000 people receive treatment in institutions for the mentally ill and mentally retarded. Most of them are confined and compressed within an antiquated, vastly overcrowded, chain of custodial State institutions. The average amount expended on their care is only $4 a day—too little to do much good for the individual, but too much if measured in terms of efficient use of our mental health dollars. In some States the average is less than $2 a day.

The total cost to the taxpayers is over $2.4 billion a year in direct public outlays for services—about $1.8 billion for mental illness and $600 million for mental retardation. Indirect public outlays—in welfare costs and in the waste of human resources—are even higher. But the anguish suffered both by those afflicted and by their families transcends financial statistics—particularly in view of the fact that both mental illness and mental retardation strike so often in childhood, leading in most cases to a lifetime of disablement for the patient and a lifetime of hardship for his family.

This situation has been tolerated far too long. It has troubled our national conscience—but only as a problem unpleasant to mention, easy to postpone, and despairing of solution. The Federal Government despite the nation-wide impact of the problem, has largely left the solutions up to the States. The States have depended on custodial hospitals and homes. Many such hospitals and homes have been shamefully understaffed, overcrowded, unpleasant institutions from which death too often provided the only firm hope of release.

The time has come for a bold new approach. New medical, scientific, and social tools and insights are now available. A series of comprehensive studies initiated by the Congress, the Executive Branch, and interested private groups have been completed and all point in the same direction.

Governments at every level—Federal, State, and local—private foundations, and individual citizens must all face up to their responsibilities in this area. Our attack must be focused on three major objectives:

First, we must seek out the causes of mental illness and mental retardation and eradicate them. Here, more than in any other area, "an ounce of prevention is worth more than a pound of cure." For prevention is far more economical and it is far more likely to be successful. Prevention will require both selected specific programs directed especially at known causes, and the general strengthening of our fundamental community, social welfare, and educational programs which can do much to eliminate or correct the harsh environmental conditions which often are associated with mental retardation and mental illness. The proposals contained in my earlier Message to the Congress on Education and those which will be contained in a later message I will send on the Nation's Health will also help achieve this objective.

Second, we must strengthen the underlying resources of knowledge and, above all, of skilled manpower which are necessary to mount and sustain our attack on mental disability for many years to come. Personnel from many of the same professions serve both the mentally ill and the mentally retarded. We must increase our existing training programs and launch new ones; for our efforts cannot succeed unless we increase by several-fold in the next decade the number of professional and subprofessional personnel who work in these fields. My proposals on the Health Professions and Aid for Higher Education are essential to this goal; and both the proposed Youth Employment Program and a national service corps can be of immense help. We must also expand our research efforts, if we are to learn more about how to prevent and treat the crippling or malfunction of the mind.

Third, we must strengthen and improve the programs and facilities serving the mentally ill and the mentally retarded. The emphasis should be upon timely and intensive diagnosis, treatment, training, and rehabilitation so that the mentally afflicted can be cured or their functions restored to the extent possible. Services to both the mentally ill and to the mentally retarded must be community based and provide a range of services to meet community needs.

It is with these objectives in mind that I am proposing a new approach to mental illness and to mental retardation. This approach is designed, in large measure, to use Federal resources to stimulate State, local and private action. When carried out, reliance on the cold mercy of custodial isolation will be supplanted by the open warmth of community concern and capability. Emphasis on prevention, treatment, and rehabilitation will be substituted for a desultory interest in confining patients in an institution to wither away.

In an effort to hold domestic expenditures down in a period of tax reduction, I have postponed new programs and reduced added expenditures in all areas when that could be done. But we cannot afford to postpone any longer a reversal in our approach to mental affliction. For too long the shabby treatment of the many millions of the mentally disabled in custodial institutions and many millions more now in communities needing help has been justified on grounds of inadequate funds, further studies and future promises. We can procrastinate no more. The national mental health program and the national program to combat mental retardation herein proposed warrant prompt Congressional attention.

President Kennedy went on to propose to the Congress a comprehensive approach encompassing prevention, community services, research, and training.

LEGISLATION

President Kennedy's proposal to combat mental retardation resulted in two significant pieces of federal legislation, both enacted by Congress in 1963. Public Law 88–156 amended the maternal and child health provisions of the Social Security Act to include comprehensive maternity and infant care projects aimed at high-risk mothers. This law also authorized grants to states for comprehensive planning in the field of mental retardation.

The major piece of legislation to be enacted was Public Law 88–164, entitled the Mental Retardation Facilities and Community Mental Health Centers Construction Act of 1963. This law launched the first major federal program for construction of facilities for the mentally retarded and mentally ill. Title I of the act provided grants for construction of research centers and grants for facilities for the mentally retarded. There were three pertinent parts in Title I.

Part A—*Grants for Construction of Centers for Research for Mental Retardation and Related Aspects of Human Development.* This part provided matching grants to pay up to 75% of the cost of constructing regional research facilities devoted to the problems of mental retardation.

Part B—*Project Grants for Construction of University-Affiliated Facilities* (UAF) *for Mental Retardation.* This part provided matching grants to pay up to 75% of the cost of constructing UAF facilities for research and training of persons specializing in the diagnosis, treatment, and care of the mentally retarded.

Part C—*Grants for Construction of Facilities for Mental Retardation.* This part provided matching grants to pay for a portion of the cost of constructing state and local facilities for the care of the mentally retarded.

Title II of the Act dealt with community mental health centers. The 1963 legislation launched major federal programs in the area of mental retardation. In 1966, Lyndon B. Johnson created—and in his turn Richard M. Nixon supported—the President's Committee on Mental Retardation, which continued to affirm the need for federal assistance in constructing and operating such facilities. The need for new legislation, however, became apparent in 1969 and 1970. The existing programs of grants for constructing and staffing facilities to serve the mentally retarded needed to be extended. In addition, many people recognized the need for expanding the scope of coverage of the programs. Victims of other neurologically handicapping conditions required care similar to that required by persons who suffer mental retardation. By 1969 it was also clear that the 1963 legislation had been underfunded, which put serious constraints on what could be accomplished.

Both the House and the Senate committees concerned with this proposed new legislation held hearings. This 1969–1970 legislative process of continuing the 1963 legislation and broadening the scope of its coverage provided the catalyst for the evolution of the concept of handicapping developmental disabilities. Eminent professionals from various disciplines associated with the field of mental retardation as well as representatives from the United Cerebral Palsy Association, the Association of Retarded Citizens, and others all testified. Several key points were made. First, many common needs of individuals were classified under different diagnostic labels. Second, many of the retarded were also suffering other handicaps that needed attention. Third, those afflicted with multiple handicaps required attention to *all* their problems, physical and mental. Fourth, many people whose diagnostic label was not that of mental retardation but something else had needs closely related to those of the mentally retarded and required similar services. The proposed legislation reflected the views of the scientific community and was considered an ecumenical bill since it brought under one umbrella disabled persons with common needs but different diagnostic labels.

The legislative result of these hearings was Public Law 91–517, passed on October 1970 and entitled the Developmental Disabilities Service and Facilities Construction Amendments of 1970. Their purpose was to amend the Mental Retardation Facilities and Community Mental Health Facilities Construction Act of 1963. The key amendments of Public Law 91–517 struck out the words "mental retardation" and "clinical training" in the original 1963 Public Law 88–164 and replaced them with "developmental disabilities" and "interdisciplinary training." Title I, Part B of the 1963 Public Law 88–164 had authorized project grants for the construction of University Affiliated Facilities for the mentally retarded. Public Law 91–517 extended this program for three additional years and expanded it to include developmental disabilities other than mental retardation. Title I, Part C of Public Law 88–164 had authorized construction of community mental retardation facilities. Public Law 91–517 replaced that authority and mandated a federal-state formula grant program to: (a) assist the states in developing and implementing a comprehensive state plan to meet the needs of the developmentally disabled; (b) assist public or other nonprofit agencies in the construction of facilities used in the provision of services; (c) provide services to persons with developmental disabilities; (d) support costs of planning, administration, or technical assistance to states and local agencies; (e) train specialized personnel needed in this area; and (f) provide for the demonstration or development of new techniques for the delivery of services.

Public Law 91–517 established a definition for developmental disabilities.

> Disabilities attributable to mental retardation, cerebral palsy, epilepsy, or another neurological condition of an individual found by the secretary [Health, Education, and Welfare] to be closely related to mental retardation or to require treatment similar to that required for a mentally retarded individual, which disability originates before such individual attains age 18, which has continued or can be expected to continue indefinitely, and constitutes a substantial handicap to the individual.

Public Law 91–517 also established a National Advisory Council on Services and Facilities for the Developmentally Disabled, which was to advise the Secretary of Health, Education, and Welfare on regulations and also to study and evaluate programs authorized by the law.

In June 1973, the authorization for the Developmental Disabilities Program expired, but it was continued under a supplemental appropriations bill. At the same time, legislation was being considered to extend and to improve the programs initiated under the 1970 law. Hearings were again held, and representatives from many professional and consumer organizations testified. Among these groups were the National Society for Autistic Children, the National Association for Retarded Children, the National Association for Private and Residential Facilities for the Mentally Retarded, the Muscular Dystrophy Association of America, the American Speech and Hearing Association, the United Cerebral Palsy Association, Inc., the American Physical Therapy Association, the National Easter Seal Society for Crippled Children and Adults, the National Association for Mental Health, Inc., and the National Association of State Mental Health Program Directors. In the opinion of many leaders in various professions and fields, the definition of developmental disabilities under the 1970 act was narrowly restrictive. Thus, a large number of persons who were in fact developmentally disabled and who could greatly benefit from the services mandated by the act were omitted. It was recommended that the definition be expanded to include autism and specific learning disabilities. An estimated 6 million or more American citizens suffered from mental retardation, 2 million from epilepsy, 750 thousand from cerebral palsy, 80 thousand from autism, and nearly half a million children of the school age population from specific learning disabilities.

The result was Public Law 94–103, Developmentally Disabled Assistance and Bill of Rights Act, which was signed into law on October 4, 1975, by President Ford. The legislation authorized a three-year extension of State Formula Grants authorized under Public Law 91–517 to assist in planning and implementing programs on behalf of the developmentally disabled and continued support for the University-Affiliated Programs. It also included efforts to safeguard and protect the rights of the developmentally disabled person. The definition of developmental disability was, as had been recommended, broadened to include autism. However, all specific learning disabilities were not included. Disabilities attributable to dyslexia were included, but only if these resulted from a disability attributable to mental retardation, cerebral palsy, epilepsy, or autism. Public Law 94–103 provided a new operating definition for the developmentally disabled population.

The term "developmental disability" means a disability of a person which:

A i is attributable to mental retardation, cerebral palsy, epilepsy, or autism;

   ii is attributable to any other condition of a person found to be closely related to mental retardation because such condition results in similar impairment of general intellectual functioning or adaptive behavior to that of mentally retarded persons or requires treatment and services similar to those required for such persons; or

   iii is attributable to dyslexia resulting from a disability described in clause i or ii of this subparagraph;

B originates before such person attains age eighteen;

C has continued or can be expected to continue indefinitely;

D constitutes a substantial handicap to such persons' ability to function normally in society.

Public Law 94–103 also required the Secretary of Health, Education and Welfare to contract for an independent objective study of the definition of developmental disability, with respect to which disabilities should be included and which should be excluded. Subsequent to the study, a report to the Congress was required. A contract was awarded to Abt Associates, Inc. of Cambridge, Massachusetts, to conduct the study. A National Task Force on the Definition of Developmental Disabilities was selected to ensure as broad a representation of perspectives, experience, knowledge, and geographic location as possible. This 47 member task force met for three working sessions and had the responsibility and authority to make the final recommendations.

The Task Force made its final recommendations in November 1977. They attempted to make clear that the term "developmental disabilities" was not a general catch-all for an arbitrary collection of existing labels or conditions. Rather, the "developmentally disabled" are a group of people experiencing a chronic disability which substantially limits their functioning in a variety of broad areas of major life activity central to independent living. A majority of the Task Force advocated a generic or functional definition that cut across specific categories or conditions. It was thought that this would lead to better access to services and the appropriate use of services related to capacity for functioning or need rather than to diagnostic category. The Task Force recommended the following definition of developmental disabilities. For purposes of the Developmental Disabilities Act, a developmental disability is a severe, chronic disability of a person which:

1. is attributable to a mental or physical impairment or combination of mental and physical impairments;
2. is manifest before age 22;
3. is likely to continue indefinitely;
4. results in substantial functional limitations in three or more of the following areas of major life activity:
   a. self-care,
   b. receptive and expressive language,
   c. learning,
   d. mobility,
   e. self-direction,
   f. capacity for independent living, or
   g. economic self-sufficiency; and
5. reflects the need for a combination and sequence of special, interdisciplinary, or generic care, treatment, or other services which are
   a. of lifelong or extended duration and
   b. individually planned and coordinated.

The major changes over the existing definition involve the elimination of specific references to categories of disabling conditions, such as mental retardation and epilepsy, and the emphasis on substantial functional limitations. The use of the term "impairment" was advocated because categories or conditions were thought to be confusing and potentially devisive, creating antagonism between groups representing included and excluded conditions. Furthermore, identifying all conditions which might result in developmental disabilities would have resulted in a very long, but probably incomplete list. However, some Task Force members believed that the terms "mental" or "physical impairments" were too vague and would result in endless interpretation of who was and who was not developmentally disabled. A major concern was that the developmental disabilities program could not be successfully administered at the state and local levels without identifiable categories of disability. Consequently, a minority report was included which proposed the followed substitution for Part 1 of the definition:

> is attributable to mental retardation, cerebral palsy, epilepsy, or autism; or is attributable to any other condition of a person similar to mental retardation, cerebral palsy, epilepsy, or autism *because* such condition results in similar impairment of general intellectual functioning and adaptive behavior, and requires treatment and services similar to those required for such persons.

Those advocating the minority definition shared the goal of the majority of improving access and more appropriate use of developmental disabilities services. However, they believed that this could best be accomplished by retaining the existing categorical disabilities named in the act and strongly emphasizing serving other individuals who met the criteria of similar impairment and similar needs.

In considering legislation to extend the developmental disabilities program, the majority definition was adopted in the Senate bill and the minority definition was adopted in the House bill. In October 1978, a joint House-Senate conference committee recommended that the House bill be adopted, but that the majority definition replace the minority definition. This recommendation was accepted and became PL 95–602 entitled Rehabilitation, Comprehensive Services, and Developmental Disabilities Amendments of 1978 when signed by President Carter on November 6, 1978. Thus, this law provides a new operating definition for developmental disabilities. Given that the concept of developmental disabilities is continually evolving, it is likely that the effort at definition will continue also.

DETERMINATION OF DEVELOPMENTAL DISABILITIES

The broad definition of developmental disabilities, written to appease the legislative process, provides only a general outline. It is necessary to consider what constitutes a disability. Developmental disabilities are assessed in relation to normal development of systems, capabilities, and functioning. When comparisons are made against the norm, it is meaningful to differentiate among developmental *delay*, developmental *deficit* or *disorder*, and developmental *disability*. Wherever an aspect of functioning is not demonstrated by an individual at an age when the majority of children of similar age demonstrate it, the individual is considered to be exhibiting a developmental delay or a developmental disorder. If the system in question appears to be intact and not damaged, the discrepancy between functioning level and expectancy may reflect a slowness in rate of development (i.e., developmental delay). If the system in question is not functioning appropriately, the discrepancy in functioning may reflect a developmental disorder. Any developmental delay or disorder that persists throughout life and hampers a person's functioning or adjusting can be considered a developmental disability although, as we have seen, there is a specific current legislative definition of what disabilities constitute the field of developmental disabilities. For example, an infant may be demonstrating a developmental delay in the motor area if he is not sitting at nine months of age. Later it may be determined that the motor problem is not a delay but a deficit or disorder such as cerebral palsy, which significantly hampers functioning throughout life and constitutes a developmental disability.

SCHEMA FOR DEVELOPMENTAL DISABILITIES

Given the legislative definition of "developmental disabilities," what is needed is a conceptual schema that will depict the multiple interactions of the many factors that affect the human organism at various periods of its development and that manifest themselves in various systems of functioning. The Developmental Disabilities Cube in Figure 1.1 provides such an integrating schema. One axis represents the etiologic factors, the second represents the time sequence of major developmental periods, and the third represents the interdependent systems affected. Etiologic factors can be considered as either genetic or environmental. Developmental periods can be broken down into prenatal, perinatal, and postnatal. Human functioning can be viewed as comprised of a number of interdependent systems

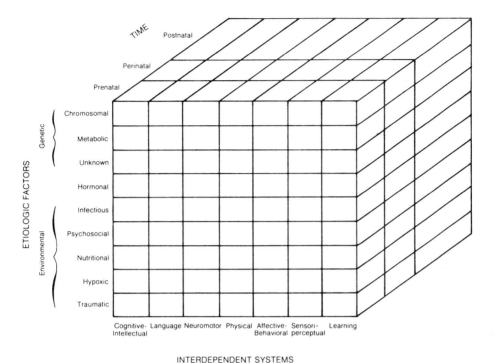

FIGURE 1.1 Developmental Disabilities Cube depicting the interaction of etiologic factors occurring during a time period of development resulting in manifestations in various systems.

including the cognitive-intellectual, language, neuromotor, physical, affective-behavioral, sensoriperceptual, and learning. The consequences of the etiologic factors depend not only on the type of factor but also on the developmental period in which they occur. An etiologic factor can be operative during one developmental period, but its functional consequences may not show themselves until a later period. This is particularly true of the chromosomal disorders and inborn errors of metabolism, which are prenatal in etiology but which may not be recognized until the perinatal or postnatal period. Etiologic factors operating in any developmental period may produce manifestations across a number of dimensions or systems such as intelligence, language, and learning; or they may affect only one system, such as the neuromotor. In addition, the various genetic and environmental etiologic factors can act singly or together, during one developmental period or across several, producing manifestations in one system or across several.

The conceptual schema of the Developmental Disabilities Cube provides not only a method for considering the etiology and manifestations of various developmental disabilities but also a method for integrating these components with treatment and prevention. Both treatment and prevention involve environmental manipulations of some kind designed to affect manifestations. Knowledge of the possible multiple causative factors of a recent or remote occurrence for patterns of manifestations can lead, however, to a specificity of intervention. In the case of manifestations attributable to genetic chromosomal causes, prevention by genetic counseling before subsequent conceptions or treatment in the form of hormone replacement can be used for some syndromes. In the case of a genetic inborn error of metabolism, dietary procedures after birth can actually be used to prevent disability. Our ability to integrate knowledge about etiology, manifestations, and specificity of intervention needs to be enhanced through research; it is hoped that this schema will foster such integration.

Now that the evolution of the concept of developmental disability has been traced from its origins in the area of mental retardation, we are prepared to examine in more detail the etiology, diagnosis, and treatment of developmental disabilities.

References

Developmental Disabilities Services and Facilities Construction Act, 1970 (PL 91–517). Available HEW/SRS publication #72–25035.

Hormuth, R. P. A proposed program to combat mental retardation. *Children*, 1963, *10*, 29–31.

Mayo, L. W. Report of the President's Panel on Mental Retardation. *Health, Education and Welfare Indicators*, February 1963, v–xiv.

National Plan to Combat Mental Retardation. Washington, D.C., U.S. Government Printing Office, October 1962.

President John F. Kennedy. Special message to the Congress on mental illness and mental retardation. *Public Papers of the Presidents*, February 5, 1963, 126–37.

President's Committee on Mental Retardation. *MR 76. Mental Retardation: Past and Present*. Washington, D.C., U. S. Government Printing Office, 1977. [Stock no. 040-000-00385-1]

2

Mental Subnormality

"Like the poor, the mentally retarded have always been with us" (Crissey, 1975, p. 800). The recognition that some individuals have been impaired in their ability to cope with their environment has also always been with us. However, the concepts concerning mental subnormality have undergone considerable modification since the beginning of this century (Wechsler, 1958). There have been changes in our thinking on the nature of intelligence and what constitutes normal and subnormal mental ability. It is important to recognize that the thinking and the concepts concerning mental abilities have been greatly influenced by prevailing attitudes and thinking. "Mental deficiency is a particularly clear instance of the contention that no field of scientific investigation is independent of the larger society in which it is embedded" (Sarason and Doris, 1969, p. 5).

Mental subnormality is defined as "subnormal general intellectual functioning which originates during the developmental period and is associated with impairment of either learning and social adjustment, or both" (Knobloch and Pasamanik, 1974, p. 149). There are several important components to this concept of subnormality. First, the impairment is in *general* intellectual functioning which can affect maturation, learning, and social adjustments (which differentiates the impairment from a specific deficit such as a language disorder). Second, it can have numerous organic and environmental etiologies. Third, it occurs during the developmental period (which differentiates the impairment from other later life phenomena such as senility).

It has been gradually recognized that mental subnormality needs to be subdivided so that we can differentiate mental deficiency and mental retardation. "Mental deficiency" refers to subnormal intellectual ability due to a pathologic condition of the brain which could result from a variety of disease processes. The intellectual manifestations may also be accompanied by other manifestations of chronic organic brain disease—such as sensation, perception, and neuromotor difficulties—or they may be the only expression. "Mental retardation" refers to intellectual and educational deficits that appear, to an undetermined but important extent, to be related to a constellation of social, familial, and cultural factors rather than to organic central nervous system pathology. While it is appropriate and necessary to make the distinction between mental deficiency and mental retardation, it is also important to recognize that if situations of poor physical and psychological environments persist over time, a condition of mental retardation can progress to mental deficiency.

What constitutes general intellectual functioning or ability? To most people, the answer would be "intelligence." The concept of intelligence itself has undergone considerable development during this century and still there is substantial disagreement about what is meant by intelligence. It is beyond the scope of this book to consider in detail the history of the concept of intelligence or of the mental testing movement. However, a brief consideration of the evolution of thinking in these areas is necessary for an appreciation and understanding of mental deficiency and mental retardation.

THE CONCEPT OF INTELLIGENCE

Individual differences in abilities have long been an area of interest. However, in the mid-nineteenth century Charles Darwin published *On the Origin of Species* (1859) and substantially influenced the study of individual differences. Darwin not only suggested that man inherited his body from animal ancestors, but "raised the question as to whether there is continuity in respect to mind between animals and man" (Boring, 1950, p.471). This suggestion stimulated interest in animal and comparative psychology as well as in problems of heredity and mental inheritance.

In 1869, Sir Francis Galton published *Hereditary Genius* in which he provided evidence for the tendency of genius to run in families. He also published *English Men of Science, Their Nature and Nuture* (1874), *Inquiries into Human Faculty and Its Development* (1883), and *Natural Inheri-*

tance (1889). The eugenics movement—the efforts at substituting intelligent selection for natural selection in the interest of racial improvement—also began at this time. To foster this intelligent selection, Galton began a survey of man's abilities and in the process developed mental tests. James McKeen Cattell established a laboratory at the University of Pennsylvania to develop a set of tests, 50 of which he described in his 1890 paper, "Mental Test and Measurement." Subsequently, in both Europe and America, the new tool of mental testing was used to assess human faculties.

Another major advance came in the early 1900s through the efforts of Alfred Binet. While Cattell's mental tests had primarily been of sensory discrimination capacity, Binet proposed tests of so-called higher mental functions, such as memory, imagery, imagination, attention, comprehension, suggestibility, esthetic appreciation, moral sentiments, strength of will, and motor skills (Boring, 1950, p.572). In 1903, Binet published *L'etude experimentale de l'intelligence*, and published the first scale of intelligence in 1905 with Theodore Simon.

Binet replaced the idea of separate functions, which was previously emphasized by Galton and Cattell, with the concept of general intelligence. The Binet-Simon Scale was built around three main assumptions about the nature of intelligence: (1) that there is goal direction to the mental processes involved and (2) that it involved the ability to show adaptive solutions and (3) selectivity of self-judgment and self-criticism of choices (Chaplin and Krawiec, 1968). In addition to Binet's specific assumption about the nature of intelligence, there was a basic assumption underlying his original scale devised to measure intelligence. Persons were considered normal if they were able to do the things that persons of their age normally did; retarded if their test performance corresponded to the performance of persons younger than themselves; and accelerated if their performance levels exceeded that of persons their own age (Terman, 1960). Thus, a person's performance on the test was measured in terms of mental age (MA) which was compared to his or her chronological age (CA) and expressed as a quotient of intelligence (MA/CA x 100).

The work of Binet was followed by that of others who thought about intelligence somewhat differently. Charles Spearman (1863–1945) advocated a two-factor theory of intelligence and assumed that all mental tests required a general ability (G) and a specific ability (S). With the advent of the statistical tool of factor analysis, there was an active search for additional factors. L. L. Thurstone (1887–1955) advocated a theory of seven primary mental abilities (verbal, numerical, spatial, perceptual, memory, reasoning, and work fluency) and undertook a program of test construction to measure these (Chaplin and Krawiec, 1968). In the 1940s, the Wechsler Scale of Intelligence was devised by David Wechsler, who continued his efforts to define intelligence (1958). He stressed that it was a construct and, as such, maintained that we cannot reasonably expect to know what intelligence *is* but only "what it involves and eventually, what it distinguishes" (p.4). Stressing that intelligence is more than the sum of its parts and includes drive and incentive, Wechsler proposed a definition: "Intelligence, operationally defined, is the aggregate or global capacity of the individual to act purposefully, to think rationally and to deal effectively with his environment" (p. 7).

The Wechsler Scales for measuring intelligence contain verbal subtests (information, comprehension, arithmetic, similarities, vocabulary, and digit span) and performance subtests (picture completion, picture arrangement, block design, object assembly, and digit symbol) which yields verbal, performance, and full-scale IQ scores. These scales continue to be revised and utilized extensively today. The specific subtests are not conceived as measures of primary mental abilities but as a means through which intelligence can manifest itself. With the advent of the use of the Wechsler Scales, a new method of determining intelligence quotients was devised to depict a person's relative standing among the group with which he is being compared. Rather than using MA/CA to generate an IQ, a statistical method was used based on the mean score and standard deviation (σ) around the mean of the reference group. These scores were standardized and distributed according to the normal curve in order to arrive at a distribution that

TABLE 2.1 American Association of Mental Deficiency (AAMD) classification of mental subnormality[a]

AAMD Category	σ	Stanford-Binet ($\sigma = 16$)	Wechsler ($\sigma = 15$)
Mild	−2 to −3	67–52	69–55
Moderate	−3 to −4	51–36	54–40
Severe	−4 to −5	35–20	39–25 (Extrapolated)
Profound	>5	<19	<24 (Extrapolated)

[a] Based on standard deviations (σ) below the mean ($\bar{X} = 100$) with corresponding intelligence scores for the Stanford-Binet and Wechsler Scales.

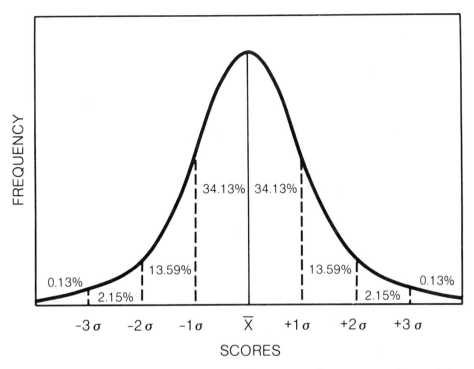

FIGURE 2.1 Normal curve distribution of IQ scores with percentage of scores falling within successive standard deviations from the mean.

would be utilized to classify IQ. The mean scores for each group were assigned the IQ score of 100.

Figure 2.1 depicts the theoretical normal curve distribution of IQ scores and the percentage of the population included within successive σ from the mean. Using the method, the American Association of Mental Deficiency (AAMD; Grossman, 1977) has established an intellectual classification system based on the number of standard deviations below the mean. Table 2.1 presents this classification system and the range of scores for each category for the Stanford-Binet and Wechsler Tests. It can be seen that approximately 68% of the population would be expected to obtain IQ scores within ± 1σ around the mean and 95% between ± 2σ (i.e., between IQ scores 68–70 and 130–132). Mental subnormality, by this method, refers to those who obtain IQ scores more than 2σ below the mean, and this group encompasses approximately 2.5% of the population.

Since IQ is used as a method of defining relative intelligence, from both a conceptual and statistical view point, it is absolutely necessary for IQ score to remain constant. From a statistical standpoint, a test must be reliable to have any utility and validity. It would not be a valid or useful instrument if an individual obtained one IQ score one day and a drastically different score the very next day with the same test. Also, a person's relative standing or IQ score is expected to remain roughly the same throughout life under ordinary conditions (Wechsler, 1958). However, the interaction of these conceptual and statistical necessities with the hereditary-genetic view of retardation led to an erroneous emphasis on the immutability of intelligence and the idea of a "fixed IQ." Thus, whatever score an individual obtained was thought to reflect his functioning forever. Indeed, the concept of a "fixed IQ" was "in accord with the social mores of the time and was agreeably accepted" (Crissey, 1975, p. 803).

In order for the concept of immutability to be restored to its proper statistical and conceptual place, a change in the view that intelligence and retardation reflect only hereditary and genetic factors was needed. Gradually, evidence began to accumulate which showed that "children could move from retardation to normalcy or normalcy to retardation. A sober look at the correlates to poverty suggested that poor nutrition, inadequate health care, prematurity, multiple sensory and neurological defects even though minor, and an impoverished environment were at least as deleterious as genetic factors" (Crissey, 1975, p. 805).

Another factor that contributed to the change in emphasis from just hereditary and genetic factors to a consideration also of environmental factors was an awakening of national interest in the problems of mental subnormality. In terms of national policy, mental subnormality was largely ignored prior to World War II, but the war forced an assessment of our human resources (Sarason and Doris, 1969). This assessment showed that there were many individuals who were functionally retarded—not because of mental deficiency, but because of poor education, nutrition, health, and other environmental factors. A new national policy emerged, fostered by the civil rights movement and the "war on poverty," in which our society began to see itself obligated to help others who, for reasons beyond their control, required some form of external help (Sarason and Doris, 1969).

Those affected with mental subnormality, as we indicated in the first chapter, came to be included among those seen as needing this help.

The nature of intelligence continues to be studied and theoretical models continue to evolve. For example, Guilford proposes a structure of the intellect model which has three interacting dimensions which yield a possibility of 120 factors (Bouchard, 1968). The three dimensions and their components are:

Operations: cognitive, memory, convergent thinking, divergent thinking and evaluation

Content: figural, symbolic, semantic and behavioral

Products: units, classes, relations, systems, transformation, and implication.

Thus, we have progressed to the point where one model of intelligence is really a dynamic information processing system in which "the scientific understanding of intelligence is a matter of describing the structure of cognition and thought, and of specifying the biological and environmental conditions that control its growth and development" (Bouchard, 1968, p.29).

Although some recent conceptualizations of intelligence emphasize cognition, others stress intelligence as a construct that stands for more than cognition and includes motivational factors as well. In a recent endeavor to clarify the consideration of intelligence, Wechsler (1975) argues that intelligence is not a quality of the mind but an aspect of behavior. Intelligence is not a singular and unique trait, but it is one that has many facets; it is not a type of faculty or combination of cognitive faculties. Wechsler indicates that confusion persists in distinguishing between the concept of intelligence and the modalities by which it is expressed. Thus, there is a continuing failure to distinguish between tasks used as measures of ability or aptitude and their use as measures of intelligence. This highly relativistic view of intelligence is exemplified by Wechsler's contention (1975) that intelligence includes awareness of what one is doing, goal directiveness or meaningfulness, rationality (i.e., that which is capable of being logically deduced and consistent), and worthwhileness (i.e., that which is valued and deemed useful by group opinion).

The complex multifaceted nature of the concept of intelligence provides a base from which to assess once again the definition of mental subnormality as given by the American Association of Mental Deficiency. For mental subnormality to be present, it is essential that the impairment in general intellectual functioning be manifested in one or more aspects of a person's adaptation to his or her environment. Adaptive behavior is defined by the AAMD as "the effectiveness or degree with which the individual meets the standards of personal independence and social responsibility expected of his age and cultural group" (Grossman, 1977, p. 11). Thus, adaptive behavior is also multifaceted, and the individual's capabilities for independence and social responsibility need to be assessed in relation to community demands and to age-specific expectations.

Utilizing this schema, AAMD (Grossman, 1977), has also categorized adaptive behavior into four levels scaled from significant but mild deviation from population norms to almost total lack of adaptation at the profound level. Because general intellectual functioning is an integral component of adaptive behavior and because behaviors sampled by current intelligence tests contribute to overall adaptation, there will be a high correlation between measures of intelligence and assessments of adaptive behavior. Between these two dimensions, however, there frequently are, in individual cases, discrepancies that can be of significance in determining etiology and prognosis and in planning education and vocational training.

We hope this brief review will foster an appreciation of the nonstatic, evolving conceptualization of what constitutes intelligence, both normal and subnormal, and how it is measured. Studies of intelligence focus at present on assessing the current levels of functioning of individuals with the goal of raising levels of performance insofar as possible. The remedial potential of environmental factors such as stimulation and special education "must always be considered in relation to the organizational integrity of the child's central nervous system, which ultimately determines the degree and mode of reaction to the environment" (Knobloch and Pasamanick, 1974, p.177). It is now recognized that both genetic and hereditary factors and environmental factors can contribute to the integrity of the child's central nervous system and to the adequacy of care, stimulation, and education. We will explore some of these factors as we consider the etiology and manifestations of mental subnormality.

ETIOLOGY, MANIFESTATIONS, AND MANAGEMENT

The known etiologies of mental subnormality—though they are many—are still few compared with those that are obscure or totally unknown. We propose to discuss the known causes of mental subnormality under categories marked by three developmental stages: prenatal, perinatal, and postnatal.

Certain inherent difficulties arise in such a discussion. One is that the specific reason for the mental subnormality is precisely known only rarely. That is, all the genetic and environmental influences that we will discuss are *associated* with mental subnormality. But what actually happened in the central nervous system on a cellular and subcellular level to result in the clinical picture of mental subnormality is not known. We are getting closer to some answers however. For example, we now know that intelligence is not located in a particular anatomic location in the brain. We are becoming more cognizant of the fact that mental subnormality implies a problem in neuronal communication. Whether this is the result of abnormal or nonfunctional dendritic arborization (Huttenlocher, 1974; Purpura, 1974; Williams, Ferrante, and Caviness, 1975), the result of biochemical-metabolic imbalances, or whether there are combinations of these factors or others yet unknown, the fact remains that in mental subnormality the transfer of information from the environment to storage and retrieval areas of the brain and then to decision making or action does not take place properly. Much work remains to be done to further our understanding, and it continues to be among the most exciting areas of research and collaboration between basic scientists and clinicians.

Another difficulty in this kind of categorization is that the etiology of mental subnormality may well be related to an interaction of events, both genetic and environmental in different developmental periods, so that determination of one single specific etiology becomes not only extremely simplistic but also relatively useless. This is well illustrated by the discussion regarding case J.C. (p. 75).

Still another inherent difficulty in this kind of categorization is that though the etiology of subnormality may occur in one time period, its manifestation as a subnormality may not appear until a much later period. This time lag is particularly noticeable in chromosomal disorders, which may not be recognized (though genetic and therefore prenatal in etiology) until birth or thereafter and in the inborn errors of metabolism, which may not be recognized until infancy. Furthermore, it is difficult to determine precisely when in the prenatal period an influence might have been operative. The prenatal period extends, by definition, from conception until the birth of the infant and is divided into three trimesters. The first is called

TABLE 2.2 Etiologic classification of mental subnormality according to factors during developmental periods with representative examples

	Incidence per 1,000 live births	Average age of diagnosis	Average life expectancy
PRENATAL PERIOD			
A. GENETIC FACTORS			
Inborn errors of metabolism			
Cerebral lipidoses	——	prenatal–infancy	2–6 yrs.
Infantile Gaucher's	——	——	——
Niemann-Pick	——	——	——
Tay-Sachs	0.28 among Ashkenazi Jews	——	——
Mucopolysaccharidoses	0.04		
Hurler's syndrome	——	prenatal possible	variable
Hunter's syndrome	——	prenatal achieved	——
Sanfilippo syndrome	——	prenatal achieved	——
Disorders of protein metabolism			
Aminoacidopathies			
Phenylketonuria	0.05–0.1	newborn	adult
Homocystinuria	0.01	prenatal possible	variable
Lesch-Nyhan syndrome	——	prenatal possible childhood	variable
Disorders of carbohydrate metabolism			
Galactosemia	.013	prenatal–infancy	adult
Glycogen storage disease	——	childhood	variable
Chromosomal Disorders	5	prenatal	variable
Disorders of the autosomes			
Down's syndrome (trisomy 21)	1.5	prenatal–newborn	variable
Edward's syndrome (E) (trisomy 18)	0.15	prenatal–newborn	<1 yr.
Patau's syndrome (D) (trisomy 13)	0.13	prenatal–newborn	<1 yr.
Cri-du-chat syndrome	0.02	prenatal–newborn	adult

Disorders of the sex chromosomes			
Klinefelter's syndrome	0.7	puberty	adult
Turner's syndrome	0.25	puberty	adult
Multiple Malformations			
Neural tube defects			
Anencephaly	0.1–6.7	prenatal or birth	perinatal
Meningomyelocele	1–2	prenatal or birth	variable
Syndromes of multiple malformation			
Neurofibromatosis	———	mid-childhood	adult
(Von Recklinghausen's)			
Tuberous sclerosis	———	variable	adult
Other inherited syndromes			
Muscular dystrophy	———	2–5 yrs.	early adult
Kernicterus as a result of	———		
blood group incompatibility		perinatal	
B. ENVIRONMENTAL FACTORS			
Congenital infections			
Toxoplasmosis	1.3	perinatal	variable
Rubella	Rare	preventable due to vaccine	variable
Cytomegalovirus (CMV)	10	perinatal	variable
Herpes simplex virus	0.01	perinatal	variable
(HSV)		variable	
Other maternal factors			
Psychosocial disadvantage			
Malfunction of the materno-placento-			
fetal unit			
PERINATAL PERIOD			
A. METABOLIC FACTORS			
Hypoglycemia		perinatal	adult
Hypocalcemia		perinatal	adult
B. ENVIRONMENTAL FACTORS			
Hypoxia-asphyxia-ischemia	variable	perinatal	variable
Trauma	variable	perinatal	variable
Malnutrition	variable	perinatal	variable
Infection (meningitis)	0.4	perinatal	variable
POSTNATAL PERIOD			
A. METABOLIC-HORMONAL FACTORS			
Congenital hypothyroidism	0.12	infancy	adult
Hypoglycemia	———	variable	variable
B. ENVIRONMENTAL FACTORS			
Trauma	———	———	———
Hypoxia	———	———	———
Infection			
Meningitis (bacterial)	———	———	———
Meningoencephalitis (viral)	———	———	———
Poisoning	———	———	———
Psychosocial disadvantage	frequent	infancy–childhood	adult

29

the embryonic period or the period of organogenesis. The last two trimesters are referred to as the fetal period and represent the time during
which fetal growth and development occur. The perinatal period overlaps
somewhat with the prenatal period in that it is considered to begin during
the second half of pregnancy and to continue through the first four weeks
after birth. Because of this overlap and somewhat artificial division, it is not
always completely clear whether an environmental influence is prenatal,
perinatal, or both. Given these conditions, we will attempt to be as accurate as possible both about the etiology of mental subnormality and the
time period to which it is related. Table 2.2 illustrates this etiological
approach by portraying various factors during the three major developmental periods and by indicating representative specific disorders.

PRENATAL PERIOD

The factors of importance in the etiology of mental subnormality in
this period are both genetic and environmental. In recent years it has
become increasingly common to make prenatal diagnoses by amniocentesis
of suspected inherited syndromes, including inborn errors of metabolism,
chromosomal disorders, and multiple malformations, so that pregnancies so
affected may be terminated. An excellent review of the state of the art of
prenatal genetic diagnosis has been published by Nadler (1976). Furthermore, Milunsky (1976) has listed the diagnoses that are now possible prenatally, most of which are associated with mental deficiency.

GENETIC FACTORS

The genetic factors of concern, then, include inborn errors of metabolism, chromosomal disorders, and multiple malformations. The concept of
"inborn errors of metabolism" was introduced by Sir Archibald Garrod in
the Croonian Lectures (1908), in which he discussed alkaptonuria, cys-
tinuria, albinism, and pentosuria. He found these diseases interesting because they were present from birth, they seemed to lack progression of
symptomatology with age, and because they helped to elucidate metabolic
pathways. He credited Bateson with the discovery of the autosomal recessive mode of inheritance of alkaptonuria in 1902. With this type of inheritance, each parent is a carrier of a recessive gene resulting in a 1 in 4
chance of having an affected child. The more prevalent the gene is in the

general population, the more common the condition. For example, in phenylketonuria, the gene incidence is 1 in 100 and the incidence of the disorder is 1 in 10,000 to 20,000 live births. In Tay-Sachs, the gene incidence in Ashkenazi Jews is 3 to 4 in 100 and the incidence of disorder in that population is 1 in 3,600 live births.

Garrod developed the theory that these metabolic disorders arise because an enzyme governing a single metabolic step is altered or missing altogether. Subsequently, Beadle (1945) worked out the concept of "one gene–one enzyme." He proposed that each enzyme is under the control of a single gene and that a mutation in that gene results in an alteration of the ability of cells to carry out a single biochemical reaction, a disability that manifests itself in various organ systems.

Inborn Errors of Metabolism

The inborn errors that affect the central nervous system include disorders of lipid, mucopolysaccharide, protein, and carbohydrate metabolism. Screening tests have been devised for some (Renuart, 1966). In all, they probably account for only 4% to 7% of mental deficiency (Knobloch and Pasamanick, 1974, p.174). We will discuss several of these inborn errors.

CEREBRAL LIPIDOSES   The cerebral lipidoses, including infantile Gaucher's disease, Niemann Pick disease, Tay-Sachs disease, Krabbes disease, and metachromatic leukodystrophy, are among the rare causes of mental deficiency (Malone, 1976). They are transmitted by autosomal recessive inheritance. When not detected prenatally by amniocentesis, they present within the first year of life (except metachromatic leukodystrophy, which presents within the first two years of life) with progressive neurologic deterioration and death in early childhood.

The defect in infantile Gaucher's disease is an almost complete absence of the enzyme β-glucosidase resulting in an excess of glucocerebroside in the liver and spleen (hepatosplenomegaly) and the accumulation of a lipid material compatible with a cerebroside within the neurons of the brain stem, basal ganglia, and cerebellum. The bone marrow contains Gaucher cells which are pathognomonic. Neurologically, the affected child presents in the first year of life with brain-stem signs, including strabismus, opisthotonus, and dysphagia, and progressively deteriorates. There is no known treatment.

The defect in Niemann-Pick disease is a marked deficiency of the enzyme sphingomyelinase with a subsequent accumulation of sphingomyelin in the liver and spleen (hepatosplenomegaly) and in the cerebral cortex. The bone marrow contains "foam cells," which are characteristic of this disease. Clinically, one third of the patients will demonstrate a cherry red spot in the macula (indistinguishable from Tay-Sachs disease) and pale optic discs. The course of the disease is similar to that of infantile Gaucher's.

Tay-Sachs disease is perhaps the best studied of all these lipidoses and will be discussed in more detail. It is largely confined to children of Ashkenazi Jewish parents, in whom there is a high incidence of consanguinity. The biochemical defect is a deficiency of hexosaminidase A, with a resultant increase in brain content of G_{M2}-ganglioside. A report on genetic screening from the National Academy of Sciences (1975) indicates that 3% to 4% of Ashkenazi Jews are carriers; in that population, Tay-Sachs disease occurs with a frequency of 1 in 3600 live births. In other populations, it is quite rare, with a gene frequency of 1 in 380 (Malone, 1976).

If undetected prenatally, the disease usually makes itself known in a previously normal infant around 4 to 6 months of age. Hypotonicity develops with a gradual loss of previously acquired motor skills; concomitantly, the infant develops a seeming hyperacusis (sensitivity to sound) and visual impairment, and the characteristic "cherry red spot" in the macula may be seen. This represents the red fovea surrounded by an accumulation of whitish ganglioside. The initial hypotonicity of the infant is gradually replaced by evidence of decerebration and spasticity. Convulsions may occur. Death usually occurs between 2 and 3 years of age. There is no known treatment for Tay-Sachs or for any of the other lipidoses, but there has been recent evidence that enzyme replacement might indeed be possible through liposomes (Gregoriades, 1976; Weissman, 1976). The best current management is prevention.

MUCOPOLYSACCHARIDOSES   The mucopolysaccharidoses including Hurler's syndrome, Hunter's syndrome, and Sanfilippo's syndrome, are characterized by the accumulation of mucopolysaccharides in brain, skin, skeletal tissues, cornea, and/or viscera. They follow the laws of autosomal recessive inheritance except Hunter's syndrome, which is X-linked recessive.

Hurler's and Sanfilippo's syndromes both present with severe mental retardation, corneal clouding, skeletal deformities, and coarse features.

Hunter's presents with moderate mental retardation, skeletal changes, and early deafness. In all, the course is one of gradual neurologic deterioration with death usually occurring by 30 years of age. Screening tests on urine for the detection of the mucopolysaccharidoses can be done with a 5% solution of cetyltrimethyl ammonium bromide (C-Tab) (Shih, 1973) or by the Berry spot test (1960) using toluidine blue. Diagnosis rests on the demonstration of increased excretion of mucopolysaccharides. Legum, Schorr, and Berman (1976) have recently published an excellent review of the mucopolysaccharidoses.

DISORDERS OF PROTEIN METABOLISM   Disorders of protein metabolism associated with mental deficiency include the aminoacidopathies and the Lesch-Nyhan syndrome. The aminoacidopathies are probably the best known of the inborn errors of metabolism, and as a group include phenylketonuria, branched-chain ketoaciduria (maple syrup urine disease), methylmalonic acidemia, and homocystinuria. They too, follow the laws of autosomal recessive inheritance. Frimpter (1973, part 2) has summarized the pertinent information about maple syrup urine disease, and methylmalonic acidemia.

Phenylketonuria, described by Fölling, a Norwegian biochemist, in 1934 and known as PKU, has probably received the greatest amount of attention and has been the subject of the greatest screening effort of newborns. As of January 1974, 45 states had enacted legislation for mandatory newborn screening and treatment (National Academy of Sciences, 1975). Initially, the ferric chloride test was used as a screening test to detect the elevated levels of phenylpyruvic acid in the urine (grey-green color). Then Guthrie (1961) first announced the use of a microbiologic assay for detecting elevated blood phenylalanine levels; later Guthrie and Susi (1963) elaborated upon the technique for use in newborn screening.

The metabolic defect in classic PKU is a deficiency of phenylalanine hydroxylase with a resultant elevation of blood phenylalanine levels and decrease in tyrosine; these metabolic changes are thought to interfere with the myelination of the brain. However, the exact reason for mental deficiency in phenylketonuria is not known. The incidence of PKU is one out of 10,000 to 20,000 births.

The manifestations of classic untreated PKU are as follows. In the cognitive-intellectual area, moderate to severe mental retardation is typical. Language is affected in relation to the mental retardation, as is learning. In neuromotor functioning, individuals with PKU are clumsy, particularly in fine motor coordination, but are not definitely athetoid or spastic. Irritability is a noted behavioral characteristic early on, but later, affected individuals are "good-tempered" (Penrose, 1962). Knobloch and Pasamanick (1974) have indicated that seizures and "autistic behavior" are frequently present. Physically, babies with PKU often have a "mousy odor" and eczema. Later, they are typically blond, blue-eyed, and fair. Some affected individuals manifest a seizure disorder.

The intensive screening effort has served to identify affected individuals at birth and therefore has made possible treatment with a low phenylalanine (Lofenalac) diet soon after birth. It has also taught us the variation which can exist in phenylalanine levels and the criteria which must be met before the diagnosis of phenylketonuria is made. The criteria are as follows: a phenylalanine level at or >20 mg% and a tyrosine level <5 mg% on two separate occasions, as well as a response to a phenylalanine challenge test of a rise to 20 mg% (National Academy of Sciences, 1975). Frimpter (1973) has discussed four relatively benign forms of hyperphenylalaninemia which typically do not require dietary management. More recently, two very rare forms of hyperphenylalaninemia have been described that can result in neurologic disorder and that are caused by deficiency of factors other than phenylalanine hydroxylase and in which dietary control of phenylalanine levels does not prevent neurologic impairment (Bartholome et al, 1977; Kaufman et al., 1978). Our knowledge in this area continues to expand.

Knobloch and Pasamanick (1974) summarize the current view of treatment of the classic form of PKU. "Almost all articles and texts state that untreated patients are severely mentally defective, that all are normal at the time of birth, and that each week treatment is delayed results in some loss of intellectual function, because damage occurs progressively in the postnatal period" (p. 175).

The Collaborative Project regarding PKU has provided information which corroborates this summary statement. They have found thus far that "near normal" IQs (mean of 93 ± 16) are attained as a result of early treatment (by 65 days of age), and that dietary management need not be extremely rigid. That is, when the phenylalanine level was maintained at 9.9 mg%, children did as well on cognitive-intellectual evaluation as did those maintained at a level of 5.4 mg%. The mean IQ for those who started the diet in the first month was 95, whereas it was 85 for those who started it in the second month (Dobson et al., 1977). The diet, however, needs close following so that enough, but not too much, phenylalanine is allowed.

Apart from prevention of mental retardation, one effect of the diet may be to control seizures and "autistic" behaviors (Knobloch and Pasamanick, 1974) and in this way contribute to an improvement in functioning. For these reasons, and because some individuals with PKU become irritable and distractible with elevated phenylalanine levels, the diet may need to be continued into adulthood. However, as the child grows, the restrictive nature of the diet is poorly tolerated psychologically and "cheating" is common. Therefore, most PKU diets are considerably liberalized by 5 years of age. The optimal time for discontinuing the diet is still being evaluated. Treatment procedures and prognostic statement, therefore, need to be made on the basis of monitoring the development of each individual with PKU rather than on the basis of generalities about PKU as a whole.

Special mention needs to be made of the potential hazard created by the pregnant mother who has PKU and who is not put on a restrictive diet during pregnancy. All her children will be exposed to high phenylalanine levels in utero, and all will be retarded, though the children themselves may not have phenylketonuria (Efron, 1965; Perry et al., 1973).

The following case illustrates the unfortunate fact that in spite of the mandatory state screening programs, an occasional affected individual is missed. The case also demonstrates the multidimensional manifestations in affected individuals.

CASE S.B.F.

S.B.F. was referred for evaluation of developmental delay at 4 years 8 months of age. He was the product of a term uncomplicated pregnancy and delivery and weighed 8 lb 8½ oz at birth. The initial PKU screening test revealed a phenylalanine level of 8.8 mg% after one day of milk feedings. For unknown reasons, a followup on this elevated level (normal up to 3.6 mg%) was not done.

Motor milestones (rolling, sitting, pulling to stand) were achieved appropriately during the first year. However, S.B.F. did not walk until 18 months of age. He began to follow simple commands at 24 months of age, and to speak in a few 2 to 3 word combinations by 2 years 6 months. Now, at 4 years of age, he is unable to dress himself, is messy in feeding himself, and his coordination has been slow to develop. His behavior has been difficult to manage because of frequent temper tantrums and screaming.

On developmental testing elsewhere at 3 years 11 months of age, he was found on the Stanford-Binet to have a mental age of 2 years 4 months and an IQ of 50. At that time his language was echolalic and perseverative. The family did not follow through with further developmental evaluation and therapy.

When he was seen for the first time at the Duke Developmental Evaluation Center, he presented as an attractive, blond, blue-eyed youngster who looked bright and smiled readily. He seemed to be in terror of the physical examination, however. His height was in the 60th percentile, weight in the 85th percentile, and head circumference in the 10th percentile. The remainder of the examination was unremarkable. Phenylalanine level was grossly elevated at 30 mg% with a tyrosine level of 1.6 mg%.

A repeat of the Stanford-Binet yielded a mental age of 2 years 3 months and an IQ of 35. Essentially, this represented a lack of progress rather than a degeneration in that his mental age (MA) remained relatively constant while his chronological age (CA) increased 9 months. Speech and language skills receptively were at the 2-year–4-month level and expressively at the 24-month level. Fine motor skills were at the 20–24-month level, and gross motor at the 24–28-month level.

Dietary modification will be undertaken so as to substantially decrease the intake of phenylalanine. Whether this will be tolerated at this time or whether it will produce any amelioration of the retardation or behavior remains to be seen.

Homocystinuria is an extremely interesting aminoacidopathy with an incidence of one per 100,000. Three years after the first case reports, Schimke et al. (1965) reported on studies of 20 families with 38 affected members. Frimpter (1973) has included a perceptive review of homocystinuria among the causes of aminoaciduria. The metabolic defect is a reduction in the activity of the enzyme cystathionine synthase resulting in accumulation of homocystine in the blood and urine. Urinary screening for elevated homocystine levels with cyanide-nitroprusside usually produces a deep red color (O'Brien, 1970). Currently, 10 states routinely screen newborns for homocystinuria.

The manifestations of homocystinuria are as follows. In the cognitive-intellectual area, affected individuals usually function in the moderate to severe range of mental retardation with commensurate functioning in the areas of language and learning. Neuromotor functioning is affected by the retardation, by the tendency for bony anomalies, and by the results of cerebrovascular thromboses (strokes) to which these individuals are prone. Life expectancy is greatly reduced because of the occurrence of in-

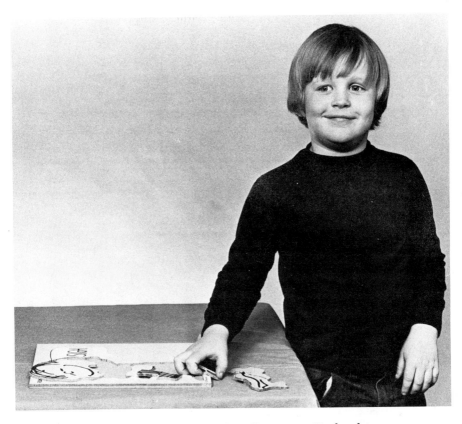

S.B.F. is now 6 years of age and has phenylketonuria. His handsome appearance has made it difficult for the family to accept his current level of intellectual functioning, which is in the moderate range of retardation.

travascular thromboses (Perry, 1974). Physically, affected individuals have a Marfan-like habitus (tall, thin, with long fingers and toes), and may have ectopic lenses (displaced down), sparse fair hair, fragile skin, and bony anomalies such as pes cavus, pectus excavatum, osteoporosis, and kyphoscoliosis. Behaviorally, they tend to be excessively nervous.

Dietary treatment with a low methionine diet has been recommended, but its efficacy in reducing disability is not known. Interestingly, there is a form of homocystinuria which is responsive to large doses of pyridoxine (Vitmain B_6) (Hillman, 1976; Sardharvalla, 1976).

The Lesch-Nyhan syndrome is transmitted as an X-linked recessive and is a metabolic disorder in which the absence or inactivity of the enzyme hypoxanthine-guanine phosphoribosyltransferase results in excessive purine synthesis and elevated uric acid levels in blood and urine. The manifestations of the Lesch-Nyhan syndrome are as follows. In the cognitive-intellectual area, functioning is usually within the moderate range (IQ of 30–65) of mental retardation (Kelley and Wyngaarden, 1972), but dysarthria and choreoathetosis might interfere with speech and communication and give a spuriously low result. In the neuromotor area, hypotonia and delay in achievement of motor milestones in early infancy, are followed later by the development of definite spasticity and choreoathetosis. A major behavioral manifestation is compulsive self-mutilation, especially lip and finger biting, for which restraints are often necessary. Seizures are not uncommon. Learning is affected by the mental retardation, neuromotor involvement, and behavioral manifestations. Treatment is aimed primarily at reducing the uric acid levels with allopurinol in order to prevent obstructive uropathy which can result from an excess of uric acid crystals in the urine. Although the central nervous system sequelae are not reversible, improvement in self-mutilation may be noted (Kelley and Wyngaarden, 1972).

DISORDERS OF CARBOHYDRATE METABOLISM   Disorders of carbohydrate metabolism which are associated with mental deficiency include galactosemia and glycogen storage disease, and they are also transmitted in an autosomal recessive manner.

In galactosemia, the enzyme galactose-1-phosphate uridyltransferase is lacking and galactose accumulates. Usually infants are normal at birth, but within the first month, they develop poor feeding, failure to thrive, cataracts, jaundice, and an enlarged liver. If untreated, mental deficiency results. Galactose may be identified in the urine by the presence of reducing substance (Clinitest Tablets) which is not glucose. In 13 states there is mandatory routine screening of newborns for galactosemia. Treatment requires the withdrawal of milk and milk products from the diet, as well as iridectomy as needed for the cataracts (Sardharvalla, 1976).

Glycogen storage diseases (glycogenoses) were the first of the inborn errors to have the enzymatic defect delineated (Cori, 1953). Types 1, 3, and 6 result in the accumulation of glycogen in the liver due to lack of the enzymes needed for proper breakdown of glycogen into glucose. As a re-

B.R. is a 9-year-old youngster with a slow progressive degenerative central nervous system disorder of unknown etiology. He is shown here to emphasize that in spite of the fact that we have learned a great deal about inborn errors of metabolism since Garrod, there are still children who present with disorders for which we can find no etiology. This becomes a problem in terms of appropriate management and prognosis as well as genetic counseling.

sult, hypoglycemia in infancy may be a prominent symptom, and may lead to seizures and mental retardation. Von Gierke's disease (type 1) glycogenosis is the one most frequently associated with mental retardation, though Sidbury (1967) indicates the IQ is usually normal even in type 1. Muscle weakness is a common manifestation.

Chromosomal Disorders

Chromosomal disorders constitute the next large group of genetic, prenatal causes of mental deficiency. At least 3% of all early conceptuses have an altered chromosomal number (Smith and Marshall, 1972). The majority end in spontaneous abortion (Kajii et al. 1973), leaving approximately 1 out of 200 live-born infants with a chromosomal disorder (Jones, 1975). The altered chromosome number or arrangement might occur in the autosomes or in the sex chromosomes. Down's syndrome (trisomy 21) is probably the most common of the autosomal disorders with an incidence of one out of 600 live births. The trisomy 18 and trisomy 13 syndromes have also been very well described. The deletion syndromes, including the deletion of the short arm of chromosome 4 and the deletion of the short arm of chromosome 5 (cri-du-chat syndrome) are rare but well recognized among the autosomal causes of mental deficiency. Klinefelter's (XXY) and Turner's (XO) syndromes are common disorders of the sex chromosomes. We shall discuss each of these giving more emphasis to Down's syndrome and Klinefelter's syndrome.

DISORDERS OF THE AUTOSOMES   In 1866, John Langdon Down described a syndrome of mental deficiency associated with mongoloid features which he termed "mongolism." This term will still be found in use occasionally but objections to an ethnic classification have resulted in the more appropriate designation of "Down's syndrome." Little was known about the etiology of this congenital syndrome until Lejeune, Gautier, and Turpin (1959) described the first abnormality of human chromosomes, which was the association of 47 chromosomes in Down's syndrome. The extra chromosome material was attached to the 21–22 group, and it came to be known as trisomy 21.

Trisomy 21 accounts for 95% of all cases of Down's syndrome and is thought to occur as a result of nondisjunction in the first or second meiotic division of gametogenesis, which produces an abnormal ovum with a functional extra chromosome. There is no clear explanation why this happens, but there is a higher incidence of Down's syndrome in children of older mothers. One hypothesis is that the older an ovum gets, the more likely it is to exhibit nondisjunction. Solomons (1969) reported that 65% of all children with Down's syndrome are born to mothers over 30 years of age. Mothers over 40 years of age run a risk 30 times greater of having a Down's child than mothers below 20 years of age. The recurrence risk of having another child with trisomy 21 for any given family is 1–2 out of 100.

Of all children with trisomy 21, 1% to 2% are mosaic—one cell line being normal and the other being trisomy 21. In general, the mosaic form of Down's is more mildly affected. Fishler, Koch, and Donnell (1976) report that 25 mosaic Down's had a significantly higher mean IQ level (67) than trisomy 21 Down's (52) matched for sex and age. Mosaic Down's have better verbal facility and less visual-perceptual difficulty than is typical of the trisomy 21 population (Fishler, 1975).

Translocation accounts for 3.5% of all cases of Down's syndrome and occurs when chromosome material from chromosome 21 attaches itself to another chromosome, usually in group D (13–15) or less frequently in group G (21–22). Thus, a mother who is a balanced carrier for D-G translocation would have 45 chromosomes rather than 46 and would look perfectly normal. The translocation may be sporadic or familial, but if it is of the D-G type, 10% of her offspring would have Down's syndrome (Gorlin, 1977). If the father is the carrier, the incidence is less, probably owing to a competitive disadvantage with normal sperm. The expected risk of a Down's child if the mother has a G-G translocation is 9% if the translocation is 21–22, but 100% if the translocation is 21–21 (Gorlin, 1977). The child who has Down's syndrome on the basis of translocation will actually have a chromosome count of 46 but will have extra genetic material in the long arm of chromosomes in group G or D.

The manifestations of Down's syndrome are as follows:

1. In the cognitive-intellectual area, Down's syndrome is typically characterized by moderate mental retardation, although intelligence quotients range from 25–70. "There is a tendency to score higher during the first and second years of life when using the Gesell Development Scales. There is a gradual decrease in D.Q. to a plateau at the age of three and four years. In fact, the scores on developmental tests at those age levels appear to be reliable predictors of the child's subsequent intellectual functioning" (Fishler, 1975, p. 89). Historically, there has been a pessimistic prognosis about intellectual development, probably because of studies using only institutionalized children. Kirman (1964) was among the first to stress the need

for communities to plan for better facilities for children with Down's syndrome, emphasizing the improved prognosis for survival and for development when they are not institutionalized. Benda (1969) has maintained that many Down's children are in the educable (mild) range. In Golden and Pashayan's recently reported study (1976), parental educational level was an important determinant of IQ level in Down's syndrome children. The mean IQ of those with parents in the higher educational levels was in the lower end of the mildly retarded range, whereas the mean IQ of children with parents in the lower educational levels was found to be in the lower end of the moderately retarded range. Speech and language delays are a particular problem in Down's syndrome, with expressive language delay more marked than receptive. These children frequently have oral-motor problems, nasal speech, recurrent otitis media accompanied by intermittent and variable hearing impairment, and articulation problems.

2. In the neuromotor area, the Down's syndrome infant follows a relatively normal motor pattern during the first six months. Thus, "many parents have difficulty accepting the retardation based on early physical measures alone. However, from then on there is a gradual, but growing, discrepancy in the subsequent progress. By the time the infant reaches one year of age, he is often developmentally 4 to 5 months behind his chronological age. This lag nearly doubles by the time the child reaches his second birthday" (Share, 1975, p. 80). Walking often does not occur until age 2 or 3. Hyperextensible joints and generalized hypotonia are characteristic.

3. In the area of physical appearance, individuals are often diagnosed as having Down's syndrome on the basis of simple inspection and physical examination (Smith & Berg, 1976). Hall (1966) listed the following ten signs and their frequency of occurrence in Down's syndrome in infancy: flat facial profile (90%), absent Moro reflex (85%), muscle hypotonia (80%), dysplastic ears (60%), excessive skin at the back of the neck (80%), oblique palpebral fissures (80%), hyperflexible joints (80%), dysplastic pelvis (70%), dysplastic middle phalanx of fifth finger (50%), and transverse palmer (simian) crease of palms (45%). Other common characteristics are as follows. The skull is brachycephalic with prominence of the forehead, shortening of the anteroposterior diameter, and flattening of the occiput. The oral cavity is small and contributes to the protrusion of the tongue. Drooling and delay in dentition are common. The palate is normal in height but is narrow and short. The eyes usually slant upward, and Brushfield spots (small whitish-yellow dots on the periphery of the iris) are common. Blepharitis (inflammation of the eyelids) is also common as are myopia, strabismus, and cataracts. The ears are small, often having an overfolded helix (Holmes et al., 1972; Sarason and Doris, 1969; Solomons, 1969). Congenital heart defects (ventricular septal defect, A-V communis, atrial septal defect, patent ductus) occur in approximately 40% of all Down's children (Gorlin, 1977) and acute leukemia is three to fifteen times more common than in normal controls (Solomons, 1969).

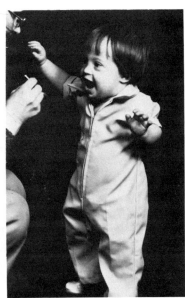

E.A.W., a 12-month-old youngster with trisomy 21 Down's syndrome, is the first and only child in his family. He has achieved his motor milestones as expected for children without the disorder. He is a lively, active youngster who has been fortunate in terms of the amount of time, love, and stimulation for learning and education to which he has been exposed. He has a small ventricular septal defect, but has been relatively free of upper respiratory infections.

4. In the behavioral-affective area of development, the Down syndrome child has been noted to have a generally amicable disposition. Nevertheless, stubbornness has been used to describe a characteristic behavior pattern (Benda, 1969). Although studies are somewhat unclear, there is no greater risk of emotional disturbance in Down syndrome than in other children (Sarason and Doris, 1969). However, hyperactivity is not uncommon. Social maturity is likely to exceed intellectual maturity.

The overall incidence of Down's syndrome in the United States is estimated at one per 600 live births (Solomons, 1969) to one per 700 (Holmes et al., 1972). About 50% succumb during the first five years with respiratory infections and congenital heart disease (Holmes et al., 1972; Kirman, 1964) Benda (1969) estimated a conservative life expectancy of about 30 years. This was based on institutionalized individuals, as no information was available on those who lived and died in the community (Benda, 1969). Males are sterile but the literature indicates that more than a dozen females have produced 16 children. Eleven were normal and 5 had Down's syndrome. All the mothers were trisomy 21 as were all the affected infants. (Solomons, 1969). The following case reports and photographs are included so that parental concerns and developmental achievement at different ages may be better understood in trisomy 21 (Down's syndrome).

CASE K.D.

K.D. is an 11-month-old child who was diagnosed as having Down's syndrome and was referred for evaluation and program planning. He is the third child but the only son of parents who are under 30 years of age. The diagnosis was made at birth, and the child had been healthy, apart from upper respiratory infections. On examination, he had the stigmata of Down's syndrome, but no Brushfield's spots, or simian line, and no congenital heart disease. On fine and gross motor evaluation, he was at the 6–7-month level. In language, he was at the 5–6-month level receptively and expressively.

Chromosome studies revealed trisomy 21. A home program for motor and language development was outlined in contemplation of plans for placement in developmental day care when he was 2 years 6 months old.

CASE E.J.C.

E.J.C., a 10-year-old child with Down's syndrome, was referred for help with future educational and vocational training as well as for consideration of an alternate living situation in the future.

She was the seventh and last child of a mother who was 39 years old at the time of E.J.'s birth. She had been enrolled in developmental day care at an early age, and then had been in the public schools in classes for the trainable mentally retarded. She had learned to read (but with little comprehension). Her speech had been very difficult to understand, and she had had palatal surgery as well as speech therapy, which helped considerably.

On psychological assessment, she was found to be functioning in the moderately retarded range. She had particular difficulty in the verbal area. Her behavior was variable and included overactivity and stubbornness, with assertive and negativistic qualities. Educational assessment revealed an ability to learn quickly by rote instruction, and her major strength was in reading and word-attack skills. By chromosome study, she was found to have trisomy 21 (Down's syndrome).

Recommendations included continuation in a TMR setting with continued language input and future placement in a vocational training center.

Infants with trisomy 18 syndrome (Edwards') are usually small and feeble. Males usually do not survive as long as females (Weber, 1967). Only 10% survive the first year and usually these are severely mentally retarded. Edwards et al. (1960) first described the syndrome. Common anomalies are prominent occiput, low-set malformed ears, small oral opening and narrow palatal arch, clenched hands with a tendency for overlapping of the index finger over the third and of the fifth finger over the fourth, prominent cutis marmoratum, rocker-bottom feet, and congenital heart disease—usually ventricular septal defect or patent ductus arteriosus (Smith, 1970). Estimates of the incidence of trisomy 18 vary between 0.28 per 1,000 (Gorlin, 1977) and 0.15 per 1,000 live births (Nevin, 1976).

E.J.C. is a 10-year-old youngster with trisomy 21 Down's syndrome who is the youngest of 7 children. Figure 12 shows the epicanthal folds and oblique slant of her eyes. Figure 13 shows her breathing with her mouth open.

She has had recurrent upper respiratory infections, ear infections, and speech and language problems.

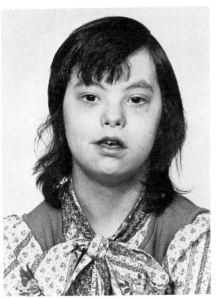 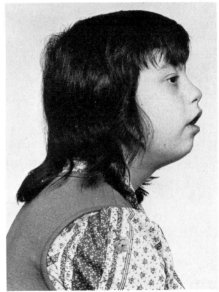

Infants with the trisomy 13 syndrome (Patau's) also rarely survive past a year of age, although one child is known to have survived to 10 years of age (Gorlin, 1977). Patau et al. (1960) first described this syndrome. The etiology of the trisomy is usually nondisjunction, although 20% of cases are caused by translocation (Gorlin, 1977). Affected infants tend to have localized scalp defects in the parietooccipital area, hypertelorism, iris coloboma with retinal dysplasia, cleft lip and palate, congenital heart defect including ventricular septal defect, patent ductus arteriosus, atrial septal defect, cryptorchidism, minor motor seizures, apneic spells in early infancy, and apparent deafness (Gorlin, 1977; Smith, 1970). Musculoskeletal anomalies include overlapping flexed fingers and rocker-bottom feet. Severe mental retardation is a common finding. The incidence has been estimated to be 0.13 per 1,000 live births (Nevin, 1976).

Children with cri-du-chat (the deletion of a portion of the short arm of chromosome 5) have a characteristic mewing sound in the newborn period. The syndrome was first described by Lejeune et al. (1963). Approximately 10%–15% of cases occur because of translocation. Affected children are usually severely mentally retarded, and have failure to thrive, hypotonia in infancy, microcephaly, a rounded face, and hypertelorism (Smith, 1970). The frequency is 0.02 per 1,000 live births (Nevin, 1976). The syndrome has been found to be present in about 1% of institutionalized individuals with an IQ <35 (Gorlin, 1977).

DISORDERS OF THE SEX CHROMOSOMES   Klinefelter, Reifenstein, and Albright (1942) described nine men with gynecomastia, aspermatogenesis, small testes, and increased excretion of follicle-stimulating hormone. This condition, now known as Klinefelter syndrome, is usually detected after puberty when the underdeveloped secondary sex characteristics and the testicular atrophy become apparent. The incidence is reported to be approximately 1 in 1,400 live births (Holmes et al., 1972).

In the same year that the abnormal chromosome count in Down's syndrome was reported, Jacobs and Strong (1959) reported a case of Klinefelter's syndrome which was found to have 47 chromosomes. On the basis of size and shape, the extra chromosome was thought to be an X chromosome yielding a male with an XXY genetic constitution rather than the normal XY male constitution. Nondisjunction is the postulated cause of the extra X chromosome and can be of maternal or paternal origin. For the

XXY form of Klinefelter's (80% of cases) maternal age is significantly advanced (Gorlin, 1977). Urinary levels of 17-ketosteroids are at the low range of normal and gonadotropins are usually increased (Myhre et al., 1970).

The manifestations of Klinefelter's syndrome are as follows:

1. In the cognitive-intellectual area, the majority of affected individuals are intellectually normal (Sarason and Doris, 1969; Holmes et al., 1972). Initially, a high incidence of mental retardation was recorded in association with Klinefelter's. However, these reports reflected a sample of institutionalized people of whom 0.5–1% were found to have the syndrome (Gorlin, 1977). Speech and language development is delayed in about 25% (Gerald, 1976).
2. The physical features include long legs with a slim body build, small penis and testes, and excessive development of male mammary glands (gynecomastia). Bradyclinodactyly (short, in-curved finger) and limitation of pronation-supination of the forearm are more subtle features that may not be noticed.
3. In the affective-behavioral area, there is no common pattern of psychopathology, but there have been reports of psychosexual confusion, disturbances of body image and self-concept, some feminine identification, and a lability of affect with poor planning (Kvale and Fishman, 1965).

Treatment consists of androgen replacement, which has been effective when administered during adolescence, both in decreasing gynecomastia and in aiding the maturation of secondary sex characteristics. It has been noticed that behavior can change in terms of better self-concept and increased assertiveness and goal directiveness, coincidental with the physical changes (Myhre et al., 1970). However, Gerald (1976) has noted that many patients will fail to continue their medication. Individuals with Klinefelter's syndrome have a normal life span.

Turner (1938) reported on seven females with sexual infantilism, webbing of the neck, short stature and deformity of the elbow (cubitus valgus). Again in 1959, a case was reported of Turner's syndrome with chromosomal analysis showing only 45 chromosomes, the missing one assumed to be an X, thus presenting as an XO (Ford et al., 1959). The monosomy is thought to be brought about either by meiotic nondisjunction or by loss of a sex chromosome (either X or Y) during an early cleavage division of the zygote. Holmes et al. (1972) report the frequency to be about 1 in 3,300 live births. Approximately 60% of cases of Turner's syndrome are XO, whereas the remainder have X chromosome partial deletion or replication, or are mosaic (Gorlin, 1977). Three-fourths of the neonatally ascertained patients found in surveys of newborn females by buccal smear were mosaic (Gerald, 1976).

The manifestations of Turner's syndrome are as follows:

1. In the cognitive-intellectual area, individuals with Turner's syndrome are generally normal, and when retardation is present, it is usually not severe (Sarason and Doris, 1969). Speech and language are not usually affected nor is neuromotor functioning. There have been some reports of learning problems related to a defect in spatial orientation and perception (Gorlin, 1977).
2. Physical characteristics include short stature, broad shieldlike chest, low hair line over the nape of the neck, webbed neck (40%), congenital lymphedema of the extremities, especially the hands and feet, coarctation of the aorta (20%), cubitus valgus, high-arched palate, tendency for recurrent otitis media, and renal anomalies such as horseshoe kidney (80%). Ovaries are absent. Instead there is a ridge of connective tissue devoid of germinal elements (gonadal dysgenesis). Therefore, individuals with Turner's syndrome are amenorrheic and develop none of the secondary sexual characteristics expected at puberty except sexual hair. Diagnosis both by buccal smear and chromosome analysis is usually made at puberty because of short stature, amenorrhea, and lack of secondary sexual characteristics.

Little is mentioned in the literature about affective-behavioral manifestations, and in our experience there is no outstanding characteristic presentation, apart from poor self-concept. In order to promote psychosexual development, cyclic estrogen therapy is indicated at adolescence and usually helps with adaptation. Affected individuals usually have a normal life span.

Multiple Malformations

NEURAL TUBE DEFECTS   Recently neural tube defects, which include anencephaly and meningomyelocele, have been receiving a great deal of attention because of the recent availability of methods for prenatal diagnosis. By measuring amniotic fluid α-fetoprotein or maternal serum α-fetoprotein (Brock, 1972; Milunsky, and Alpert, 1974), it has become possible to detect anencephaly or meningomyelocele prenatally with accuracy ranging from 60% to 92% for the former and 29% to 50% for the latter (Milunsky and Alpert, 1976). It may well be that before long, screening maternal serum for α-fetoprotein will become part of the routine obstetric evaluation. If not made prenatally, the diagnosis of a neural tube defect is made at birth.

Anencephaly occurs in from 0.1 to 6.7 per 1,000 live births (Shulman, 1972) and is the most common central nervous system malformation incompatible with life. The infant usually dies soon after birth.

Meningomyelocele is a sac that contains spinal fluid, incompletely formed meninges and malformed spinal cord; often it is weeping and may become infected. It is most common in the lumbosacral area and there is neurologic deficit below the level of the mass. The most serious complication is the development of hydrocephalus, which might occur subsequent to a block in spinal fluid flow, either because of the obliteration of subarachnoid pathways or subsequent to ascending infection from the sac. Hydrocephalus occurs in 80% of cases.

The frequency of meningomyelocele is accepted as one per 500 to one per 1,000 live births. Milunsky speaks about an increased incidence of one per 300 in infants whose mothers are over 35 years of age. The estimated recurrence risk usually given in genetic counseling to a family who has had one child with a neural tube defect is 5%. However, according to Holmes (1976), genetic counseling needs to be done with the realization that there are different causes for neural tube defects. If etiology is not considered, the overall recurrence rate in siblings is 1.7%. If it is considered, recurrence rate varies from 0% to 25%.

There has always been a difference of opinion about the management of children with meningomyelocele and hydrocephalus (Lorber, 1976). Those children who are not treated may or may not survive. However, even in Lorber's series of 848 infants, *all* of whom were treated aggressively surgically, only 50% survived. Those children who are treated by repair of the meningomyelocele soon after birth, and the early shunting of the hydrocephalus may manifest the following.

1. In the cognitive-intellectual area, there is a wide range of variability from above average to severely retarded functioning. In Lorber's series (1976), 41% of the severely physically handicapped children (81.4% of survivors) demonstrated an IQ <80. The level of functioning seems to be related to the thickness of the cortex at the time of the shunt as well as to the history of central nervous system infection such as encephalitis and meningitis (Hunt and Holmes, 1976).
2. In the affective-behavioral area of development many children with meningomyelocele are extremely pleasant and cooperative. They tend to be optimistic and happy and some demonstrate the "cocktail-party chatter" syndrome.
3. The physical findings are primarily related to neurologic deficit below the

level of the defect. Some children have been able to walk if the lesion is below L4–5. Most are wheelchair dependent, however, and are subject to decubiti. Scoliosis is common. Repeated fractures are common. Affected individuals are also subject to hip dislocation and to chronic problems with lack of sphincter control. Recurrent urinary tract infections because of inability to empty the bladder are common, and diversionary surgery has to be considered. Even then, urinary tract infections may be frequent; and a need for revision of the surgery is not unusual. The other major area of physical difficulty is the problem with the ventricular shunts that are needed to relieve hydrocephalus. It is not unusual for the shunts to become occluded or infected so that revisions of these are also needed. Of the survivers in Lorber's series (1976), only 1.4% have no handicap; 17.2% have moderate handicap, and the remainder have severe multisystem physical defects. The projected cost of lifetime care for one child with open spina bifida has been estimated at $100,000–$250,000 (Milunsky and Alpert, 1976). As a result of their experience, Lorber (1976) has set forth guidelines for selection of cases for treatment, and has made a plea for more antenatal detection.

SYNDROMES OF MULTIPLE MALFORMATION   There are many syndromes of multiple malformations associated with mental deficiency some of which are genetic in etiology and some of which are multifactorial. Among them are the Prader-Willi syndrome (Hall and Smith, 1972), Rubenstein-Taybi syndrome (Rubenstein and Taybi, 1963), Cornelia de Lange syndrome (Berg et al., 1970; Ptacek et al., 1963), Williams syndrome (Williams, Barratt-Boyes, and Lowe, 1961; Jones and Smith, 1975), tuberous sclerosis (Bourneville's Disease), and neurofibromatosis. We will briefly discuss neurofibromatosis and tuberous sclerosis as representative examples of this group.

Neurofibromatosis first described by Friedrich Daniel von Recklinghausen (1882) is one of the neurocutaneous syndromes and is dominantly inherited. The manifestations are physical and cognitive-intellectual. In the area of cognitive-intellectual functioning, 10% to 25% of patients with neurofibromatosis are retarded, and most of these are in the mild range (Jones, 1975). The physical manifestations consist of café au lait spots on the skin, neurofibromas involving both the peripheral and central nervous system, and localized areas of osteosclerosis. Seventy-five percent of patients with neurofibromatosis have six or more café au lait spots measuring 1.5 cm or larger in diameter. In many, the café au lait spots are the only manifestations of neurofibromatosis. Although peripheral neurofibromas can be unsightly, central gliomas of the optic or acoustic nerves can cause

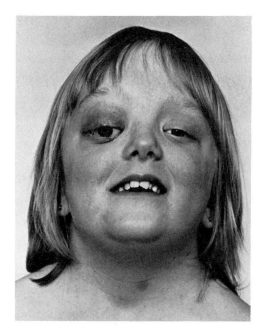

D.T. is a 7-year-old youngster with neurofibromatosis which was diagnosed after she developed an optic glioma. In Figure 14, one can see the artificial eye on the right as well as a prominent café au lait spot on her neck. Figure 15: Examination of her mother's back revealed several large café au lait spots as well as neurofibromas. In addition, the mother had been treated for hypertension which was thought to be related to the disorder.

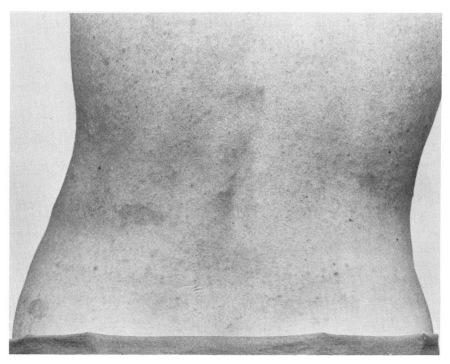

vision or hearing loss. Scoliosis may be associated with the presence of neurofibromas on the spinal nerve roots. Hypertension related to pheochromocytoma has been reported in increased incidence in neurofibromatosis. A more complete description of neurofibromatosis may be found in Ford (1966).

Tuberous sclerosis, first described by Bourneville (1880), is another dominantly inherited neurocutaneous disorder with variable expression, whose manifestations are also in the physical and cognitive-intellectual areas. Physical manifestations include "ashleaf spots," which are dull white macules often present at birth, the "shagreen patch" (orange-peel consistency), which is found on the trunk and lower extremities, and adenoma sebaceum, which develops in the nasolabial folds in adolescence. Hamartomas (benign, tumorlike nodules resulting from an overgrowth of normal tissue) of the brain, kidney, and heart occur frequently and are the most common cause of death in children with this disorder. Seizures are related to the extent of hamartomatous change in the brain. Sixty-nine percent of those without mental deficiency have seizures. Of those with mental deficiency, 100% develop seizures (Smith, 1970). The presence and degree of mental retardation is related to the extent of hamartomatous change in the brain.

Other Inherited Syndromes

MUSCULAR DYSTROPHY The pseudohypertrophic dystrophy of Duchenne, or childhood muscular dystrophy, is transmitted as a sex-linked recessive and is characterized as a rapidly progressive myopathy that begins in early childhood (Zundel and Tyler, 1965). The principal manifestation is in the motor area, and the commonest presenting symptoms are clumsiness and gait abnormality. Muscle weakness usually begins in the pelvic girdle and is responsible for a waddling gait. Pseudohypertrophy affects the gastrocnemius in 80% of the cases and is usually striking. Gower's sign is the particular way that patients with muscular dystrophy have of "walking up their legs" in order to get to a standing position from a seated one on the floor. Cognitively, mild to moderate mental retardation is not unusual. The progressive nature of the disease makes survival beyond age 20 a rarity.

KERNICTERUS Kernicterus resulting from blood group incompatibility (both Rh and ABO) can also be considered among the genetic causes of mental retardation. In kernicterus, bilirubin, which is an end product of hemoglobin degradation, is deposited in the nuclei of the basal ganglia, particularly the lenticular and caudate nuclei (Ford, 1966). The subsequent clinical picture in surviving infants, includes hypotonia, paralysis of upward gaze, nerve deafness, and opisthotonus. Later, choreiform and athetotic movements develop. Those severely affected may have seizures and failure to thrive i.e., height and weight <3rd percentile. Cognitively, variable degrees of retardation may be manifest depending on the serum level of bilirubin. The treatment of kernicterus is prevention. This has been accomplished in recent years through the use of hyperimmune globulin (Freda et al., 1978) or fetal transfusions prenatally, and/or the use of exchange transfusions and phototherapy (Lucey, 1972; Lucey et al., 1968) postnatally.

ENVIRONMENTAL FACTORS

The environmental factors of importance in the etiology of mental deficiency in the prenatal period include intrauterine infection (TORCH), poor maternal health, psychosocial factors, and poor functioning of the materno-placento-fetal unit.

Congenital Infections

Recently, there has been much interest in the manifestations of prenatal infection by the TORCH Group. The TORCH acronym stands for TOxoplasmosis, Rubella, Cytomegalovirus, and Herpes, and is a reminder that the manifestations of each may be clinically similar to the others. A newborn infant who is small for gestational age and microcephalic (occasionally hydrocephalic), one presenting with jaundice, hepatosplenomegaly, rash (vesicular, petechial), and chorioretinitis, or cataracts, shows presumptive evidence of a generalized infection with one of the TORCH agents. Many affected infants do not survive the newborn period. In those who do, severe central nervous system involvement with retardation and/or cerebral palsy has been considered the rule. However, there has been considerable interest recently in the breadth of the entire clinical spectrum caused by TORCH agents since it is now recognized that "severe infection" represents only a small percentage of TORCH symptoms.

TOXOPLASMOSIS   Congenital toxoplasmosis was first described by Wolf, Cowen, and Paige, (1939) with manifestations of encephalitis, seizures, chorioretinitis, and intracranial calcification. It is caused by *Toxoplasma gondii*, a protozoon, and is passed transplacentally from an infected mother to the fetus. The manifestations of infection in the mother often go unnoticed or may be expressed as posterior cervical lymphadenopathy or the "flu." Infection is thought to occur by eating poorly cooked meat or by contacts with animals, specifically cats.

The manifestations of congenital toxoplasmosis are variable depending on the gestational age at which the infection was acquired by the mother. Infection acquired before pregnancy probably will not result in congenital infection (Feldman and Miller, 1956; Desmonts and Couvreur, 1974). Infection acquired during the first two trimesters may result in abortion or in the birth of a severely involved infant with microcephaly, chorioretinitis, cerebral calcifications, mental retardation, and seizure disorder. When the infection is acquired in the third trimester, the infant will have more mild or "subclinical" involvement at birth (Desmonts and Couvreur, 1974). In a long-term follow-up study of nine infants born with "subclinical" involvement (Alford, Stagno, and Reynolds, 1975), two of the infants have developed significant chorioretinitis, one has a sensorineural hearing deficit, and one has manifested microcephaly, chorioretinitis, mild hepatosplenomegaly, and intracranial calcifications. Cognitive-intellectual evaluation has revealed an average reduction of 17 points in IQ (110 to 93) as compared with matched controls.

The incidence of toxoplasmosis in France has been reported as 6.3 per 100 per year. Of 183 pregnant women with high antibody titers whose infection was acquired during the pregnancy, 59 (33%) had infants with toxoplasmosis and seven pregnancies ended in abortion. Fifteen percent of the 59 had severe disease, 19% had mild disease (i.e., normal at birth except for chorioretinitis), and 66% had subclinical illness (i.e., developed chorioretinitis and/or cerebral calcifications after several months of age) (Desmonts and Couvreur, 1974). In Birmingham, Alabama, the incidence of IgM-positive newborns has been reported as 1 out of 750 (Alford et al., 1975). Diagnosis may be made serologically by serial antibody titers in the mother and/or infant, or by isolation of the organism. Spinal fluid protein elevation has been reported to be the best prognostic indicator regarding severity of disease. That is, those patients with a grossly elevated spinal fluid protein (>500 mg%) during the first month after delivery had a poorer prognosis than those with less marked elevation (150–285 mg%) (Alford et al., 1975). They have recommended treatment of those with spinal fluid or eye findings with sulfadiazine and pyrimethamine for a month, beginning shortly after delivery, in order to reduce disability. In France, Desmonts and Couvreur (1974) have recommended treatment of infected mothers during pregnancy with spiramycin. By using this therapy, the incidence of healthy, uninfected infants was raised from 44% to 76%.

RUBELLA   Rubella is the congenital infection that has received the most publicity. Lundstrom (1962) first described the high rate of severe sequelae that may follow first trimester infection of the fetus. Infants may be born with obvious involvement (low birth weight—51% are less than 2500 grams (Cooper, 1975)—jaundice, hepatosplenomegaly, thrombocytopenic purpura, microcephaly, and hemolytic anemia), or they may appear normal only to manifest mild or severe involvement later. Some infants may appear normal and remain normal. However, 35% of those whose mothers have rubella in the first month of pregnancy are affected. Similarly, 25% of those whose mothers have rubella in the second month, and 10% of those whose mothers have rubella in the third month are affected (Babson et al., 1975). In the epidemic of 1964, an estimated 20,000 (Weller, 1971) to 30,000 (Cooper, 1975) children with rubella-associated birth defects were born in the United States. Of these, 1,790 are retarded, 8,000 are deaf, and 3,500 are blind. The direct cost has been estimated at $920,000,000 (Weller, 1971).

The Rubella Project (Cooper, 1975) begun in 1964, is a longitudinal follow-up study of nearly 400 children with congenital rubella who were referred because of relatively serious polyorgan disease. Cognitive-intellectual functioning was evaluated at 8 to 9 years of age, at which time 26% of 210 children tested were in the mentally retarded range. Of these, 2 were in the borderline category, 3 were in the mild range, 7 were in the moderate, 15 were in the severe, and 21 were in the profound range of mental retardation. The degree of retardation was not specified in six. Language is affected in relation to the retardation and to the deafness.

The percentages of major physical manifestations are as follows: 87% show loss of hearing (Organ of Corti and central); 34%, cataract (glaucoma); and 46% congenital heart disease. The 1964 epidemic was responsible for the swelling of the deaf-blind population from less than 200 reported cases being served in educational facilities in 1968 to 4,000 in 1975. Rubella children have been found to be at risk for developing diabetes and thyroid disorders.

In a separate study, Peckham (1972) found that 23% of 84 babies who appeared normal at birth, but who had serologic evidence for rubella, manifested rubellalike defects (usually deafness associated with retinopathy) at 1 to 4 years of age. By 6 to 8 years of age, an additional nine children demonstrated defects (three with bilateral deafness, four with unilateral deafness, and two with retinopathy).

In the behavioral-affective area, 50% of the children in the Rubella Project had no psychiatric disorder, 18% had a "reactive behavior disorder," 3% had a neurotic behavior disorder, and 12% manifested "cerebral dysfunction." Of paramount interest is the fact that 6% were autistic. (The usual incidence of autism in the general population is 0.045%.) More detail about affective disturbance in children with congenital rubella is available in the study by Chess, Korn, and Fernandez (1971).

Learning is seriously affected. The Rubella Project demonstrated that only 10% of the children could negotiate school without resource help. The others needed resource room help or special schools, that is, schools for the deaf and/or multiply handicapped. Thirty-six percent are enrolled in special education for single handicaps and 17% are in special education for multiple handicaps. Eleven percent are institutionalized and 2% are not placed.

Treatment has been aimed primarily at prevention by immunization prior to pregnancy. Termination of pregnancy is recommended for laboratory-confirmed cases during the first trimester. Diagnosis may be accomplished both by serologic evidence of maternal infection and by isolation of virus from amniotic fluid (Levin et al., 1974).

CYTOMEGALOVIRUS (CMV)   In spite of the publicity that rubella has received, CMV is the infectious agent most frequently associated with congenital injury and damage in the United States today (Lang, 1975, p.35). CMV is a member of the herpesvirus family and has the ability to establish latent or active infection. Infection occurs in about 1% of all live-born infants, and it is estimated that at least 10% of these will eventually manifest "significant damage" (Lang, 1975). Diagnosis can be made by culture or by serology.

CMV has been recovered from urine, saliva, semen, cervical secretions, breast milk, and blood. By childbearing age, 40% to 50% of white, middle-class American women are CMV antibody positive. There is an even higher incidence in lower socioeconomic groups, and there has been some thought that the spread of CMV might be related to poor hygiene and/or communal living. The type of infection seems to depend somewhat on the age and immunocompetency of the patient. Acquired CMV infection in adults may present as heterophile-negative infectious mononucleosis, interstitial pneumonia, hepatitis, or mild and subclinical illness (flu). Once established, the infection tends to persist either continuously or intermittently. Reactivation of latent virus is associated with organ transplantation, blood transfusions, malignancy, and pregnancy—and seems to be related to the presence of foreign antigens or to depressed immunologic reactivity (Lang, 1975).

Congenital CMV infection may follow reactivation or reinfection as well as primary maternal infection during pregnancy. The relationship of the serologic response to infection/reinfection/reactivation of CMV is being examined because the usual rule, namely, that a prior infection with a demonstrated specific antibody rise conveys protection against future infection, does not seem to apply to CMV. The wisdom of preparing a vaccine is thus being questioned (Lang, 1975). There is no known treatment.

The degree to which the fetus is involved, depends on the gestational age and the virulence of the organism. Infection might also occur during the birth process by contact with cervical secretions. The entire spectrum of disability due to CMV is not known. Certainly the syndrome of the severely affected infant with growth and mental deficiency, microcephaly, intracranial calcification, hepatosplenomegaly, jaundice, and hearing deficit is well known and may well be the result of a particularly virulent organism affecting the fetus early in gestation. Manifestations may be limited to the central nervous system (Hanshaw, 1975) and present as microcephaly, intracranial calcifications, retardation, seizures, and cerebral palsy.

One unanswered question is whether inapparent infection present at birth can result in sequelae later in life. It is known that most of the 1% of newborns affected at birth are clinically normal. Nevertheless, it is worthwhile to examine a recent follow-up study of "inapparent" congenital CMV infection. Hanshaw et al. (1975) found the cord blood of 53 out of 8,644 newborns tested (1:163) to be positive for CMV-IgM antibody. This antibody is formed by the fetus in response to prenatal exposure to CMV. Of those 53, 44 were available for testing and were evaluated at 3 years 6 months to 7 years of age, with an equal number of control children matched for age, sex, race, birth weight, and social class. A second random control group consisted of the 44 children born immediately after the birth of the positive CMV-IgM baby.

In the cognitive-intellectual area, those infants with a positive CMV-IgM antibody titer achieved a mean IQ of 102.5 compared with the matched controls who achieved a mean IQ of 111.7 compared with the random controls who achieved a mean IQ of 119.2. Of the positive CMV-IgM babies, 15.8% had an IQ 79 or below. None of the controls had an IQ < 80. Physical manifestations included microcephaly in 16.3%, hearing loss bilaterally in 12.5% (with a questionable hearing loss in an additional 15%), and chorioretinitis in 2.3%. Because of intellectual, behavioral, or sensory abnormalities, a prediction was made that 36.3% of the positive CMV-IgM babies would need "special education not available in the usual school setting" (Hanshaw et al., 1975, p. 50). This was in contrast to the matched controls of whom 13.6% were predicted to experience school failure, and the random controls of whom only 4.5% were predicted to manifest school failure. School failure was closely related to social class as well, but 2.7 times as many school failures occurred among the positive CMV children in social classes IV and V (Hollingshead index), compared with the controls in the same classes.

The value of such comprehensive longitudinal studies is inestimable as we try to understand the etiology and manifestations of developmental disabilities, and as we consider prevention, treatment, and allocation of resources. The question about who is at risk for what remains extremely important, and studies such as this help us to better understand the interrelationship of organic and environmental factors so that informed decisions can be made in the future regarding prevention and treatment.

HERPES SIMPLEX VIRUS (HSV)   Asymptomatic herpes simplex virus (HSV) infection is thought to be relatively infrequent. The fetus may be involved locally (CNS, eye, skin, oral cavity) or in a disseminated fashion by either HSV_1 or HSV_2. According to Nahmias et al. (1975), only HSV_2 has been shown to be associated with chorioretinitis. Blattner (1974) reported that the majority of neonatal herpes virus infections in the newborn are Type 2, and Nahmias et al. (1975) indicated that 30% of neonatal herpes is caused by Type 1 and 70% by Type 2. Of 89 cases with Type 2 followed by Nahmias et al. (1975), 78% had disseminated disease or encephalitis, and 52% of them died. Only 20% survived without sequelae. Of 40 cases with Type 1, 70% had disseminated disease or encephalitis, and 71% died; only 7% survived without apparent sequelae.

If the infection is local (e.g., vesicles on skin, mouth ulcers), then prognosis for survival without sequelae is fairly good, though reports about school performance and cognitive functioning are not available. If the infection is disseminated or localized to the central nervous system, the prognosis for survival is poor (30%), and in survivors, sequelae are common (Nahmias et al., 1975). Treatment with idoxuridine or cytosine arabinoside has been discouraging. Therefore, the approach has been one of prevention (e.g., delivering by cesarean section since it is believed that the infant is often infected through contact with maternal genital herpes). The preparation and use of hyperimmune globulin is under consideration.

SYPHILIS   Syphilis is another of the congenital infections frequently considered with the TORCH Group. The incidence of congenital syphilis has more than doubled over the past 10 years, and in 1972 1,932 cases were reported to the U. S. Public Health Service (Taber and Huber, 1975). Usually, congenital syphilis is the result of an infection after the 16th week of gestation. The product of the pregnancy may be normal, may be aborted, may be stillborn, may be born with obvious disease at the time of birth, or may have onset of disease later in life.

Some newborn manifestations of congenital syphilis include hepatosplenomegaly, pneumonia alba, periostitis, jaundice, and snuffles. Later, interstitial keratitis with subsequent decrease in visual acuity, sensorineural deafness, Hutchinson's teeth, and Clutton's joints may all be manifestations of congenital syphilis. Involvement of the central nervous system is the most serious consequence. Untreated congenital neurosyphilis may present in childhood (10–15 years) with learning problems in school and progressive degeneration of central nervous system functioning. Dullness, apathy, and forgetfulness are among the first symptoms. Antisocial acts are not uncommon. Mild euphoria is quite common. Speech and language become unintelligible and progressive motor deterioration occurs. The course is slow and progressive until the child becomes completely demented. Diagnosis can be confirmed in the infant by specific serologic (VDRL) and immunologic [IgM, FTA-ABS (IgM)] studies. Treatment in the newborn period is an adequate dose of penicillin (Taber and Huber, 1975).

Maternal Factors

The other environmental prenatal factors that place an individual at high risk for mental retardation are maternal ill health during pregnancy, including high or low weight, anemia, diabetes, drug exposure and addiction, alcoholism, renal disease, and seizure disorder. Other factors that play important roles are socioeconomic status, maternal age, maternal emotional status, and the functioning of the materno-placento-fetal unit.

MATERNAL WEIGHT: EXCESSIVE GAINS AND LOSSES   Maternal weight gain has always been of concern to obstetricians, primarily because of the close relationship of excessive weight gain and fluid retention to eclampsia (edema, proteinuria, and hypertension with possible convulsions and coma). Pre-eclampsia and eclampsia in the mother are associated with higher perinatal mortality (8%–20% compared with an overall incidence of about 2%) in the fetus (Jaffe et al., 1976). Those who survive are at risk for being born with a low birth weight, whether they are born prematurely or at term, and for being hypotonic and asphyxiated. For these reasons, there has been a strict rule that only a weight gain of 20 lb during pregnancy would be tolerated. In recent years, however, because it is realized that not all who gain more than 20 lb will be stricken with eclampsia or pre-eclampsia, the more lenient weight gain of 24 lb is allowed (Babson et al., 1975).

Alternatively, maternal weight gain has been a concern when a mother's health is in jeopardy or she runs a risk of being malnourished. The mother is then less likely to be able to fight off infection. Moreover, abnormal bleeding and premature labor are more common with maternal malnutrition (Babson et al., 1976). Finally, the fetus itself will suffer when its mother is malnourished. Mothers exposed to famine during pregnancy give birth to babies of lower birth weight (Gruenwald et al., 1967; Smith, 1947). Animal studies have demonstrated that starvation during pregnancy results in less DNA, RNA, and protein content of fetal brains (Winick, 1974). These studies have caused concern that human maternal malnutrition may result in mental deficiency and other serious CNS insults in offspring. However, Stein et al. (1972) found no effect on the mental performances of young Dutch men who were preparing for induction to the army and who had been exposed prenatally to the famine in Holland in 1944–1945. Levine and Wiener (1976, p. 131) also concluded that "although malnutrition is a major insult to the developing organism, the organism has a remarkable resiliency, and following nutritional rehabilitation shows very few major deficits in later performance as a consequence of the early malnutrition."

At present, then, there is no unanimity of opinion regarding the long-term effects of fetal malnutrition. The most that can be said is that there may well be meaningful measurable biochemical effects, but the issue is very much confused by the adequacy of the postnatal nutritional and learning environment. Anemia in the mother, which may or may not be related to maternal malnutrition, is known, however, to be associated with prematurity and low birth weight in the infant.

DIABETES   Diabetic and prediabetic mothers have babies who are large for gestational age, predisposed to the respiratory distress syndrome (Robert et al., 1976), and physiologically "immature for dates" (Pildes, 1973). The severity of maternal diabetes has been classified by White (1974) from Class A (mild) to Class E (severe). As the severity increases, the infant is more likely to be small for gestational age owing to vascular disease in the mother. It is not unusual for infants of diabetic mothers to be delivered by cesarean section when the chances of extrauterine survival seem more promising than those offered by the intrauterine environment. Assessment of survival chances begins by the measurement of serial urinary estriol levels, by the oxytocin challenge test, and by the examination of amniotic fluid. Infants of diabetic mothers are at risk for hypoglycemia in the newborn period.

OVERUSE OF DRUGS AND ALCOHOL   Little is yet known with certainty about the effect on the fetus of maternal exposure to drugs, but there is evidence that many commonly used pharmaceutical products when taken in early pregnancy may be responsible for teratogenesis and/or retardation (Korones, 1976; Milkovich and van den Berg, 1974; Pomerance and Yaffe, 1973). Infants exposed prenatally to chronic maternal alcoholism are subject to craniofacial, limb, and cardiovascular defects as well as to growth deficiency and mental subnormality (Jones et al., 1973; Streissguth, 1976). In a prospective study of the fetal alcohol syndrome at the Boston City Hospital, Ouellette and Rosett (1976; Ouellette et al., 1977) reported that 65% of infants of mothers who abstained or drank moderately were normal on the initial neurological examination at two to three days of life. In contrast, only 29% of the infants of mothers who drank heavily (average 174 ml of absolute alcohol per day) were normal on the initial neurological examination. The abnormalities consisted of hypotonia or jitteriness, and poor suck. Furthermore, five of 42 infants (12%) were microcephalic. The babies were small, some on the basis of prematurity (17%). Others were small for gestational age (27%). More long-term followup studies are in progress.

Infants who are exposed prenatally to heroin through the addiction of the mother tend to be small for gestational age and to have withdrawal symptoms characterized by tremor, irritability, hypotonicity, high-pitched cry, decreased sleeping time, diarrhea, sucking alterations, and fever soon after birth. Respiratory distress and hyperbilirubinemia are distinctly unusual (Rothstein and Gould, 1974). Those infants exposed to methadone, however, are prone to even more marked withdrawal, and to hyperbilirubinemia (Zelson, Sook, and Casalino, 1973). Treatment of the withdrawal symptoms is indicated in the neonatal period. The long-term sequelae of heroin exposure in utero are not known.

Other maternal factors that may adversely affect the developing fetus and the manner in which the fetus might be affected are indicated below. This is not an exhaustive list or discussion, but will serve to acquaint the reader with some of the more frequent problems encountered.

Mothers with renal disease are subject to eclampsia, and the fetus is then at high risk owing to low birth weight. Seizure disorder in the mother exposes the fetus both to the deleterious effects of the seizures themselves (hypoxia, acid-base changes) and to the effects of the anticonvulsant drugs (Korones, 1976, p.39). Adolescent mothers are more likely to have low birth weight appropriate for gestational age (premature) babies. In unwed mothers, the incidence of low birth weight babies and of perinatal mortality is doubled (Babson et al., 1975). Mothers over 35 are at high risk for having infants with chromosomal disorders.

Psychosocial Disadvantage

Adverse psychosocial and emotional factors can affect not only the pregnant mother but also the fetus, though the mechanism is unknown. The designation of "low socioeconomic status" implies certain characteristics that include low income, poor job status or unemployment, lack of adequate and appropriate nutrition, and lack of appropriate clothing. It is a global picture, but all aspects may not apply to every individual characterized as being of "low socioeconomic status." Nevertheless, there has been documentation that in this group of people there is a higher incidence of prematurity and perinatal mortality. In quoting 1966 statistics from Oregon, Babson et al. (1975) showed that there was more than a doubling of the incidence of prematurity—and more than a tripling of the incidence of perinatal mortality—in comparing the infants of farm laborers and farmers. Myerowitz and Lipkin (1976, p.267) conclude, "Adverse economic, social and family circumstances for the pregnant woman are associated with . . . prematurity, low birth weight and subsequent developmental problems for their infants." Gordon (1975, p.6) cites a 1973 study of the National Academy of Sciences in which mothers at "no risk" who received adequate prenatal care "bore 5.8% of their live-born infants weighing 5½ pounds or less; the comparable figure for women at risk and who received inadequate care was 19.6%." It has been impossible to separate out which of the many factors involved are responsible for the poor outcome.

Certainly these mothers are "at risk" for physical problems such as poor nutrition, anemia, eclampsia, poor or nonexistent prenatal care, and infection. The effects of poor education; of feelings of inadequacy, hopelessness, anger, and despair; of noisy and crowded living conditions; and of inadequate clothing are unknown. Stott (1971) has discussed the relationship of psychologic stress during pregnancy to the occurrence of malformation and mental retardation. Babson et al. (1975, p.12) mentions "family distress" as a "possible cause" of early delivery or fetal deprivation. More needs to be learned about the effect of these prenatal environmental stresses on the developing fetus.

Malfunction of the Materno-Placento-Fetal Unit

The proper functioning of the materno-placento-fetal unit is essential to fetal well-being, and any interference in blood supply (oxygen and nutritional supply) to the fetus could result in the malfunction of essential organs, especially the central nervous system (Dancis, 1975). Premature placental separation, infarcted placenta, a prolapsed cord (or one wrapped tightly around the neck), and trauma that injures the placenta and/or fetus are representative of the kinds of environmental influences that might result in mental deficiency because of impaired blood flow and subsequent hypoxia. Furthermore, those pregnancies complicated by diabetes, hypertension, eclampsia, and preeclampsia are at risk for developing uteroplacental dysfunction that would interfere with the proper exchange of oxygen, carbon dioxide, and nutrients between mother and fetus and could lead to fetal hypoxia, prematurity and/or growth retardation.

TESTING FOR MALFUNCTION   At present there are several available methods by which to follow pregnancies and determine early if the fetus is in trouble. An informed decision can then be made about the welfare of the fetus in utero versus the health of the newborn if the pregnancy is terminated. In the prenatal period, the normal pattern of maternal estriol levels is a valuable indicator of fetal health because the synthesis of estriol requires a normal placenta and normal fetal adrenal cortex. A decrease in estriol production is believed to indicate that the fetus is in jeopardy. When the fall is precipitous, as might occur with maternal diabetes, it may well be an indication for intervention.

Ultrasound is used for estimating fetal head size and gestational age as well as for locating the placenta prior to amniocentesis. As mentioned earlier, the examination of amniotic fluid obtained by amniocentesis early in pregnancy has become a useful tool in making prenatal diagnoses of inborn errors of metabolism and chromosomal disorders. It is also useful later in pregnancy in evaluating fetal maturity by chemical analysis. A creatinine of 2 mg% is associated with a fetal weight of at least 2,500 grams, and a lecithin to sphingomyelin ratio of 2 or more is associated with fetal lung maturity and essentially no chance of death from hyaline membrane disease (the idiopathic respiratory distress syndrome). If the amniotic fluid is found to be meconium stained, this is considered to be an indication of fetal asphyxia and the need for intervention. When uteroplacental dysfunction is suspected prior to the onset of labor, the oxytocin challenge test can be used to monitor the fetal response to labor. If a "late deceleration" pattern is seen on monitoring the fetal heart rate, the fetus may well be subject to hypoxia during labor so that prevention of labor, and delivery by cesarean section would be warranted. By utilizing these new techniques and determining the welfare of the fetus, some mental subnormality can be prevented. Quilligan and Collea (1976) and Symonds (1976) review these techniques in more detail.

PERINATAL PERIOD
ENVIRONMENTAL FACTORS

Hypoxia–Asphyxia–Ischemia

The environmental factors of concern in the etiology of mental deficiency in the perinatal period are, in summary, fetal hypoxia-asphyxia-ischemia—which may be related to malfunction of the placenta and/or cord prior to and during labor and delivery—birth trauma, malnutrition, and infection. As indicated earlier, the advances in recent years in monitoring the progression of pregnancy have made it possible to prevent some morbidity and mortality. The current efforts at collaboration between obstetricians and neonatologists in the field of perinatal medicine should further improve matters. And in fact, neonatal (first 28 days) mortality rates have decreased from 20.5 per 1,000 live births in 1950 to 11.7 in 1975 (Wegman, 1976). A more complete discussion of improved neurologic outcome will be found on page 67.

The process of labor presents many opportunities for fetal hypoxia and possible asphyxia. Umbilical cord compression or prolapse, premature placental separation, and/or maternal hypotension as a result of bleeding, medication, or positioning can result in fetal hypoxia. Monitoring the fetal heart rate during labor is used to determine as early as possible any sign of fetal distress. For example, a pattern of "variable deceleration" in fetal heart rate is suggestive of umbilical cord compression and might be improved by a change in maternal position, for example from the supine position to lying on her side. On the other hand, if improvement is not noted and the pattern becomes one of "late deceleration," then labor might need to be slowed and cesarean section performed. The goal is to prevent hypoxia-asphyxia.

When this is not accomplished and the fetus is deprived of sufficient oxygen, the infant at birth is usually depressed and has a low Apgar score (James and Adamsons, 1972, p. 71). Every attempt at quick resuscitation must be made; the procedure may include endotracheal intubation with adequate oxygenation, external cardiac massage, and the administering of appropriate fluids and nutrients, for example glucose and bicarbonate. A low five-minute Apgar (< 6) is closely related to both an increased incidence of perinatal mortality (up to 15 times) and to an increased incidence of neurologic abnormality (Korones, 1976; Fitzhardinge, 1975). The degree of neurologic abnormality depends on the severity and duration of hypoxia and on the condition of the infant prior to delivery (maturity and nutritional state). There is no definitely known time period of perinatal hypoxia–asphyxia which the infant can withstand and remain unscathed. There is a high correlation of perinatal asphyxia and birth trauma, and subsequent neonatal seizures. In fact, these perinatal complications account for 36% of the cases of neonatal seizures among full-term infants (Volpe, 1973).

Infants who are of low birth weight (Battaglia and Lubchenco, 1967; Dubowitz et al., 1970; Lubchenco et al., 1963) and are appropriate in size for their gestational age (preterm) are at high risk for asphyxia at birth and for hyaline membrane disease after birth. In this group, 50% of neonatal seizures are the result of perinatal asphyxia and trauma (Volpe, 1973). Hyaline membrane disease or the idiopathic respiratory distress syndrome is associated with possible hypoxia and acidosis, so that prevention of mortality and morbidity demands strict monitoring of blood gases with attention to adequate ventilation. Though the idiopathic respiratory distress syndrome may occur in any infant, the largest number of cases occurs in small preterm infants. The overall incidence is 0.5% to 1.0% of all deliveries (Klaus, 1972). In the study by Fitzhardinge (1975), 46% of 67 infants whose gestational age was <33 weeks and whose mean birth weight was 1,403 grams had hyaline membrane disease.

The survival rate of infants with the respiratory distress syndrome who require assisted ventilation (most severe) ranges from 30% for infants <1,250 grams to 61% for those >1500 grams (Fitzhardinge, 1975). Intracranial hemorrhage is the leading cause of death and is present in 65% to 75% of all autopsies of respiratory distress babies (Krishnamoorthy, 1976). Volpe (1976) has summarized the pathology that occurs as a result of perinatal hypoxic-ischemic brain injury.

The quality of survival depends on the severity of the respiratory distress syndrome (hypoxia-asphyxia), the degree of prematurity, and the presence of intracranial bleeding and seizure phenomena. Johnson et al. (1974) reported that 17% of 55 infants who required assisted ventilation had moderate-severe neurologic handicap. Krishnamoorthy (1976) found that 15% of 202 such infants had moderate-severe neurologic sequelae that included spastic diplegia, hydrocephalus, quadriplegia, choreoathetosis, DQ less than 80 in all and less than 50 in most, strabismus, and/or deafness. Twenty-two percent of those less than 1,500 grams were in this moderate-severe group. Seventeen percent of those who weighed between 1,501 and 2,500 grams at birth were in this category. Fitzhardinge (1975) found that 22.5% of the boys who were less than 1,500 grams had "gross central nervous system defects," more than half of which were hydrocephalus. In that series, no "gross" defects were found in the girls.

Hydrocephalus is the most common complication in survivors of intraventricular hemorrhage, which occurs in 25% of preterm infants who weigh less than 1,000 grams. Krishnamoorthy et al. (1977) have found computerized tomography to be useful in diagnosing intraventricular and sub-arachnoid hemorrhage in infants whose clinical course deteriorates inexplicably. Of those who survive, 40% are normal, 20% have had mild sequelae, and 40% have had moderate-severe sequelae. Because prematurity, the respiratory distress syndrome, assisted ventilation, and intracranial hemorrhage often occur in the same infant, it is hard to single out any one factor as etiologic in neurologic handicap. What seems amazing is that so many of these infants do so well. A comparison of two studies, the one published 17 years before the other, attests to the improvement in the quality of survival now possible through modern perinatal care. Drillien's report (1958) of infants who weighed less than 1,360 grams at birth and of whom 28.2% survived with approximately 66% definitely handicapped mentally and physically becomes more notable in its data when compared with Fitzhardinge's report (1975) of preterm infants who weighed <1,440 grams at birth and of whom 52% survived with less than 10% having "gross central nervous system defects" and a mean DQ of 110 for the girls and 108 for the boys. Even more improvement should be possible in these figures and percentages with the development of regional perinatal centers.

The infant who is of low birth weight and small for gestational age (SGA) presents a different set of perinatal problems and is also at risk for mental deficiency. This group includes those infants with chromosomal aberrations, congenital infections, congenital anomalies, and placental dysfunction. Hypoglycemia, hyperbilirubinemia, hypocalcemia, and polycythemia are some of their special problems. Fitzhardinge and Steven (1972) reported on a five-year prospective study of 96 infants who were small for gestational age with no obvious cause for their low birth weights. Approximately 30% of the children had some speech problem, 59% of the boys and 69% of the girls had abnormal EEG tracings, and more than 40% of the children did poorly in school although the average IQ was 95 for the boys and 101 for the girls. It is not known whether the neurologic problems are the result of poor intrauterine growth, postnatal metabolic problems, or both.

Trauma

Mechanical trauma as might be associated with the delivery of a large baby born by difficult labor, or the use of forceps may result in subdural hemorrhage in the newborn period. Breech delivery is associated with 18% perinatal mortality and 16% morbidity, including asphyxia and intracranial hemorrhage. This may present as the early onset of seizures, as rapid obtundation from anemia and increased intracranial pressure, or as a hemiparesis. Treatment consists of repeated subdural taps to lower the pressure. Outcome depends on early recognition and treatment, and prevention. Subarachnoid hemorrhage may be related to both mechanical trauma and perinatal asphyxia. It is three times more common in the premature infant but is the most common cause of intracranial bleeding in the full-term infant. Again, with modern perinatal care, improvement in outcome can be expected.

Malnutrition

Nutritional problems may occur in any infant, but they are more common in the preterm infant and include inability to suck, difficulty in feeding because of severe respiratory problems, and functional abnormality of the gastrointestinal tract (e.g., anomalies, pneumatosis intestinalis), which make regular feeding impossible for variable time periods. Therefore, other methods for providing protein, calories, vitamins, and minerals have been devised. These include peripheral intravenous fluids and nutrients and central hyperalimentation. When the infant is ready, gavage feedings may be attempted. Some advocate the feeding of breast milk initially as it is better tolerated by the infant and also provides some potentially important defenses against infection (Wilfert, 1975). Recently, breast-milk banks have been organized in order to provide sufficient breast milk to perinatal centers. The primary concern, of course, is to provide all the essential nutrients to the infant during the time of excessive need so that growth and development can continue in as normal a fashion as possible. Again, just as is the case during the prenatal period, the effect of malnutrition on brain development in infancy is not known. Winick (1974) and Martin (1973) present convincing evidence about the stunting of brain growth which is caused by early infant malnutrition. On the other hand, Lloyd-Still et al. (1974) found that severe malnutrition in infancy associated with cystic fibrosis, can affect intellectual performance as measured in the first five years of life, but that after that, no differences were observed between those who were malnourished and their control siblings. It may be that brains stunted in size can still work well with exposure to a stimulating environment.

Infection

The neonate, and particularly the preterm infant, is at risk for developing serious infections such as pneumonia, sepsis, or meningitis. The reasons are twofold. First, the neonate is immunologically incompetent both with regard to humoral immunity (immunoglobulins) and cellular immunity (Miller, 1973; Wilfert, 1975). Second, the neonate is exposed to organisms during the birth process and postnatally in the delivery room and nursery for which he is immunologically unprepared, or which may be "hospital strains" and therefore resistant to antibiotics. Strict handwashing rules and attention to aseptic technique in handling neonates as well as bacteriologic surveillance of nursery and delivery room equipment are essential in the prevention of infection.

When severe infection does occur, prompt recognition and appropriate antimicrobial therapy are important in preventing morbidity and mortality. The incidence of meningitis in full-term neonates is 0.13 per 1,000 births, whereas it is 2.24 per 1,000 in preterm births (Bell and McCormick, 1975). The breakdown of causative organisms in a recent study of 133 infants listed by Bell and McCormick (1975) is *Escherichia coli* in 38%, group B beta hemolytic streptococcus in 31%, and *Listeria monocytogenes* in 5%. The mortality of bacterial meningitis in the neonatal period runs as high as 60% to 74% in most series (Bell and McCormick, 1975). Prompt attention to the minimal symptomatology in this age group and appropriate therapy can reduce this to 18.5% (McCracken, 1972).

Sequelae among survivors have been estimated at 31% to 56% (Bell and McCormick, 1975). Fitzhardinge et al. (1974) reported that of 37 patients with neonatal meningitis 54% survived. Of those, 55% were "functionally normal" at evaluation from 1–10 years of age (mean 4 years 10 months). Sequelae were most severe after gram negative meningitis. Volpe (1973) reports a 30% or less chance for normal development in neonates with seizures who survive meningitis. Hydrocephalus, mental deficiency, seizure disorder, cerebral palsy, and hyperactive behavior are among the more notable subsequent deficits.

METABOLIC FACTORS

The metabolic problems in the perinatal period which are related to mental deficiency are hypoglycemia and hypocalcemia, both of which predispose the infant to neonatal seizures and the added risk of hypoxia.

Hypoglycemia and Hypocalcemia

Senior (1973) has listed the causes of neonatal hypoglycemia. Infants who are small for gestational age and those who are infants of diabetic mothers (Cornblath and Schwartz, 1966; Pildes, 1973) are particularly prone to these complications. Preterm infants, especially those under 1,500 grams at birth, are also at risk for developing hypocalcemia and hypoglycemia. Furthermore, hypocalcemia is seen following obstetric trauma. Infants with early onset hypocalcemia have a 50% chance of normal development; those with late onset hypocalcemia have an 80% to 100% chance of normal development, and those with hypoglycemia have a 50% chance of normal development (Volpe, 1973).

These metabolic disturbances are the second leading cause of neonatal seizures, which can themselves result in further morbidity according to Volpe (1973). In a study of 347 infants who had neonatal seizures during the period 1960 to 1972, 53% were normal, 17% died, and 30% had sequelae. In full term infants, a normal EEG in the neonatal period was associated with an 86% chance for normal development at 5 years of age whereas an EEG with multifocal abnormalities was associated with only a 12% chance of normal development. The EEG has not been shown to be helpful in prognosis with regard to the preterm infant with neonatal seizures.

POSTNATAL PERIOD
METABOLIC-HORMONAL FACTORS

There are two metabolic-hormonal factors of concern in the etiology of mental deficiency in the postnatal period. These are congenital hypothyroidism and hypoglycemia.

Congenital Hypothyroidism

Congenital hypothyroidism, or in its extreme form, cretinism, can lead to physical and mental deficiency if undetected. The frequency of congenital hypothyroidism in the United States is 1 out of 8,500 (Klein, Agustin, and Foley, 1974). It is thought to be a treatable and preventable form of mental deficiency if appropriate thyroid therapy is initiated by four months of age (Rosman, 1976). Because of this, some states have begun neonatal screening programs to ensure early detection. However, Topper (1951) found that 39% remained mentally defective in spite of adequate therapy—although therapy was begun at different times—and postulated a "static encephalopathy" as the cause.

The manifestations of congenital hypothyroidism are as follows. Cognitively, untreated patients with hypothyroidism are mentally retarded, usually in the moderate-severe range. Speech and language are severely affected and usually partial or complete deafmutism is an essential part of cretinism. In the neuromotor area, delay in walking is characteristic. Rosman (1976) has described the older child or adolescent as follows.

> He . . . stands and walks with slightly flexed knees, internally rotated legs, adducted thighs, and a lordotic back. His movements in walking are stiff, awkward, and careless. In each step, the toe touches the ground before the heel, and the limbs never straighten fully, always being held slightly flexed at the knees and hips because of pseudocontractures. . . . The arms are affected less than the legs. (p.585)

Incoordination of motor control, awkwardness, and jerky movements are frequent. The physical findings in infancy include constipation, coarse dry skin, large tongue, umbilical hernia, hoarse cry, jaundice, and poor feeding. Later, cretinism is characterized by short stature, porcine facies, coarse hair, thinning of the outer two-thirds of the eyebrows, dry coarse skin, myxedema, and slowness of deep tendon reflexes. Behavior is characterized by impairment of psychic functions during which little notice is taken of one's surroundings. Bizarre behavior and abnormal ideation may develop. Treatment of cretinism after the first four months of age will not result in significant improvement in mental functioning, though growth and motor functioning can be positively affected (Rosman, 1976).

Hypoglycemia

Severe prolonged hypoglycemia resulting from excessive insulin levels either from an endogenous or from an exogenous source is another cause of postnatal hormonal mental deficiency. One of the important functions of insulin, a pancreatic hormone, is to lower blood sugar by its action on cell membranes. When there is excessive insulin, blood sugar drops, and symptoms of hypoglycemia occur progressing from hunger and jitteriness to somnolence, coma, and seizures. Administering glucose relieves the symptoms temporarily, but only a reduction in the insulin level to normal will result in permanent improvement. When the symptoms are recognized and treated early, no permanent brain damage occurs. It is only when the brain, which requires glucose for energy, is deprived of glucose for too long that mental deficiency might occur. Stanley and Baker (1976) have reviewed the pathology, treatment, and outcome of hyperinsulinism in infants and children.

ENVIRONMENTAL FACTORS

The major environmental factors of concern in the etiology of mental deficiency in the postnatal period are trauma, hypoxia, infection, poisoning, and psychosocial disadvantage.

Trauma

Trauma is reportedly the leading cause of death in the pediatric age group and is responsible for more than half of all childhood deaths. "In 1973, 29,000 children died and thousands more were permanently disabled as a result of trauma" (Grosfeld, 1975, p.267). Accidental trauma may result in bony fractures and/or soft tissue injury. When trauma is associated with hypoxia or hypovolemia, secondary brain damage and mental deficiency may result. Trauma to the central nervous system is of primary concern in a discussion of mental deficiency. This may be direct trauma with skull fracture and extrusion of brain, or more indirect with subdural or epidural hematoma, and increased intracranial pressure. The extent of the injury and the availability of proper medical care determine the final outcome. Heiskanen and Kaste (1974) reported that only 17 of 36 children who suffered severe brain injury and were unconscious for more than 24 hours were able to function normally in school.

Nonaccidental trauma or child abuse has received a great deal of attention in the years since Kempe et al. (1962) first described the battered child syndrome. An excellent review by Newberger and Hyde (1975) summarizes the current status of child abuse. The incidence is unknown. In 1972, when 22,000 cases of abuse were officially reported, Kempe estimated there were 60,000 incidents, and David Gil projected an estimate of 2.5 to 4 million cases per year (Newberger and Hyde, 1975). In Kempe's recent article (1976), the statistics cited are 300,000 reports per year, including 60,000 children with significant injuries, 2,000 deaths, and 6,000 with permanent brain injury. One-third of the children who are abused are less than 6 months of age, another one-third are 6 months to 3 years of age, and the final one-third are over 3 years of age. Preterm infants in particular are at risk. Mealey (1975) reported that of 80 infants with subdural hematomas, 20 were confirmed as "battered babies," 9 were classified as "abuse and neglect probable," and 9 were designated as "uncertain, trauma presumed." The outlook is poorest in those with subdurals diagnosed in the first 3 months of life (Mealey, 1975).

The development of abused children has been studied by Martin et al. (1974). One three-year followup study of 42 physically abused children, found 33% of the children to be "functioning retarded" with a developmental quotient below 80. A history of skull fracture or subdural hematoma was found more than four times more frequently in the retarded than in the nonretarded. Neurologic damage was three times more frequent in those functioning in the retarded range. Failure to thrive at the time of identification was two times as common in the retarded. Forty-three percent of the children with normal intellect had language delay.

A second followup study of 58 children showed that 19 had IQ scores one or more standard deviations below the expected mean, while only 8 children had scores one or more standard deviations above the mean. The mean IQ in those with moderate-severe neurologic dysfunction and with a history of head trauma was 17 to 21 points below, in both verbal and performance areas, the mean IQ in those without such findings or history. Ninety percent of those with severe neurologic dysfunction had had skull fracture and/or subdural hematoma, and 80% of them had an IQ of 85 or below. On the Beery Test of Visuomotor Integration, 29 of the 49 children to whom it was given scored more than 6 months below their age level while only five scored more than 6 months above their age level. Again, the history of head trauma and moderate-severe neurologic dysfunction adversely affected performance.

Martin et al. (1974) also studied the effect of the abusive environment on cognitive functioning. Frequent home changes were not found to have a significant effect on a child's cognitive functioning. However, the instability of a present home environment (frequent unemployment, high geographic instability. excessive disorganization, poor management) and the presence of an abusive environment (excessive physical punishment, obvious rejection or hostility toward the child) were found to be statistically significant correlates of lower cognitive functioning. The median IQ of those in unstable homes was 96.2 whereas that of those in stable homes was 107.4. The median IQ of those in an abusive environment was 98.5 whereas that of those in a nonabusive environment was 108.5. Martin and his associates concluded that "a home environment in which physical abuse takes place has a detrimental effect on the child's development even without the additional presence of undernutrition, maternal deprivation, sexual abuse, psychotic parents or inadequate social or family function." (p.36)

The personality-emotional-behavioral status of abused or neglected children has not yet been systematically studied, but some observations have been made. Morris, Gould, and Matthews (1964) described abused children who were hospitalized as less afraid than other children but as constantly on the alert for danger. Martin et al. (1974) noted that performance on intellectual testing was hindered in at least 25 of 58 children by "resistance to the testing procedure, withdrawal and hesitancy due to anxiety, hyperactivity, fatigue, and in one case, hunger" (p.64). A study of 101 abused children conducted in 1968 by the Denver Department of Welfare, described the children as follows: " 'The children under 5 years of age were whiney, fussy, chronically crying, demanding, stubborn, etc. . . . The children over 5 years of age were seen typically as gloomy, unhappy or depressed. . . . and as being ungratifying and difficult to enjoy.' " (Martin et al., 1974, p. 28) Siblings were not considered to be different in personality characteristics. In our own evaluation of 31 children who have been followed by protective services for abuse and/or neglect, five were described as assertive, hostile, unsocialized, while 12 others were described as sad, fretful, shy, low self-esteem, depressed, sullen, cautious and/or negativistic.

The physical findings of abuse and neglect have been well described (Kempe et al., 1962; Helfer and Kempe, 1968; Kempe and Helfer, 1972) and include soft tissue injury (bruises, burns), bony injury (fractures, metaphyseal separation, subperiosteal hemorrhages), and failure to thrive. The treatment of abuse and neglect is both immediate and long term. Ultimately, the goal is prevention. Immediate treatment consists of the medical care of the child to get him over his injuries, and the long-term treatment involves developmental, educational, and emotional help to the child, and help to the family so that abuse and/or neglect will not recur. This might involve additional services through the department of social services (homemaker services, living arrangements, finances), and through other community agencies that are committed to the welfare of these children. Lay therapy, parents anonymous groups, crisis nurseries, and stimulating day care combined with play therapy are some of the modalities that have been found to be helpful. In a recent article, Kempe (1976) discussed his views of the need for preventing child abuse through more careful observations of parents in the prenatal and postpartum period and at pediatric clinic visits, to determine if there is a *potential* to abuse. A second modality for the prevention of abuse advocated by Kempe (1976) is the use of lay health visitors, who could visit in the home of every newborn and give support to the mother and become the "lifeline" for the family. The following family study is illustrative of the setting in which abuse and neglect might occur, and shows the effect of the dynamic interplay of prenatal, perinatal, and postnatal factors in the etiology of mental subnormality and its outcome. An appreciation is gained regarding the importance of early intervention.

CASE J.C.

J.C. was referred at 2 years 6 months of age for evaluation of developmental delay. He was the product of a 32-week gestation and weighed 1,000 grams at birth. His Apgar at 1 minute was 0, and after intubation and resuscitation, his Apgar at 5 minutes was 6. He was hospitalized for 2 months after birth during which time his mother was minimally involved in his care. At 4 months of age, he was hospitalized for a second time because of failure to thrive.

His parents were unmarried but were living together. His mother presented herself as a woman who was concerned but who had difficulty managing the household. Subsequently, she was found to be functioning in the moderately retarded range of intelligence. His father had grown up in one of the state insitutions for the retarded and was employed as a laborer. They lived in public housing and "stayed to themselves." Neighbors had reported the family to the Protective Services Division of the Department of Social Services on several occasions because of suspected neglect. A caseworker was assigned.

When J.C. was a year of age, his brother B.C. was born. B.C. was a full-term baby and had no perinatal problems. Because of the caseworkers's concerns about their development, both children were seen at the Developmental Evaluation Center at Duke approximately 18 months later. At that time, J.C.'s height and weight were below the 3rd percentile, and his head circumference was at the 75th percentile. There was a large hematoma of the scalp in the occipital area and several smaller ones on his forehead. He was lethargic and did not interact with the examiner. His right arm was edematous and tender and his right hip was edematous, with limitation of motion and ecchymoses. On radiographic examination, he was found to have a fracture-dislocation of the right arm. He was hospitalized for treatment of suspected abuse and subsequently was discharged to the care of foster parents. Further developmental testing while he was in foster care indicated he was functioning in the moderately retarded range.

Meanwhile, B.C. was also found to be retarded in his growth and development, but there was no suspicion of abuse. At 18 months of age, he was less than 3rd percentile in height and weight and 25th percentile for head circumference. On developmental testing, his mental age was 7 to 10 months which placed him in the mild-moderate range of mental retardation. A plan of intervention was developed whereby he could remain with his parents. Weekly home visits were begun in order to teach the mother how to play with and stimulate B.C. A homemaker from Social Services provided help in meal planning and grocery buying. The boy was seen every other week in a neighborhood health center to evaluate his growth. The results were gratifying. By 2 years of age (6 months later), his weight was in the 25th percentile, and he had gained 4 to 5 months developmentally. At 2 years 6 months, he entered a developmental day-care center for stimulation. Subsequently, he was reevaluated at 3 years 6 months. At that time, his height was in the 60th percentile and weight and head circumference were in the 75th percentile. He was social-age appropriate, and was in the borderline-mild range of intellectual functioning. Progress in his language and motor skills paralleled that in his cognitive functioning.

Meanwhile, J.C. was returned to the home after a year in foster care. When last seen, he was in the 60th percentile for height and weight, but unfortunately, cognitively, remained in the moderate range of mental retardation.

In this family, the first child, J.C., was at risk for neurologic problems because of his preterm birth and perinatal asphyxia. The intensive nursery care he needed prevented his mother from being involved in his care in the neonatal period and probably interfered with the process of maternal attachment. This plus the mother's own limitations placed him at extremely high risk for abuse (Klaus et al., 1972; Klein and Stern, 1971). The abuse itself, the abusive environment, and the documented failure to thrive are additional contributing factors involved in the multifaceted etiology of his mental subnormality. One can only speculate that if the mother had been more involved with his care as a neonate and if a health visitor program had been in effect, then some of this disability might have been prevented. By contrast, B.C. came out better. He did not have the perinatal problems and to our knowledge was not abused, although he experienced the abusive environment and was malnourished until 18 months of age. In spite of this deprivation, when intervention was instituted, he was able to make considerable gains in growth and development over the ensuing two years. Again, the availability of a health visitor program might well have provided intervention earlier, and thus *prevented* this younger's difficulties. As it is, they have been ameliorated—for the time being.

Hypoxia

Hypoxia–asphyxia, which might occur in near drowning (Fandel and Bancalari, 1976), in respiratory infections (croup, epiglottitis, bronchiolitis, pneumonia), in asthma, in aspiration, and in severe chest trauma, may be etiologic in the onset of postnatal mental deficiency. The mechanism of damage in hypoxia is as follows. A gradual reduction in arterial oxygen saturation to 85% results in minor neurologic aberrations. Further reduction below 65% results in faulty judgment, impaired coordination, unconsciousness, and a progressive depression of central nervous system functioning. Acute and complete cerebral hypoxia will result in histologic changes in the cortex and thalamus after 3 to 4 minutes. The cerebellum is more resistant to hypoxic damage and the brainstem is most resistant. More than 5 minutes of anoxia usually results in irreversible damage (Wollman and Smith, 1975).

Infection

Infections of the central nervous system (meningitis, meningoencephalitis) may cause mental deficiency in the postnatal period. Meningitis is an infection of the meninges surrounding the brain and the symptoms include headache, vomiting, stiff neck, fever, lethargy, and irritability. Meningoencephalitis implies involvement of both the meninges and the brain substance in the inflammatory process.

MENINGITIS   In children between 4 months and 3 years of age, *Hemophilus influenzae* is the leading cause of meningitis. The subsequent course depends on the time interval between the onset and diagnosis of meningitis and on the adequacy of treatment. In severe cases, *H. influenzae* meningitis has been shown in angiographic studies to cause narrowing of major intracranial arteries. Furthermore, subdural effusions, which may or may not be pyogenic, present a further possible complication with regard to causing increased intracranial pressure and seizures. The mortality rate is approximately 5% to 8% (Bell and McCormick, 1975). Sequelae in survivors include hearing loss, retardation, hydrocephalus, seizure disorder and motor disturbances. Sell et al. (1972) reported that 29% of 86 patients treated for *H. influenzae* meningitis between 1960 and 1964 had serious or significant neurologic handicap, that an additional 14% had mild residual deficits, and that 43% were normal.

Pneumococcal meningitis ranks second to *Hemophilus influenzae* as a cause of meningitis in the age range of 4 months to 3 years. It, too, usually occurs secondary to pneumococcal infection elsewhere (pneumonia, otitis) or to sepsis or bacteremia. The mortality rate is 19% in children less than 10 years of age (Bell and McCormick, 1975). The central nervous system sequelae are similar to those with *Hemophilus influenzae*.

Tuberculous meningitis is declining in incidence but still accounted for 7.6% of bacterial meningitis in a study of 248 cases from 1961–1965 (Allison and Dalton, 1967). In children, the age range of highest incidence is 6 to 24 months. The course is slow and typically presents as fever, lethargy and/or irritability with gradual progression to headache, vomiting, stiff neck, and coma. Convulsions and papilledema (indicative of increased intracranial pressure) are not uncommon. If the diagnosis is not made and treatment not begun early enough, death results. The mortality rate is about 40% (Bell and McCormick, 1975). Lincoln, Sordillo, and Davies (1960) found neurologic sequelae in 24% of survivors and these ranged from cranial nerve palsies to mental deficiency, spasticity, blindness, and seizures. Damage to the auditory nerve (cranial nerve VIII) secondary to treatment with streptomycin is another possible problem.

MENINGOENCEPHALITIS Enteroviral (ECHO, Coxsackie) meningoencephalitis in the first year of life may result in neurologic impairment. Sells, Carpenter, and Ray (1975) have found smaller head circumference, lower mean IQ, and depressed speech and language skills in such children compared to controls. Enteroviral meningoencephalitis after the first year of life does not adversely affect neurologic performance. At present, other studies are in progress to elucidate further the significance of enteroviral meningoencephalitis in infancy.

Other viral encephalitides may be acute or chronic. The chronic ones include rubella, CMV, herpes, and measles (rubeola) as the causative agent. Subacute sclerosing panencephalitis (SSPE) is the chronic encephalitis associated with rubeola. It is characterized by progressive neurologic deterioration in middle childhood (8–11 years of age) which is often heralded by a progressive decline in school performance and the development of myoclonus. It has been reported to follow both infection with rubeola and immunization with measles vaccine, though the latter is rare (Katz, 1976). The prolonged incubation period is characteristic.

Herpes and measles can also cause an acute encephalitis characterized by somnolence, fever, and seizures. With measles, the frequency of occurrence of encephalitis has been reported as one case in 600 to one in 1,000. The mortality is 10% to 15%, and neurologic sequelae are found in 20% of survivors (Bell and McCormick, 1975). Herpes simplex encephalitis may represent either a primary or a reactivation process. The incidence is not known, but it is considered to be the most frequent severe nonseasonal encephalitis (Bell and McCormick, 1975). The clinical features include fever, vomiting, headache, lethargy, confusion, and convulsions. Signs of increased intracranial pressure and deepening coma are ominous. Frontotemporal areas are more frequently involved. The mortality rate is considered to be 60% to 70% (Bell and McCormick, 1975), and sequelae including seizures, speech and language disorders, and intellectual impairment are common in survivors.

Poisoning

Still another environmental cause of mental deficiency in the postnatal period is poisoning. The ingestion of agents that might cause hypoxia due to hypoventilation and central nervous system depression include tranquilizers, sedatives, antihistamines, and narcotics. Ingestion of petroleum distillates may cause hypoxia due to pneumonitis. Digitalis, quinidine, and the tricyclic antidepressants (Tofranil and Elavil) may induce cardiac arrhythmias and subseqnent hypoxia.

Lead poisoning is not an infrequent cause of encephalopathy in young children. The prodrome consists of anorexia, apathy, anemia, incoordination, irritability, and vomiting. These symptoms then intensify over a period of weeks if lead ingestion continues until acute encephalopathy occurs characterized by ataxia, acute persistent vomiting, lethargy, coma, seizures, and increased intracranial pressure (Chisholm, 1972). Chronic lead poisoning "may also present as nonspecific mental retardation, behavior disturbance, convulsive disorder, or any combination thereof" (Chisholm, 1972, p.544). Symptoms begin to occur at blood levels of 80 to 100 μg per 100 gm whole blood. Treatment consists of the elimination of lead from the environment and chelation therapy. The incidence of lead poisoning is greatest in urban areas where 10% to 25% of the children 12 to 36 months of age may have evidence of increased lead absorption and where 2% to 5% may have manifestations of intoxication (Chisholm, 1972).

Psychosocial Disadvantage

In the postnatal period, psychosocial disadvantage is one of the leading causes of mental retardation in the mild range. Children in this situation are normal in infancy, but by school age are demonstrating difficulties in the cognitive-intellectual area. Knobloch and Pasamanick (1974) cite several studies that support this view and relate IQ in early childhood to socioeconomic status, maternal educational level, and quality of maternal care. For example, Heber (1971) found that low socioeconomic status and maternal IQ of 75 or below resulted in a progressively poorer test performance from an IQ of 100 at 2 years of age to 70 at 18 years of age.

The etiology of this form of mental retardation is the total milieu of low socioeconomic status. It includes inadequate nutrition and medical care, poor living conditions that are often noisy and crowded, lack of an academic orientation, suppression of verbal communication and curiosity, feelings of hopelessness, and inferior educational facilities in a ghetto (Knobloch and Pasamanick, 1974). Hurley (1969) further characterizes the "culture of poverty" as one of alienation, powerlessness, meaninglessness of struggle, depression and degradation, feeling of failure, emotional exile, and low self-image. He sees poverty as excluding individuals from an environment in which proper human development can take place.

Recognition of the importance of psychosocial disadvantage in the etiology of mental retardation and in the perpetuation of the poverty cycle led to ideas about intervention with programs in early childhood education. Heber and Garber (1975) have been involved in a prospective study of the effects of a home and study-center stimulation program beginning at 3 months of age in the infants of those mothers of low socioeconomic status and an IQ of 80 or below (Milwaukee Project). They found that at 12 months of age, there was no difference in developmental quotient (115) between the 20 children in the control group and the 20 in the stimulation group. However, by 5 years 6 months of age, the children in the stimulation group scored a mean of 31 points higher than controls on the Stanford-Binet. The recent review by Caldwell, Bradley, and Elardo (1975) highlights the history of the development of other early education programs and discusses the various program models that have been designed. Overall, most of these appear to be helpful and effective.

Project Headstart was one of the earliest and has been the largest program of early intervention education. It was geared to providing a preschool experience to 3- and 4-year-old disadvantaged youngsters as well as encouraging parental participation so that carryover of learning from the school to the home could occur. The quality of teaching has been variable, however, as has been parental participation and the current overall consensus is that Headstart has been "less than successful" (Marquis, 1976). One concern of critics is that gains are not sustained. Proponents of the Headstart Program explain that intervention programs should start earlier than 3 to 4 years of age, that the home should be more involved in cognitive stimulation, and that the public educational system needs to be changed so that the child can continue to make cognitive gains.

A different approach to the problem has been to identify factors in the early mother-child interaction that lead to competency in later life (Marquis, 1976). These include the ample use of language and visual teaching techniques, the encouragement of exploratory behavior, and the limitation of restrictive techniques in an effort to foster curiosity and independence. "Human interaction in a stimulating environment replete with conversation and personal attention is at the crux of human growth" (Hurley, 1969, p. 25). The home-based stimulation program of Gutelius et al. (1972) is geared toward facilitating the mother-child relationship in just these ways and is actually quite similar in concept to Kempe's idea of the health visitor in the prevention of abuse and neglect.

The manifestations of psychosocial disadvantage are as follows. In the cognitive-intellectual area, borderline to mild mental retardation is common. Speech and language are usually delayed and that which is used is at a younger developmental level (Deutsch, 1965). There are no specific characteristic patterns. Neuromotor function is usually well developed in gross motor tasks and in self-help. However, fine motor proficiency involving paper and pencil tasks may be delayed owing to inexperience. Physically, some disadvantaged children may show failure to thrive and have an unkempt appearance. Behaviorally, by the time they are of school age, they typically present either as passive, shy, apathetic children, or as unsocialized and overly active, aggressive youngsters. Learning presents difficulties for these children, but with resource help, they can learn. A pattern that is observed all too frequently is repeated school failure and school dropout. Treatment involves prevention that includes facilitation of the early mother-child interaction, preschool experience with family involvement, and much-needed—but often unattainable—social change.

CONCLUSION

This chapter has outlined the major etiologic factors concerned with mental subnormality. The genetic and environmental factors related to mental deficiency and the environmental factors related to mental retardation have been described with respect to the time period in which they originate. It is clear that adverse genetic and environmental factors may exist singly or in combination and result in mental subnormality. Furthermore, mental subnormality may exist alone or in combination with language, neuromotor, physical, educational, and behavioral difficulties.

Much remains to be learned about the specific pathology of the brain which results in mental subnormality. It is hoped that as the pathology of mental deficiency is elucidated and as mental deficiency is understood pathologically, more active preventive measures can be utilized. For the present, we will have to rely on diagnosing genetic defects in the prenatal period, providing good prenatal and perinatal care, on minimizing the deleterious postnatal environmental influences, and on utilizing the environment to foster the attainment of maximum functioning in each individual.

Much also remains to be learned about the nature of intelligence and about the effect of environmental influences on a person's "intelligence" as evidenced in his or her functioning. Likewise, our understanding of the functional capacities of a person at particular levels of intelligence in relation to the demands made by environment will continue to evolve. We have progressed through the period in which definite immutable expectancies were held in relation to IQ scores and corresponding levels of mental subnormality. We have learned to appreciate the complex multidimensionality of functioning and the capacity for change at all levels. Rather than assuming fixed expectancies, we are now in a period in which the major approach is to expose each person to the best program of stimulation and education we can devise, to meet him at his current level of functioning, and to use his progress as a guide to future expectancies and programs.

We are going to have to come to grips, however, with the complicated problem of weighing a given amount of gain in relation to the resources expended in terms of time, money, and effort in achieving that gain. The need for this kind of assessment holds true not only for individual persons but also for entire national programs. The time may come when we will have to allocate our limited resources to programs that produce the greatest demonstrable gains in functioning for the largest number of persons. Much attention in the future will be directed toward answering the question of which specific programs work best for what specific problems in what specific situations.

In this chapter we have tried to elucidate the complexity of the problem of mental subnormality and to provide the reader not only with facts of its various etiologies and manifestations but also with firm foundations of the nature and definition of intelligence and of the way our understanding of the levels of intellectual functioning is changing.

References

Alford, C.A., Stagno, S. & Reynolds, D.W. Toxoplasmosis: Silent congenital infection. In S. Krugman & A.A. Gershon (Eds.), *Infections of the fetus and the newborn infant.* (Progress in Clinical and Biological Research, Vol. 3). New York: Alan R. Liss, 1975, 133–57.

Allison, M.J. & Dalton, H.P. Etiology of meningitis at the Medical College of Virginia, 1961–1965. *Virginia Medical Monthly*, 1967, 94, 317–19.

Babson, S.G., Benson, R.C., Pernoll, M.L. & Benda, G.I. *Management of High-Risk Pregnancy and Intensive Care of the Neonate.* St. Louis: C.V. Mosby, 1975.

Bartholomé, K., Byrd, D.J., Kaufman, S. & Milstien, S. Atypical phenylketonuria with normal phenylalanine hydroxylase and dihydropteridine reductase activity in vitro. *Pediatrics*, 1977, 59, 757–61.

Battaglia, F.C. & Lubchenco, L.O. A pratical classification of newborn infants by weight and gestational age. *Journal of Pediatrics*, 1967, 71, 159–63.

Beadle, G.W. Biochemical genetics. *Chemical Reviews*, 1945, 37, 15–96.

Bell, W.E. &McCormick, W.F. *Neurologic Infections in Children.* Philadelphia: W.B. Saunders, 1975.

Benda, C.E. *Down's Syndrome.* New York: Grune & Stratton, 1969.

Berg, J.M., Mcreary, B.D., Ridler, M.A.C. & Smith, A.F. *The DeLange Syndrome.* Oxford: Pergamon Press, 1970.

Berry, H.K. & Spinanger, J.A. Paper spot test useful in study of Hurler's syndrome. *Journal of Laboratory and Clinical Medicine*, 1960, 55, 136–38.

Blattner, R.J. The role of viruses in congenital defects. *American Journal of Diseases of Children*, 1974, *128*, 781–86.

Boring, E.G. *A History of Experimental Psychology*. New York: Appleton-Century-crofts, 1950.

Bouchard, T.J., Jr. Current conceptions of intelligence and their implications for assessment. In P. McReynolds (Ed.), *Advances in Psychological Assessment* (Vol. 1). Palo Alto: Science and Behavior Books, 1968.

Bourneville, D. Scléreuse tubéreuse des circonvolutions cérébrales, Idiote et épilepsie hémiplégique. *Archives de Neurologie* (Paris), 1880, *1*, 81.

Brock, D.J.H. & Sutcliffe, R.G. Alpha-fetoprotein in the antenatal diagnosis of anencephaly and spina bifida. *Lancet*, 1972, *2*, 197–99.

Caldwell, B.M., Bradley, R.H. & Elardo, R. Early stimulation. In J. Wortis (Ed.), *Mental Retardation and Developmental Disabilities* (Vol. 7). New York: Brunner/Mazel, 1975. 152–94.

Chaplin, J.P. & Krawiec, T.S. *Systems and Theories of Psychology*. New York: Holt, Rinehart and Winston, 1968.

Chess, S., Korn, S.J. & Fernandez, P.B. *Psychiatric Disorders of Children with Congenital Rubella*. New York: Brunner/Mazel, 1971.

Chisholm, J.J. Lead poisoning. In H.L. Barnett & A.H. Einhorn (Eds.), *Pediatrics*. New York: Appleton-Century-Crofts, 1972.

Cooper, L.Z. Congenital rubella in the United States. In S. Krugman & A.A. Gershon (Eds.), *Infections of the fetus and the newborn infant*. (Progress in Clinical and Biological Research, Vol. 3). New York: Alan R. Liss, 1975, 1–22.

Cori, G.T. Glycogen structure and enzyme deficiencies in glycogen storage disease. *Harvey Lectures*, 1953, *48*, 145–71.

Cornblath, M. & Schwartz, R. *Disorders of Carbohydrate Metabolism in Infancy*. Philadelphia: W.B. Saunders, 1966.

Cronbach, J.J. Five decades of public controversy over mental testing. *American Psychologist*, 1975, *30*, 1–15.

Crissey, M.S. Mental retardation: Past, present, and future. *American Psychologist*, 1975, *30*, 800–809.

Dancis, J. Feto-maternal interaction. In G.B. Avery (Ed.), *Neonatology: Pathophysiology and Management of the Newborn*. Philadelphia: J.B. Lippincott, 1975.

Desmonts, G. & Couvreur, J. Congenital toxoplasmosis. A prospective study of 378 pregnancies. *New England Journal of Medicine*, 1974, *290* (20), 1110–16.

Deutsch, M. The role of social class in language development and cognition. *American Journal of Orthopsychiatry*, 1965, *35*, 78–88.

Dobson, J.C., Williamson, M.L., Azen, C. & Koch, R. Intellectual assessment of 111 four-year-old children with phenylketonuria. *Pediatrics*, 1977, *60*, 822–27.

Drillien, C.M. Growth and development in a group of children of very low birth weight. *Archives of Disease in Childhood*, 1958, *33*, 10–18.

Dubowitz, L.M.S., Dubowitz, V. & Goldberg, C. Clinical assessment of gestational age in the newborn infant. *Journal of Pediatrics.*, 1970, 77 (1), 1–10.

Edwards, J.H., Harnden, D.G., Cameron, A.H., Crosse, V.M. et al. A new trisomic syndrome. *Lancet*, 1960, *1*, 787–89.

Efron, M.L. Aminoaciduria. *New England Journal of Medicine*, 1965, *272*, 1058–67; 1107–13.

Fandel, I. & Bancalari, E. Near drowning in children: Clinical aspects. *Pediatrics*, 1976, *58* (4), 573–79.

Feldman, H.A. & Miller, L.T. Congenital human toxoplasmosis. *Annals of the New York Academy of Science*, 1956, *64*, 180–84.

Fishler, K. Mental development in mosaic Down's syndrome as compared with trisomy 21. In R. Koch & F.F. de la Cruz (Eds.), *Down's Syndrome: Research, Prevention, Management.* New York: Brunner/Mazel, 1975, 87–98.

Fishler, K., Koch, R. & Donnell, G.N. Comparison of mental development in individuals with mosaic and trisomy 21 Down's syndrome. *Pediatrics*, 1976, *58*, (5), 744–48.

Fitzhardinge, P.M. Early growth and development in low birth weight infants following treatment in an intensive care nursery. *Pediatrics*, 1975, *56* (2), 162–72.

Fitzhardinge, P.M. & Steven, E.M. The small-for-date infant: II. Neurological and intellectual sequelae. *Pediatrics*, 1972, *50*, 50–57.

Fitzhardinge, P.M., Kazemi, M., Ramsay, M. & Stern, L. Long-term sequelae of neonatal meningitis. *Developmental Medicine Child Neurology*, 1974, *16*, 3–10.

Fölling, A. Über Ausscheidung von Phenylbrenztraubensaure in den Harn als Stoffwechselanomalie in Verbindung mit Imbezillität. *Hoppe-Seyler's Zeitschrift für Physiologische Chemie*, 1934, *227*, 169–76.

Ford, F.R. *Diseases of the Nervous System in Infancy, Childhood, and Adolescence*, 5th ed. Springfield, Illinois: Charles C Thomas, 1966.

Ford, C.E., Jones, K.W., Polani, P.E., de Almeida, J.C. et al. A sex-chromosome anomaly in a case of gonadal dysgenesis (Turner's syndrome). *Lancet*, 1959, *1*, 711–13.

Freda, V.J., Pollack, W & Gorman, J.G. Rh disease: How near the end? *Hospital Practice*, June 1978, 61–69.

Frimpter, G.W. Aminoacidurias due to inherited disorders of metabolism. *New England Journal of Medicine*, 1973, *289* (16), 835–41; (17), 895–90.

Garrod, A.P. Inborn errors of metabolism (Croonian Lectures). *Lancet*, 1908, *2*, 1–7; 73–79; 142–48; 214–20.

Gerald, P.S. Sex chromosome disorders. *New England Journal of Medicine*, 1976, *294* (13), 706–8.

Golden, W. Pashayan, H.M. The effect of parental education on the eventual developmental of non-institutionalized children with Down syndrome. *Journal of Pediatrics*, 1976, *89* (4), 603–5.

Gordon, H.H. Perspectives on Neonatalogy–1975. In G.B. Avery (Ed.), *Neonatology: Pathophysiology, and Management of the Newborn*. Philadelphia: J.B. Lippincott, 1975.

Gorlin R.J. Classical chromosome disorders. In J.J. Yunis (Ed.), *New Chromosomal Syndromes*. New York Academic Press, 1977, 59–117.

Gregoriades, G. The carrier potential of liposomes in biology and medicine. *New England Journal of Medicine*, 1976, *295* (13), 704–10: *295* (14), 765–70.

Grosfeld, J.L. Symposium on childhood trauma. *Pediatric Clinics of North America*, 1975, *22* (2), 267.

Grossman, H.J. (Ed.). *Manual on Terminology and Classification in Mental Retardation*. American Association on Mental Deficiency. Baltimore: 1977.

Gruenwald, P., Funakawa, H., Mitani, S., Nishimura, T. et al. The influence of environmental factors on fetal growth in man. *Lancet*, 1967, *1*, 1026–28.

Gutelius, M.F., Kirsch, A.D. MacDonald, S., Brooks, M.R. et al. Promising results from a cognitive stimulation program in infancy. *Clinical Pediatrics*, 1972, *11*, 585–93.

Guthrie, R. Blood screening for phenylketonuria. *Journal of the American Medical Association*, 1961, *178* (8), 863.

Guthrie, R. & Susi, A. A simple phenylalanine method for detecting phenylketonuria in large populations of newborn infants. *Pediatrics*, 1963, *32*, 338–43.

Hall, B. Signs of mongolism in newborns. *Modern Medicine*, 1966, *34*, 171.

Hall, B.D. & Smith, D.W. Prader-Willi syndrome. *Journal of Pediatrics*, 1972, *81* (2), 286–93.

Hanshaw, J.B., Scheiner, A.P., Moxley, A.W., Gaev, L. et al. CNS sequelae of congenital cytomegalovirus infection. In S. Krugman & A.A. Gershon (Eds.), *Infections of the fetus and the newborn infant*. (Progress in Clinical and Biological Research, Vol. 3). New York: Alan R. Liss, 1975, 47–54.

Heber, R. Rehabilitation of families at risk for mental retardation: A progress report. *Rehabilitation Research and Training Center in Mental Retardation*, Madison: University of Wisconsin, 1971.

Heber, R. & Garber, H. The Milwaukee Project: A study of the use of family intervention to prevent cultural-family retardation. In B.Z. Friedlander, G.M. Sterritt & G.E. Kirk (Eds.). *Exceptional Infant* (Vol. 3). New York: Brunner/Mazel, 1975.

Heiskanen, O. & Kaste, M. Late prognosis of severe brain injury in children. *Developmental Medicine and Child Neurology*, 1974, *16*, 11–14.

Helfer, R.E. & Kempe, C.H. *The Battered Child*. Chicago: University of Chicago Press, 1968.

Hillman, R.E. Megavitamin responsive aminoacidopathies. *Pediatric Clinics of North America*, 1976, *23* (3), 557–67.

Holmes, L.B., Driscoll, S.G. & Atkins, L. Etiologic heterogeneity of neural-tube defects. *New England Journal of Medicine*, 1976, *294* (7), 365–69.

Holmes, L.B., Moser, H.W., Halldórsson, S., Mack, C. et al. *Mental Retardation: An Atlas of Diseases with Associated Physical Abnormalities*. New York: Macmillan, 1972.

Hunt, G.M., & Holmes, A.E. Factors relating to intelligence in treated cases of spina bifida cystica. *American Journal of Diseases of Children*, 1976, *130*, 823–27.

Hurley, R. *Poverty and Mental Retardation: A Causal Relationship*. New York: Vintage, 1969.

Huttenlocher, P.R. Dendritic development in neocortex of children with mental defect and infantile spasms. *Neurology*, 1974, *24*, 203–10.

Jacobs, P.A. & Strong, J.A. A case of human intersexuality having a possible XXY sex-determining mechanism. *Nature*, 1959, *183*, 302–3.

Jaffe, R.B., Schruefer, J.J., Bowes, W.A., Creasy, R.K. et al. High risk pregnancies: Maternal medical disorders. In R.L. Brent & M.I. Harris (Eds.), *Prevention of Embryonic, Fetal, and Perinatal Disease*. (DHEW Pub. # [NIH] 76–853). Bethesda, Maryland: 1976, 28.

James, L.S. Adamsons, K., Jr. Labor delivery and the beginning of independent life. In H.L. Barnett and A.H. Einhorn (Eds.), *Pediatrics*, 15th ed. New York: Appleton-Century-Crofts, 1972.

Johnson, J.D., Malachowski, N.C., Grobstein, R., Welsh, D. et al. Prognosis of children surviving with the aid of mechanical ventilation in the newborn period. *Journal of Pediatrics*, 1974, *84*, 272–76.

Jones, K.L. Congenital malformations: The general problem. In J. Wortis (Ed.), *Mental Retardation and Developmental Disabilities* (Vol. 7). New York: Brunner/Mazel, 1975, 112–29.

Jones, K.L. & Smith, D.W. The Williams elfin facies syndrome. *Journal of Pediatrics*, 1975, *86* (5), 718–23.

Jones, K.L., Smith, D.W., Ulleland, C.N., & Streissguth, A.P. Pattern of malformation in offspring of chronic alcoholic mothers. *Lancet*, 1973, *1*, 1267–71.

Kajii, T., Ohama, K., Niikawa, N., Ferrier, A. et al. Banding analysis of abnormal karyotypes in spontaneous abortion. *American Journal of Human Genetics*, 1973, *25*, 539–47.

Katz, S.L. Childhood immunizations. *Hospital Practice*, 1976, *11* (11), 49–59.

Kaufman, S., Berlow, S., Summer, G.K., Milstien, S. et al. Hyperphenylalaninemia due to a deficiency of biopterin. *New England Journal of Medicine*, 1978, *299*, 673–79.

Kaufman, S., Holtzman, N.A., Milstien, S., Butler, I.J. et al. Phenylketonuria due to a deficiency of dihydropteridine reductase. *New England Journal of Medicine*, 1975, *293*, 785–90.

Kelly, W.N. & Wyngaarden, J.B. The Lesch-Nyham syndrome. In J.B. Stanbury, J.B. Wyngaarden & D.S. Frederickson (Eds.), *The Metabolic Basis of Inherited Disease*. New York: McGraw-Hill, 1972, 969–91.

Kempe, C.H. Approaches to preventing child abuse. The health visitor concept. *American Journal of Diseases of Children*, 1976, *130*, 941–47.

Kempe, C.H. & Helfer, R.E. *Helping the Battered Child and his Family*. Philadelphia: J.B. Lippincott, 1972.

Kempe, C.H., Silverman, F.N., Steele, B.F., Drogenmueller, W. et al. The battered-child syndrome. *Journal of the American Medical Association*, 1962, *181*, (1), 17–24.

Kirman, B.H. The patient with Down's syndrome in the community. *Lancet*, 1964, 2, 705–9.

Klaus, M.H. Pulmonary diseases of the newborn. In H.L. Barnett and A.H. Einhorn (Eds.), *Pediatrics*, 15th ed. New York: Appleton-Century-Crofts, 1972, 1261–73.

Klaus, M.H., Jerauld, R., Kreger, N.C., McAlpine, W. et al. Maternal attachement: Importance of the first postpartum days. *New England Journal of Medicine*, 1972, *286*, 460–63.

Klein, A.H., Agustin, A.V. & Foley, T.P. Successful laboratory screening for congenital hypothyroidism. *Lancet*, 1974, 2, 77–79.

Klein, M. & Stern, L. Low birth weight and the battered-child syndrome. *American Journal of Diseases of Children*, 1971, *122*, 15–18.

Klinefelter, H.F., Jr., Reifenstein, E.C., Jr. & Albright, F. Syndrome characterized by gynecomastia, aspermatogenesis without A-Leydigism, and increased excretion of follicle stimulating hormone. *Journal of Clinical Endocrinology*, 1942, 2, 615–27.

Knobloch, K. & Pasamanick, B. (Eds.) *Gesell and Amatruda's Developmental Diagnosis*, 3rd ed. Hagerstown, Maryland: Harper & Row, 1974.

Kolodny, E.H. Lysosomal storage diseases. *New England Journal of Medicine*, 1976, *294*, 1217–20.

Korones, S.B. *High-Risk Newborn Infants. The Basis for Intensive Care Nursing*. St. Louis: C.V. Mosby, 1976.

Krishnamoorthy, K.S., Neurologic outcome of neonatal intensive care. Lecture presented at the post-graduate course in pediatric neurology by Harvard Medical School. November, 1976.

Krishnamoorthy, K.S., Fernandez, R.A., Momose, K.J. DeLong, G.R. et al. Evaluation of neonatal intracranial hemorrhage by computerized tomography. *Pediatrics*, 1977, *59*, 165–72.

Kvale, J.N. & Fishman, J.R. The psychosocial aspects of Klinefelter's syndrome. *Journal of the American Medical Association*, 1965, *193*, 567–72.

Lang, D.J. The epidemiology of cytomegalovirus infections: Interpretation of recent observations. In S. Krugman & A. Gershon (Eds.) *Infections of the fetus and the newborn infant.* (Progress in Clinical and Biological Research, Vol. 3). New York: Alan R. Liss, 1975.

Legum, C.P., Schorr, S. & Berman, E.R. The genetic mucopolysaccharidoses and mucolipidoses: Review and comment. In I. Schulman (Ed.), *Advances in Pediatrics* (Vol. 22). Chicago: Year Book Medical Publishers, 1976, 305–47.

Lejeune, J., Gautier, M. & Turpin, R. Les chromosomes humains en culture de tissues. *Comptes Rendus Hebdomadaires des Séances de l'Académie des Sciences, Série D: Sciences Naturelles*, 1959, *248*, 602–3.

Lejeune, J., Lafourcade, J., Berger, R., Vialatte, J. et al. Trois cas de deletion partielle du bras court d'un chromosome 5. *Comptes Rendus Hebdomadaires des Séances de l'Académie des Sciences, Série D: Sciences Naturelles*, 1963, *257*, 3098–3102.

Levin, M.J., Oxman, M.N., Moore, M.G., Daniels, J.B. et al. Diagnosis of congenital rubella in utero. *New England Journal of Medicine*, 1974, *290*, (21), 1187–88.

Levine, S. & Wiener, S. A critical analysis of data on malnutrition and behavioral deficits. In I. Schulman (Ed.), *Advances in Pediatrics* (Vol. 22). Chicago: Year Book Medical Publishers, 1976, 113–36.

Lincoln, E.M., Sordillo, S.V.R. & Davies, P.A. Tuberculous meningitis in children. *Journal of Pediatrics*, 1960, *57*, 807–23.

Lloyd-Still, J.D., Hurwitz, I., Wolff, P.H. & Schwachman, H. Intellectual development after severe malnutrition in infancy. *Pediatrics*, 1974, *54* (3), 306–11.

Lorber, J. Ethical problems in the management of myelomeningocele and hydrocephalus. In T.E. Oppé & F.P. Woodford (Eds.), *Early Management of Handicapping Disorders.* Amsterdam: Associated Scientific Publishers, 1976, 31–43.

Lubchenco, L.O., Hansman, C., Dressler, M. & Boyd, E. Intrauterine growth as estimated from liveborn birth-weight data at 24 to 42 weeks of gestation. *Pediatrics*, 1963, *32*, 793–800.

Lucey, J.F. Neonatal jaundice and phototherapy. *Pediatric Clinics of North America*, 1972, *19* (4), 827–39.

Lucey, J., Ferreiro, M. & Hewitt, J. Prevention of hyperbilirubinemia of prematurity by phototherapy. *Pediatrics*, 1968, *41*, 1047–54.

Lundström, R. Rubella during pregnancy: A follow-up study of children born after an epidemic in Sweden, 1951, with additional investigations on prophylaxis and treatment of maternal rubella. *Acta Pediatrica*, 1962, *51* (suppl. 133), 1–110.

McCracken, G. H., Jr. The rate of bacteriologic response to antimicrobial therapy in neonatal meningitis. *American Journal of Diseases of Children*, 1972, *123*, 547–53.

Malone, M. J. The cerebral lipidoses. *Pediatric Clinics of North America*, 1976, *23* (2), 303–26.

Marquis, P. Cognitive stimulation. *American Journal of Diseases of Children*, 1976, *130*, 410–15.

Martin, H. P. Nutrition: Its relationship to children's physical, mental, and emotional development. *American Journal of Clinical Nutrition*, 1973, *26*, 766–75.

Martin, H. P., Beezley, P., Conway, E. F. & Kempe, C. H. The development of abused children. In I. Schulman (Ed.), *Advances in Pediatrics* (Vol. 21). Chicago: Year Book Medical Publishers, 1974, 25–73.

Mealey, J., Jr. Infantile subdural hematomas. *Pediatric Clinics of North America*, 1975, *22* (2), 433–42.

Meyerowitz, S. & Lipkin, M., Jr. Psychosocial aspects. In R. L. Brent & M. I. Harris (Eds.), *Prevention of Embryonic, Fetal, and Perinatal Disease*. (DHEW Pub. # [NIH] 76–853). Bethesda, Maryland: 1976, 263–86.

Milkovich, L. & van den Berg, B. J. Effects of prenatal meprobamate and chlordiazepoxide hydrochloride on human embryonic and fetal development. *New England Journal of Medicine*, 1974, *291* (24), 1268–71.

Miller, M. E. The immunodeficiencies of immaturity. In E. R. Stiehm & V. A. Fulginiti (Eds.), *Immunologic Disorders in Infants and Children*. Philadelphia: W. B. Saunders, 1973, 168–83.

Milunsky, A. Prenatal diagnosis of genetic disorders. *New England Journal of Medicine*, 1976, *295*, (7), 377–80.

Milunsky, A. & Alpert, E. The value of alpha-fetoprotein in the prenatal diagnosis of neural tube defects. *Journal of Pediatrics*, 1974, *84*, 889–93.

Milunsky, A. & Alpert, E. Antenatal diagnosis, alpha-fetoprotein, and the FDA. *New England Journal of Medicine*, 1976, *295* (3), 168–69.

Morris, M. G., Gould, R. W. & Matthews, P. J. Toward prevention of child abuse. *Children*, 1964, *11*, 55–60.

Myhre, S. A., Ruvalcaba, R. H. A., Johnson, H. R., Thuline, H. C. et al. The effects of testosterone treatment in Klinefelter's syndrome. *Journal of Pediatrics*, 1970, *76*, 267–76.

Nadler, H.L. Prenatal detection of genetic defects. In I. Schulman (Ed.), *Advances in Pediatrics* (Vol. 22). Chicago: Year Book Medical Publishers, 1976, 1–81.

Nahmias, A.J., Visintine, A.M., Reimer, C.B., Del Buono, I., Shore, S.L. & Starr, S.E. Herpes simplex virus infection of the fetus and newborn. In S. Krugman & A.A. Gershon (Eds.), *Infections of the fetus and the newborn infant.* (Progress in Clinical and Biological Research, Vol. 3). New York: Alan R. Liss, 1975, 63–77.

National Academy of Sciences, National Research Council. *Genetic Screening Programs, Principles, and Research.* Washington, D.C., 1975.

Nevin, N.C. Aetiology of genetic disease. In A.C. Turnbull, F.P. Woodford (Eds.), *Prevention of Handicap through Antenatal Care.* (IRMMH Reviews of Research and Practice, Vol. 18). Amsterdam: Associated Scientific Publishers, 1976.

Newberger, E.H. & Hyde, J.N., Jr. Child abuse- Principles and implications of current pediatric practice. *Pediatric Clinics of North America*, 1975, *22* (3), 695–715.

O'Brien, D. *Rare Inborn Errors of Metabolism in Children with Mental Retardation.* (DHEW Pub. # [USPHS] 2049). Washington, D. C.: U. S. Government Printing Office, 1970.

Ouellette, E.M. & Rosett, H.L. A pilot prospective study of the fetal alcohol syndrome at the Boston City Hospital. The infants. *Annals of the New York Academy of Science*, 1976, *273*, 123–29.

Ouellette, E.M., Rosett, H.L., Rosman, N.P. & Weiner, L. Adverse effects on offspring of maternal alcohol abuse during pregnancy. *New England Journal of Medicine*, 1977, *297*, 528–30.

Patau, K., Smith, D.W., Therman, E., Inhorn, S.L. & Wagner, H.P. Multiple congenital anomaly caused by an extra autosome. *Lancet*, 1960, *1*, 790–93.

Peckham, C.S. Clinical and laboratory study of children exposed *in utero* to maternal rubella. *Archives of Disease in Childhood*, 1972, *47*, 571–77.

Penrose, L.S. *The Biology of Mental Defect*, Rev. ed. New York: Grune & Stratton, 1962.

Perry, T.L. Homocystinuria. In W.L. Nyhan (Ed.), *Heritable Disorders of Amino Acid Metabolism: Patterns of Clinical Expression and Genetic Variation.* New York: John Wiley, 1974.

Perry, T.L., Hansen, S., Tischler, B., Richards, F.M. & Sokol, M. Unrecognized adult phenylketonuria. *New England Journal of Medicine*, 1973, *289* (8), 395–98.

Pildes, R. Infants of diabetic mothers. *New England Journal of Medicine*, 1973, *289* (17), 902–4.

Pomerance, J.J. & Yaffe, S.J. Maternal medication and its effect on the fetus. *Current Problems in Pediatrics*, 1973, *4*, 3–60.

Ptacek, L.J., Opitz, J.M., Smith, D.W., Gerritsen, T. & Waisman, H.A. The Cornelia de Lange syndrome. *Journal of Pediatrics*, 1963, *63* (5), 1000–20.

Purpura, D.P. Dendritic spine "dysgenesis" and mental retardation. *Science*, 1974, *186*, 1126–28.

Quilligan, E.J. & Collea, J.V. Fetal monitoring in pregnancy. In I. Schulman (Ed.), *Advances in Pediatrics* (Vol. 22). Chicago: Year Book Medical Publishers, 1976, 83–112.

Renuart, A.W. Screening for inborn errors of metabolism associated with mental deficiency or neurologic disorders or both. *New England Journal of Medicine*, 1966, *274*, 384–87.

Robert, M.F., Neff, R.K., Hubbell, J.P., Toeusch, H.W. & Avery, M.E. Association between maternal diabetes and the respiratory distress syndrome in the newborn. *New England Journal of Medicine*, 1976, *294* (7), 357–60.

Rosman, N.P. Neurological and muscular aspects of thyroid dysfunction in childhood. *Pediatric Clinics of North America*, 1976, *23* (3), 575–94.

Rothstein, P. & Gould, J.B. Born with a habit: Infants of drug-addicted mothers. *Pediatric Clinics of North America*, 1974, *21* (2), 307–21.

Rubenstein, J.H. & Taybi, H. Broad thumbs and toes and facial abnormalities. A possible mental retardation syndrome. *American Journal of Diseases of Children*, 1963, *105*, 588–608.

Sarason, S.B. & Doris, J. *Psychological Problems in Mental Deficiency*, 4th ed. New York: Harper & Row, 1969.

Sardharvalla, I.B. Treatment of galactosemia and homocystinuria. In T.E. Oppé & F.P. Woodford (Eds.), *Early Management of Handicapping Disorders*. Amsterdam: Associated Scientific Publishers, 1976, 25–30.

Schimke, R.N., McKusick, V.A., Huang, T. & Pollack, A.D. Homocystinuria. Studies of 20 families with 38 affected members. *Journal of the American Medical Association*, 1965, *193* (9), 711–19.

Sell, S.H.W., Merrill, R.E., Doyne, E.O. & Zimsky, E.P., Jr. Long-term sequelae of *Hemophilus influenzae* meningitis. *Pediatrics*, 1972, *49*, 206–11.

Sells, C.J., Carpenter, R.L. & Ray, C.G. Sequelae of central-nervous system enterovirus infections. *New England Journal of Medicine*, 1975, *293* (1), 1–4.

Senior, B. Neonatal hypoglycemia. *New England Journal of Medicine*, 1973, *289* (15), 790–92.

Share, J.D. Developmental progress in Down's syndrome. In R. Koch and F. de la Cruz (Eds.), *Down's Syndrome: Research, Prevention, & Management*. New York: Brunner/Mazel, 1975, 78–86.

Shih, V.E. *Laboratory Techniques for the Detection of Hereditary Metabolic Disorders*. Cleveland: CRC Press, 1973.

Shulman, K. Defects of the closure of the neural plate. In H.L. Barnett & A.H. Einhorn (Eds.), 15th ed. *Pediatrics*. New York: Appleton-Century-Crofts, 1972, 868.

Sidbury, J.B. Jr., The genetics of the glycogen storage diseases. *Progress in Medical Genetics*, 1967, 5, 32–58.

Smith, C.A. Effects of maternal undernutrition upon the newborn infant in Holland (1944–1945). *Journal of Pediatrics*, 1947, 30, 229–43.

Smith, D.W. *Recognizable Patterns of Human Malformation*. Philadelphia: W.B. Saunders, 1970.

Smith, D.W. & Marshall, R.E. *Introduction to Clinical Pediatrics*. Philadelphia: W.B. Saunders, 1972.

Smith, G.F. & Berg, J.M. *Down's Anomaly*. Edinburgh: Churchill Livingstone, 1976.

Solomons, G. Mongolism. *Hospital Medicine*, 1969, 5 (10), 58–69.

Stanley, C.A. & Baker, L. Hyperinsulinism in infants and children: Diagnosis and therapy. In L.A. Barness (Ed.), *Advances in Pediatrics* (Vol. 23). Chicago: Year Book Medical Publishers, 1976, 315–55.

Stein, Z., Susser, M., Saenger, G. & Marolla, F. Nutrition and mental performance. *Science*, 1972, 178, 708–13.

Stott, D.H. The child's hazards in utero. In J.G. Howells (Ed.), *Modern perspectives in International Child Psychiatry*. New York: Brunner/Mazel, 1971.

Streissguth, A.P. Psychologic handicaps in children with the fetal alcohol syndrome. *Annals of the New York Academy of Sciences*, 1976, 273, 140–45.

Symonds, E.M. The evaluation of fetal well-being in pregnancy and labour. In D. Hull (Ed.), *Recent Advances in Paediatrics*. Edinburgh: Churchill Livingstone, 1976, 1–34.

Taber, L.H. & Huber, T.W. Congenital syphilis. In S. Krugman & A.A. Gershon (Eds.), *Infections of the Fetus and the Newborn Infant*. (Progress in Clinical and Biological Research, Vol. 3). New York: Alan R. Liss, 1975.

Terman, L.M. & Merrill, M.A. *Stanford-Binet Intelligence Scale*. Boston: Houghton Mifflin, 1960.

Topper, A. Mental achievement of congenitally hypothyroid children. *American Journal of the Diseases of Children*, 1951, 81, 233–49.

Turner, H.H. A syndrome of infantilism, congenital webbed neck, and cubitus valgus. *Endocrinology*, 1938, 23, 566–74.

Volpe, J.J. Neonatal seizures. *New England Journal of Medicine*, 1973, 289 (8), 413–16.

Volpe, J.J. Perinatal hypoxic-ischemic brain injury. *Pediatric Clinics of North America*, 1976, 23 (3), 383–97.

Von Recklinghausen, F. *Über die multiplen Fibroma der Haut und ihre Beziehung zu den multiplen Neuromen*. Berlin: A. Hirschwald, 1882.

Weber, W.W. Survival and the sex ratio in trisomy 17–18. *American Journal Human Genetics*. 1967, *19*, 369–73.

Wechsler, D. Intelligence defined and undefined: A relativistic appraisal. *American Psychologist*, 1975, *30*, 135–39.

Wechsler, D. *The Measurement and Appraisal of Adult Intelligence*. Baltimore: Williams and Wilkins, 1958.

Wegman, M.E. Annual summary of vital statistics—1975. *Pediatrics*, 1976, *58* (6), 793–99.

Weissman, G. Experimental enzyme replacement in genetic and other disorders. *Hospital Practice*, September 1976, 49–58.

Weller, T.H. The cytomegaloviruses: Ubiquitous agents with protean clinical manifestations. *New England Journal of Medicine*, 1971, *285*, 203–14; 267–74.

White, P. Diabetes mellitus in pregnancy. *Clinics in Perinatology*, 1974, *1*, 331–47.

Wilfert, C.M. The neonate and gram negative bacterial infections. In S. Krugman & A.A. Gershon (Eds.), *Infections of the fetus and the newborn infant*. (Progress in Biological and Clinical Research, Vol. 3). New York: Alan R. Liss, 1975, 167–81.

Williams, J.C.P., Barratt-Boyes, B.G. & Lowe, J.B. Supravalvular aortic stenosis. *Circulation*, 1961, *24*, 1311–18.

Williams, R.S., Ferrante, R.J. & Caviness, V.S., Jr. Neocortical organization in human cerebral malformations: A Golgi-EM study. *Neuroscience Abstracts*, 1975, *1*, 776.

Winick, M. Malnutrition and the developing brain. *Research Publications Association for Research in Nervous and Mental Disease*, 1974, *53*, 253–62.

Wolf, A., Cowen, D. & Paige, B.H. Toxoplasmic encephalomyelitis III. A new case of granulomatous encephalomyelitis due to a protozoon. *American Journal of Pathology*, 1939, *15*, 657–94.

Wollman, H. & Smith, T.C. The therapeutic gases: Oxygen, carbon dioxide, and helium. In L.S. Goodman, A. Gilman, A.G. Gilman & G.B. Koelle (Eds.), *The Pharmacological Basis of Therapeutics*, 5th ed. New York: Macmillan, 1975.

Zelson, C., Sook, J.L. & Casalino, M. Neonatal narcotic addiction. Comparative effects of maternal intake of heroin and methadone. *New England Journal of Medicine*, 1973, *289* (23), 1216–20.

Zundel, W.S. & Tyler, F.H. The muscular dystrophies. *New England Journal of Medicine*, 1965, *273*, 537–43; 596–601.

3

Early Infantile Autism

HISTORY

The term autism was coined by Bleuler in 1911 to label a disorder of thought process in the schizophrenic syndrome. In 1943, Kanner used the term differently to describe eleven children whose condition he characterized as "autistic disturbance of affective contact." Kanner thought that these children exhibited certain basic schizophrenic phenomena, such as extreme autism, obsessiveness, stereotypy, and echolalia, but that they differed from other schizophrenics in that onset of the disease occurred not in the second or third year of life but much earlier. Kanner also pointed out that the parents of these children were lacking in "warmth." His identification of possible involvement of parent-child relationships, his hypothesis of an inborn component and poor prognosis, and his descriptive clarity in writing were factors that contributed to the impact of Kanner's work (Sarason and Doris, 1969) and led to considerable controversy in the literature concerning the etiology, manifestations, diagnosis, and treatment of "early infantile autism." Much of the initial controversy surrounding infantile autism resulted from Kanner's assertion that inability to relate was the fundamental pathognomic disorder and that the other behavioral abnormalities stemmed from the affective disturbance of desire for aloneness and sameness. Although many hailed the clarity of Kanner's behavioral observations, others questioned whether affective disturbance was a sufficient cause of some of the observed behaviors. For example, Scheerer, Rothmann, and

Goldstein (1945) asked whether the disturbance in relating to humans was not secondary or parallel to a defect in abstraction.

A more wide-ranging problem was the classification of the disorder as described by Kanner. Although Kanner thought that autism differed from childhood schizophrenia, some authors thought that it could be included within the general framework of schizophrenia (Bender, 1956; O'Gorman, 1967). The debate has continued. Others, including the authors of this book, hold autism to be a separate disorder (van Krevelin, 1952; Rutter, 1965), a belief concisely stated by Tanguay (1976, p.76): "Early infantile autism and childhood schizophrenia are distinctly different illnesses. Early infantile autism is a syndrome which occurs quite early in life and is related to that spectrum of illnesses termed the 'developmental disabilities.' Childhood schizophrenia is the downward extension of adult schizophrenia into childhood."

ETIOLOGY

Not only was there controversy about whether the major disturbance was affective or not and whether or not autism was distinct from childhood schizophrenia, but also whether it was induced by environmental or by inborn factors. In their review of the literature up to the late 1950s, Sarason and Gladwin (1958) tried to indicate that the available evidence did not support such an either/or view. Writers continued, however, to posit a causal dichotomy, yet no treatment based on an exclusive concern for environment or for heredity yielded any "solid evidence to support the theoretical position from which it evolved" (Ornitz, 1973).

The controversy surrounding the etiology of infantile autism centers around psychogenic theories and biological theories, including deficit, biochemical, viral, and genetic theories.

PSYCHOGENIC THEORY

Although Kanner concluded that autistic children had some inborn defect, he also maintained that it was partly a psychogenic disorder originating in lack of affection from the parents, i.e., "emotional refrigeration" (Kanner, 1949). Other writers have agreed that autism is mainly due to psychogenic factors (Despert, 1951; Goldfarb, 1961; Kaufman et al., 1957;

Bettelheim, 1967). But evaluation of the possibility of a psychogenic basis for autism has been complicated by the large number of different hypotheses, the ambiguity and vagueness of the hypotheses (Rutter, 1968), and the differing criteria for the diagnosis of autism. Psychogenically, autism is seen as the child's response to general qualities of his parents' personalities or as a reaction to prolonged stress or other adverse situations.

Rutter (1968) points out the main objections to the hypothesis that specific parental abnormalities directed at one child have caused the autism. First, since autism occurs so early in life, it would have to be a very severe parental abnormality to cause such a disturbance rather than the subtle parental abnormalities reported by most writers. Second, parental abnormalities may result from the pathology of the child rather than vice versa. This point has received considerable recent support in light of the evidence pointing to the stimulus value of the child and the infant's ability to shape parental behavior (Lewis and Rosenblum, 1974). Third, there may be both an organic and psychogenic variety of autism, but this has not been supported by existing data.

Essential psychodynamic approaches to autism protray the condition as a disturbance of development because of anxiety and stress. Bettelheim (1967) is the leading proponent of a psychogenic theory. He suggests that the source of the stress and anxiety for the infant is his fear for his life. The child perceives the environment as hostile and threatening and the emotions of significant figures in his environment as negative in relation to him. The child's response is pervasive rage and rejection of his environment, especially his social environment. Thus, infantile autism is seen as a "fortress" erected to shut out the world, but at the price of internal emptiness.

Rutter points out that while it is plausible that autism could result from stress, this explanation would necessitate a regression model. The majority of autistic children, however, appear abnormal from infancy. Also the effects of prolonged social deprivation are different from the behaviors characteristic of autism. For example, obsession features seen in autistic children are not usually seen in children reared in institutional settings (see Provence and Lyston, 1962). Rutter (1968, p.9–10) remarks that Bettelheim's hypothesis may possibly be correct but probably is not since "neither he nor anyone else has demonstrated that autistic children have in fact experienced these supposed extreme experiences. . . . The balance of evidence seems against the view that autism is psychogenically determined but there are no decisive findings one way or the other."

BIOLOGICAL THEORY

In the causal dichotomy controversy, biological theories emphasize inborn factors as opposed to environmental factors. These inborn factors include defects in specific aspects of functioning, biochemical imbalances, infectious agents, and genes.

Deficit Theories

In 1964, Rimland published *Infantile Autism: The Syndrome and its Implication for a Neural Theory of Behavior.* He asserted that no evidence at present supports the psychogenic point of view but that some evidence suggests an organic pathology. He speculated that a primary factor could be an impairment in the function of the reticular formation of the brainstem.

More recent research has centered on other defects and their implications for etiology. Tanguay (1976) groups these deficit theories into three categories:

THE THEORY OF PERCEPTUAL INCONSISTENCY   Ornitz and Ritvo (1968) postulated a deficit in the homeostatic regulation of sensory input and motor output. "As a result of this defect, the child fails to gain a stable inner representation of his environment, and hence, he cannot learn to interact normally with others or to use communicative speech" (p. 77). Support for this theory comes from electrophysiological research focused on phenomena mediated by the vestibular nuclei in the brainstem. Autistic children demonstrate markedly diminished vestibular reactivity (as measured by the duration of the ocular nastagmus) in comparison with normal subjects (Ornitz et al., 1974). Additional supportive evidence comes from the findings in autistic children of a "significant reduction in the tendency of the rapid eye movements of REM sleep to cluster into bursts" (Ornitz et al., 1969, p. 77).

THE THEORY OF A DEFECT IN CROSS-MODAL ASSOCIATIONS   Typically children are adept at receiving information in one modality, such as the auditory, visual, and tactile, and at responding in another. Bryson (1970) demonstrated that autistic children have great difficulty responding in a modality different from that in which the stimulus is presented. Lelord et al. (1973) demonstrated that auditory-evoked responses are enhanced when auditory stimuli are followed 300 msec later by a strong flash in normals but not in autistics. Another source of evidence comes from Lovaas et al. (1971), who demonstrated that conditioned responses to complex stimuli (auditory, visual, and tactile) could be produced by any one of the several components in normal children but by only one of the components in autistic children.

THE THEORY OF CENTRAL COGNITIVE DEFECT   This theory is based on the autistic child's inability to comprehend or use communicative speech, which Rutter (1968) hypothesizes lies at the base of autism. Studies have shown that autistic children have difficulty encoding auditory and visual information (Tubbs, 1966) and in processing sequentially patterned information (DeMyer et al., 1972) and temporally patterned information (Hermelin, 1972). In a study matching autistic children with normals on the basis of mental age, Frith (1970) has shown that in contrast with normals autistic children fail to recall meaningful sentences better than random words.

Tanguay (1976) summarizes consideration of these theories of etiology based on defects of autistic children and points out that these defects in language and in processing linear information involve functions for which the gradients are predominantly in the left hemisphere of the brain. Furthermore, the abilities of the autistic children, i.e., relative strength on the performance tasks of the WISC and holistic processing of information are right hemisphere functions. He suggests that autistic children may fail to develop hemispheric specialization in the normal way.

Another source of support for left hemisphere involvement in infantile autism is the pneumoencephalographic findings in 17 autistic children reported by Hauser, DeLong, and Raman (1975). None of the children had specific diagnosable neurological disease or gross motor disorders. In fact, the motor, visual, auditory, and somaesthetic systems were intact and showed no striking abnormalities in hypothalamic functions and no global defect in alertness, attention, or cognitive ability. The pneumoencephalograms in 15 of 17 children demonstrated "ventricular enlargement, indicating a deficiency of brain substance in the left cerebral hemisphere" (p. 680) primarily of the left temporal horn. The authors suggested that "dysfunction of the medial temporal lobe is a major factor in the pathogenesis of the syndrome of infantile autism" (p. 683).

Biochemical Theories

More recently, attention has been directed toward biochemical theories and findings. Nerve cells communicate by chemical messengers called neurotransmitters. One group of transmitters is the monoamines (dopamine, norepinephrine, and serotonin). Monoamines are found in areas of the brain which control emotions and behavior and are involved in the therapeutic activity of the psychoactive drugs (Yuviler, Geller, and Ritvo, 1976). A number of investigators have been evaluating serotonin levels in autistic children and comparing them with those in normals to determine the influence of this monoamine in autism. In a report on a study of 72 autistics and 71 controls, Peterson and Torrey (1976) confirmed several trends regarding endogenous serotonin levels in autistic children: "The levels are higher on the average than in controls" and "the levels show marked variability, much greater than that recorded in controls" (p. 62). Additional support comes from the work of Yuviler, Geller, and Ritvo (1976): "Our results do suggest that autistics have higher blood serotonin, higher platelet counts, and somewhat higher serotonin per platelet than age matched non-autistic children" (p. 103). However, these authors point out that they have not studied either activity level or chronic dietary intake systematically and thus are not yet certain that their results are directly related to autism.

Viral Theories

Another approach has been to investigate the role that infectious agents, especially viruses, may play in the etiology of autism and childhood schizophrenia. Peterson and Torrey (1976) offer as evidence the data that children with childhood psychosis have abnormal dermatoglyphic patterns (Sank, 1968; Hilburn, 1970), more physical stigmata (Steg and Rapaport, 1975), and more perinatal complications than normal children. They maintain that all these difficulties could be caused by intrauterine infections. In conclusion, they point to several agents that could affect the CNS of the fetus and produce an infant with behavioral symptoms consistent with autism and/or childhood schizophrenia. The hypothesized teratogenic agents would have several distinctive characteristics. They would have a "seasonal influence" and a "minimal influence on the clinical course of the pregnancy except for first or second trimester bleeding." They would be "capable of producing subtle, but definite physical abnormalities, such as the physical stigmata in toes, etc. and would possibly influence the dermatoglyphic patterns of the newborn child. Such a possible group of teratogens would include many common and well-studied viral agents" (p. 26–27). Among them would be rubella virus, cylomegalovirus (CMV), herpes simplex virus (HSV), and measles virus.

Genetic Theories

The role that genes play in autism has yet to be determined because of a number of complications. First, there are insufficient data. In genetic studies, information on all family members, and not just the affected individual, is needed; and that information, for ethical and practical reasons is difficult to gather. Second, most of the work to date has had to utilize the diagnostic dichotomy of presence or absence of autism rather than a gradation or continuum. Spence (1976) points out that there is no evidence that a single gene mechanism is responsible for autism. Instead, he suggests that polygenic or multifactorial inheritance is a possibility. "It may be that several mechanisms are responsible for some or all of the cases. Or, it may be that only certain aspects, symptoms, of the condition are inherited. Since these possibilities exist, each symptom of the condition and cluster of the symptoms will have to undergo separate genetic analyses, testing the data against the existing genetic hypothesis" (p. 173).

INTEGRATION OF INDIVIDUAL THEORIES

As is often the case when dealing with human phenomena, the study of autism has gone through a period of narrow, highly specialized theories, high on polemic but low on integration. We are currently in a period in which researchers are attempting to integrate findings into a more unified mind-body approach to the etiology of infantile autism. More specifically they are rediscovering that it is difficult to separate nature–nurture and are redirecting their attention toward the interaction of biological and psychological factors. "A genetically determined biological vulnerability is just that. It can be exaggerated by a destructive and/or impoverished environment and can be compensated for by a constructive environment. Only when the initial neurobiological disorder is of devasting proportions is it the overriding determinant of outcome" (Fish, 1976, p. 178).

In discussing Rutter's (1968) hypothesis that a cognitive deficit involving language comprehension lies at the basis of autism, Baker et al. (1976) remark that "the role of psychosocial factors cannot be entirely dismissed, as it may be necessary for certain environmental circumstances to occur in order for the syndrome of autism to develop in children who have the necessary (but not sufficient) cognitive defect" (p. 134).

Concerning the interaction of psychological and biochemical factors, Coleman (1973) reports on the acknowledged links between the two.

The neurologists are willing to concede that, in some cases, biochemistry can be significantly changed and compromised by the emotional environment of an individual patient. Even in patients with unequivocal organic etiologies of central nervous system disease, data is now available that demonstrates an environmental effect on the patient's biochemistry, particularly the metabolic systems at risk in that particular patient. (DeMyer et al. 1971, p.3)

Given this focus on etiological integration and interaction, we can consider two attempts at a definition of autism. Ritvo (1976) states that autism is a physical disease of the brain. Patients who present with it "share a neuropathophysiologic process which interferes with developmental rate, and the modulation or integration of sensory input within the brain. These malfunctions then lead to other symptoms typical of the disorder—disturbances of motility, disturbances of language, and disturbance of personality development expressed by psychosis and the inability to relate to others" (p.5). Coleman's opinion (1976), though differing markedly in other ways, is not dissimilar. She does not think that autism is a disease entity. Rather, it is a constellation of symptoms, i.e., "a syndrome, one of the limited patterns that the infant central nervous system has in reaction to injury or genetic misinformation" (p.2). Since there appear to be three distinct subgroups within the syndrome, she prefers the plural term "autistic syndromes" to the singular term "autism."

THE CLASSIC AUTISTIC SYNDROME   Onset is in the prenatal, perinatal, neonatal, or early infancy period. There is no observed neurological or EEG impairment. The clinical course can begin improving between 5 and 7 years of age. Three organic etiological groups are proposed to account for the syndrome: familial, celiac, and purine autistic syndromes.

CHILDHOOD SCHIZOPHRENIA—AUTISTIC TYPE   There are no neurological or EEG abnormalities and no evidence of degenerative disease. Onset is after 30 months of age. Additional psychiatric symptoms are present.

THE NEUROLOGICALLY IMPAIRED AUTISTIC SYNDROME   There is evidence of organic brain disease and neurological and EEG abnormalities. The following etiologies are proposed:

metabolic syndrome (PKU, metachromatic leukodystrophy, and Hurler's
   syndrome)
gestational viral syndrome (rubella)
sensory deprivation syndrome (deafness, blindness)
sequelae of the infantile spasms syndrome

Whether one considers autism to be infantile autism or autistic syndromes, the field has come a long way since the 1958 review of Sarason and
Gladwin. Also the investigative research is becoming more systematic so
that Kanner's comment in the introduction to Rimland's 1964 book no
longer characterizes the field: "The concept of 'early infantile autism' (I
could not think of a better name) was diluted by some to deprive it of its
specificity, so that the term was used as a pseudodiagnostic wastebasket for
a variety of unrelated conditions, and a nothing–but psychodynamic etiology was decreed by some as the only valid explanation, so that further curiosity was stifled or even scorned."

MANIFESTATIONS

Now that we have examined where we have been and how etiologies
are currently conceptualized, we can focus on the manifestations dimension
of the Developmental Disabilities Cube. As there has been increasing
specificity in the area of theory and clinical research, there has also been an
increased specificity concerning manifestations that serve as increasingly
stringent criteria for the diagnosis of autism.

DIAGNOSTIC CRITERIA

In his initial discussion Kanner (1943) indicated three necessary criteria for the diagnosis of autism: (1) extreme self-proccupation and lack of
relationship with people, (2) onset during the first 2 years of life, and (3)
lack of severe motor retardation. Later (Eisenberg and Kanner, 1956) a
fourth criteria was added—the insistence on the preservation of sameness.
Subsequently, there has been considerable disagreement about the diagnostic criteria. Clancy, Dugdale, and Rendle-Short (1969) suggest that what
leads to this disagreement—and to the resulting difficulty in making a diagnosis of infantile autism—is the lack of any pathognomic signs or symptoms.

This lack of unique identifying signs is not limited to the disorder of infantile autism. Many disorders are comprised of symptoms and signs which are also present in other disorders. Frequently the uniqueness of the condition lies in the pattern of signs. Furthermore, initial postulation of a disorder or condition as a separate entity typically is based upon clinical observations. Efforts are then made to specify the conglomeration of symptoms and signs that comprise the postulated disorder. Comprehensiveness typically surpasses specificity. Once there is sufficient specificity of the conglomeration of symptoms and signs and their pattern, consensual clinical diagnosis is possible. The next step, which frequently comes a long time after diagnosis, is empirical differentiation of aspects which are necessary and sufficient for the postulated disorder.

Efforts to establish the relative importance or diagnostic usefulness of specific signs and preliminary empirical efforts are beginning to occur with infantile autism. An attempt was made by the British Working Party to clarify and describe what was meant by the term psychosis in childhood. The diagnostic criteria that were formulated were known as the "Nine Points" and were reported by Mildred Creak, chairman of the group (Creak, 1961, 1964). Clancy et al. (1969) used Creak's nine-point scale to derive 54 individual behavior items. These items were then given to the parents of 25 children diagnosed as autistic, 32 normal controls, 25 subnormal controls (IQ between 40 and 80), 25 rubella-deaf controls, and 15 cerebral-palsied controls. Fourteen behaviors were isolated as ones most consistently present in the condition of infantile autism, and the authors contend that these may be regarded as the major manifestations of the disease. In decreasing order of frequency, the 14 items are:

1. Great difficulty in mixing and playing with other children.
2. Seeming deafness: No reaction to speech or noise.
3. Strong resistance to any learning, either new behavior or new skills.
4. Lack of fear about realistic dangers, e.g., may play with fire, climb dangerous heights, run into busy road or into the sea.
5. Resistance to change in routine: Change in the smallest things may result in acute, excessive, or seemingly illogical anxiety, e.g., child rejects new or all but a few foods.
6. Preference for indicating needs by gestures. Speech may or may not be present.
7. Laughter and giggling for no apparent reason.
8. Not cuddly as a baby. Either holds himself still or clings limply.

9. Marked physical overactivity. Child may wake and play for hours in the night and yet be full of energy the next day.
10. No eye contact. Persistent tendency to look past or turn away from people especially when spoken to.
11. Unusual attachment to a particular object or objects. Easily preoccupied with details or special features of this object, and has no regard to its real use.
12. Tendency to spin objects, especially round ones. Can become totally absorbed in this activity and distressed if interrupted.
13. Repetitive and sustained odd play, e.g., linking pieces of string, rattling stones in a tin, tearing paper.
14. Standoffish manner. Communicates very little with other people. Treats them as objects rather than people.

Clancy et al. (1969) maintain that for the diagnosis of autism to be made, at least seven of these behaviors should be present. They also maintain that when a diagnostician uses these criteria, it is unlikely that an autistic child will be missed, although some children exhibiting another condition could be misdiagnosed as autistic. In their study, six controls demonstrated seven or more of these manifestations.

Coleman (1976) as we have seen has advocated the term "autistic syndromes" because there appear to be several distinct subgroups within the syndrome. In her approach, there are six primary criteria:

1. Early age of onset of clinical symptoms.
2. Profound inability to relate to other people.
3. Language retardation including impaired comprehension and unusual use of language.
4. Ritualistic and compulsive behavior.
5. Disturbance of motility and appearance of stereotypes.
6. Abnormal perceptual responses to auditory, visual, and tactile sensory stimuli but usually not olfactory stimuli.

Recently, Ritvo and his coworkers (1976) have advocated diagnostic criteria based on a grouping of symptoms and characteristics into areas of manifested dysfunction. "We reserve the diagnosis 'autism' for patients who clearly show, prior to thirty-six months of age, irregularities of development and disturbances of the modulation of sensory input, relatedness and language. . . . The presence of these symptoms is necessary and sufficient to establish the diagnosis. Motility disturbances, while frequently present, are not necessary to establish the diagnosis" (p. 13).

SYSTEM DYSFUNCTIONS

With this background, we can see the progession of diagnostic criteria from several characteristics to an array of behaviors to a grouping of behaviors and characteristics into areas of manifested dysfunction. We can extend this by considering the manifestations of autism in terms of the Developmental Disabilities Cube presented earlier (p. 17). Specifically, we will consider cognitive-intellectual, neuromotor, language, physical, affective-behavioral, and sensori-perceptual manifestations. Hopefully, the integrating conceptual schema of the Developmental Disabilities Cube will be conducive to future efforts to empirically differentiate necessary and sufficient aspects of infantile autism.

Cognitive-Intellectual Dysfunctions

Initially there were claims that autistic children were basically of normal intelligence (Kanner, 1943; Bettelheim, 1967) and appeared retarded only because of profound social withdrawal. Rutter (1968) argues that social withdrawal does not account for the cognitive-intellectual dysfunctions, nor is the presence of mental subnormality sufficient to account for autism. He reports that some autistic children demonstrate low IQ scores but many demonstrate IQ scores in the normal range. He maintains that the IQ score of the autistic child is just as stable as that of other children and IQ scores obtained in early childhood predict remarkably well later intellectual, social, and behavioral adjustment (Lockyer and Rutter, 1968). Furthermore, it has been shown that loss of the symptom of social withdrawal had little effect on the IQ of autistic children (Rutter et al., 1967).

Another characteristic of the intellectual functioning of autistic children is the wide variability of scores in the area being assessed. Autistic children tended to score well on nonverbal tasks and poorly on verbal tasks. This suggests that to "some extent the autistic child's poor level of intellectual attainment is related to specific defects in language rather than to a global deficiency of intellect" (Rutter, 1968, p.5).

That point of view is not supported, however, by Ritvo (1976), who points out that mental retardation and autism can coexist. He argues that the idea that primary affective deficiency of autistic children interferes with their cognitive potentials is giving way to the recognition that "their intellectual deficiencies are every bit as real as in patients with primary retardation. Accumulating clinical experience indicates that two-thirds to three-fourths of all autistic patients will perform throughout life at retarded levels" (p. 16).

Concerning the hypotheses that what is exhibited is a language deficit rather than impairment of intellect, Baker et al. (1976) report that "research to date seems to suggest that a number of the cognitive skills necessary for language are impaired in autism, and that it is to be expected that these are skills not unique to language" (p. 145). The emerging pattern of cognitive strength reflected in nonverbal skills, and weakness reflected in skills necessary for language provide additional support for the idea of possible left hemispheric weakness in autistic children and should be an impetus for further neuropsychological research.

Language Dysfunctions

Not only is language disturbances a criterion symptom, but it is frequently one of the first symptoms to be recognized and reported. Although a substantial literature exists about the characteristics of autistic language, most studies have been primarily impressionistic case reports. Baker et al. (1976) comment that "systematic studies of the language of autistic children are few, and a reliable and specific profile of autistic language does not yet exist" (p. 122). A variety of language characteristics have been reported, but there is little agreement in the findings. For example, there are reports both of a difference in pronoun usage by autistic children (Weiland and Legg, 1964; Goldfarb et al., 1972) and no difference between autistic children and controls (Cunningham, 1968). The amount of questioning present in the language of autistic children is also contested with reports of lack of questioning as a characteristic (Hingtgen and Bryson, 1972; Wolf and Chess, 1965) and denials that this is a characteristic (Cunningham, 1968; Rutter, Greenfield, and Lockyer, 1967).

Baker et al. (1976) point to the lack of uniformity of diagnostic criteria and samples varying in age and intellectual level as well as to various procedures of language sampling and analysis as factors contributing to the inconsistent findings. They report on a number of studies with a group of 19 autistic children (who met the criteria of infantile autism; Rutter, 1971) and 23 aphasic children. The aphasic children were diagnosed as having "an uncomplicated developmental language disorder which included impairment in comprehension as well as in the production of language" (p. 125). The mean age of the autistic group was 7 years and 0 months and of the aphasic group 8 years and 2 months.

The results of a language analysis of a half-hour sample of conversation between mothers and their children indicated that the two most common language categories of both groups were answers and spontaneous remarks. The autistic group had significantly more utterances in the categories of delayed echoes and thinking aloud. There was also a significant difference in the imitative behavior of the two groups, with the autistic group exhibiting more inappropriate delayed repetitions and the aphasics more appropriate repetition of self and appropriate repetition of others. It was suggested that autistic children may have a greater abnormality in the use of language than in the structural acquisition of language as compared with aphasic language.

In a review article of language in childhood psychosis, Baltaxe and Simmons (1975) address the issue of delayed versus deviant language development in autistic children. They report a number of studies to support the contention that the language of autistics is not only delayed but also deviant. Deviation of pitch, stress, inflection; manneristic style and idiosyncratic use of words (DeHirsch, 1967); prelinguistic vocalizations (Ricks, 1972); use of the past tense marker (Bartolucci and Albers, 1974); difficulties in the transfer from one sensory modality to another; poor use of gestures; difficulties understanding the meaning of spoken words (Tubbs, 1966); and differences in language acquisition (Baltaxe and Simmons, 1974; Simmons and Baltaxe, 1975) are offered as evidence for language defects.

Ritvo et al. (1976) includes muteness and echolalia of feelings and words as common disturbances of speech and language in autistic children. If functional speech develops, "it is usually atonal and arrhythmic, lacking inflection and failing to convey subtle emotion" (p.11). Furthermore, he maintains that these qualities are usually present into adulthood.

Language has frequently been considered as a prognostic indicator. Eisenberg (1956) maintained that if there was no language by 5 years of age, there was likely to be gross retardation and disturbed behavior in later life. However, Rutter et al. (1967) maintain that this is not always so and that some individuals do gain speech later in life. Rutter et al. (1967) did find a significant association between presence or absence of language and outcome. Lack of language development, particularly when accompanied by an IQ below 60, was considered to be indicative of a very guarded outcome (Rutter and Sussenwein, 1971). Baker et al. (1976) summarize the current status of language as a prognostic indicator.

Thus, while it has been generally recognized that there is a relationship between language and prognosis, this relationship has typically been stated in
terms of the expected progress for the child with some language as opposed to
the expected progress for the child with no language. A precise character-
ization of the prognosis that may be expected for children with different levels
of language acquisition at different ages has not been made. (p. 132)

Another area of concern relating to language, has been the mother-
child interaction in terms of the hypothesis of deviant maternal language
model. Although this is not a manifestation of autism, this is probably the
most appropriate point to consider this hypothesis. Baltaxe and Simmons
(1975) report that the most carefully analyzed data on mother-child interaction and language development has been produced by Brown and his coworkers (Brown and Belluge, 1964; Brown, Cayden, and Bellugi, 1970;
Brown and Hanlon, 1970). The authors go on to say that although further
work is needed, the findings on linguistic models by Brown et al. (1970)
show that some of the differences in verbalization of psychotic and normals
appear to reflect types of models. Goldfarb, Goldfarb, and Scholl (1966)
reached the conclusion that poorer linguistic models were provided by
mothers of schizophrenic children than by the mothers of normal children.
However, this study has been criticized on design factors (Klein and Pollack, 1966). Furthermore, the comparisons were made between the language models of mothers of autistic children and those of normal children.
As Barker et al. (1976, p. 138) point out: "There is now a considerable body
of evidence (Snow, 1972; Olin, 1970) that the mother modified her language level according to the language level of her child." What is needed if
normal controls are used in comparison with autistic children is to match
on the basis of language age instead of chronological age.

Another method is to compare the language models provided by
mothers of autistic children with models provided by mothers and other
language impaired children. Baker et al. (1976) used mothers of aphasic
children in such a comparison and found no significant differences between
the two groups of mothers for any of the linguistic measures. They concluded that "the mothers of autistic children have language behavior which
is typical for mothers of language disabled children" (p. 139).

Neuromotor Dysfunctions

The primary motor characteristics are behavior stereotypes, usually involving the hands and arms in flapping movements. Walking on the toes, staccato lunging of the trunk, body rocking or swaying, and head rolling or banging are also reported (Ritvo et al., 1976). "Repetitive and sustained odd play," for example, tearing paper, and spinning objects, are criteria advanced by Clancy et al. (1969) and ritualistic and compulsive behavior are listed by Coleman (1976) as criteria. Walker and Coleman (1976) used a camera to study the characteristics of adventitious movements in autistic children. Three groups of adventitious movements were seen: flapping, clapping, and posturing. "Facial grimacing, choreic and athetotic movements, jumping and rocking and behaviors focusing on the ears and mouth were also observed" (p. 143).

Physical Dysfunctions

Walker (1976) reports that the incidence of minor physical anomalies in autistic children was found to be significantly greater than in controls matched by socioeconomic level and by age. Low seating of ears, syndactyly, and hypertelorism were significantly more frequent among autistic children than normals. There was also a significantly higher incidence of abnormal cranial circumference and high palate in the autistic children than would have been expected on the basis of normal frequencies. Walker argued that the results suggested that congenital factors are associated with the development of autism.

Affective-Behavioral Dysfunctions

Primary disturbance of affective contact is a cardinal characteristic of autistic children. This disturbance of affective contact has been noted from very early infancy. One of the 14 criteria proposed by Clancy (1969) indicates an infant who is not cuddly, holds himself still, or clings limply. Kanner (1943) pointed out the "extreme autistic aloneness" in his group of children. Coleman (1976) also lists profound inability to relate to other people as a criterion. Clancy et al. (1969) also includes other criteria that indicate affective disturbance such as no eye contact, evidenced in a turning away when spoken to, and in laughing and giggling for no apparent reason.

Ritvo et al. (1976) summarize an array of behaviors reflecting disturbances of relating which are characteristic of autistic children. They exhibit "poor or deviant eye contact (McConnell, 1967), delayed or absent social smile, delayed or absent anticipatory response to being picked up, apparent aversion to physical contact, a tendency to react to only a part of another person, disinterested in playing games with others, and delayed, absent, or overreactive stranger anxiety" (p. 11).

While there is little disagreement about the existence of affective manifestations, it needs to be pointed out that these manifestations can be somewhat intermittent. Also, these affective manifestations are not unique to autistic children and may be considered as reactive or secondary to disturbances in language or perception (Churchill, 1972; Reichler and Schopler, 1971). Furthermore, some controlled studies challenge the belief based on clinical experience that some affective manifestations can be considered as pathognomic of autism. Churchill and Bryson (1972) found no support for the hypothesis that adult attention causes autistic children to withdraw or that autistic children are significantly different from normal children in their behaviors of looking at and approaching a strange adult.

Sensoriperceptual Dysfunctions

As discussed above, disturbance in modulation and integration of sensory input is a major manifestation of autistic disturbance according to Ritvo and his coworkers (1976). This disturbance includes, hypo- and hyperreactivity to visual, auditory, and pain stimuli. Also reported is an "impaired ability to use internal sensory input to make discrimination in the absence of feedback from motor responses" (Hermelin and O'Conner, 1970, p. 9).

INCIDENCE: The study of Lotter (1966) in England and that of Torrey et al. (1975) in the United States have estimated that frequency of autism to be roughly one in every 2,200 live births or between 4 and 5 out of every 10,000. Kanner (1954) reported a male/female ratio of 4:1. Lotter's ratio (1966) was 2.5:1 while Spence et al. (1973) reported a ratio of 4.8:1. The age of onset is generally considered to be at birth, but it can extend up to 30 months of age.

TREATMENT AND MANAGEMENT

As mentioned previously, the severe disturbances comprising the manifestation of autism usually persist throughout a child's life and thus constitute a major developmental disability. Given the present state of knowledge, cures of autism are not likely, so the goals become management and stimulation of maturation and development. To accomplish these goals, a combination of approaches is used. "Basically, there are two major modalities of treatment; one is biological and the other is social educational" (Fish, 1976, p.108).

PHARMOCOTHERAPY

The primary intention of pharmocotherapy for autistic children is to promote development by improving the child's receptivity to social and educational therapies. Fish (1976) maintains that one is attempting basically "to modify the disturbance of physiological patterning of attention, affect and of motor behavior" (p.109).

Psychoactive drugs have been shown to be effective in treatment of adult psychoses, but the nature of the psychoses of infantile autism is a different matter. In psychotic adults, functions are present but deviant (disturbed), and administration of a major tranquilizer such as chlorpromazine results, among other effects, in correction of schizophrenic mentation" (Campbell, 1975).

Autistic children exhibit delays and deficits in development in addition to psychoses. Consequently, many functions such as language and adaptive skills have to be developed, not merely returned to normal levels. Thus, while a reduction in reactivity of the adult psychotic may be desirable, it is not desirable in the young autistic child in whom one needs to promote development. Campbell (1975) also points out other problems with pharmocotherapy with autistic children including the uncertain effect on cognition; the influence of long-term pharmocotherapy on growth, weight, endocrine systems, and organs; and the poor prognosis with any available treatment modality.

In addition to the general problems in using psychoactive drugs with autistic children, additional problems occur in relation to choice of drug and dosage level. Fish (1976) reports that the specific medication and specific dosage level are basically determined by treatment and modification. Moreover, the optimal dosage level is not always constant. Both Fish (1976) and Campbell (1975) report that stimulants make autistic children worse. Fish (1976) maintains that in general the major neuroleptics or tranquilizers are the most effective drugs available for autistic children. However, the sedative effects are often deterrents for usage with young children. Some success has been reported with Haloperidol (Engelhardt et al., 1973) and Campbell (1975) reports that "the combination of stimulating and anti-psychotic properties make this drug superior to phenothiazines" (p. 413).

Although there are difficulties with pharmocotherapy for autistic chil-dren, the search for an effective drug without undesirable side effects on cognition and development is continuing. Also, drugs have been shown at times to be effective in rendering the autistic child more amenable to other therapies (Campbell, 1975). Fish (1976) summarizes the situation well. "What drugs do, when they are effective, is to make a child more receptive to educational and social therapies which must go on all the time for the child's development to be promoted and his improvement to continue" (p. 109).

DEVELOPMENTAL THERAPY

Schopler and his coworkers (Schopler et al., 1971; Schopler & Reich-ler, 1971) have devised a developmental therapy program. This program is based on several factors. First, the view that autism is most likely caused by biochemical and neurological brain abnormalities. Second, these abnor-malities result in perceptual inconstancies with impairment of speech and communication. Third, review of the evidence, which indicates that parents' personalities fall within the "normal range," and thus they are not the cause of the child's autism. In this approach, parents are helped to function as primary developmental agents with treatment being focused on the autistic child's relatedness, competence motivation, cognitive, and per-ceptual motor functioning. A central aspect of the therapy program is a direct demonstration by the therapist, which contributes in two general ways. First, by offering the therapist as a model for general attitudes and approaches and second, by demonstrating specific teaching methods. The therapists help the parents gain a realistic appraisal of the child, which is viewed as enabling them to make their best energies available to maintain or improve family adjustment. Schopler and Reichler (1971) are somewhat less pessimistic about outcome than other writers. "Depending on the se-verity of the underlying impairment and the consistency of appropriate ed-ucation, the child may reach optimal or normal levels of development" (p. 101).

However, the point is also made that there is a link between progress and IQ. When the IQ level is less than 50, a poor prognosis for normal development exists. When the IQ level is over 50, there is a greater variability in prognosis.

Rutter and Sussenwein (1971) have also formulated a developmental and behavioral approach to treatment which also has an emphasis on inclusion of the parents. This treatment program is based on their view of autism as "a central defect in the cognitive functions associated with language comprehension (and production) and with the processing of symbolic or sequenced information" (p. 377). Social and behavioral abnormalities are viewed as secondary to the central cognitive defect. The goals of this developmental and behavioral approach are to foster development of social skills, especially normal attachment behavior and language, and to eliminate both rigid stereotyped deviant behaviors as well as less specific deviant behaviors such as sleep disturbance and aggression. Parents are worked with directly to help them foster appropriate imitative behavior in their children. Parental counseling is provided to help them deal with the problems created by an autistic child and to deal with their own feelings and emotions.

SPECIAL EDUCATION

The efforts to modify and develop educational techniques to enhance learning in children with other developmental disabilities such as mental retardation have also been applied to autistic children. The task of education with autistic children is particularly challenging because of the constellation of inattention, poor communication, and related deficits and inappropriate behaviors that characterize these children. In addition, educational programs have attempted to provide treatment benefits in terms of stimulating development as well as to increase academic skills. A comprehensive effort to evaluate different educational approaches in terms of their behavioral, social, and learning outcomes has been conducted by Bartak and Rutter (1973). Their findings also included a followup of participants 3.5 to 4 years later (Rutter and Bartak, 1973).

In this study, a comparison was made between three educational units, differing in theoretical orientation, in organization and structure, and in style of staff-child interactions. One unit was primarily psychotherapeutic, with little emphasis on teaching; a second was a permissive classroom environment, in which a combination of special education methods and relationship and regressive techniques were employed; a third was a structured and organized setting for the teaching of specific skills. The authors report that "the differences between units in organization, structure and style of staff-child interaction were associated with marked differences in the children's scholastic attainment but with few differences in any other sphere of progress" (p. 259).

Children in all three units showed improvement in behavior and social responsiveness in the units, but not outside the units; and there were no significant differences among the units in amount of improvement. The children of the unit that most emphasized structure organization and the teaching of specific skills produced the most gains in scholastic attainments. "It appears that this emphasis led to greater attainment and that an autistic unit with large amounts of specific teaching in a well-controlled classroom situation is likely to bring the greatest benefits in terms of scholastic progress" (p. 257).

Additional evidence that structure is beneficial with autistic children comes from an evaluation of functioning in structured versus unstructured therapy (Schopler et al., 1971). Autistic children demonstrated better attention and more appropriate affect; they also related better, and behaved more appropriately in the structured therapy sessions than in the unstructured sessions. There were no significant differences in quality of vocalizations. This study, which pointed out the marked individual differences in children, is consistent with other studies (Schopler and Reichler, 1971) in finding that functioning is related to level of development. The greatest disorganizing effect of the unstructured situation is exhibited by those with the lowest levels of development.

INTEGRATION OF THEORY AND TREATMENT

It can readily be seen that therapeutic and management approaches do stem from theoretic views of autism. The psychogenic view of autism with its emphasis on parental deficits led to parentectomy therapy typified by Bettelheim's approach of separating the child from his parents and substituting warm, accepting parent surrogates (Schopler and Reichler, 1971). With the evidence now supporting a biological therory or view of autism with emphasis upon developmental, central cognitive, sensoriperceptual, and language deficits, the therapeutic and management approaches have changed. The model now advocated combines pharmocotherapy to promote development and receptivity, with behavioral and educational therapies. Rather than parentectomy, an essential component of this approach is an active inclusion of the parents as cotherapists. Efforts are taken to teach parents specific techniques to promote the development of more appropriate language, cognition, relatedness, and behavior in their children. It appears that the moving admonition of a few years ago has been heeded. "It is time to recognize the autistic child's parents as the integral agent to the solution of his child's problems rather than as having caused them" (Schopler and Reichler, 1971, p. 101).

Perhaps this recognition has been the greatest advance in the past decade and has lifted the unwarranted burden of guilt from the shoulders of people who are daily having to confront the draining challenges presented by an autistic child. This recognition has not only provided a basis for the parent's direct inclusion in the treatment programs but also has freed them from feelings of guilt and shame which heretofore seemed to be responsible for the absence of a strong national parent group such as exists with parents of retarded children in the National Association of Retarded Citizens. The National Society for Autistic Children, founded by Rimland in the middle 1960s, is growing and is becoming increasingly able to advocate and lobby for funding for research and services for autistic children.

References

Baker, L., Cantwell, D. P., Rutter, M. & Bartak, L. Language and autism. In E. Ritvo, B. Freeman, E. Ornitz & P. Tanguay (Eds.), *Autism: Diagnosis, Current Research, and Management.* New York: Spectrum Publications, 1976.

Baltaxe, C. & Simmons, J. Q. Language patterns in autistic and Down's syndrome adolescents, a comparison. Paper presented at the annual meeting of the American Association of Mental Deficiency, Toronto, 1974.

Baltaxe, C. A. & Simmons, J. Q. Language in childhood psychosis: A review. *Journal of Speech and Hearing Disorders,* 1975, 439–58.

Bartak, L. & Rutter, M. Special education treatment of autistic children: A comparative study–1: Design of study and characteristics of units. *Journal of Child Psychology and Psychiatry,* 1973, *14,* 161–79.

Bartolucci, G. & Albers, R. Deictic categories in the language of autistic children. *Journal of Autism and Childhood Schizophrenia,* 1974, *4,* 131–41.

Bender, L. Schizophrenia in childhood: Its recognition, description, and treatment. *American Journal of Orthopsychiatry,* 1956, *26,* 499–506.

Bettelheim, B. The Empty Fortress. New York: Free Press, 1967.

Bleuler, E. Dementia praecox oder Gruppe der Schizophrenien. Leipzig: Franz Deuticke, 1911. Trans. by J. Zimkin. New York: International Press, 1952.

Brown, R. & Bellugi, V. Three processes in the child's acquisition of syntax. Harvard Education Review, 1964, 34, 133–51.

Brown, R., Cayden, C. & Bellugi, V. The child's grammar from 1 to 11. In R. Brown (Ed.), Psycholinguistics (Selected Papers). New York: Free Press, 1970, 100–54.

Brown, R. & Hanlon, C. Derivational complexity and order of acquisition in child speech. In J.R. Hayes (Ed.), Cognition and the Development of Language. New York: John Wiley, 1970, 11–53.

Bryson, C.Q. Systematic identification of perceptual disabilities in autistic children. Perceptual and Motor Skills, 1970, 31, 239–46.

Campbell, M. Pharmocotherapy in early infantile autism. Biological Psychiatry, 1975, 10, 399–423.

Churchill, D. The relation of infantile autism and early childhood schizophrenia to developmental language disorders of childhood. Journal of Autism and Childhood Schizophrenia, 1972, 2, 182–97.

Churchill, D. & Bryson, C.Q. Looking and approach behavior of psychotic and normal children as a function of adult attention or preoccupation. Comprehensive Psychiatry, 1972, 13, 171–77.

Clancy, H., Dugdale, A. & Rendle-Short, J. The diagnosis of infantile autism. Developmental Medicine and Child Neurology, 1969, 11, 432–42.

Coleman, M. Serotonin in Down's Syndrome. Amsterdam: North-Holland, 1973.

Coleman, M. (Ed.). The Autistic Syndromes. Amsterdam: North-Holland, 1976.

Creak, M. Schizophrenic syndrome in childhood. Progress report of a working party. British Medical Journal, 1961, 2, 889–90.

Creak, M. Schizophrenic syndrome in childhood. Further progress report of a working party. Developmental Medicine and Child Neurology, 1964, 6, 530–35.

Cunningham, M. A comparison of the language of psychotic and non-psychotic children who are mentally retarded. Journal of Child Psychology and Psychiatry, 1968, 9, 229–44.

DeHirsch, K. Differential diagnosis between aphasic and schizophrenic language in children. Journal of Speech and Hearing Disorders, 1967, 32, 3–10.

DeMyer, M. Research in infantile autism, a strategy and its results. Biological Psychiatry, 1975, 10, 433–52.

DeMyer, M., Schwier, H., Bryson, C., Solow, E. & Roeske, N. Free fatty acid response to insulin and glucose stimulation in schizophrenic, autistic, and emotionally retarded children. Journal of Autism and Childhood Schizophrenia, 1971, 1, 436–52.

DeMyer, M., Alper, G.D., Barton, S., DeMyer, W.E., Churchill, D.W., Hingtgen, J.N., Bryson, D.Q., Pontius, W. & Kimberlin, C. Imitation in autistic, early schizophrenic and non-psychotic subnormal children. *Journal of Autism and Childhood Schizophrenia*, 1972, 2, 264–287.

Despert, J.L. Some considerations relating to the genesis of autistic behavior in children. *American Journal of Orthopsychiatry*, 1951, 21, 335–50.

Eisenberg, L. The autistic child in adolescence. *American Journal of Psychiatry*, 1956, 112, 607–12.

Eisenberg, L. & Kanner, L. Early infantile autism. *American Journal of Orthopsychiatry*, 1956, 26, 556–66.

Engelhardt, D.M., Polezos, P., Waezer, J. & Hoffman, S.P. A double-blind comparison of fluphenazine and haloperidol in outpatient schizophrenic children. *Journal of Autism and Childhood Schizophrenia*, 1973, 3, 128–37.

Fish, B. Pharmocotherapy for autistic and schizophrenic children. In E. Ritvo, B. Freeman, E. Ornitz & P. Tanguay (Eds.), *Autism: Diagnosis, Current Research, and Management*. New York: Spectrum Publications, 1976.

Frith, U. Studies in pattern detection in normal and autistic children. *Journal of Experimental Child Psychology*, 1970, 10, 120–35.

Goldfarb, W. *Childhood Schizophrenia*. Cambridge, Massachusetts: Harvard University Press, 1961.

Goldfarb, W., Goldfarb, N., Braunstein, P. & Scholl, H. Speech and language faults of schizophrenic children. *Journal of Autism and Childhood Schizophrenia*, 1972, 2, 219–33.

Goldfarb, W., Goldfarb, N. & Scholl, H.H. The speech of mothers of schizophrenic children. *American Journal of Psychiatry*, 1966, 122, 1220–27.

Hauser, S., DeLong, G. & Raman, N. Pneumographic findings in the infantile autism syndrome. A correlation with temporal lobe disease. *Brain*, 1975, 98, 667–88.

Hermelin, B. Locating events in time and space: Experiments with autistic, blind, and deaf children. *Journal of Autism and Childhood Schizophrenia*, 1972, 2, 288–98.

Hermelin, B. & O'Conner, N. *Psychological Experiments with Autistic Children*. London: Pergamon Press, 1970.

Hilburn, W.B. Dermatoglyphic findings on a group of psychotic children. *Journal of Nervous and Mental Diseases*, 1970, 151, 352–58.

Hingtgen, J. & Bryson, C. Recent developments in the study of early childhood psychosis: Infantile autism, childhood schizophrenia, and related disorders. *Schizophrenia Bulletin*, 1972, 5, 8–55.

Kanner, L. Autistic disturbance of affective contact. *Nervous Child*, 1943, 2, 217–50.

Kanner, L. Problems of nosology and psychodynamics of early infantile autism. *American Journal of Orthopsychiatry*, 1949, *19*, 416–26.

Kaufman, I., Rosenblum, E., Herms, L. & Willer, L. Childhood schizophrenia: Treatment of children and parents. *American Journal of Orthopsychiatry*, 1957, *27*, 683–90.

Klein, D.L. & Pollack, M. Schizophrenic children and maternal speech facility. *American Journal of Psychiatry*, 1966, *123*, 232.

Lelord, G., Laffant, F., Jusseaume, P. & Stephant, J.L. Comparative study of conditioning of averaged evoked responses by coupling sound and light in normal and autistic children. *Psychophysiology*, 1973, *10*, 415–25.

Lewis, M. & Rosenblum, L.A. *The Effect of the Infant on its Caregiver*. New York: John Wiley, 1974.

Lockyer, L. & Rutter, M. A 5- to 15-year follow-up study of infantile psychosis. III– Psychological aspects. *British Journal of Psychiatry*, 1969, 115, 865–82.

Lotter, V. Epidemiology of autistic conditions in young children. I–prevalence. *Social Psychiatry*, 1966, *1*, 124–37.

Lovaas, O., Schreibman, L., Koegel, R. & Rehm, R. Selective responding by autistic children to multiple sensory input. *Journal of Abnormal Psychology*, 1971, 77, 211–22.

McConnell, O.L. Control of eye contact in an autistic child. *Journal of Child Psychiatry*, 1967, *8*, 249–55.

O'Gorman, G. *The Nature of Childhood Autism*. London: Butterworth, 1967.

Olin, E. Maternal language styles and children's cognitive behavior. *Journal of Special Education*, 1970, *4*, 53–67.

Ornitz, E.M. Childhood autism: A review of the clinical and experimental literature. *California Medicine*, 1973, *118*, 21–47.

Ornitz, E. & Ritvo, E. Perceptual inconstancy in the syndrome of early infantile autism and its variants. *Archives of General Psychiatry*, 1968, *18*, 76–98.

Ornitz, E.M., Ritvo, E.R., Brown, M.B., LaFranchi, S., Parmelee, T. & Walter, R.D. The EEG and rapid eye movements during REM sleep in normal and autistic children. *Electroencephalography and Clinical Neurophysiology*, 1969, *26*, 167–75.

Ornitz, E.M., Brown, M.B., Mason, A. & Putnam, N.H. Effect of visual input on vestibular nystagmus in autistic children. *Archives of General Psychiatry*, 1974, *31*, 369–75.

Peterson, M.R. & Torrey, E.F. Viruses and other infectious agents as behavioral teratogens. In M. Coleman (Ed.), *The Autistic Syndromes*. Amsterdam: North-Holland, 1976.

Provence, S. & Lipton, R.C. *Infants in Institutions*. New York: International Universities Press, 1962.

Reichler, R.J., & Schopler, E. Observations on the nature of human relatedness. *Journal of Autism and Childhood Schizophrenia*, 1971, *1*, 283–96.

Ricks, D.M. Vocal communication in pre-verbal normal and autistic children. In N. O'Conner (Ed.), *Language, Cognitive Deficits, and Retardation*. London: Butterworth, 1972.

Rimland, B. *Infantile Autism*. New York: Appleton-Century-Crofts, 1964.

Ritvo, E., Freeman, B., Ornitz, E. & Tanguay, P. (Eds.). *Autism: Diagnosis, Current Research, and Management*. New York: Spectrum Publications, 1976.

Rutter, M. The influence of organic and emotional factors on the origins, nature, and outcome of childhood psychosis. *Developmental Medicine and Child Neurology*, 1965, *7*, 518–28.

Rutter, M. Concepts of autism: A review of research. *Journal of Child Psychology and Psychiatry*, 1968, *9*, 1–25.

Rutter, M. The description and classification of infantile autism. In D. Churchill, G. Alpern, & M. DeMyer (Eds.), *Infantile Autism Proceedings of the Indiana University Colloquium*. Springfield, Illinois: Charles C Thomas, 1971.

Rutter, M. & Bartak, L. Special education treatment of autistic children: A comparative study. II–Follow-up findings & implication for services. *Journal of Child Psychology and Psychiatry*, 1973, *14*, 241–70.

Rutter, M., Greenfeld, D. & Lockyer, L. A 5- to 15-year follow-up study of infantile psychosis: II–Social and behavioral outcome. *British Journal of Psychiatry*, 1967, *113*, 1183–99.

Rutter, M. & Lockyer, L. A 5- to 15-year follow-up study of infantile psychosis: I–Description of sample. *British Journal of Psychiatry*, 1967, *113*, 1169–82.

Rutter, M. & Sussenwein, F. A developmental and behavioral approach to the treatment of preschool autistic children. *Journal of Autism and Childhood Schizophrenia*, 1971, *1*, 376–97.

Sank, D. Dermatoglyphics of childhood schizophrenia. *Acta Genetica et Statistica Medica*, 1968, *18*, 300–14.

Sarason, S.B. & Gladwin, T. Psychological and cultural problems in mental subnormality: A review of research. *Genetic Psychology Monographs*, 1958, *57*, 3–290.

Scheerer, M., Rothmann, E. & Goldstein, K. A case of "idiot savant": An experimental study of personality organization. *Psychological Monographs*, 1945, *58* (4).

Schopler, E., Brehm, S.S., Kinsbourne, M. & Reichler, R.J. Effect of treatment structure on development in autistic children. *Archives of General Psychiatry*, 1971, *24*, 415–21.

Schopler, E. & Reichler, R.J. Parents as cotherapists in the treatment of psychotic children. *Journal of Autism and Childhood Schizophrenia*, 1971, *1*, 87–102.

Simmons, J.Q. & Baltaxe, C. Language patterns of autistic children who have reached adolescence. *Journal of Autism and Childhood Schizophrenia*, 1975, *5*, 299–307.

Spence, A.M. Genetic studies. In E. Ritvo, B. Freeman, E. Ornitz & P. Tanguay (Eds.), *Autism: Diagnosis, Current Research, and Management.* New York: Spectrum Publications, 1976.

Spence, M.A., Simmons, J.Q., Brown, N.A. & Wehler, C. Sex ratios in families of autistic children. *American Journal of Mental Deficiency*, 1973, *77*, 405–7.

Tanguay, P. Clinical and electrophysiological research. In E. Ritvo, B. Freeman, E. Ornitz & P. Tanguay (Eds.), *Autism: Diagnosis, Current Research, and Management.* New York: Spectrum Publications, 1976.

Torrey, E.F., Hersh, S. & McCabe, K. Early childhood psychosis and bleeding during pregnancy. *Journal of Autism and Childhood Schizophrenia*, 1975, *5*, 287.

Tubbs, V.K. Types of linguistic disability in psychotic children. *Journal of Mental Deficiency Research*, 1966, *10*, 223–40.

Van Krevelin, A. Early infantile autism. *Zeitschrift für Kinderpsychiatrie*, 1952, *19*, 91.

Walker, H. Incidence of minor physical anomalies in autistic patients. In M. Coleman (Ed.), *The Autistic Syndromes.* Amsterdam: North-Holland, 1976.

Walker, H. & Coleman, M. Characteristics of adventitious movements in autistic children. In M. Coleman (Ed.), *The Autistic Syndromes.* Amsterdam: North-Holland, 1976.

Weiland, M. & Legg, D. Formal speech characteristics as a diagnostic aid in childhood psychosis. *American Journal of Orthopsychiatry*, 1964, *34*, 91–94.

Wolff, S. & Chess, S. An analysis of the language of fourteen schizophrenic children. *Journal of Child Psychology and Psychiatry*, 1965, *6*, 29–41.

Yuwiler, A., Geller, E. & Ritvo, E. Neurobiochemical research. In E. Ritvo, B. Freeman, E. Ornitz & T. Tanguay (Eds.), *Autism: Diagnosis, Current Research, and Management.* New York: Spectrum Publications, 1976.

4

Cerebral Palsy

Gradually, the concept has evolved that cerebral palsy is a disorder of the central nervous system caused by one or more of several possible insults to the developing brain in the first three years of life, a disorder resulting primarily in neuromotor dysfunction but one also possibly involving intellectual, learning, behavioral, speech and language, and sensoriperceptual difficulties. The neuromotor dysfunction may affect one or more extremities with weakness, incoordination, spasticity, contractures, or involuntary movements. Implicit in the use of the term "cerebral palsy" is the understanding that no active disease is present at the time of the diagnosis. In arriving at the above concept, the path proved arduous and uncertain, given the multiplicity of possible etiologies, the variety of manifestations, and the range of variable responses to the many approaches to therapy. Our plan in this chapter is to assist the reader in understanding the historical evolution of the concept of cerebral palsy as well as to provide the framework for considering the multidimensional and interactive aspects of etiology, manifestations, treatment, and prognosis. There is still much to learn, and the story will continue to evolve.

HISTORY

Like mental retardation, cerebral palsy has always been with us as a condition of human pathology. However, it was not until the early nineteenth century that descriptive reports began to appear. Sigmund Freud, in his monograph entitled *Infantile Cerebral Paralysis* (Russin, 1968), presented a historical survey of the contributions of those early observers, and credited Cazauvielh with the first description of congenital spastic hemiplegia. He described it as a disorder that occurred more often in girls than in boys, on the right side more often than on the left, and which often resulted in a shortening of the extremities on the involved side, decreased mobility, contractures, and impaired intelligence. He postulated that the etiology was related to a developmental arrest of the cerebral hemisphere on the side opposite the hemiplegia. In a series of lectures delivered at the Royal Orthopedic Hospital of London, W. J. Little, an orthopedist, presented in 1843 the first clinical description of cerebral palsy with a modern philosophy of treatment (Denhoff and Robinault, 1960). His interest in cerebral palsy continued and broadened so that in 1861 he presented his theory of the etiology of cerebral palsy to the Obstetrical Society of London in a paper entitled, "On the influence of abnormal parturition, difficult labour, premature birth, and asphyxia neonatorum on the mental and physical condition of the child especially in relation to deformities" (Little, 1861). He introduced the concept that cerebral injury, both mechanical and hypoxic, occurring at birth, could result in cerebral palsy and tried to emphasize to the obstetricians present that even though these infants lived, "the act of birth did occasionally imprint upon the nervous and muscular systems of the nascent organism very serious and peculiar evils" (p. 379). He indicated that "spastic rigidity" was the result of abnormal parturition in 47 of his cases. He also claimed that seizures could be the result of asphyxia and that mental retardation could follow birth trauma and asphyxia. Although he recognized that hemiplegia could occur in infants from six months to two years of age after febrile seizures, he emphasized the problems at birth as being etiologic in many other cases. This was the first time that such an etiology for cerebral palsy had been considered, and from the few comments made by the obstetricians present, they were clearly surprised. According to a Dr. Barnes, "the difficulty there appeared to be in discussing this excellent paper, arose no doubt from the entire novelty and originality of the subject" (p.379).

Between 1861 and the turn of the century, further progress was made in the recognition of other etiologies for cerebral palsy (prematurity, infectious diseases) and in the appreciation that a relationship existed between cerebral palsy, mental retardation, and epilepsy. J. Hughlings Jackson and Bourneville were among those who wrote about the relationship between cerebral palsy and epilepsy (Russin, 1968). As more interest developed in

the disorder and as more information became available, it became necessary to classify what was known. This was not an easy task in view of the
various manifestations and etiologies. The one commonality was that all
those affected demonstrated a disorder of neuromotor functioning. Freud's
classification (Russin, 1968) included five main types of cerebral palsy and
was based on the neuromotor manifestations. It was the system most
frequently relied upon until the middle of the twentieth century. The five
types were:

1. Hemiplegic infantile cerebral paralysis
2. General cerebral stiffness—characterized by increased tension and caused
   by abnormal birth (Little's disease)
3. Paraplegic stiffness
4. Bilateral hemiplegia
5. General chorea and bilateral athetosis

Thus, although the earliest descriptive papers pointed out the possibility of associated intellectual deficits, and although later authors pointed out
the association between epilepsy and cerebral palsy, these neuromotor
manifestations came to assume primary importance as the above classification system became more broadly recognized. In this country for example,
in the early twentieth century Dr. Winfield Phelps, an orthopedist who
devoted his life to the treatment of cerebral palsy and who actually popu-
larized the term, was so involved with the neuromotor aspects of the disorder that he defined cerebral palsy as a combination of motor and sensory
disturbances in a group of handicapped individuals who were not primarily
mentally retarded (Denhoff and Robinault, 1960; Wolf, 1969). Other forces
were probably influential in the primary emphasis given to deficits in
neuromotor functioning. For example, parents of cerebral-palsied children
who could get surgical and physical therapy for their children were less
inclined to accept the possibility that the children might be mentally as
well as physically impaired; in fact, many objected to the notion. As a
result, approaches to treatment were geared primarily toward neuromotor
rehabilitation for many years.

In recent years, however, the pendulum has swung back, and there
has been increasing reawareness of the multiple manifestations of cerebral
palsy. The definition of Denhoff and Robinault (1960) is particularly clear in
this respect.

Cerebral palsy is a manifestation or group of manifestations of impaired neurologic function due to aberrant structure, growth, or development of the central nervous system. The deviations making up this broad entity are protean in cause and varied in expression, and they are reflected in impairment of various functions of body and mind. . . . The manifestations of impaired neurologic function may be observed as a variety of neuromotor, intellectual, sensory, and behavioral signs and symptoms singly or in combinations and varying in degree. Cerebral palsy is designated as a clinical diagnosis when the neuromotor aspect dominates the picture. (p. 1)

MANIFESTATIONS

Before proceeding to a discussion of etiology and a description of the types of cerebral palsy, we will consider the variety of these manifestations of neurologic impairment which may accompany the neuromotor manifestations.

Disorders of special sense—vision and hearing—are relatively frequent findings in the cerebral-palsied population. The visual problems divide into severe visual impairment, e.g. cortical blindness, chorioretinitis, and retrolental fibroplasia, and less severe impairment, e.g. visual field defects and strabismus. The auditory problems may be related to auditory processing or to damage to the auditory nerve secondary to hypoxia or the side effects of certain antibiotics, or to congenital infection (rubella, cytomegalovirus). The importance of recognizing these disorders early cannot be overstressed, as developmental progress can be hindered without proper management.

The relationship between cerebral palsy and language development—particularly in infantile hemiplegia—is of special interest and in fact was commented on by the early scholars. Cotard, a student of Charcot, was of the opinion that hemiplegics from infancy never showed aphasia because the speech center in the brain was not well localized in infancy, and he postulated that the functions of one cerebral hemisphere could be taken over by the other. However, other authors of the day recognized the occurrence of aphasic symptoms in children with infantile hemiplegia but felt that the side of involvement was not of any particular significance and that aphasic symptoms were as common after lesions in the right cerebral hemisphere as after lesions in the left (Russin, 1968). This was in contrast to the situation in adults in whom aphasia has almost always been associated with a lesion in the dominant left hemisphere and a right hemiplegia. The relationship in children is still not clear today. Crothers and Paine (1959) indicated that the side of the hemiplegia made little difference in terms of the incidence of speech and language deficits and that when aphasia occurred, it was of variable duration.

> On close observation, many of our patients still showed fumbling for words and minor evidence of aphasia, even after as long as two years from the acute episode. . . . Freud & Rie (1891) originally reported on brief aphasia for not more than fifteen months follow-up in five cases, but subsequently stated that the aphasia was usually transient. One should bear in mind that such may not always be the case. (p.101)

Gold and Carter (1976) are of a different persuasion and virtually negate the notion that a youngster with acquired hemiplegia will be left with a language disorder if affected before four years of age.

> Dysphasia, more commonly encountered in older children with a dominant hemisphere lesion, is rare in children younger than four years of age; unless associated with mental retardation, it is never observed with onset before the age of two years. Dysphasia frequently occurs at the time of the acute episode, especially when associated with seizures; subsequently, normal speech patterns return after a period of 2 to 21 days, particularly in younger children. (p.421)

Our own observations are more in line with those of Crothers and Paine (1959), and we have also been impressed by the frequent relationship between the behavior problems for which parents seek help and the language problems which are found on evaluation. The time has come for elucidating and clarifying the relationship of speech and language development and cerebral palsy. Various possibilities and combinations come to mind. It may be that we have yet to look carefully enough at each child to determine if, indeed, there is language impairment. It may be that in those children who have congenital hemiplegia and who have been recognized as having a language disorder, there has been bilateral brain impairment so that the "other hemisphere" was not in a position to "take over." It may be that auditory processing (Nober, 1976) is more of a problem in some children than others. It may be that the degree of language impairment is related to experience and opportunity. Lencione (1976) has highlighted the "abundant evidence" that mothers talk less to their handicapped children. Bax and MacKeith (1975) have also been aware of this phenomenon and have expressed the view that "the development of communication . . . is more important to the cerebral palsied than learning to walk" (p.30). Therefore, they encourage mothers to talk to their cerebral-palsied youngster so he can "learn his mother tongue at mother distance" (p.30). We look forward to more investigative inquiry into these relationships.

The relationship between behavioral disturbance and cerebral palsy has been recognized and has often been considered as representative of the "brain-damaged" personality. Rutter, Graham, and Yule (1970) showed that children with brain damage (neuroepileptic) but without mental retardation have four to five times as much "psychiatric disorder" as ordinary children. The term *neuroepileptic* was used to describe those children who demonstrated an "undoubted abnormality of the brain of a type not due to maturational factors" (p.99), and referred in essence to children who present with cerebral palsy or with epilepsy. In that study, psychiatric disorder was "judged to be present when there was an abnormality of behavior, emotions or relationships which was sufficiently marked and sufficiently prolonged to cause handicap to the child himself and/or distress or disturbance in the family or community" (p.165). Although they considered both neurologic and nonneurologic factors (social status, sex, ordinal position, and familial history), they reached the conclusion that dysfunction of the brain "was the main feature associated with the finding that the rate of psychiatric disorder was higher for children with neuro-epileptic disorders" (p.185). They also found that bilateral brain damage resulted in a higher incidence of psychiatric disorder and that language retardation, which might also reflect the presence of bilateral brain damage, was associated with a higher incidence of psychiatric disorder. Again, the relationship of language, behavior, and brain dysfunction is pointed out. The type of psychiatric disorder seen was neither specific nor unusual—it was just the *rate* that was increased. Rutter et al. (1970) found that "the presence of organic brain dysfunction is associated with a high *susceptibility* to psychiatric disorder" and that "the effect of brain dysfunction is largely to render the child more liable to react adversely" to those stresses and strains that may impair the development of any child (p.208). In the cerebral-palsied population studied, 16 out of 36 demonstrated "psychiatric disorder" as compared with 144 out of 2,189 in the general population. Four had a "neurotic disorder"; three had antisocial behavior or a conduct disorder; four had a "mixed" disorder; three had the hyperkinetic syndrome; one was psychotic; and one was "other." The conclusion then was that there was no one behavioral syndrome of brain damage "but rather many different psychiatric disorders resulting from interaction between neurological dysfunction, family disturbance, and social circumstances" (p.214).

Another view has been that there is an "organic personality" manifesting behavior that can be characterized as impulsive, distractible, perseverative, and hyperactive (Strauss and Lehtinen, 1947). Dunsdon (1952) indicated that the emotional responses of the cerebral palsied are like their motor responses—poorly modulated. Several sources (Crothers and Paine, 1959; Cruickshank, Hallahan, and Bice, 1976; Oswin, 1967) have discussed the feelings of cerebral-palsied adolescents as well as the feelings of their families. Parents are described as feeling guilty, angry, and sad, and as being overprotective. The adolescents themselves are described as being angry, sad, and resentful and as having a poor self-concept. Cruickshank et al., (1976b, p.131) have stated this well in describing a typical answer of cerebral-palsied youngsters to the question of defining a "nuisance." "It means me; that's what I am." Certainly there is a wide range of variability in the feelings, personality, and interactions of cerebral-palsied youngsters. The extent of physical limitation, the frequency of therapy and hospitalizations, the frequency and quality of family interaction, the number and kind of social and school opportunities, the level of communication skills, and the nature of the brain dysfunction itself all play a dynamic role in the manifestations of affective functioning. The degree and persistence of behavioral disorder is variable and is influenced to a considerable extent by environment.

The learning problems of children with cerebral palsy are variable, but can be multiple. They may be the result of one or more of the following: sensoriperceptual problems, mental retardation, short attention span, distractibility, thought disorder, and motor incoordination. The range and severity of involvement is broad. Some children may have learning problems of a very specific nature while others may have more generalized problems. Some may have little evidence of handicap in learning while others manifest a severe handicap. Strauss and Lehtinen (1947) were modern pioneers in the elucidation of the components of learning difficulties of brain injured children and in the development of strategies for educating them—strategies that remain relevant. William Cruickshank has also been in the forefront of educational planning for children with cerebral palsy. In one of his more recent contributions (1976) he has outlined the ways in which educators who deal with cerebral-palsied children can utilize interdisciplinary evaluations to plan educationally for these handicapped children. The recent enactment of Public Law 94–142 mandating the public schools to provide for the education of handicapped children is seen as a first step in meeting the educational needs of the cerebral palsied. The problems to be encountered are considerable and complex, and their solution will not be easy. The challenge and opportunity are here to provide educational and vocational planning experiences of such quality that these handicapped children will be able to assume a more independent role in society. Cohen (1976) has provided a historical overview of the development of vocational guidance for the cerebral palsied and has pointed out the difficulties currently encountered in their employment.

ETIOLOGY

Over the years the evolution in thought concerning the manifestations of cerebral palsy has been paralleled by an evolution in thought about its etiology. Various etiologies were postulated in earlier times: developmental arrest of the brain, infection, birth trauma, and prematurity. The difficulty in accepting any proposed set of causal connections arose in trying to establish clinicopathologic correlations. Frequently, postmortem examinations revealed no specific lesion in association with specific clinical manifestations. For example, the pathology seen in a case of spastic diplegia might not be different from that seen in spastic quadriplegia. Nevertheless, Mc-Nutt (1885) did present pathologic evidence demonstrating that birth trauma could cause meningeal hemorrhage and subsequent "shrinkage of convolutions" resulting in spastic paralysis. And Sigmund Freud noted at a postmortem examination that calcification was present in the contralateral lenticular nucleus (one of basal ganglia) of a patient who had had athetosis (Russin, 1968).

It is now clear that cerebral palsy may result from any insult to the developing brain, that the insult may occur in the prenatal, perinatal, or postnatal period and that it may result from genetic and/or environmental causes. The Developmental Disabilities Cube (p. 17) provides a useful and clear method of considering the interaction of these multiple etiologic factors with developmental periods resulting in manifestations in various systems of functioning, and that change over time as development, treatment, and environmental influences dynamically interact.

PRENATAL PERIOD

A discussion of the factors of importance during this developmental period is fraught with difficulty because our information and knowledge are still imprecise. For example, we can say that congenital malformations of the fetus, low birth weight, evidence of prenatal hypoxia–asphyxia, congenital infection (TORCH), and intracranial hemorrhage are commonly associated subsequently with a clinical picture of cerebral palsy. Nevertheless, children can be born with those prenatal risk factors operative and not manifest cerebral palsy. And oftentimes in any given case we might not know whether a combination of factors or just one factor was operative. Or a child may present with cerebral palsy, and no etiology will be forthcoming. We know of "associations" more often than we know of specific etiologies. An exception to this is the now well-appreciated relationship between Rh (or ABO) incompatibility and hyperbilirubinemia that, if untreated and severe, can result in kernicterus and athetoid cerebral palsy.

Several studies have described the increased frequency of congential malformations in youngsters with cerebral palsy (Drillien, 1974; Malamud et al., 1964). In the post-mortem study of 68 patients with cerebral palsy who died in a chronic care institution for the mentally deficient, Malamud et al. (1964) found that 35.3% had malformations of the brain (arrests or distortions in development). Drillien (1974), in a study of the etiology of low birth weight, found that 15% of the children studied were "developmentally abnormal"; that is, they had either a major malformation or three or more minor ones. Of these, 50% had moderate or severe neurologic deficit at one to three years of age. The questions then arise about whether the same prenatal factor(s) resulted in both the low birth weight and the malformations, and what precisely they were, and why indeed the other 50% of children so affected did *not* have moderate to severe neurologic deficit. The questions at this point are not answerable.

Factors in pregnancy which have been identified as being associated with an increased likelihood of congenital malformation in the fetus are hydramnios (excessive amniotic fluid), convulsive disorder in the mother, exposure to certain drugs, and maternal chronic hypertension (Heinonen,

Slone, and Shapiro, 1977). Malamud et al. (1964) found a history of vaginal bleeding during the gestational period in 42% of the mothers of the cases he described. The etiology of these malformations is probably multifactorial.

The infectious agents that are known to affect the central nervous system adversely in the prenatal period are the TORCH agents, any of which can cause cerebral palsy. (See discussion in chapter 2.) The maternal factors that might predispose a fetus to intracranial bleeding and to hypoxia–asphyxia are primarily those that might also result in the birth of a low weight infant, or to stillbirth or perinatal death. These include eclampsia, hypertension, adolescent mother, low socioeconomic status, maternal weight, vaginal bleeding during pregnancy, excessive vomiting, and hydramnios. Other maternal factors include organic heart disease, chronic asthma, hypothyroidism, urinary tract infection, and convulsions (Drillien, 1974; Niswander and Gordon, 1972).

In the postmortem examination of the central nervous system of approximately 470, 22 to 35-week-old fetuses whose mothers had been enrolled in the Collaborative Perinatal Study, Towbin (1970) reported that hypoxia and/or mechanical trauma were the cause of the three basic types of central nervous system damage seen. The most common finding in the preterm fetus was "hypoxic cerebral periventricular damage," with intraventricular hemorrhage. The series of events postulated to lead to this outcome are (1) fetal hypoxia (often related to maternoplacental problems), (2) circulatory failure in the fetus, and (3) stasis of blood with local cerebral tissue death. In the 22 to 35-week-old fetus brain tissue differentiation is most active in the deep periventricular structures and in the deposits of cerebral matrix which protrude into the lateral ventricles; therefore, they are particularly vulnerable to hypoxia and cell death. The expected neurologic sequelae in survivors would be involvement of the pyramidal fibers to the lower extremities resulting in spastic diplegia. With more extensive involvement, the nerve tracts to the upper extremities could also be involved resulting in quadriplegia, and intraventricular hemorrhage could occur. Krishnamoorthy et al. (1977) examined 28 infants with a mean gestational age of 33 weeks, by computerized tomographic (C-T) brain scan, after sudden clinical deterioration. Three infants were found to have subarachnoid hemorrhage (SAH). Twenty others were found to have had intraventricular hemorrhage and of those, only 6 survived (30%). Those who survived had less extensive hemorrhage and 2 of the 6 later required shunting procedures after the development of progressive hydrocephalus. One of the infants with SAH also developed hydrocephalus. Follow-up of survivors is currently being undertaken.

The interrelationships then, between low birth weight, hypoxia, and intracranical hemorrhage, can begin to be appreciated. More discussion will follow in the section on the perinatal period. It should be understood however that no definite 1:1 correlation exists between maternal factors and fetal difficulties. Likewise no 1:1 correlation exists between fetal difficulties and the clinical symptoms of cerebral palsy. At this stage of our knowledge, these are associations.

PERINATAL PERIOD

The separation of the prenatal from the perinatal period in terms of neurologic sequelae and the etiology of cerebral palsy is somewhat artificial. Adverse prenatal influences may continue to operate during the perinatal period resulting in low birth weight (preterm and small for gestational age), and in cord and placental complications. The perinatal events of importance in the etiology of cerebral palsy are hypoxia–asphyxia, intracranial bleeding, and central nervous system infection, all of which are capable of causing structural brain damage. The preterm infant is particularly susceptible to these factors, and the younger the gestational age, the more susceptible he is (Drillien, 1972b; Fitzhardinge, 1975; Johnson et al. 1974; Lubchenco et al., 1974). Clifford and Drorbaugh (1970), in relating findings of the Collaborative Perinatal Study, indicated that the incidence of cerebral palsy and severe retardation was about 7 per 1,000 live births in the Boston population, and that the incidence was 36 per 1,000 in preterm infants compared with 5.6 per 1,000 for full-term infants. According to Babson (1975), up to 40% of patients in cerebral palsy clinics have been low birth weight infants, and more than 75% with spastic diplegia have been of low birth weight.

Preterm infants are more likely than term infants to be born depressed and asphyxiated, possibly because of their susceptibility to intracranial bleeding before birth, or during the birth process. However this is a two-way street as asphyxia can predispose to intracranial bleeding. Towbin (1970) found that subdural hemorrhage in the posterior fossa (probably occurring as a result of vertical molding during delivery) and that epidural hemorrhage in the spinal cord and brainstem (occurring as a result of fetal malposition or during labor and delivery) were manifestations of trauma that result in central nervous system damage and are likely to occur in the preterm fetus. Ford, Crothers, and Putnam (1927) indicated that intracranial hemorrhage was 16 times more frequent in the preterm than in the full-term infant. In infants with known intracranial hemorrhage who have been followed for 11 to 20 months, 40% are normal, 20% have mild neurologic deficits, and 40% have moderate-severe deficits: spastic diplegia, hydrocephalus, quadriplegia, choreoathetosis (Krishnamoorthy, 1976). Another possible reason for the asphyxia at birth is the high incidence of breech presentation (Nebel et al. 1962), and placenta and cord problems (Drillien, 1974; Lilienfeld and Parkhurst, 1951; Niswander et al., 1966 a–d; Niswander, Gordon, and Drage, 1975). Furthermore, asphyxia in the newborn period as a result of the respiratory distress syndrome is more common in the preterm infant. And as mentioned earlier, hypoxia–asphyxia predisposes an infant to intracranial hemorrhage. Krishnamoorthy (1976) indicated that in their series, 65% to 75% of infants who had respiratory distress syndrome and came to autopsy were found to have intracranial hemorrhage. In several series, 15% to 20% of survivors of the respiratory distress syndrome have been left with moderate–severe neurologic handicap (Fisch et al., 1975; Johnson et al., 1974). Brown et al. (1974) found that 51% of cases of perinatal asphyxia were due to prepartum disorders (shock, placental insufficiency, hemorrhage, cord around neck, cardiac arrest), 40% were due to intrapartum disorders (forceps, breech, cesarean section, complicated delivery), and 9% were due to postpartum difficulties. Of the 94 infants studied, half either died or were left with significant handicap, including microcephaly, dystonia, spasticity, hemiplegia, and choreoathetosis. Those preterm neonates with persistent hypotonia had a particularly poor prognosis.

Because the neonate is relatively immunologically incompetent, central nervous system infection, such as bacterial meningitis, occurs more readily and is particularly devastating at this time of life when symptoms are minimal and brain growth is proceeding (Bell and McCormick, 1975; Feigin and Dodge, 1976; Fitzhardinge, 1974; McCracken, 1972).

Infants who are term and are either appropriate or large for gestational age may be exposed to the deleterious effects of asphyxia owing to prolonged labor, abnormal presentation, and/or trauma associated with delivery. Towbin (1970) has demonstrated the cortical cerebral, spinal cord, and brainstem hemorrhage that can be associated with difficult labor and delivery. Breech birth is associated with 18% perinatal mortality and 16% morbidity (Babson, 1975). Subdural hemorrhage can be seen as a result of obstetric trauma but is declining in incidence with improved obstetric practice. Subarachnoid hemorrhage is the most common form of intracranial bleed in the full term infant and is associated with mechanical trauma and perinatal asphyxia. Five out of the six infants with known subarachnoid hemorrhage on the basis of C-T scan who were followed for 11 months were either normal or had only mild central nervous system sequelae (Krishnamoorthy, 1976). Volpe (1976) has presented the asphyxial and ischemic changes that can occur in the full-term newborn and correlated these pathologic findings with the development of choreoathetosis and spasticity in survivors.

POSTNATAL PERIOD

In the postnatal period, the etiologic factors are usually environmental, but hemiplegia can result from complications of illnesses which have a genetic basis. Sickle cell disease is a genetically determined hemoglobinopathy that predisposes those patients to cerebral thromboses and subsequent hemiplegia. Those children born with cyanotic congenital heart disease are also at risk for developing hemiplegia on the basis of cerebral thrombosis. Gold and Carter (1976) in reviewing a 21-year survey of 86 children with acquired hemiplegia seen by the child neurology service of Columbia Presbyterian Medical Center found that 11 were the result of trauma, 11 had central nervous system infections, 10 had congenital heart disease, 5 had sickle cell disease, 16 had occlusive vascular disease, 4 had a vascular malformation, and 25 had no specific etiology. Four others had miscellaneous conditions.

The environmental factors of importance in the postnatal period are infection of the central nervous system and trauma. Head trauma occurs in approximately 3% of children in the first seven years (Gold and Carter, 1976) and may be accidental or part of the battered child syndrome. The damage to the brain may be caused by skull fracture with concomitant subdural hemorrhage or intracerebral bleeding, cerebral edema, and/or hypoxia and hypovolemia if the trauma is more generalized. Over 80% of subdural hematomas of childhood occur in the first year of life, and although we tend to think more often of car accidents in this regard, in a series of 80 infants with subdurals, 36% were related to child abuse, 28% were related to "falls and blows," and only 4% were the result of automobile accidents (Mealey, 1975). The treatment is evacuation of the hematoma, which may require taps, craniotomy, or shunting. In a series of 40 infants with subdurals treated prior to 1968, 50% were normal at followup of 1 to 6 years, and 25% were "defective." The other 25% were either lost to followup or had died. Spinal injuries may well produce a picture which looks like cerebral palsy (quadriplegia or paraplegia) in young children, but these are relatively uncommon (Babcock, 1975).

The central nervous system infections that are important in the postnatal etiology of cerebral palsy are meningitis, encephalitis, and brain abscess. The latter is unusual except in the setting of cyanotic congenital heart disease with bacteremia. Encephalitis of viral origin is somewhat unusual in the age group 0 to 3 years, though it may follow either active infection or immunization (rubella, rubeola, mumps) and may result in hemiplegia (Gold and Carter, 1976). Bacterial meningitis in the first three years of life can result in cerebral palsy. The usual organisms responsible are *Hemophilus influenza*, type B, and *Streptococcus pneumoniae;* and where endemic, tuberculosis. Feigin and Dodge (1976) indicate that the risk of a child developing bacterial meningitis by 5 years of age has been estimated at between one in 400 and one in 2,000. In their followup of 88 children with bacterial meningitis in the preschool period, nine demonstrated hemiplegia or quadriplegia soon after discharge, but a year later, only three demonstrated these findings. Two children demonstrated persistent ataxia. Ten children had an IQ <80, and three had a clinically significant hearing loss. Thus 11% were left with intellectual deficit and 6% were cerebral palsied. This study gives hope for a better prognosis in bacterial meningitis than have previous ones (Sell et al., 1972).

Although acute hemiplegia of infancy may result from trauma, infection, or preexisting medical conditions, there is no known cause in at least 25% of the cases. Often the history obtained is that the child (usually <3 years of age) had a high fever, began having seizures, and as he recovered was left with a hemiparesis without a known etiology for any of it. Gold and Carter (1976) indicate that these neurologic sequelae are more permanent if the insult occurs in the first year of life and if status epilepticus and coma are present. Sequelae include motor findings of hemiplegia, sometimes quadriplegia, mental retardation in 30% to 50%, and seizures in 50%. Prognosis for speech recovery is good, but behavior problems are not unusual.

It can be seen, then, that in cerebral palsy the etiology may be any static insult to the developing brain; that the manifestations—though primarily neuromotor—may well involve more than this one system; and that attention needs to be paid to the intellectual, sensoriperceptual, learning, speech and language, and behavioral aspects of functioning. Only then will appropriate intervention such as specific educational experience, and/or environmental manipulation have the best chance of improving levels of functioning.

Incidence

The incidence of cerebral palsy has been documented in various studies around the world and the rate varies between 1 and 5.9 per 1,000 depending more upon the variety of methods used for identification rather than the actual incidence. Rutter, Graham, and Yule (1970) indicate that "the most thorough investigations are agreed in finding a rate of cerebral palsy of about 2.0 to 2.5 per 1,000 among school age children" (p.113). In describing the British Columbia Health Surveillance Registry, Miller (1976) indicated that at year end 1974 4.7% of the 31,707 disabled children and 5.2% of the 57,841 disabled children and adults had cerebral palsy. As the population of British Columbia was 2.5 million at that time, the incidence of cerebral palsy in the general population was approximately 1.2 per 1,000. According to the Public Health Service in 1971, there were 750,000 individuals in the United States with cerebral palsy (3.8 per 1,000) at an annual care cost of $1.6 billion (Brent and Harris, 1976).

Among preterm infants, the incidence has always been higher. Ford, Crothers, and Putnam (1927) indicated that 7% of premature infants would either be mentally defective or would develop spastic paralysis. Churchill et al. (1974) reported that in the Collaborative Perinatal Study (1958–1965) the incidence of prematurity was 639/49,430 or 13 per 1,000 live births, and that the incidence of cerebral palsy in those premature infants was 44/639, or approximately 7%.

It seems useful now to consider the types of cerebral palsy along with the incidence of each of these. The classification proposed by Freud in 1897 was relied upon until about 1950. Since then, several other classifications have been proposed and a comparison of two of these follows. Based on the examination of 466 cases, Crothers and Paine (1959, p. 38) offered the following classification and percentages of occurrence.

Spasticity	64.6%
Paraplegia	2.8%
Monoplegia	0.4%
Hemiplegia	40.5%
Tetraplegia	19.0%
Triplegia	1.9%
Extrapyramidal	22.0%
Mixed	13.1%

Denhoff (1976) proposed the following classification and percentages of occurrence.

Spasticity	50%–60%
Paraplegia (legs only)	10%–20%
Monoplegia	rare
Hemiplegia	35%–40%
Diplegia (legs > arms)	0%–20%
Quadriplegia	15%–20%
Triplegia	rare
Dyskinesia	20%–25%
Ataxia	1%–10%
Mixed	15%–40%

As pointed out by Molnar (1973), some authors have used the terms paraplegia and diplegia synonymously, and others have used diplegia and quadriplegia synonymously, which has led to a fair amount of confusion. In this chapter, we will refer to spastic diplegia and paraplegia synonymously. Furthermore, it should be pointed out that Crothers and Paine's term "extrapyramidal" (1959) is equivalent to Denhoff's "dyskinesia" (1976). We will now proceed to discuss the manifestations of spastic hemiplegia (congenital and acquired), spastic quadriplegia, spastic diplegia, and extrapyramidal cerebral palsy in more detail as these constitute the majority of cases in all series.

TYPES OF CEREBRAL PALSY
CONGENITAL SPASTIC HEMIPLEGIA

Congenital spastic hemiplegia of prenatal or perinatal onset (66.6% of cases) is the result of an upper motor lesion or pyramidal tract lesion which occurs in the brain above the level of the brain stem, opposite the side affected. It is usually noted in the early months of life because of the presence of a fisted hand on the involved side and asymmetry of movement between the two sides of the body. The establishment of handedness before 12 months of age is presumptive evidence for congenital hemiplegia (Crothers and Paine, 1959). As first noted by Cazauvielh in 1827, the right side is affected more often than the left. Taft (1973) has described the early physical and neuromotor findings associated with the identification of "hemisyndrome" and has found the "cover test" to be particularly helpful. In this test, a light cover is put on the baby's face. Ordinarily, a 5-to-6-month-old infant will use both hands to remove it. When a child uses only one hand, suspicion is raised about his ability to use the other hand effectively and is further evaluated by holding the hand that originally reached to pull off the cover and watching the quality of movement of the hand in question. Furthermore, by 7 to 9 months of age, use of the lateral propping and parachute responses will bring out any asymmetry that might exist (Taft, 1973). On further neuromotor examination, the hemiplegic extremities are found to be weak, flaccid, and hyporeflexic initially, with a gradual progression to an increase in tone, the development of hyperactive deep tendon reflexes, a stretch reflex, and an extensor plantar response (Babinski's sign). The characteristic posture is of adduction and flexion of the upper extremity and adduction and extension of the lower, with a tendency to contractures. These are the physical findings associated with spasticity. Occasionally, especially after 2 years of age, athetotic posturing may accompany the hemiplegia.

Walking is usually delayed; nevertheless, 39% walk by 18 months, 66% by 24 months, and 90% by 36 months (Crothers and Paine, 1959). When there is sufficient strength for walking, the gait is characterized by circumduction and toe walking on the affected side. It is not uncommon to find sensory deficit on the involved side (Crothers and Paine, 1959; Molnar, 1973) and over a period of time, hemiatrophy (poor growth on the involved side) often becomes noticeable. A kind of visual field defect, homonymous hemianopsia, can be seen in those with sensory deficit and was actually first described by Freud. Other eye findings include strabismus, which is the commonest expression of cranial nerve involvement. Furthermore, approximately 30% of all children with congenital hemiplegia develop a seizure disorder (Crothers and Paine, 1959).

In the area of cognitive-intellectual functioning, Crothers and Paine

(1959) reported that those children with congenital hemiplegia had a better intellectual prognosis than those with acquired hemiplegia. Specifically, 5% were in the superior range, 32% were in the average range, 26% were in the "below average" range (defined as those who did poorly in school and who needed "concessions and protection"), 17% were in the "inadequate" range (trainable rather than educable), and 20% were "grossly defective" (required complete protection) (p. 171). Cruickshank, Hallahan, and Bice (1976a) reported that in a study of cerebral-palsied children on the New Jersey crippled-children's rosters who were available for intellectual assessment, the mean IQ of 130 individuals with right hemiplegia was 74.73 with a standard deviation of 24.47 as compared with a mean IQ for those with a left hemiplegia (N = 120) of 79.73 with a standard deviation of 28.46. Unfortunately, there was no mention of how many had hemiplegia that was acquired rather than congenital. The incidence of speech and language problems is not known, though Crothers and Paine (1959) indicate that articulation problems are not so common in congenital hemiplegia as they are in acquired. We have discussed earlier in this chapter our concerns about language development and cerebral palsy.

ACQUIRED OR POSTNATAL SPASTIC HEMIPLEGIA

Acquired or postnatal spastic hemiplegia (33.3% of cases) is defined as hemiplegia that comes on gradually or suddenly in a child who was less than 3 years of age and had previously been normal. Head trauma, central nervous sytem infection (e.g., encephalitis or meningitis), and prolonged seizures are among the most common causes, though frequently the etiology is not known. On physical examination a difference will be noted in the child's ability to use the affected side, and strabismus and hearing deficit may also be noted. Approximately 55% of these children will have a seizure disorder (Crothers and Paine, 1959; Gold and Carter, 1976). The neuromotor examination reveals weakness and clumsiness of movement of the affected side as well as the characteristic posturing, hyperactive reflexes, and stretch reflex previously described. The right side is more often involved than the left (Gold and Carter, 1976).

Cognitively, "approximately 25% may be overtly retarded" (Gold and Carter, 1976). Crothers and Paine (1959) noted that those who acquired hemiplegia after 2 years of age had a more favorable prognosis cognitively than those who were affected before 2 years of age. Both Crothers and

Paine (1959) and Gold and Carter (1976) noted that the mean IQ usually was lower when a seizure disorder accompanied the hemiplegia. According to Crothers and Paine (1959), the distribution of cognitive functioning in the postnatal hemiplegic group was as follows: 2% were in the superior range, 16% in the average range, 36% in the "below average" range, 26% in the "inadequate" range, and 20% in the "grossly defective" range.

SPASTIC QUADRIPLEGIA

Spastic quadriplegia connotes involvement of all four extremities with the physical findings of spasticity. This is the type of cerebral palsy in which deformities and contractures requiring orthopedic intervention are most frequently seen. Although the onset is usually prenatal or perinatal, it is usually not possible to diagnose spastic quadriplegia in the newborn period. One should have concern, however, about preterm infants as being at risk, and about those term infants who are overly irritable, have seizures, and/or a high-pitched cry as well as those who are apathetic, overly sleepy, and have sucking and swallowing problems. The latter may be manifested later in the child's development as chewing and swallowing difficulties, dysarthria, and persistent drooling.

In the first year of life, infants with spastic quadriplegia typically are delayed in the attainment of motor milestones, have abnormal muscle tone, have a persistence of primitive reflexes, and frequently have chewing, sucking and swallowing problems. On neuromotor examination, persistence beyond 4 to 6 months of age of the *asymmetric tonic neck* reflex (turning the infant's head when supine results in extension of the arm and leg on the jaw side and flexion of the limbs on the occiput side as in a fencing posture), and the *tonic labrynthine* reflex (when the child is prone, the flexor posture predominates, and the child will be unable to lift his head; when the child is supine, extensor tone predominates, resulting in opisthotonus and difficulty in bringing his hands to the midline) are cause for concern. Furthermore, an *obligatory asymmetric tonic* neck reflex (lasting >30 sec) is always abnormal and is indicative of motor deficit (Taft, 1973). The presence of these primitive postural reflexes interfere with the normal progression of fine and gross motor development. Furthermore, abnormalities of tone noted during passive movement of the extremities (e.g., floppiness or hypotonia initially, followed later by hypertonia) can be early signs in quadriplegia. Holding the infant upright and observing a scissoring of the lower extremities is indicative of increased tone in the adductors of the hip. It is the increased tone that results in contractures. Although there is considerable variability in the severity of motor disability, 30% never achieve standing balance for walking (Crothers and Paine, 1959) and fine motor coordination is usually poor bilaterally. Sensory disturbances also occur as do hearing deficit and strabismus. The sensory disturbances are associated with poor growth of the extremities, which is often noted in those who are more severely involved. Only 13% have a seizure disorder though 20% more have a history of having had seizures in the past (Crothers and Paine, 1959).

Cognitively, individuals with quadriplegia are more severely affected than any other group with spasticity. In the New Jersey study quoted by Cruickshank et al. (1976a), the mean IQ of 107 individuals was 57.39 with a standard deviation of 30.86. Crothers and Paine (1959) listed the following range of intellectual functioning: 2% are in the superior range, 12% in the average range, 16% in the "below average" range, 25% in the "inadequate" range, and 45% in the "grossly defective" range. Of those under 21 years of age, 75% are noncompetitive (Crothers and Paine, 1959). From 30% to 50% of patients exhibit some degree of dysarthria (Molnar, 1973), which compounds their difficulty in communication.

SPASTIC PARAPLEGIA

Spastic paraplegia, or spastic diplegia, though seen most often in preterm children, has been declining in incidence in recent years (Davis and Tizard, 1975; Volpe, 1976). In the Perinatal Collaborative Study, it was seen in approximately 7% or in 44 of the 639 preterm infants examined at one year of age (Churchill et al., 1974). In the infant, persistence of the crossed extensor reflex is an early sign of spastic diplegia (Taft, 1973). The other physical and neuromotor findings are delay in the achievement of motor milestones involving the lower extremities and varying degrees of spasticity. The prognosis is better in this form of cerebral palsy as seizure disorder and speech and language disorder are less frequent. Cognitively, Crothers and Paine (1959) found that 7 out of 13 of their patients had an "adequate" IQ, 5 were in the borderline range, and 1 was mentally deficient. In the New Jersey Study (Cruickshank et al., 1976a), the mean IQ of 115 individuals was 76.76 with a standard deviation of 28.38.

EXTRAPYRAMIDAL CEREBRAL PALSY

Extrapyramidal cerebral palsy is a disorder of movement and coordination which may affect the trunk and extremities as well as the muscles of chewing, sucking, and swallowing. Rigidity is considered to be a form of extrapyramidal cerebral palsy and is characterized by increased tone in the extremities, particularly when range of motion and tone are tested slowly.

R.C. is a 4-year 6-month-old youngster with spastic quadriplegia and strabismus. He was the product of a pre-term birth; he developed hydrocephalus and required a shunt. For the past 2 years he has been attending a Developmental Day Care Center and has been receiving physical therapy, speech and language therapy, and an appropriate educational plan. In spite of the physical therapy, he will need surgical intervention for the contractures which result in scissoring and toe walking. Nevertheless, he is a happy, pleasant youngster who is able to speak understandably and who is a joy to his parents.

The two most common forms of movement disorder are *chorea*, which is characterized by involuntary, spasmodic twitching contractions of individual muscles or small muscle groups of the extremities or of the face and is associated with weakness and ineffectualness in attempted activity; and *athetosis*, which is characterized by a succession of slow, involuntary, smooth writhing movements of the distal musculature such as the digits and hands as well as of the face, tongue, and throat. Occasionally these are seen together as *choreoathetoid* movements. The usual etiology is kernicterus or hypoxia after these conditions have adversely affected the basal ganglia or their connections. At present, kernicterus (bilirubin encephalopathy) is quite rare because it is a preventable disease. In the newborn, it would present with the following neuromotor manifestations: high-pitched cry, poor Moro reflex, opisthotonus (arching of the back), poor feeing, and increased tone. In the report by Crothers and Paine (1959), 60 out of 80 died before the sixth day of life. Those infants who survived developed hypotonia and were noted between 2 and 12 months of age to have a persistent asymmetric tonic neck reflex. In the second year of life, athetosis and dysarthria become noticeable. Other common physical problems are a high-frequency hearing loss and difficulty with vertical gaze. Intellectual function is usually well preserved and seizures are unlikely (Molnar, 1973).

Hypoxia is a more common cause of extrapyramidal cerebral palsy today, and in cases with this etiology, seizure disorder and mental retardation are more common (Molnar, 1973). In the first year of life, hypotonia, persistence of the asymmetric tonic neck and tonic labrynthine reflexes, delay in the attainment of milestones, and sucking, chewing, and swallowing problems are common. Athetosis becomes noticeable in the second year of life as do drooling and dysarthria. Strabismus is frequent and sensorineural hearing deficit is not uncommon (Crothers and Paine, 1959; Nober, 1976). The athetosis is characteristically observed as grimacing with talking, writhing of the distal extremities, and a "lurching gait." Because of the dysarthria and hearing loss, speech and language skills are delayed and deviant. Failure to say intelligible words by two years of age is associated with a moderate-severe dysarthria in two-thirds of cases, whereas only a mild dysarthria is seen in those who are able to say intelligible words by two years of age (Crothers and Paine, 1959).

Cognitively 12% of all patients with extrapyramidal cerebral palsy are in the superior range, 35% are in the average range, 20% in the below

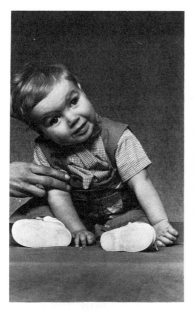

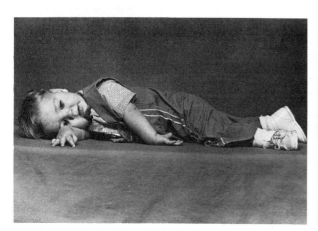

This 2-year-old boy (T. H.) has spastic quadriplegia, although he may well develop more findings of athetosis in the future; he would then present as a mixed form of cerebral palsy. He currently has a seizure disorder, decreased visual acuity, is extremely fretful, and is floppy or hypotonic. The difficulty encountered in sitting alone, in being pulled to sit, and in turning over can be readily appreciated. Nevertheless, the mother-child interaction has been a source of strength in terms of providing love and opportunity for improvement. This youngster is enrolled in an infant program for handicapped children.

145

average range, 18% are in the "inadequate" range, and 15% are in the "grossly defective" range (Crothers and Paine, 1959). In the New Jersey study (Cruickshank et al., 1976a) the mean IQ of 249 individuals was 72.60 with a standard deviation of 30.41. Spuriously low results may be the consequence of communication difficulty caused by the athetosis and dysarthria.

A note of caution is in order. The manifestations of cerebral palsy in the first year of life are usually the result of prenatal or perinatal brain insult, though they can result from postnatal brain trauma or central nervous system infection as well. When cerebral palsy is suspected at that early age, one must be absolutely certain that the manifestations are indeed the result of a static lesion in a developing individual rather than representative of an inborn error of metabolism, or a degenerative lesion or of increased intracranial pressure that may be reversible, each of which can mimic cerebral palsy for a while but in which the nature of the lesion becomes clear by careful and repeated examination. A clear example of this is the Lesch-Nyhan syndrome, an inborn error of metabolism, in which the presence of an inactive enzyme results in the accumulation of uric acid in urine and blood (see chapter on mental subnormality). The functional impairment which can result is hypotonia in infancy followed by motor delay, spasticity, and choreoathetosis. Self-mutilation, especially lip and finger biting, is a frequent behavioral manifestation. Treatment with allopurinol to reduce the uric acid level is indicated, but neurologic findings reveal no beneficial effect.

Furthermore, Brown and Drillien (1971) and Drillien (1972a, 1973) have described an entity of "transient dystonia" in low birth weight infants which deserves mention. In the course of a prospective study of low birth weight infants, attention was focused upon those who showed abnormal neurologic signs before a year of age. In 60% of the infants who showed moderate or severe dystonia (unequivocally abnormal neurologic signs such as increased tone, retarded motor development, exaggerated reflexes or persistence of primitive reflexes from 2-8 months of age), the abnormality disappeared between 8 and 12 months. A further 20% were normal at 1 year, but abnormal signs reappeared later; the remaining 20% remained abnormal and had definite cerebral palsy. One-third of the children with moderate-severe dystonia were "markedly hyperactive and restless in the second and third years" (Drillien, 1972b, p.577), as opposed to only 7% of those who had been neurologically normal. Though Drillien's intention was to follow these children through 7 years of age to look for a relationship to language development, learning difficulties, and behavior problems, the necessary permission could not be obtained. This study is important with regard to prognostication when abnormal neurologic signs are present in the first year of life. Certainly it shows that cerebral palsy may well be the result, but it is likely that the abnormal neurologic signs will not be prominent in most children as they get older; rather, the children may be normal or they may have mild motor involvement, and/or behavioral, learning, perceptual and speech and language difficulties.

In several ways, these children with transient dystonia represent the "gap" in the "continuum of reproductive wastage" proposed by Lilienfeld and Parkhurst (1951). First, the study demonstrates that the incidence of abnormal neurologic signs increases with decreasing birth weight (55% of surviving infants with a birth weight <1250 grams as opposed to 16% of those with a birth weight 1,751–2,000 grams) (Drillien, 1973). Second, it demonstrates the range of sequelae possible after the finding of abnormal neurologic signs in the first year of life from normality through behavioral problems (and suspected learning and language problems) to frank cerebral palsy.

TREATMENT AND MANAGEMENT

The treatment of cerebral palsy has traditionally been through orthopedic surgery and physical therapy and more recently has included occupational therapy, special educational techniques, and speech and language therapy. The interested reader is referred to the following sources for more information about specific techniques (Bobath, 1967; Cruickshank, 1976; Gillette, 1974; Marks, 1974; Pearson and Williams, 1972; Samilson, 1975). The aim in treatment has been to prevent contractures, to promote ambulation, and to promote independence. It is intersting to read the views of Paine and Crothers (1959) with regard to (1) the family's attitude toward therapy over a period of time, (2) the role of time, (3) the need for health professionals to allow patients flexibility and initiative in their treatment, and (4) the need to know when to stop therapy. For example, they found that parental expression of anxiety by "energetic optimism" in the early years changed to less interest in the details of treatment as time passed and to more "restlessness" about the future. They developed the policy that "overoptimism is dangerous and that unjustified pessimism is worse"

(p. 16). They pointed out that "one fact which is frequently ignored is that a considerable number of older hemiplegic children and adults without conventional therapy are essentially without handicap" (p. 190). They acknowledged the importance of the parent-child interaction and of the physician's interaction with the family. But they urged doctors to broaden their interests in each patient beyond providing physical care. Otherwise, "they may encourage docility instead of welcoming experiments in independence by the child. It is our impression that respect for ingenuity and tolerance to resistence and even rebellion by the child will lead, in many cases, to modification or even abandonment of rigid therapeutic and educational procedures. Certainly there is singularly little evidence that sufficient thought has been devoted to the problem of reappraising treatment, and perhaps abandoning it as the child grows older" (p. 283). Although specific methods and techniques of therapy may well be modified as time goes by, these principles of therapy advanced by Paine and Crothers (1959) should be guideposts for all time.

In 1962, Paine published a report on the outcome of 177 patients with cerebral palsy, 74 of them having been totally untreated because of (1) medical advice against it, (2) parental disinterest, (3) late diagnosis, and (4) lack of treatment facilities in their locale. It is one of the few opportunities to compare results of various forms of treatment in cerebral palsy with natural outcomes without treatment. Some of the findings were as follows: in moderate to severe hemiplegia and quadriplegia, the treated group had a better gait and fewer contractures; in these patients, intensive physical therapy did not obviate the need for orthopedic surgery. In extrapyramidal cerebral palsy, there was little difference between the treated and untreated groups, and coordination and function seemed to improve in both with age.

As one considers the needs of patients with cerebral palsy, one really does tend to think in terms of locomotion and independence in ambulation. What one needs to reflect upon, however, are the innumerable needs of the child in achieving independence in living—with educational, training, psychological, and speech and language needs all getting their proper attention. For example, it might be that an individual with cerebral palsy could better spend his time and effort in perfecting his speech and language and learning a trade, rather than in going from wheelchair to crutches. Bax and MacKeith (1975) have stated this quite well:

The motor disability in cerebral palsy is the most overt and obvious sign of the child's dysfunction. It is not, perhaps, the most disabling, in so far as other problems of communication and of learning may be more significant in terms of the child's overall function. It may be wiser to pay more attention to these problems than to spend too much time attempting to achieve the impossible in physical therapy. Perhaps the order of importance of abilities is being able to communicate, being able to sit, being independent in dressing and toileting, and then walking. (p.29)

In considering treatment, then, the needs of the child, the timing, and the needs of the parents all need to be considered. Bax and McKeith (1975) recognize four common crisis periods in family life. (1) The early period when the deficits are diagnosed. (2) The time when school approaches. (3) The time when school is over and the handicapped individual needs to assume as much of an independent role as possible in employment, marriage, etc. (4) The time when the parents realize they will not always be around to take care of the child who by this time is an adult. Providing anticipatory guidance and helping the family make decisions are among the most important therapeutic roles a health professional can play.

Crothers and Paine talked of these same issues almost twenty years ago. O'Reilly (1975) compared the outcome of cerebral palsy adult patients then and now and found that there has been little change. Only about a quarter of affected adults are employed; 28% died or were in institutions; almost 40% are sitting at home without productive activity. His plea was for the establishment of more educational and training opportunities for these handicapped citizens.

Treatment of cerebral palsy needs to be multifaceted. Prevention with an improved prenatal and perinatal environment would be ideal. But there will probably always be some affected individuals. The emphasis of treatment needs to be toward a goal of independent living for people so affected. Their neuromotor dysfunction may well be accompanied by all or some of the following: vision and hearing deficits, speech and language impairments, behavioral difficulties, learning problems, cognitive impairments, and seizure disorders. Their treatment needs to be planned in such a way that all aspects of a handicapped person's disability are given proper attention.

References

Babcock, J.L. Spinal injuries in children. *Pediatric Clinics of North America*, 1975, *22*, 487–500.

Babson, S.G., Benson, R.C., Pernoll, M.L. & Benda, G.I. *Management of High Risk Pregnancy and Intensive Care of the Neonate.* St. Louis: C.V. Mosby, 1975.

Bax, M.C.O. & MacKeith, R. The pediatric role in the care of the child with cerebral palsy. In R.L. Samilson (Ed.), *Orthopaedic Aspects of Cerebral Palsy.* (Clinics in Developmental Medicine, Vol. 52/53). London: William Heinemann, 1975.

Bell, W.E. & McCormick, W.F. *Neurologic Infections in Children.* Philadelphia: W.B. Saunders, 1975.

Bobath, B. The very early treatment of cerebral palsy. *Developmental Medicine and Child Neurology*, 1967, *9*, 373–90.

Brent, R.L. & Harris, M.I. (Eds.). *Prevention of Embryonic, Fetal, and Perinatal Disease.* (DHEW Pub. #[NIH] 76-853). Bethesda, Maryland, 1976.

Brown, J.K. & Drillien, C.M. The dystonic syndrome of the low birth-weight infant. *Archives of Disease in Childhood*, 1971, *46*, 739–40.

Brown, J.K., Purvis, R.J., Forfar, J.O. & Cockburn F. Neurological aspects of perinatal asphyxia. *Developmental Medicine and Child Neurology*, 1974, *16*, 567–80.

Churchill, J.A., Masland, R.L., Naylor, A.A. & Ashworth, M.R. The etiology of cerebral palsy in preterm infants. *Developmental Medicine and Child Neurology*, 1974, *16*, 143–49.

Clifford, S.H. & Drorbaugh, J.E. Obstetric history of grossly retarded children in the Boston Sample of the Collaborative Study. In C.R. Angle & E.A. Bering, Jr. (Eds.), *Physical Trauma as an Etiological Agent in Mental Retardation.* (DHEW, NIH Public Health Service). Proceedings of a Conference on the Etiology of Mental Retardation, October 13–16, 1968. Omaha, Nebraska, 1970.

Cohen, J.S. Vocational guidance and employment. In W.M. Cruickshank (Ed.), *Cerebral Palsy: A Developmental Disability*, 3rd rev. ed. Syracuse, New York: Syracuse University Press, 1976.

Crothers, B. & Paine, R.S. *The Natural History of Cerebral Palsy.* Cambridge: Harvard University Press, 1959.

Cruickshank, W.M. (Ed.). *Cerebral Palsy: A Developmental Disability*, 3rd rev. ed. Syracuse, New York: Syracuse University Press, 1976.

Cruickshank, W.M., Hallahan, D.P. & Bice, H.V. The evaluation of intelligence. In W.M. Cruickshank (Ed.), *Cerebral Palsy: A Developmental Disability*, 3rd rev. ed. Syracuse, New York: Syracuse University Press, 1976a.

Cruickshank, W.M., Hallahan, D.P. & Bice, H.V. Personality and behavioral characteristics. In W.M. Cruickshank (Ed.), *Cerebral Palsy: A Developmental Disability.* 3rd rev. ed. Syracuse, New York: Syracuse University Press, 1976b.

Davies, P.A. & Tizard, J.P.M. Very low birthweight and subsequent neurological defect. *Developmental Medicine and Child Neurology,* 1975, *17,* 3–17.

Denhoff, E. Medical Aspects. In W.M. Cruickshank (Ed.), *Cerebral Palsy: A Developmental Disability,* 3rd rev. ed. Syracuse, New York: Syracuse University Press, 1976.

Denhoff, E. & Robinault, I.P. *Cerebral Palsy and Related Disorders: A Developmental Approach to Dysfunction.* New York: McGraw-Hill, 1960.

Drillien, C.M. Abnormal neurologic signs in the first year of life in low birth weight infants: Possible prognostic significance. *Developmental Medicine and Child Neurology,* 1972a, *14,* 575–84.

Drillien, C.M. Aetiology and outcome in low-birthweight infants. *Developmental Medicine and Child Neurology,* 1972b, *14,* 563–74.

Drillien, C.M. Fresh approaches to prospective studies of low birth weight infants. *Research Publications Association for Research in Nervous and Mental Disease,* 1973, *51,* 198–209.

Drillien, C.M. Prenatal and perinatal factors in etiology and outcome of low birth weight. *Clinics in Perinatology,* 1974, *1,* 197–211.

Dunsdon, M.I. *The Educability of Cerebral-Palsied Children.* London: National Foundation for Educational Research, 1952.

Feigin, R.D. & Dodge, P.R. Bacterial meningitis: Newer concepts of pathophysiology and neurologic sequelae. *Pediatric Clinics of North America,* 1976, *23,* 541–56.

Fisch, R.O., Bilek, M.K., Miller, L.D. & Engel, R.R. Physical and mental status at four years of age of survivors of the respiratory distress syndrome. *Journal of Pediatrics,* 1975, *86,* 497–503.

Fitzhardinge, P.M. Early growth and development in low birth weight infants following treatment in an intensive care nursery. *Pediatrics,* 1975, *56,* 162–72.

Fitzhardinge, P.M., Kazemi, M., Ramsay, M. & Stern, L. Long-term sequelae of neonatal meningitis. *Developmental Medicine and Child Neurology,* 1974, *16,* 3–10.

Ford, F., Crothers, B. & Putnam, M.C. Birth injuries of the central nervous system. In *Medicine Monographs* (Vol. 11). Baltimore, Maryland: Williams & Wilkins, 1927.

Gillette, H.E. *Systems of Therapy in Cerebral Palsy,* Springfield, Illinois: Charles C Thomas, 1974.

Gold, A.P. & Carter, S. Acute hemiplegia of infancy and childhood. *Pediatric Clinics of North America,* 1976, *23,* 413–33.

Heinonen, O.P., Slone, D. & Shapiro, S. *Birth Defects and Drugs in Pregnancy.* Acton, Massachusetts: Publishing Sciences Group, 1977.

Johnson, J.D., Malachowski, N.C., Grobstein, R., Welsh, D. et al. Prognosis of children surviving with the aid of mechanical ventilation in the newborn period. *Journal of Pediatrics,* 1974, *84,* 272–76.

Krishnamoorthy, K.S. Neurologic outcome of neonatal intensive care. Lecture presented at the postgraduate course in pediatric neurology. Harvard Medical School, November, 1976.

Krishnamoorthy, K.S., Fernandez, R.A., Momose, K.J., DeLong, G.R. et al. Evaluation of neonatal intracranial hemorrhage by computerized tomography. *Pediatrics,* 1977, *59,* 165–72.

Lencione, R.M. The development of communication skills. In W.M. Cruickshank (Ed.), *Cerebral Palsy: A Developmental Disability,* 3rd rev. ed., Syracuse, New York: Syracuse University Press, 1976.

Lilienfeld, A.M. & Parkhurst, E. A study of the association of the factors of pregnancy and parturition with the development of cerebral palsy. *American Journal of Hygiene,* 1951, *53,* 262–82.

Little, W.J. On the influence of abnormal parturition, difficult labour, premature birth, and asphyxia neonatorum on the mental and physical condition of the child especially in relation to deformities. *Lancet,* October 19, 1861, 378.

Lubchenco, L.O., Bard, H., Goldman, A.L., Coyer, W.E. et al. Newborn intensive care and long-term prognosis. *Developmental Medicine and Child Neurology,* 1974, *16,* 421–31.

McCracken, G.H., Jr. The rate of bacteriologic response to antimicrobial therapy in neonatal meningitis. *American Journal of Diseases of Children,* 1972, *123,* 547–53.

McNutt, S. Apoplexia neonatorum. *American Journal of Obstetrics,* 1885, *18,* 73–81.

Malamud, N., Itabashi, H.H., Castor, J. & Messinger, H.B. An etiologic and diagnostic study of cerebral palsy. *Journal of Pediatrics,* 1964, *65,* 270–93.

Marks, N.C. *Cerebral-Palsied and Learning-Disabled Children.* Springfield, Illinois: Charles C Thomas, 1974.

Mealey, J., Jr. Infantile subdural hematomas. *Pediatric Clinics of North America,* 1975, *22,* 433–42.

Miller, J.R. Description of a handicapped population. The British Columbia Health Surveillance Registry. *Birth Defects: Original Article Series,* 1976, *12,* 1–11.

Molnar, G.E. Clinical aspects of cerebral palsy. *Pediatric Annals,* 1973, *2,* 10–27.

Nebel, W.A., Flowers, C.E., Jr., Jones, O.H., Peete, C.H. et al. Obstetric factors in cerebral palsy, a North Carolina study. *North Carolina Medical Journal,* 1962, *23,* 329–35.

Niswander, K.R., Friedman, E.A., Hoover, D.B., Pietrowski, H. et al. Fetal morbidity following potentially anoxigenic obstetric conditions. Abruptio placenta. *American Journal of Obstetrics and Gynecology*, 1966a, 95, 839–45.

Niswander, K.R., Friedman, E.A., Hoover, D.B., Pietrowski, H. et al. Fetal morbidity following potentially anoxigenic obstetric conditions. Placenta previa. *American Journal of Obstetrics and Gynecology*, 1966b, 95, 846–52.

Niswander, K.R., Friedman, E.A., Hoover, D.B., Pietrowski, H. et al. Fetal morbidity following potentially anoxigenic obstetric conditions. Prolapse of the umbilical cord. *American Journal of Obstetrics and Gynecology*, 1966c, 95, 853–58.

Niswander, K.R., Friedman, E.A., Hoover, D.B., Pietrowski et al. Fetal morbidity following potentially anoxigenic obstetric conditions. Occult prolapse of the umbilical cord. *American Journal of Obstetrics and Gynecology*, 1966d, 95, 1099–1103.

Niswander, K.R. & Gordon, M. *The Collaborative Perinatal Study of the National Institute of Neurological Diseases and Stroke. The Women and their Pregnancies.* Philadelphia: W.B. Saunders, 1972.

Niswander, K.R., Gordon, M. & Drage, J.S. The effect of intrauterine hypoxia on the child surviving to 4 years. *American Journal Obstetrics and Gynecology.* 1975, *121*, 892–99.

Nober, E.H. Auditory processing in cerebral palsy. In W.M. Cruickshank (Ed.), *Cerebral Palsy: A Developmental Disability*, 3rd rev. ed. Syracuse, New York: Syracuse University Press, 1976.

O'Reilly, D.E. Care of the cerebral palsied: Outcome of the past and needs for the future. *Developmental Medicine and Child Neurology*, 1975, *17*, 141–49.

Oswin, M. *Behavior Problems Amongst Children with Cerebral Palsy.* Bristol, England: John Wright, 1967.

Paine, R.S. On the treatment of cerebral palsy. The outcome of 177 patients, 74 totally untreated. *Pediatrics*, 1962, 29, 605–16.

Pearson, P.H. & Williams, C.E. (Eds.). *Physical Therapy Services in the Developmental Disabilities.* Springfield, Illinois: Charles C Thomas, 1972.

Russin, L.A. (Trans.). *Infantile Cerebral Paralysis* by Sigmund Freud. Coral Gables, Florida: University of Miami Press, 1968.

Rutter, M., Graham, P. & Yule, W. *A Neuropsychiatric Study in Childhood.* (Clinics in Developmental Medicine, Vol. 35/36). London: William Heinemann, 1970.

Samilson, R.L. (Ed.). *Orthopaedic Aspects of Cerebral Palsy.* (Clinics in Developmental Medicine, Vol. 52/53). London: William Heinemann, 1975.

Sell, S.H.W., Merrill, R.E., Doyne, E.O. & Zimsky, E.P., Jr. Long-term sequelae of *Hemophilus Influenzae* meningitis. *Pediatrics*, 1972, 49, 206–11.

Strauss, A.A. & Lehtinen, L.E. *Psychopathology and Education of the Brain-Injured Child* (Vol. 1). New York: Grune & Stratton, 1947.

Taft, L.T. Early recognition of cerebral palsy. *Pediatric Annals*, 1973, 2, 30–46.

Towbin, A. Central nervous system damage in the human fetus and newborn infant. *American Journal of Diseases of Children*, 1970, *119*, 529–42.

Volpe, J.J. Perinatal hypoxic-ischemic brain injury. *Pediatric Clinics of North America*, 1976, *23*, 383–97.

Wolf, J.M. (Ed.). *The results of treatment in cerebral palsy*. Springfield, Illinois: Charles C Thomas, 1969.

5

Seizure Disorders

In this chapter, the terms epilepsy and seizure disorder will be used interchangeably to denote a condition of recurrent episodes of cerebral electrical discharge which result in altered states of awareness or consciousness, and/or partial or generalized motor, sensory, autonomic, and affective disturbance. The magnitude of this disorder can be appreciated by considering incidence and cost estimates. Approximately 7% of the population suffer at least one convulsion per lifetime (O'Leary and Goldring, 1976). The prevalence rate of epilepsy ranges from a low of one per 1,000 in Finland (Olivares, 1972) to a high of 15 per 1,000 in one tribe in Tanganyika in which epileptics are ostracized and thereby forced to intermarry (Rodin, 1972a). The average prevalence rate in Europe and North America is 4.5 per 1,000 and in Africa it is 5.7 per 1,000 (Rodin, 1972a). In terms of costs, the Epilepsy Foundation of America (1975) reports that in 1972 $4.37 billion were spent in the United States alone on epilepsy.

Epilepsy is not a single disorder but includes a diversity of types. The previously presented Developmental Disabilities Cube (See Figure 1.1) is useful for conceptualizing the multifactorial etiologies occurring during particular developmental periods, giving rise to manifestations across various dimensions of functioning, and necessitating comprehensive integrated management. A brief review of the history of acquisition of knowledge about epilepsy, from pre-Hippocratic times to the present, will precede a description and discussion of the various types of epilepsy and their etiologies, manifestations, treatments, and prognoses.

155

HISTORY

Temkin (1971) has written a detailed historical account tracing the development of thought about the etiology and treatment of epilepsy from the time of the Hippocratic writings (400 B.C.) to the time of J. Hughlings Jackson (late nineteenth and early twentieth centuries). According to Temkin (1971), the ancient Greeks before Hippocrates called epilepsy the "sacred disease" because they thought a deity had entered the stricken one. However, the Hippocratic writers astutely proposed that a disturbance of the brain, which was hereditary and not divine, was the cause. They thought the specific pathology was a stagnation of the cold humors (phlegm and black bile) within the ventricles or cavities of the brain, and therefore treatment consisted of "warm-and-dry" dietetic and pharmacologic approaches. The "sacred disease" was considered by Hippocrates to be incurable although there was some thought that patients could avoid attacks by binding their arms and avoiding unpleasant odors that might provoke attacks. This latter statement is particularly interesting in view of our current knowledge that the aura of some forms of epilepsy consists of an unpleasant odor.

Though the ancient Greeks had described it as the "sacred disease," the Romans called epilepsy the "falling sickness" or "falling evil." There were many theories of etiology which came to the fore then and have subsequently enjoyed popularity over the centuries. Among them are: (1) "possession by a demon," which was a prominent theory from Roman times until the Age of the Enlightenment; (2) uncleanliness owing to contagion and "evil breath" (Middle Ages, 500–1500) and; (3) the adverse influence of certain phases of the moon, which lead to the periodicity of the attacks (Roman times until Tissot in 1770). In ancient times there was no real distinction between epilepsy and "madness" or mental disorder, and patients with either were considered to be "lunatics" in that they suffered from abnormal states manifested in periodic attacks that seemed to coincide with phases of the lunar calendar. During those years, treatment consisted of religious cures in the name of Christ, special herbs and diets including peony and mistletoe, and various superstitious incantations.

Between the eighteenth and nineteenth centuries, many of these theories about epilepsy were laid to rest. However, they were replaced by theories that continued to attach a stigma to the disorder. For example, a Swiss physician, Simon Tissot (1728–1797), wrote in 1770 in his *Treatise on*

Epilepsy that masturbation was etiologic (Temkin, 1971). In 1887, Lombroso linked epilepsy and criminality and indicated that epileptics and criminals comprised a distinct and degenerate class (Temkin, 1971).

Gradually, however, progress has been made during the last 150 years in elucidating the etiology(ies) of seizure disorders and in changing social attitudes. This has occurred because of (1) opportunities to observe, categorize, and treat seizure disorders and to recognize them as constituting entities separate from emotional disturbances (2) advances made in localizing brain function and correlations now possible between the clinical presentation of seizures and the pathologic anatomy of the brain found at surgery or autopsy, (3) interests in and opportunities to investigate *microscopically*, both normal and pathological central nervous system anatomy, and (4) efforts to record the electrical activity of the brain, both during seizure activity and at rest.

By the middle of the nineteenth century, many of the clinical aspects of epilepsy had been described. For example, according to Temkin (1971) Calmeil in 1824 described "absence" as a "passing mental confusion," and "status epilepticus" as a prolonged seizure constituting a medical emergency; Bravais in 1827 and Bright in 1828 described hemiplegic epilepsy and the "march" of associated motor symptoms. Bright also described the brain pathology in his patient, which consisted of a tumor on the surface of the upper part of the posterior lobe of the left hemisphere. "Grand mal" was considered a "fully developed fit" and "petit mal" was the name attached to those seizures that were not grand mal. W. J. West (1840) reported on salaam seizures or infantile spasms after observing them in his own son, and Romberg in 1853 described the "aura" of seizures as any prodromal symptom. Sir Charles Locock in 1858 introduced bromide therapy, which became the first successful pharmacologic agent in the treatment of epilepsy. In 1873, the renown neurologist, J. Hughlings Jackson (1835–1911) formulated a description of epilepsy that is still useful today.

"Epilepsy is the name for occasional, sudden, excessive, rapid and local discharges of grey matter." . . . The cells of the discharging lesion are diseased. Their disease is brought about by "morbid nutrition," which in turn can be the effect of various pathological processes. Their morbid condition causes the cells to discharge excessively and too readily. These cells have become "a mad part" and while the discharge spreads, other "sane cells" are made to "act madly." "The more excessive the discharge the severer the fit." (Temkin, 1971, p.337, 342)

Concurrently, progress was made in the localization of brain function and in the correlation of the clinical presentation of seizures and the pathologic anatomy observed at autopsy. In 1825, Bouchet and Cazauvielh described pathologic changes in Ammon's horn (part of the temporal lobe) in epileptics. Broca in 1861 localized the function of speech to the left third frontal convolution. In 1864, J. Hughlings Jackson attributed aphasia, or loss of speech, to an interruption in the blood supply to Broca's area, as might occur when the middle cerebral artery was involved in a pathologic process (tumor, embolus, thrombus, inflammation). He further noted that paralysis occurred after destruction of cells but that convulsions occurred secondary to "discharging" lesions of the grey matter. In 1870, he described the "Jacksonian march" (previously described by Bravais and Bright, but Jackson's name was now attached to the disorder) as "those [convulsions] in which the fit begins by deliberate spasm on one side of the body, and in which parts of the body are affected, one after another" (Temkin, 1971, p.305). Jackson is credited by Temkin (1971) with aligning the epilepsies with modern views of the physiology of the nervous system and being indifferent to whether the behavior of those affected was "ridiculous, pathetic, or criminal" (p.381).

Meanwhile, others were involved in developing dissection and fixation techniques for improved microscopic delineation of normal and pathologic central nervous system anatomy. O'Leary and Goldring (1976) provide a historical account of these accomplishments. In 1833, Ehrenberg first observed neurons under the microscope; in 1837, Purkinje, discovered neurons in the cerebellar cortex; and in 1850, Koelliker found that the nerve cells in the grey matter make connections with the axons in the white matter. Flechsig (1847–1929) found that myelination of the different systems of the brain and spinal cord occurred at different times in fetal life. Golgi discovered in 1871 a staining method that used a silver chromate precipitate which encrusted neuron bodies, dendrites, and axons selectively. Ramón y Cajal then used this technique to explore systematically the nervous system and was able to demonstrate that axons invariably make free (synaptic) contacts with nerve bodies (somata) and dendrites. Impulse conduction along dendrites was found to occur toward the soma and outwards along the axon. In 1906, Cajal and Golgi shared the Nobel Prize for their work on the elucidation of the fine structure and function of the central nervous system.

As more was learned about the electrical activity of the brain, experiments were carried out first in animals and then in humans, using electrical stimulation to localize function. As a result, by 1954 Penfield presented a detailed map of the cerebral cortex with regard to localization of function. During those early experiments, it was noted that excessive electrical stimulation could result in convulsions. Meanwhile, other investigators became more interested in recording the brain's own electrical activity, and in 1929 Hans Berger described the first human electroencephalogram (EEG).

The following is a modern and somewhat simplified explanation of brain ultrastructure and function as it relates to epilepsy (O'Leary and Goldring, 1976).

> All brain activities are induced by electrochemical processes, in particular such generalized nervous phenomena as conduction, excitation, and inhibition. Generators of weak electric currents lie in the surface membranes of the somata (bodies) of nerve cells, their dendrites, and axons. A whole cell, made up of these several parts, is called a *neuron*. The membrane coverings of somata and dendrites provide many spot contacts (synapses) with the terminal tendrils of axons arising from other cells, each such spot showing a narrow cleft at the interface between presynaptic (axonal) and postsynaptic (soma-dendritic) components. These junctures permit one-way conduction from the axon terminus to the dendritic part with which it is in touch. . . . Communication between neurons is achieved when signal bursts are transferred from the terminal endbulbs of an axon to the body or dendrites of a succeeding neuron. . . . Most synapses utilize a chemical transmitter that conveys the impact of succeeding signals of a burst across the cleft. . . . During an epileptic attack, the currents produced are considerably greater than those required for normal brain activity. These stromal currents result from abnormal recruitment and timing of many unit potentials. . . . (p. 61–62)

For example, normal neurons tend to fire at the nominal rate of about 20 per second. "Pacemaker" neurons in an epileptic focus fire at a rate of 200 to 900 per second in bursts that occur 5 to 15 times per second and that last 10 to 40 msec. The density of connections with adjacent normal neurons allows recuitment of normal neurons, "kindling" them to fire more rapidly and widening the focus. Therefore, the critical mass of bursting neurons in the focus is variable and can enlarge or shrink. Only 0.13% of the 60,000 synapses of a normal cortical neuron need to be bursting to convert that cell into another bursting cell. As adjacent cellular hyperactivity continues, seizure activity results (Ward, 1975).

Current emphasis in epilepsy research regarding etiology is in two directions. One is to elucidate the role of the neurotransmitters in more detail, and the second is to use the Golgi technique in electron microscopy to evaluate neuronal ultrastructure. Maynert, Marczynski, and Browning (1975) have reviewed the role of neurotransmitters in the epilepsies and indicate that the "expression of a seizure" involves abnormalities in synaptic transmission. The hope is to manipulate the quantity of transmitters, either by inhibition or enhancement, at synapses in order to stop seizures. O'Leary and Goldring (1976) indicate that dendritic abnormalities have been identified in electron microscopic studies of epileptogenic cortex consisting of (1) a loss of spines that adhere to dendrites, (2) a "string-of-beads" appearance on the dendritic shaft, (3) the presence of bulbous outgrowths on the dendrites, and (4) a windblown look to the dendritic arbors (p. 173). Some of these have also been noted in the electron microscopic examination of neurons of mentally deficient persons (Purpura, 1974; Huttenlocher, 1974). Certainly both mental deficiency and epilepsy can occur in the same individual. In fact, Boshes and Gibbs (1972) have stated that mental deficiency occurs with a 3 to 4 times higher incidence in the epileptic population. Conversely, EEG abnormalities are seen twice as often among the severely retarded (IQ <60) as among those with lesser retardation (Boshes and Gibbs, 1972). And as the severity of retardation increases so does the likelihood of seizures (Corbett et al., 1975). Perhaps, then, it should not come as a surprise that the electron microscopic findings in Golgi preparation of dendrites from the brains of patients with mental deficiency and seizure disorders share some common features. Further investigation should increase our understanding not only of each condition separately but also of the relationship between the two.

TYPES OF EPILEPSY

Before proceeding to a discussion of selected types of seizure disorders, we will present with some modification, the international classification of epilepsy introduced by Gastaut (1970) and Merlis (1970) and the relative frequency of each type of seizure disorder based on a study of 6,000 private patients (Gastaut et al., 1975).

TABLE 5.1 International classification of epilepsy

CLASSIFIABLE (76.5%)			
I. Partial seizures	62.3%		
A. With elementary symptomatology		10.0%	
1. Motor symptoms (Jacksonian)			
2. Sensory or somatosensory symptoms			
3. Autonomic symptoms			
4. Compound forms			
B. With complex symptomotology (temporal lobe)		39.7%	
1. Impaired consciousness only			
2. Cognitive symptoms			
3. Affective symptoms			
4. Psychosensory symptoms			
5. Psychomotor symptoms (automatisms)			
6. Compound forms			
C. Secondarily generalized		12.6%	
II. Generalized seizures	37.7%		
A. Primarily generalized epilepsy		28.4%	
1. Absences (petit mal)			9.9%
a. simple			
b. complex			
2. Bilateral massive epileptic myoclonia			4.1%
3. Clonic seizures			3.2%
4. Tonic-Clonic (grand mal)			11.3%
B. Secondarily generalized epilepsy		9.3%	
1. Lennox-Gastaut			5.1%
2. Infantile spasms			1.3%
3. Other			2.8%
NONCLASSIFIABLE (23.5%)			

In analyzing further the data on their 6,000 cases by age distribution, Gastaut et al. (1975) found that partial epilepsy was more common than generalized in those older than 15 years (78% compared with 22%) and that generalized was more common than partial in those younger than 15 years (55% compared with 45%).

There are two transient forms of seizure disorder which are not included in the classification system but which we will discuss first because of their relevance to the later development of other seizure types. These are neonatal seizures and febrile seizures. We will then proceed to discuss selected types of generalized seizures (grand mal, petit mal, Lennox-Gastaut, and infantile spasms) and partial seizures (focal sensory or motor, psychomotor or temporal lobe, and hypothalmic, autonomic, or diencephalic). Throughout the discussion, the reader should remember that nature does not always respect our systems of classification and not only do mixed types of seizures occur but also seizure types may change in the same person over his or her lifetime. The discussions of each seizure type will include a description, typical EEG findings, manifestations (physical, neuromuscular, cognitive, behavioral, speech and language, and learning), etiology, and prognoses, all insofar as it is possible to be specific about them.

TRANSIENT FORMS OF EPILEPSY
NEONATAL SEIZURES

Because of immaturity of the central nervous system, seizure activity in the newborn is not "well organized" and is often difficult to recognize. There is no *one* seizure type; rather newborn seizures may manifest themselves as "subtle, multifocal clonic, focal clonic, tonic, and myoclonic" types (Volpe, 1973, p.413). The use of the EEG has become increasingly important as an adjunctive tool in the recognition of seizure activity in this early period of life, in spite of the difficulties encountered in determining EEG normality as a function of gestational age and the technical problems encountered in getting an EEG done on a critically ill newborn attached to life support systems. Engel (1975) has written an excellent monograph on the subject of the EEG in the neonatal period. Lombroso (1974) has used the EEG pattern exhibited in the newborn period as an adjunct in the formulation of long term prognosis.

The etiology of neonatal seizures may be related to prenatal factors such as developmental anomalies of the brain and congenital central nervous system infections (TORCH), and/or perinatal factors such as asphyxia, intracranial hemorrhage, metabolic derangements (hypoglycemia, pyridoxine deficiency, hypomagnesemia, or hypocalcemia), and bacterial infection (meningitis) in the central nervous system. Volpe (1973) indicates that "perinatal complications" (anoxic encephalopathy, cerebral contusion, or intracranial hemorrhage) account for the greatest percentage of cases (50% in preterm infants and 36% of 394 cases in a composite series). Metabolic derangement constitutes the next most frequent cause of neonatal seizures followed by central nervous system infection (bacterial meningitis in two-thirds and TORCH in one-third) and developmental anomalies. Withdrawal symptoms (from maternal narcotics or phenobarbital or alcohol ingestion) can also result in neonatal seizures. Treatment consists of prompt appropriate therapy to stop the seizures (Lombroso, 1974).

The prognosis for infants with neonatal seizures depends on the etiology, the time of onset of seizures, seizure type, and gestational age (Lombroso, 1974). Thus, those infants with hypocalcemia of late onset (3 to 7 days of age) have an 80% to 100% chance of being normal. Those with subarachnoid hemorrhage have up to a 90% chance of normality, and those with hypoglycemia or early onset hypocalcemia have a 50% chance of normal development; furthermore, those with central nervous system infection have a 30% chance, and those with perinatal asphyxia have a 10% to 20% chance. Infants with neonatal seizures secondary to either an intraventricular hemorrhage or to a developmental anomaly have "virtually no chance" of normality (Volpe, 1973). Recent use of computerized tomography (C-T scan) in the diagnosis of intracranial hemorrhage in newborns will improve our ability to correlate the extent of intraventricular hemorrhage with subsequent developmental status (Krishnamoorthy et al., 1977). Overall, 51% of newborns with convulsions are normal at followup (Engel, 1975). In following 137 patients with neonatal seizures for an average time of 4.8 years, Lombroso (1974) found that 20% of term babies died within infancy or early childhood, 30% had relatively severe neurologic deficit, and 50% were normal. Those with neurologic deficit tended to have multiple handicaps, including seizures, retardation, and cerebral palsy.

A possible reason for the poor prognosis in neonatal seizures may be related to the metabolic changes occurring in the brain cells during the seizure. Wasterlain and Plum (1974) have found that the metabolic rate of the brain increases at least 2.5 times during an acute seizure resulting in a fall in the concentration of energy rich compounds such as ATP, and an increase in lactate, resulting in metabolic acidosis. In rat studies, these changes have been found to interfere with protein synthesis and to result in a smaller number of brain cells and in impairment of brain development and behavior, in an age-dependent fashion.

FEBRILE SEIZURES

A febrile seizure is a brief (<5 min) generalized seizure in a previously normal child under five years of age, which occurs with fever, the source of which lies outside the central nervous system. The EEG is usually normal in simple febrile seizures. This is the most common seizure disorder, occurring in approximately 3% of children under 5 years of age (Boshes and Gibbs, 1972; Lennox-Buchthal, 1974) and accounting for half of all seizures in young children (Ouellette, 1974). In the Collaborative Perinatal Study, the prevalence rate was 3.5% for white children and 4.2% for black (Nelson and Ellenberg, 1978). The highest incidence occurs in the second year of life (van den Berg, 1972). Of the 1706 children with febrile seizures who were followed for 7 years as part of the Collaborative Study, 65% had no subsequent seizure. Thirty-two percent had at least one more febrile seizure; 1% had at least one afebrile convulsion, but were not considered to have epilepsy (recurrent afebrile seizures), and 2% developed epilepsy (Nelson and Ellenberg, 1976).

Although almost 50% of febrile seizures are of the brief, generalized variety, 14% may be prolonged (>30 min) and/or focal (Frantzen, Lennox-Buchthal, and Nygaard, 1968). For this reason, Livingston (1972) has separated out the categories of "simple febrile seizures" which by definition occur in normal children, and "seizures with fever" in which the seizures are focal and/or prolonged and thus place the child at risk for the development of recurrent afebrile seizures or epilepsy.

Much effort has been expended in learning about the etiology of febrile seizures, delineating the factors which are important in the subsequent development of epilepsy, and determining appropriate management.

The etiology of simple febrile seizures is not definitely known, but there is a strong familial tendency that is related to a low convulsive threshold for increased body temperature. In the recently reported study by Wolf et al. (1977), 42% of the group of 355 children with febrile convulsions had a relative with a history of febrile seizures, and 16% had a relative with afebrile seizures. The mode of inheritance is not clear, but Tsuboi (1976) has suggested a polygenic mode, whereas Ounsted (1971) and Frantzen et al. (1970) have concluded that inheritance is by a single autosomal dominant gene with incomplete penetrance. Those children who go on to have recurrent febrile and/or afebrile seizures seem to have other factors operative. For example, Wolf et al. (1977) have found that young age at the time of the initial febrile seizure, abnormal pregnancy, preterm birth, prolonged or focal seizures, and an abnormal neurologic examination correlate significantly with recurrence. Several studies are in agreement that the younger the child at the time of the first seizure, the greater the risk of recurrence (Frantzen et al. 1968; Lennox-Buchtal, 1974; Wolf et al., 1977). This means that when the child is under 13 months of age at the time of the initial episode, the chance of having a recurrent febrile seizure is 2:1; whereas when the child is older than 2 years 8 months, the chance of recurrence is 1:5 (Frantzen et al., 1968).

Nelson and Ellenberg (1978) have found the major predictors of epilepsy after febrile seizures to be (1) abnormal or suspect neurologic or developmental status before any seizure; (2) "complex" (multiple, focal, or prolonged) initial febrile seizure; and (3) family history of epilepsy. Those youngsters who possessed two or more of the above risk factors showed a "20-fold increase" in the risk of developing epilepsy. The question then arises about the relationship between recurrent febrile seizures and the subsequent development of epilepsy.

In the study by Wolf et al. (1977), of 355 children with febrile seizures, 4.4% of those who received either intermittent or no anticonvulsant medication had "severe recurrent febrile seizures." Previously, Nelson and Ellenberg (1976) have indicated that the risk of later epilepsy was approximately the same whether the complex febrile seizure occurred *initially* (41 per 1,000) or *subsequently* (45 per 1,000) (p. 1032). One can conceptualize the relative risks then, in a cascade fashion. Of all children with febrile seizures, those at risk for recurrent febrile seizures are the very young. Of those with recurrent seizures, 4.4% may have a complex or severe febrile seizure. The chance of developing epilepsy after a complex seizure is relatively the same whether the complex seizure occurred initially or subsequently. The risk of developing epilepsy in the course of febrile seizures is increased 20-fold when 2 or more of the following risk factors are present: (1) preexisting neurologic abnormality; (2) complex febrile seizure; and (3) positive family history.

The cognitive-intellectual functioning of children with febrile seizures has been reported by various investigators. Gates (1972) reported that the median full scale IQ of 78 seven-year-olds with a history of febrile seizures was 96.1 with a Performance IQ of 107.2 and a Verbal IQ of 90.3 on the Wechsler Intelligence Scale for Children (WISC). Ouellette (1974) has quoted Nelson's report on data from the Collaborative Perinatal Project in which all children in the group of 47,222 who developed a febrile seizure in the first year of life were considered. Those with a simple febrile seizure had a normal IQ at 4 years of age; those with several febrile seizures were significantly lower than those of their siblings. The children with the worst prognosis were those who had more than one febrile seizure on the first day of illness. "These children were reported to have a 70% chance of subsequent mental retardation" (p. 476). The most recent report from Nelson and Ellenberg (1978), however, indicates that febrile seizures are *not* associated with an increased risk of intellectual impairment *except* in those children who develop afebrile seizures (epilepsy) and those children with abnormal developmental status prior to the onset of the febrile seizures.

The neuromotor manifestations depend to some extent on the intactness of the central nervous system before the febrile seizure. On the other hand, acute infantile hemiplegia can occur after a prolonged febrile seizure. (see Chapter 4 on cerebral palsy). Gates (1972) has reported "abnormal neurologic findings" in 3.7% of 78 seven-year-olds with a history of febrile convulsions. It is unclear, however, whether the findings were the result of seizure activity, or whether the "seizure with fever" was another symptom of an abnormal nervous system.

The long-term medical treatment of patients with febrile convulsions has been controversial over the years. Some have advocated the use of anticonvulsants at the start of the fever; and still others have advocated control of fever only. Nelson and Ellenberg (1978) suggest that anticonvulsant therapy should be considered for those youngsters with febrile seizures who possess two or more risk factors: (1) preexisting neurologic abnormality; (2) complicated febrile seizure; and (3) family history of epilepsy.

It seems as though anticonvulsant medication should also be considered for those who are at risk for recurrence of febrile seizures by the criteria identified by Wolf et al. (1977, p. 381). Since the children with febrile seizures who develop epilepsy are those who are more likely to evidence intellectual impairment, their cognitive-intellectual status should be followed in order to provide the most appropriate educational setting.

PRIMARILY GENERALIZED EPILEPSY
GRAND MAL

A grand mal seizure is a generalized one occurring without warning and characterized by loss of consciousness, by tonic (stiffening) and clonic (jerking) components, and by confusion and drowsiness in the postictal phase. Incontinence is not uncommon. The interseizure EEG may either show a variety of abnormalities or be normal. According to Livingston (1972), the EEG is normal in as many as 32% of patients.

The etiology of grand mal seizures is usually unknown, though they can be a result of any brain injury. In childhood, perinatal injury is the most common cause, and central nervous system infection is the second most common (Boshes and Gibbs, 1972). In the prenatal period, there are genetic and environmental risk factors that would predispose the affected person to the occurrence of grand mal seizures. The genetic factors include many of the inborn errors of metabolism (lipidoses, aminoacidopathies, Wilson's disease), some chromosomal problems (13–15 trisomy, deletion of the short arm of chromosome 4), developmental anomalies of the central nervous system—both of the cerebral circulation and of the brain substance—and certain dominantly inherited malformation syndromes such as tuberous sclerosis, neurofibromatosis, and the Sturge-Weber syndrome (Chalhub, 1976). The environmental factors include trauma to the brain, infection (TORCH), and hypoxia. In the perinatal period, the metabolic risk factors include hypocalcemia and hypoglycemia, and the environmental factors include brain trauma, asphyxia–hypoxia, and bacterial central nervous system infection. The postnatal period presents many environmental risk factors, including (1) trauma; (2) central nervous system infection (encephalitis and meningitis); (3) increased intracranial pressure as might occur in hypertensive encephalopathy, brain tumor, and Reye's syndrome (DeVivo, Keating, and Haymond, 1976); (4) toxic factors such as lead encephalopathy; and (5) metabolic factors such as hypoglycemia or electrolyte imbalance. According to Rodin (1968), the incidence of epilepsy after simple closed head injuries is 12%, and in penetrating head injuries it is 37%, with centroparietal wounds being most epileptogenic, having a maximum incidence of 65%. There is some tendency for the epileptic phenomena to change as time passes so that after five years 50% of those affected will stop having attacks, or will have only focal seizures (Walker, 1972). Although brain tumor is an unusual etiology for seizures in children, 4% of adults with epilepsy who were studied by Lennox had brain tumor (Boshes and Gibbs, 1972). A recent report regarding C-T scan results in 28 patients with grand mal epilepsy revealed an abnormality in only 3.5% (Gastaut and Gastaut, 1977).

Cognitive-intellectual functioning in indviduals with grand mal seizures is variable depending on the age of onset of seizures, control of seizures, the presence of other seizure types, and the amount of medication required. Whitehouse (1971) has reported on the cognitive-intellectual functioning of 42 patients who had grand mal seizures and were under 15 years of age. The mean IQ was 79.1 with a range from 45 to 117. Keith (1963) presented information about cognitive functioning in 125 children who ranged in age from 2 months to 14 years (with a mean age of 6 years 2 months) and had grand mal seizures. The instruments used to evaluate the children were variable, but the conclusion reached was that 40% were retarded.

Treatment consists of appropriate intervention depending upon the etiology of the seizures, proper anticonvulsant medication (Berman, 1976; Dodson, et al., 1976; Livingston, 1972; Millichap, 1972), and proper attention to educational and psychological needs. The ready availability of blood tests to measure anticonvulsant levels has made monitoring easier and treatment more precise in recent years.

PETIT MAL (TYPICAL ABSENCE OR CENTRENCEPHALIC EPILEPSY)

Petit mal, or typical absence, is a seizure disorder characterized by a momentary lapse of consciousness that starts and ends abruptly, usually lasting from 5 to 15 seconds, but lasting on occasion as long as 45 seconds, during which time the patient is "psychologically absent." Penry, Porter, and Dreifuss (1975) recorded on video tape 374 absence seizures in 48 patients and categorized what was seen clinically into simple and complex types of absence. Simple absence (suspended animation) constituted only 9.4% of the seizures. Complex absence included mild clonic movements such as eye blinking (45.5%), changes in postural tone such as spoon dropping (27%), and automatisms such as fumbling with clothing (63.1%). The occurrence of automatisms was related to the duration of the seizure, so that for seizures lasting more than 18 seconds, the probability of an automatism occurring was 95%. The authors differentiated these seizures clinically from psychomotor seizures (complex partial) on the basis of the following criteria: (1) there is no aura in absence; (2) the seizures are relatively brief (the majority were 10 seconds or less in duration); and (3) there is no postictal state. The EEG in petit mal classically shows a generalized 3/second regular spike and slow wave, though in the study by Penry et al. (1975) 39 seizures showed a 2–4/second "irregular spike and wave," 9 showed a 4/second "regular spike-wave," and 3 showed a 3/second "high voltage slowing without spikes" (p. 436). The rest showed classic EEG findings. Interestingly, there was nothing clinically that distinguished one

EEG variation from any of the others. Of the 374 seizures, 109 occurred spontaneously, 197 were induced by hyperventilation, and 68 were induced by photic stimulation.

The etiology of petit mal is not known. Livingston (1972) has found an incidence of 2.3% in their total clinic population with usual age of onset at 4 to 8 years. There is a high genetic predisposition and the mode of transmission is postulated to be autosomal dominant with age-dependent penetrance (Bray, 1972; Metrakos and Metrakos, 1974). There is, then, a 12% chance that offspring or siblings will have one or more convulsions, and an 8% chance that they will have epilepsy of the spike-wave type. Gastaut and Gastaut (1977) reported that 7% of 15 patients with simple absence and 17% of 6 patients with complex absence had an abnormal C-T scan.

The cognitive-intellectual manifestations are variable (apparently depending on patient population), but Livingston (1972) has emphasized the low incidence of brain damage and retardation (5.1%). However, he also mentions that those patients who have repeated episodes of petit-mal status are at risk for becoming intellectually impaired, and he indicated that an additional 6.3% of patients with petit mal were retarded at the termination of their study of 117 patients (p.58). Penry et al. (1975) reported the mean IQ on the Wechsler Intelligence Scale for Children (WISC) for the 48 patients who took part in the videotape study was 89 with a range of 44–131. Dreifuss (1972) has indicated that those patients in whom the seizures started after 5 years of age and who were easy to control had normal intellect. However, 32% of their entire study group (N-172) had an IQ of < 80. Lugaresi et al. (1974) reported 30% of their population of 213 patients with typical absence demonstrated an IQ of < 80. School performance is poor in those children with frequent "absence" because they miss much of what is going on in the classroom.

Treatment consists of appropriate anticonvulsant medications (Berman, 1976; Livingston, 1972; Masland, 1976) and attention to proper educational placement. Approximately 50% of patients with absence go into remission after adolescence (Penry, 1972); Livingston (1972) indicates that petit mal seldom continues into adult life. However, the later the onset of petit mal, the more likely it is that the patient will develop other seizure types, especially grand mal. Lugaresi et al. (1974) also stress the close relationships between petit mal (typical absence) and Lennox-Gastaut (atypical absence), saying "there is no hard and fast division" between the two (p.153).

SECONDARILY GENERALIZED EPILEPSY
LENNOX-GASTAUT (ATYPICAL ABSENCE, PETIT MAL VARIANT, OR MYOCLONIC EPILEPSY OF OLDER CHILDREN)

This form of seizure disorder is characterized by an impairment of consciousness which is usually briefer (<5 sec), less marked, and not so abrupt in onset or termination as typical absence. Gastaut et al. (1974) have identified two clinical types: in one form there is increased tone—particularly of eye and facial muscles; in the other there is myoclonus (sudden local twitching and jerking of muscles, most commonly involving the arms). Neither form is precipitated by hyperventilation. Akinetic or "drop attacks" may also occur in this form of seizure disorder. The median age of onset in 84 patients mentioned by Swaiman (1975) was 2 years 4 months. The EEG in the tonic form may show flattening, low-voltage, fast activity, and/or a rhythmic discharge of sharp waves at 10/sec. The myoclonic form is associated with a generalized bilateral, but asymmetrical, pattern of sharp and slow wave discharges of 1 to 2/sec. occurring in bursts of 5-second to 15-second duration (Gastaut et al., 1974).

The etiology of Lennox-Gastaut, or petit mal variant, is not known, but there is a low genetic factor and the presence of an "organic substrate"; it is associated with variants of generalized tonic, myoclonic, or akinetic seizures, poor prognosis, and inadequate response to anticonvulsant medication (Gastaut et al., 1974). A history of traumatic or hypoxic birth or some encephalopathy of infancy is found more frequently than in petit mal (Boshes and Gibbs, 1972). Gastaut and Gastaut (1977) have reported that 52% of 94 patients had an abnormal C-T Scan and 88% of these showed brain atrophy or malformation.

The cognitive-intellectual functioning of affected individuals is frequently impaired (IQ <80 in 91%; Lugaresi et al., 1974). Lennox-Gastaut is one of the types of seizure disorder that is more difficult to control and one that occasionally responds to the ketogenic diet (Dodson et al., 1976; Livingston, 1972). Children so affected often need special educational help. The prognosis is poor, both in terms of seizure control and in terms of cognitive functioning (Viani et al., 1977).

INFANTILE SPASMS (WEST'S SYNDROME OR MYOCLONIC SEIZURES OF INFANCY)

Infantile spasms or salaam seizures constitute a generalized seizure disorder occurring in the first year of life and characterized by lightning-fast quivering of the entire body, rolling of the eyes, sudden flexion of the head and/or upward flinging of the arms, usually occurring in bursts so that a hundred or more seizures may occur per day. The EEG shows the pattern of hypsarrhythmia (exceedingly abnormal).

The etiology of infantile spasms has been associated with cerebral injury such as perinatal complications (hypoxia, trauma), encephalopathy after pertussis immunization, metabolic problems such as phenylketonuria and hypoglycemia (Boshes and Gibbs, 1972), and congenital defects of cerebral development such as might occur in tuberous sclerosis. In approximately one-third of the patients, the etiology is unknown (Livingston, 1972).

The seizures are particularly difficult to control and intellectual deficits are common. In estimating the intelligence of 671 children at one year of age, Livingston (1972) found mental retardation in 96%, with most in the moderate-severe range. Corbett, Harris, and Robinson (1975) have reviewed the findings of various investigators and found that 10% to 25% of the children so affected die before their third birthday, and of the remainder, most are severely retarded. However, approximately 16% are normal and 10% are in the mild range of retardation. Those who survive and are retarded often display severe communication problems and stereotyped and unusual behaviors resembling children with early infantile autism (Corbett et al., 1975). The infantile spasms subside by the third or fourth year, but other seizure types may well continue (Boshes and Gibbs, 1972). The commonest seizure type seen is generalized tonic-clonic (Jeavons, Bower, and Dimitrakoudi, 1973). In 6% of patients, minor motor seizures (akinetic, myoclonic, and atypical petit mal) follow infantile spasms (Menkes, 1976).

The question has been asked, but not definitively answered, whether the repeated seizures result in the retardation or whether both the seizures and retardation are the result of underlying brain pathology. Probably it is not an either-or situation, but rather it is likely that both situations are possible. The difficulty in making a definitive statement arises from the fact that infantile spasms are notoriously difficult to control. Nevertheless, it is known that those patients who comprise a subgroup with known cerebral pathology, that is, those who have been neurologically abnormal from the beginning (50% to 60%) have a much worse prognosis—virtually no chance for either survival or for intellectual normality (Jeavons et al., 1973). In this subgroup, then, the infantile spasms and retardation are probably the result of the known brain pathology. Those patients who comprise a subgroup with no known etiology (cryptogenic) for the infantile spasms have a much better prognosis (37% chance of complete recovery) (Jeavons et al., 1973). One might infer that there is less pathology or that seizures are easier to control in this group, but this is not definitely known. Nevertheless, Rodin (1968) has found that those children in whom seizures can be controlled with steroids or ACTH during the first week after onset have a much better intellectual prognosis. Corbett et al. (1975) reviewed the literature regarding the effect of steroids on infantile spasms and concluded there was a "slightly better" prognosis for the steroid treated cases who were of cryptogenic etiology. Jeavons et al. (1973) found no difference between treated and nontreated groups. Livingston (1975) has probably had the largest experience and has found the most efficacious form of therapy to be the ketogenic diet. It would be extremely interesting and important to have a current assessment of how his patients have done intellectually, educationally, and behaviorally. At the present time, we conclude that the prognosis for life, seizure control, and intellectual normality is guarded for children with infantile spasms, although it is better for those in whom the etiology is cryptogenic. It is likely that known brain pathology is responsible for both the seizures and the retardation in some patients. In others, it is possible that repeated, uncontrolled seizures result in intellectual retardation.

PARTIAL SEIZURES WITH ELEMENTARY SYMPTOMATOLOGY
FOCAL SENSORY OR MOTOR SEIZURES

A focal seizure is a localized seizure disorder lasting a few minutes, characterized by motor or sensory phenomena in a hand, arm, foot, leg, and/or face, and possibly presenting as a Jacksonian march (i.e., as progressing sequentially from one area to another on the same side of the body) in which there may be no change in the level of consciousness. The EEG often shows isolated single or multiple spike discharges followed by flattening or slowing in the region of origin.

Focal seizures may occur at any age, though it is harder to elicit a history of focal sensory seizure in a young child. The most frequent age of occurrence is between 5 and 15 years (Bray, 1972). In the infant and young child, the occurrence of a focal seizure is not so indicative of localized cerebral pathology as it is with increasing age. Likewise, in the young child, an EEG focus may not represent an anatomical lesion. The location of a discharging focus is often age dependent in focal seizures. Thus, in infancy and in children with eye disorders, a focus may be recorded from the occipital area. A midtemporal lobe focus resulting in speech disturbance, fear, and some motor component is more common in school-age children, and an anterior temporal lobe focus is more commonly seen in adults (Boshes and Gibbs, 1972). There can also be a shifting of focus so that 50% of those who had an occipital lobe focus lose it by 9 years of age, and in those who do not lose it, it tends to become midtemporal and then anteriortemporal over time, and may even become thalamic or hypothalamic, i.e., demonstrate, the 14 and 6 pattern on EEG. Furthermore, 70% of children who had a midtemporal focus lose it by 15 years of age (Boshes and Gibbs, 1972).

Nevertheless, in children with acute hemiplegia of infancy and childhood, there is likely to be localization of pathology, and focal seizures may ensue. Gold and Carter (1976) indicate that 50% of children with hemiplegia will develop recurring seizures and that the likelihood is increased in children with the onset of hemiplegia before 2 years of age. It will be remembered that J. Hughlings Jackson associated the occurrence of focal seizures with pathology in the distribution of the middle cerebral artery of the opposite hemisphere. Therefore, anything that might interfere with cerebral circulation (arteriovenous malformation, infection, stroke, tumor, trauma) may result in focal seizures. Furthermore trauma that results in a subdural hematoma or other brain injury may result in focal seizures. Such seizures comprise 25% of all posttraumatic epilepsy (Walker, 1972). Bray (1972) has expressed the view that a tendency to have focal seizures, like petit mal, may be transmitted as an autosomal dominant disorder with age-dependent penetrance. A multifactorial etiology, one that is genetic and environmental, is probable in most. As Rodin (1968) and Rodin et al. (1972b) have pointed out, if the etiology is not multifactorial, why do some with the same trauma *not* develop epilepsy while others do.

The cognitive-intellectual manifestations are variable, depending on the age of onset, location, and etiology. Whitehouse (1971) has reported that the mean IQ in 12 patients under 15 years of age was 91.6 with a range of 70 to 117.

Treatment consists of control of seizures through the use of either anticonvulsant medication or, in selected cases, surgery (Dodson et al., 1976, part II; Masland, 1976).

The prognosis in individuals with focal seizures is dependent upon the etiology and therefore upon associated pathology (tumor, trauma, acute hemiplegia, etc.). When the focus is in the frontal lobes, the seizures are particularly hard to control (Gordon, 1974). By and large, those in whom the etiology is unknown have a better prognosis. Rasmussen (1974) reported excellent results in the surgical treatment of more than 1,000 patients with focal seizures who were unresponsive to anticonvulsant therapy. After a median followup period of 8 years, 43% were seizure free, and 23% were markedly improved. The remainder have had a variable reduction in seizure frequency. Interestingly, the effectiveness of surgical treatment was correlated with the completeness of removal of the focus rather than with the location of the focus or its etiology (Rasmussen, 1975).

PARTIAL SEIZURES WITH
COMPLEX SYMPTOMATOLOGY
PSYCHOMOTOR OR TEMPORAL LOBE SEIZURES

This type of seizure disorder is heralded by an aura or warning, and characterized by one or more of the following mental and motor symptoms (automatisms): distortion of perception of self or time, déjà vu, depersonalization, visual hallucinations, forced thinking, staring, lipsmacking, chewing, swallowing, mumbling, fumbling with hands or clothes, undressing, and searching. It may terminate in a grand mal seizure (Boshes and Gibbs, 1972). The automatisms tend to be stereotyped in the same patient, and consciousness and memory are impaired to variable degrees. In children, the seizures may be staring spells, sudden terror attacks, or bouts of abdominal pain. Four types of aura have been enumerated by Masland (1976): (1) autonomic (palpitation, sweating, pallor, chills); (2) visceral (epigastric discomfort); (3) somatosensory (numbness, choking sensation, bad taste, or bad smell; and (4) psychic (déjà vu, sense of unreality, flashing lights).

Temporal lobe seizures constitute the most common variety of focal epilepsy in adults. The usual age of onset is in late childhood or in early adolescence, although they may occur at any age. Up to 70% of patients have associated grand mal seizures. The EEG typically shows "discharges from the anteriortemporal areas, consisting mainly of spikes, but also of slow waves" (Livingston, 1972, p. 64), although the EEG may demonstrate more diffuse abnormality or be normal.

The etiology is probably multifactorial. There is a significant increase in positive family history. There is also a strong relationship to the pathologic finding of mesial temporal sclerosis (Ammon's horn), which is thought to be the result of hypoxia and cerebral edema after prolonged febrile seizures. Corsellis (1974) has discussed the neuropathologic changes, which interestingly were first described by Bouchet and Cazauvielh in 1825 (Temkin, 1971). Falconer (1973) found mesial temporal sclerosis in one-half of the 250 patients who underwent temporal lobectomy after they were found to have a temporal lobe focus on EEG and had failed to respond to anticonvulsant medication. Hamartomas clustered around the amygdala accounted for another one-fifth to one-fourth of the pathology demonstrated at surgery; miscellaneous lesions such as scars were found in one-tenth; and no specific lesion was found in the remainder. In a separate report on the outcome of surgery in 40 children (under 15 years of age), Davidson and Falconer (1975) found 60% to have mesial temporal sclerosis. Nineteen of these 22 patients had a clear-cut history of one or more severe febrile convulsions lasting more than one-half hour or occurring in a series.

The manifestations of temporal lobe epilepsy are diverse as the opening paragraph of this section indicates. The affective-personality-behavioral manifestations have been well described by Ounsted (1971).

> Psychiatrists have two special interests in the disorder. All the symptoms in the major psychoses may occur in brief as part of the ictal experience. Delusions, hallucinations, depersonalization, and derealization, forced thinking, autochthonous dread, transcendental ecstasy, depression, paroxysmal anxiety, affectless laughter, disorientation, confusion, the utterance of jumbled words, thought blocking and amnesia; all these symptoms can occur in both the temporal ictus, and in a more protracted form in the classic psychiatric disorders. Five chronic major abnormalities of behavior associate strongly with the syndrome: the hyperkinetic syndrome of early childhood, outbursts of cataclysmic rage on slight provocation, gross mental defect, and in later life both depressions and a schizophrenic-like syndrome emerge (p.379).

Crandall (1975) reported that only 23% of 53 patients who underwent temporal lobectomy were psychiatrically normal. Falconer (1973) has postulated the existence of a relationship between temporal lobe epilepsy, schizophrenia, and the finding of hamartomas (fibrous, nonmalignant tumor) at surgery. There has been a great deal of interest both historically and currently in the relationship between aggression, antisocial acts, delinquency, and criminality on the one hand and temporal lobe seizures on the other. Lewis and Balla (1976) have described a periodic antisocial symptomatology associated with a distortion of memory or episodes of altered consciousness or attention in 6% of court-referred delinquents and attributed these findings to temporal lobe epilepsy. Davidson and Falconer (1975) and Falconer (1973) have written of the close association between aggression and temporal lobe seizures, and Crandall (1975) has noted that the aggression is aggravated by the occurrence of frequent seizures. Livingston (1972) has differentiated between those who have temporal lobe epilepsy and those who have a behavioral disorder and an abnormal EEG. The behavioral disorders consisted of temper tantrums, rage, screaming spells, somnambulism, fugues, or attacks of amnesia in patients in whom the EEG, though not normal, did not show the abnormalities of discharge from the anteriortemporal areas. The decision is not always clear-cut regarding which behavioral disturbances and EEG findings constitute manifestations of temporal lobe epilepsy (Livingston, 1972, p.68). What is clear is that behavioral aberrations are common in psychomotor epilepsy.

The cognitive-intellectual manifestations depend somewhat on etiology. In Ounsted's series of 100 patients (1971), the mean IQ in 33 in whom the etiology was unknown was 105.4 as compared with a mean IQ of 80 in those (N = 32) with a history of prolonged febrile convulsions and a mean IQ of 82.1 in those (N = 35) with a known brain insult. Whitehouse (1972) reported a mean IQ of 99 with a range of 81 to 123 in three patients with temporal lobe seizures only. When other seizure types were also present, the mean IQ was lower. Whitehouse (1971) has indicated that the incidence of learning disabilities is high in psychomotor epilepsy.

Therapy has traditionally consisted of anticonvulsant and antipsychotic medication, as well as psychotherapeutic intervention (Masland, 1976). In recent years, surgery has been shown to be extremely helpful in selected cases. Murray Falconer has been a pioneer in the technique of temporal lobectomy. In one series of 100 patients selected because of unilateral temporal lobe seizures that were unresponsive to medication, 47 of the patients were considered to be psychopathic, 16 to be psychotic, 27 to be aggressive, and only 13 to be "mentally normal." After surgery, one-half of the 47 patients with mesial temporal sclerosis became free of all seizures, and 32 patients were considered psychiatrically normal. It is interesting that two of the three patients with schizophrenia had hamartomas, and after surgery their epilepsy was benefited, but the schizophrenia persisted (Falconer, 1973). In Crandall's very carefully studied group of 53 patients (1975), 38 underwent anterior temporal lobectomy. Sixty percent were relieved of "functional incapacity." The best rehabilitative results were achieved in those with no preoperative psychopathology. The next best results were achieved in the younger patients (15- to 25-year-olds) in whom seizure relief was associated with psychiatric improvement as well. In the older patients (25- to 45-year-olds), seizure relief was not associated with psychiatric improvement. Cognitive functioning improved as the seizures were relieved. In a separate study, Milner (1975) has compared the preoperative, the early postoperative, and the late postoperative (>5 years) cognitive functioning in 19 patients with left temporal lobectomy and in 13 patients with right temporal lobectomy as measured by the Wechsler-Bellevue Intelligence Scale. She found late postoperative improvement of 5 points in the former and 9 points in the latter.

Vaernet (1974) has used a different surgical technique—amygdalatomy (placing a discrete lesion in the amygdala)—to treat the "aggressive, dysphoric attitude" of patients with temporal lobe epilepsy who show a low threshold for provocation and a defect in inhibitory mechanisms. After surgery, the positive effects were a subduing of fear, aggression, and emotional tension; some verbal improvement; no intellectual impairment; and improved performance in storing and recall of material learned. The less positive effects were a decrease in selective attention, decreased problem-solving ability, and in those with bilateral surgery, a decreased level of spontaneity and decreased creativity.

The results achieved through surgery—particularly anteriortemporal lobectomy—are encouraging for patients with a unilateral focus when the seizures are unresponsive to medication. Led by Taylor and Falconer's concern (1968) for measuring the outcome of surgery in terms of "reduction of incapacity" rather than just in terms of seizure control, the long-term followup studies that are now becoming available are providing us with essential information about the pre- and postoperative cognitive, psychosocial, and seizure control state of patients with temporal lobe epilepsy. Currently, it looks as though more than half the patients whose seizures and behavioral problems are unresponsive to medical management are significantly improved by surgical means. Furthermore, the younger patients are benefited more than the older, though the lower age limit is still in question. Most of the studies mention 15 as the lower age of temporal lobectomy, but Davidson and Falconer (1975) have noted that 6 of the 40 children on whom they reported, were under the age of 11. We await with interest the further unraveling of the relationship of behavioral disorder, psychosis and epilepsy. In the meantime, we applaud the thorough and interdisciplinary way in which these neurosurgical patients have been evaluated, treated, and followed.

HYPOTHALAMIC EPILEPSY (DIENCEPHALIC OR AUTONOMIC EPILEPSY OR SEIZURE EQUIVALENT)

This type of seizure disorder is characterized by recurrent somatic complaints such as headaches, dizziness, nausea, vomiting, palpitations, abdominal pain, and sweating, but it also includes symptoms such as rage, involuntary crying and/or laughing, illusions, and emotional outbursts. In a way, it is a diagnosis of exclusion when other causes for the symptomatology have been ruled out and becomes more likely when there is a definite history of periodicity of attacks. The EEG findings are not specific (Livingston, 1972), but the patterns of 14 and 6 per second positive spikes, or 6/second spike and wave discharges, have been associated with autonomic epilepsy (Boshes and Gibbs, 1972). Livingston (1974) is not convinced, however, that that particular pattern is indeed a manifestation of epileptic disorder. The etiology has been related to head trauma in 20% of cases, but in most cases the etiology is unknown (Boshes and Gibbs, 1972). Whitehouse (1971) has reported that the mean IQ of six patients with diencephalic epilepsy was 100.1 with a range of 70 to 118. The symptom of rage associated with this form of seizure disorder has been discussed by Boshes and Gibbs (1972). "A person with diencephalic epilepsy can have an attack of rage that is accurately directed and appears to be purposeful. His furor may be triggered by someone or something; and it may last for several hours. It may or may not be followed by unconsciousness or sleep. . . . Epilepsy is a statistically insigificant cause of murder, but the fact remains that it can be a cause" (p. 44). Treatment consists of appropriate anticonvulsant medication (Livingston, 1972).

GENERAL CONSIDERATIONS: MANIFESTATIONS AND TREATMENT

Now that we have discussed individual seizure disorders, we will discuss some of the manifestations in a general way. The reason for this is that oftentimes seizure types may occur in combination, or one type may change to another type. Thus, it becomes necessary to speak somewhat broadly. Also, many reports provide followup information for patients with epilepsy in general rather than present data for each specific type. For these reasons, we will proceed to summarize the cognitive-intellectual manifestations, school performance, and affective-behavioral manifestations. Included in this section will be some comments about medical and social prognosis.

As indicated earlier in this chapter, the incidence of mental deficiency is higher in patients with epilepsy than in the general population. Whitehouse (1971) has reported that 9% of those with epilepsy have an IQ above 100, 34% have an IQ between 90 and 109, and 57% have an IQ of 89 or below. The percentages of controls who had IQs in the same range respectively, were 12%, 60%, and 28%. Rutter, Graham, and Yule (1970) reported a somewhat better outcome in children with "uncomplicated epilepsy." In their series, 2% had an IQ of 130, 29% were in the 116 to 130 range, 16% were in the 110 to 115 range, 36% were in the 86 to 100 range, 14% were in the 71 to 85 range, and 3% were in the 51 to 70 range. They found no significant verbal-performance discrepancy. Interestingly, Rodin (1968) has shown that patients with recurrent uncontrolled seizures have a tendency to show a decrease in IQ (primarily in performance) in spite of the fact that the scores remain in the normal range. Furthermore, Dodrill and Wilkus (1976) have shown a statistically significant lowering of full-scale IQ on the Wechsler Adult Intelligence Scale in uncontrolled epileptic adults who had generalized discharges present on EEG (89.42) compared with those in whom discharges were absent (103.81). Rodin (1968) and Rodin et al. (1972) have also shown that the earlier the onset of seizures, the lower the IQ, though it may still be in the normal range; when seizures start in the first three years of life, the verbal IQ is affected more than performance. It appears then that even those epileptic individuals within the normal range of intellectual functioning, might have experienced a shift downward in IQ from a previous "optimal" level. Rodin (1968) suggests that this "loss" could well be "reacted" to by them with depression and withdrawal. Furthermore, those with a significantly lower verbal IQ may demonstrate learning problems even if the full-scale IQ is within normal limits.

Gregoriades (1972) has found that 55% of children with epilepsy are educable in normal schools, 30% are in need of special education, and 15% are uneducable. Educational problems were found in both reading and math, and school performance was related to the control of seizures as well as to medication effects and behavior. Whitehouse (1972) has reported that over 50% of children with epilepsy have central nervous system dysfunction that precludes their being competitive in a regular curriculum. Rodin et al. (1972) found that 87% of 118 children with epilepsy were in regular classrooms, although 32% had been enrolled in special education at some previous time. Fifty-six percent were doing unsatisfactory work, and among the 118 children there were no honor students. Better educational results have been reported by Rutter et al. (1970), but even in their population, 18% of the epileptic children had significant reading difficulties as compared with only 6.8% of controls. In contrast, Stores and Hart (1976) have found no support for risk of learning problems in their patients with generalized epilepsy but did find that those children with focal spike discharges, particularly when emanating from the left hemisphere, were indeed at special risk for reading problems. It is hard to reconcile these discrepant findings but it seems that selection of patient population, adequacy of seizure control, length of followup, and medications must be responsible.

A concern, of course, is that in our desire to "normalize" the lives of children with epilepsy and to mainstream, we may well be shortchanging those children who have special educational needs. Rodin et al. (1972) have stated well the educational plight of the youngster with epilepsy. "He is likely to learn to accept and expect failure and when he has completed his tour of duty in school by age 16, he is totally unprepared to enter a highly competitive society requiring skills which he has not had the opportunity to acquire" (p. 157). The 25-year-followup study of Harrison and Taylor (1976) of children who had been hospitalized for at least one seizure indicates that 17.5% of 179 patients contacted regarded themselves (or were regarded as) completely or semiilliterate and that only 50% were self-supporting in the community. There was a statistically significant difference between those with epilepsy being overrepresented in the lower income groups and underrepresented in the higher income groups. Rodin et al. (1972) thought that poor education was probably the most powerful factor in keeping individuals with epilepsy in the lower socioeconomic strata. Although Rodin (1968) has emphasized that seizures do not preclude employment, he has related unemployment to lower intellect and/or organic mental changes, and to behavior and motivation. In 1966, the rate of unemployment of epileptics was 15% to 20% as compared with a rate of 7.4% for "disabled" and 3.7% for "normal" (Epilepsy Foundation of America, 1975). It seems appropriate now to turn our attention to the behavioral-personality manifestations seen in patients with epilepsy as they may well affect educational and employment efforts.

With seizure disorders as well as with other disorders involving some degree of "brain damage," manifestations in the area of behavior and personality development are frequent. One method of conceptualizing these is by the mnemonic "FAGS syndrome": fear, anger, guilt, and sadness. The FAGS syndrome, or portions of it, can be manifested by both the child and the family. The child is usually able to understand that there is something wrong with his head, but he may not know exactly what, how serious it is, how long it will last, or whether he will die (Voeller and Rothenberg, 1973). A most important issue is fear of loss of control with which the child is confronted, especially when his seizures are associated with loss of consciousness and incontinence. The fear is further exacerbated when there is no aura so that onset is sudden and unpredictable.

Another affective reaction is anger. The child and his family may be angry that the disorder afflicted him or their child. Furthermore, anger may arise in relation to some restrictions that may be placed on the child's behavior; these restrictions may be realistic or may constitute overprotection. Sometimes guilt feelings accompany anger, especially in parents but occasionally in the child. These are related to the parents' understanding of the causality of seizure disorders since they may blame themselves for what they perceive as their role in the etiology, such as difficulties during pregnancy or inadequate supervision of the child. Shame can affect both the child and family and is typically evident in the difficulties encountered in discussing the child's seizure disorder with family, friends, and professionals. These affective or emotional manifestations can influence behavior problems. Fear can lead at one extreme, to denial and difficulty in accepting the diagnosis; at the other extreme, it can lead to overprotecting and overgeneralizing incompetency. Denial may lead to parental refusal to cooperate in medication procedures, and overprotection may lead to needless restriction of activities and skill development. Overprotection can also be motivated by guilt feelings, and parental anger may be so great that it is easier to reject the child than to accept the child with convulsions (Voeller and Rothenberg, 1973).

A final consideration is that seizures may be psychogenic or triggered by an emotional state (Gordon, 1974). Also seizures and pseudoseizures can coexist, and seizures may be successfully "used" to extricate children from situations that they wish to flee or avoid. It can be seen from this brief con-

sideration that adequate attention must be paid to these psychosocial manifestations as well as to the physical and neuroelectrical manifestations in
both diagnosis and management endeavors.

Rutter, Graham, and Yule (1970) found that the rate of emotional and
behavior problems in neuroepileptic children was five times higher than
that in the general population. The rate was slightly higher (but not significantly) in those whose physical activities had been restricted. Dysfunction
of the brain was the single most important factor related to the higher rate
of psychiatric disorder. Of 99 children with epilepsy, 34 (34.3%) had a
"psychiatric disorder." Specifically, 12 had a neurotic disorder, 9 had an
antisocial or conduct disorder, 7 had a mixed disorder, 4 had the hyperkinetic syndrome, and 1 was psychotic. Unhappiness and solitariness was
characteristic of those with neurotic disorder.

In the study of the school progress of 85 children with epilepsy conducted by Holdsworth and Whitmore (1974), 18 (21.1%) were considered
by their teachers to be "noticeably deviant." Almost all of the children with
behavior problems were "educationally backward" and had behavior problems more frequently when seizures were poorly controlled.

It seems as though we need to reconsider the prevailing "optimistic attitude" that individuals with epilepsy will do just fine in the world and can
be educated in the regular classroom. For some, the optimistic attitude is
justified. For many others, however, it is not. Evidence is at hand indicating that the present system may well be perpetuating the problems of
behavioral control, illiteracy, poor self-concept, and poor preparation for
self-support. Recognizing that individuals with epilepsy are at risk for retardation, learning problems, behavioral problems, and unemployment, we
should provide cognitive-intellectual assessment, behavioral counseling and
management, and appropriate alternative opportunities for education and
job training that will help such individuals utilize their potential to become
independent. We can ill afford to turn a deaf ear to their special needs.

The social prognosis includes not only employability, but also driving
ability and marriage. Livingston (1972) has summarized the data concerning the length of seizure-free period required by various states as a condition for driving. It ranges from 6 months to 3 years. He also notes that the
government requires a person to be free of seizures without medication for
3 years before being permitted to drive a government vehicle. Livington's
own thought is that 6 months is too short and the government regulation is
too rigid. He advises his patients to apply for license after 4 seizure-free

years, whether on medication or not. Those patients on medication are checked every 6 months, and if the decision is made to stop medication, the patients are followed every 2 months during the period of withdrawal and every three months during the year after withdrawal. "It is obvious," Livingston concludes, "that a person with seizures should not drive an automobile, for the protection of lives and properties of others as well as for his own protection. The epileptic patient must understand that he will have to conduct his activities without having this privilege until his seizure disorder is controlled to the extent that he can fulfill the requirements for driving in his particular state" (p.538).

A survey of traffic accidents caused by epilepsy has recently been published by van der Lugt (1975). During a 10-year period, 203 accidents in the Netherlands were suspected of having been caused by epilepsy, though only 155 could be ascribed with certainty to epilepsy. The incidence was one per 10,000. In 76% of the cases the seizures were psychomotor; in 12%, the seizures were the first. And only 4% of those who knew they had epilepsy reported that fact when they applied for a license. By and large, the accidents associated with epilepsy were single-car accidents, which were less serious and occurred in less populated areas than those that were "average" accidents. These data provide some comfort with regard to the low incidence and mildness of traffic accidents, but they also are of concern with regard to the frequency with which drivers failed to report their condition to the licensing agency.

The other special issue to be discussed is marriage. Questions arise about the heredity of epilepsy as well as about the likelihood of congenital malformations in the offspring as a result of maternal epilepsy, or as a result of medication. The issues are not settled. Metrakos and Metrakos (1974) have concluded that "in at least three very divergent forms of 'epilepsy'— centrencephalic, febrile, and focal—a common genetically controlled predisposing factor exists. This genetic factor may be identified in the near relatives of the 'epileptic' probands as a typical or atypical centrencephalic EEG" (p.438). Boshes and Gibbs (1972) indicate that what is inherited is not a form of epilepsy, but "a greater or lesser degree of resistance to the types of injury that produce epilepsy" (p.85). They also credit Lennox with the statement that the chances were 1:4 that an individual with epilepsy would have an epileptic child and that that is 5 to 10 times the risk of a nonepileptic individual. However, Livingston (1972) is not convinced of the inheritability of clinical epilepsy, and in reviewing information on approximately 4,000 patients, he was impressed with the "paucity of clinical epilepsy" in the immediate families of the probands.

The issue of frequency of congenital malformations revolves around whether the symptom of epilepsy or the treatment might result in a congenital defect. After following about 500 patients on anticonvulsants through pregnancy, Livingston's (1972) experience indicated that "epileptic seizures per se do not cause abortions or adversely affect the unborn child" (p.592). Annegers et al. (1975) have confirmed the reports of others (Erickson and Oakley, 1974; Speidel and Meadow, 1972) that though the overall risk is low, there is an increased rate of malformations, particularly cardiac, and cleft lip and palate among the children of women taking anticonvulsants during pregnancy. There was not an increased rate of malformations when the pregnant woman with epilepsy did not take anticonvulsants (small number) or when the fathers had epilepsy.

Rodin (1968) in reviewing the pertinent literature about prognosis with regard to seizure control found that a commonly quoted figure was that 80% to 85% of patients would be controlled. However, he found that only 33% of all patients are likely to achieve a terminal remission of 2 years, that those with grand mal epilepsy have the best prognosis (50% to 60%), and that those with temporal lobe, the worst (20% to 30%). The factors associated with a poor prognosis were (1) age of onset in the first year of life, (2) the number of seizures prior to the onset of therapy, (3) the presence of more than one seizure type, and (4) an abnormal neurologic examination. With regard to longevity, the prognosis is somewhat guarded. According to Rodin (1968), the average time of death was 30 to 45 years of age. Approximately 25% to 35% died as a direct result of the epilepsy, 10% were found to have a brain tumor, 10% to 15% died in accidents, and 10% to 25% died as a result of suicide. The rest were "normal" causes.

There should be some appreciation now of the interrelationships of the medical, social, behavioral, and educational needs of patients with epilepsy. The following case dramatically illustrates the manifestations of a mixed seizure disorder across various dimensions of functioning: behavioral, language, cognitive, and school performance, and the need for attention to each.

CASE W.A.

W.A. was a 6-year-old girl referred to the Duke University Developmental Evaluation Center (DEC) in September 1975 by her pediatrician for evaluation of appropriate school placement and for help with controlling her behavior. She was the product of a full-term uncomplicated pregnancy and delivery, and had been entirely normal until 16 months previously when she was admitted to a local hospital after the onset of grand mal seizures. She remained in the hospital for 11 days for observation, evaluation, and treatment of seizures. During that time, it was noted that she vacillated between being happy and playful and being hostile and aggressive. A lumbar puncture and spinal fluid examination on two occasions were unremarkable, as was a brain scan. An EEG on the day after admission revealed abnormal discharges over the left temporal area; a second EEG revealed diffuse slowing—more marked over the left cerebrum. She was discharged with the diagnosis of "encephalitis" and was on phenobarbital and Dilantin at that time.

Over the next seven months, she was readmitted on five subsequent occasions for seizure control and medication readjustment. The seizures included staring spells, Jacksonian march, grand mal, and automatisms. One seizure had lasted for 3 hours before being controlled. During the last admission, her parents mentioned a personality change and talked about her irritability.

She was first admitted to Duke University Hospital in March, 1975, 10 months after the onset of her illness, with a right-sided seizure of 1 hour 30 minutes duration. Her parents again mentioned the occurrence of a personality change. An EEG during that admission revealed gross slowing "compatible with encephalitis." She was discharged on Mebaral, Dilantin, and Mysoline. Two months later, she was readmitted to the hospital because of behavior problems. She was described as "an impossible child" and was loud, overactive, and subject to easy outbursts of temper with hitting and spitting. Her seizures were still not under control, but had improved somewhat. She was then referred to the DEC.

At the time of her evaluation, which was begun in August 1975, her seizures were in fair control. Her parents had procrastinated about coming, in hopes that her seizures would be in optimal control so that we could see her at her best. They reported that W.A. was on phenobarbital, Dilantin, Valium, and Tegretol at that time. Their concerns were with regard to her behavior, to proper school placement, and to her speech and language. With regard to the latter concern, they noted that in starting a sentence, she would repeat the first word several times. She frequently forgot what she was going to say and would become quite loud and excited. If help was offered in terms of supplying a needed word, she would become upset and angry. She was able to understand what was said to her but often would not do what she was told to do. The following is an example of her expressive language difficulties. She wrote a *B* and requested that the examiner guess why. She then volunteered why "because, because—because it's my sweet lil' ole you know what—my sweet lil' ole . . ." She became angrier as she was unable to find the right word but could not be dissuaded from trying.

During the DEC evaluation, particular attention was paid to an assessment of her speech and language and of her behavioral problems as well as to proper school placement. The following formulation was derived after the individual evaluations were completed. The encephalitis experience by W.A. in May of 1974 brought about neurological insult resulting in severe expressive language difficulties particularly word-finding problems; severe, mixed, and poorly controlled seizure disorder; poor organization; short attention span; impulsivity; low frustration tolerance; anger; and perseveration. At the time of evaluation, she was in the average range of intellectual functioning in nonverbal areas, but was not testable in verbal IQ. She appeared to be acutely aware of her own language deficits and some of her behavioral difficulties. Neither W.A. nor the family had been able to work through the substantial changes that had occurred in her functioning and competencies.

Recommendations were made for (1) placement of W.A. in a special language classroom, (2) counseling for her parents regarding behavior management, and (3) play therapy for W.A. to help her work through her feelings regarding her loss of functioning and competencies. Also close collaboration would be maintained with the neurologist who was managing her seizures.

The parents accepted the recommendations, and W.A. was admitted into the special classroom which focused upon remediating language problems. Counseling sessions were held weekly with the parents who continued to find it very difficult to accept the changes in their daughter and to deal with them effectively. They continued to hope that W.A. would return to her old self. In addition, the seizures remained poorly controlled with an average of 10 to 15 grand mal seizures each week. More mild seizures were not counted, but also occurred. Numerous medications were attempted. When the seizures were better controlled, it seemed that her behavior would be intolerable because of angry outbursts and great irritability.

Over a period of time, gradually the seizures became more difficult to control and after several medication changes on an outpatient basis, she was readmitted to the hospital in May 1976 for improvement of both seizure and behavioral control, and to provide the parents with some rest. During the hospitalization, a C-T scan was normal and the EEG changes persisted showing bilateral involvement with the left hemisphere more involved than the right. It was felt that the behavioral problems were related to the diffuse nature of her encephalitic involvement. She was discharged after a two-week hospitalization, improved on Mellaril (tranquilizer), bromides, Celontin, and Dilantin, and was enrolled for the summer at a developmental day-care center.

Over the course of the next year, W.A.'s behavior gradually improved, both at home and in her two school situations (mornings in the language classroom and afternoons in the developmental day-care center), and her seizures were under better control. However, her behavior and performance remained somewhat variable from day to day and the parents were still receiving child management counseling. By midyear, she had improved to the extent that dvelopmental day care was no longer an appropriate setting for her, so she began spending a portion of each morning in a regular kindergarten and received special educational tutoring for 1 hour (three afternoons a week) as well as continuing in the language classroom.

It has now been 3 years since the onset of encephalitis and the initial hospitalization. Because of her improvement, a second evaluation was undertaken at the DEC in order to assess her current level of functioning and to make appropriate school placement recommendations. On the psychological evaluation, W.A. responded very well to directions and requests on verbal tasks. This was in marked contrast to her behavior during the previous evaluation when she complied with an attempt to do her best on only nonverbal tasks. She exhibited a minimal amount of perseveration and was willing to accept instruction, direction, and help. Her human figure drawing ranked in the 25% percentile when scored according to the Harris Standards for completeness of detail. On the WISC, W.A. obtained a verbal-scale IQ of 87, a performance-scale IQ of 83, and a full-scale IQ of 84. All these scores fell within the dull to normal range of intellectual functioning. There was considerable scatter in her abilities across the various subtests. In the verbal areas, she did quite well in comprehension and similarities which was indeed remarkable and indicated an ability to think and reason and express the product of that thought in words. These skills were particularly lacking at the time of the previous evaluation. In the nonverbal or performance areas, she demonstrated somewhat of a plateau effect in that she hadn't made as many gains as needed in order to keep her abreast of age-related expectancies. Overall, however, she demonstrated remarkable improvement in behavior and in speech and language, as well as in seizure control. Her teachers indicated she would no longer need the language classroom, and her tutor attested to the academic progress W.A. had made in the one-to-one learning sessions. It was felt she still needed considerable individual teacher time and that she needed opportunities for socialization. Accordingly, recommendations were made for enrollment in a day camp for the summer to foster development of her social skills. In the fall, W.A. will be attending a learning disabilities classroom within her local school, and the parents will continue with counseling.

Several points are worth mentioning regarding this case. Obviously, the course was more severe than is typical in most seizure disorders, but this serves to demonstrate the multifaceted pathology in a more vivid fashion. First, the effect of diffuse neurological dysfunction resulting in seizure disorder of various types, communication difficulties, and behavior problems is amply demonstrated. Second, one cannot help but wonder about the effect of the anticonvulsant medication on behavior. Little is really known about this factor as pointed out recently by Stores (1975a). Third, the difficulties faced by the family in relating to their youngster after the onset of her illness are demonstrated by their continuing need, after three years, for management counseling. The school personnel were able to manage W.A.'s behavior substantially better than the parents even when W.A. was at her worst. Furthermore, W.A. also has had difficulty in accepting the changes in her functioning and competencies. Fourth, the need with the developmentally disabled for constantly monitoring the adequacy of the treatment plan and altering it to meet the changing functioning of the individual and the family is dramatically conveyed. And fifth, it is seen that interdisciplinary treatment is as essential as interdisciplinary diagnostic evaluation.

It seems fitting to close this chapter with a statement about the present-day teaching of medical students at Oxford about epilepsy. We share with Stores (1975b) the hope that this emphasis will be more widespread.

> In the Oxford Medical School about one in eight students spend their two months' psychiatric attachment at the Park Hospital for Children where they see a wide range of general child psychiatry, and also become well versed in the seizure disorders of childhood and the effect they can have on behavior. Seminar discussions for all students are organized around the following propositions:
>
> 1. Seizures are common in the general population and are of considerable numerical importance in mentally handicapped groups.
> 2. "Epilepsy" is a symptom and not an adequate diagnosis; seizures may be due to local or general disorder.
> 3. Seizures are not either grand mal or petit mal attacks. There is a wide diversity of types of attack, including some of subtle clinical manifestation which nevertheless may seriously affect behavior. Detailed description is not just an academic exercise but can be of considerable therapeutic and prognostic importance.
> 4. Epilepsy is not only a matter of having fits, and management is not merely a matter of prescribing drugs. Emphasis is placed on the educational, psy-

chiatric and social complications that many people with epilepsy suffer in their lives, often for preventable reasons such as harmful drug-effects or adverse social pressures. The impact of epilepsy on the family, on education, and on employment and marriage prospects—as well as its other social implications—exemplifies principles of real-life social medicine. . . . Students at the Park Hospital formulate the seizure disorder in terms of aetiology, clinical and EEG type (including precipitating and inhibiting factors), as well as associated problems of a physical, educational, social or psychiatric nature. With this formulation they then plan comprehensive management in the light of the uniqueness of each individual case (Stores, 1975b, p.519).

Comprehensive care for the patient with epilepsy will come with the realization that outcome is determined by environmental and genetic opportunities and insults as illustrated in the Developmental Disabilities Cube and that professionals representing all disciplines need to work together to provide that comprehensive care.

References

Annegers, J.F., Elveback, L.R., Hauser, W.A. & Kurland, L.T. Epilepsy anticonvulsants and malformations. *Birth Defects*, 1975, *11* (5), 157–60.

Berman, P.H. Management of seizure disorders with anticonvulsant drugs: current concepts. *Pediatric Clinics of North America*, 1976, *23* (3), 443–59.

Boshes, L.D. & Gibbs, F.A. *Epilepsy Handbook*, 2nd ed. Springfield, Illinois: Charles C Thomas, 1972.

Bray, P.F. Inheritance of focal and petit mal seizures. In M. Alter & W.A. Hauser (Eds.), *The Epidemiology of Epilepsy: A workshop*. (NINDS Monograph #14; DHEW Pub. # [NIH] 73–390). U. S. DHEW, Public Health Service, 1972, 109–12.

Chalhub, E.G. Neurocutaneous syndromes in children. *Pediatric Clinics of North America*, 1976, *23* (3), 499–516.

Corbett, J.A., Harris, R. & Robinson, R.G. Epilepsy. In J. Wortis (Ed.), *Mental Retardation and Developmental Disabilities* (Vol. 7). New York: Brunner/Mazel, 1975, 79–111.

Corsellis, J.A.N. Neuropathological observations on epilepsy. In P. Harris and C. Mawdsley (Eds.), *Epilepsy: Proceedings of the Hans Berger Centenary Symposium*. Edinburgh: Churchill Livingstone, 1974, 111–14.

Crandall, P. Postoperative management and criteria for evaluation. In D.P. Purpura, J.K. Penry & R.D. Walter (Eds.), *Advances in Neurology* (Vol. 8). New York: Raven Press, 1975, 265–79.

Davidson, S. & Falconer, M.A. Outcome of surgery in 40 children with temporal lobe epilepsy. *Lancet*, June 7, 1975, *1*, 1260–63.

DeVivo, D.C., Keating, J.P. & Haymond, M.W. Acute encephalopathy with fatty infiltration of the viscera. *Pediatric Clinics of North America*, 1976, *23* (3), 527–40.

Dodrill, C.B. & Wilkus, R.J. Relationships between intelligence and electroencephalographic epileptiform activity in adult epileptics. *Neurology*, 1976, *26*, 525–31.

Dodson, W.E., Prensky, A.L., DeVivo, D.C., Goldring, S. et al. Management of seizure disorders: Selected aspects. *Journal of Pediatrics*, 1976, *89*, 527–40; 695–703.

Dreifuss, F.E. The prognosis of petit mal epilepsy. In M. Alter & W.A. Hauser (Eds.), *The Epidemology of Epilepsy: A Workshop.* (NINDS Monograph #14; DHEW Pub. # [NIH] 73–390). U. S. DHEW Public Health Service, 1972, 129–32.

Engel, R.C.H. Abnormal electroencephalograms in the neonatal period. Springfield, Illinois: Charles C Thomas, 1975.

Epilepsy Foundation of America. *Basic Statistics on the Epilepsies.* Philadelphia: F.A. Davis, 1975.

Erickson, J.D. & Oakley, G.P. Seizure disorders in mothers of children with orofacial clefts: A case-control study. *Journal of Pediatrics*, 1974, *84*, 244–46.

Falconer, M.A. Reversibility by temporal-lobe resection of the behavioral abnormalities of temporal lobe epilepsy. *New England Journal of Medicine*, 1973, *289*, 451–55.

Frantzen, E., Lennox-Buchthal, M. & Nygaard, A. Longitudinal EEG and clinical study of children with febrile convulsions. *Electroencephalography and Clinical Neurophysiology*, 1968, *24*, 197–212.

Frantzen, E., Lennox-Buchthal, M., Nygaard, A. & Stene, J. A genetic study of febrile convulsions. *Neurology*, 1970, *20*, 909–17.

Gastaut, H. Clinical and electroencephalographic classification of epileptic seizures. *Epilepsia*, 1970, *11*, 102–13.

Gastaut, H., Broughton, R., Roger, J. & Tassinari, C.A. Generalized nonconvulsive seizures without local onset. In P.J. Vinken and G.W. Bruyn (Eds.), *Handbook of Clinical Neurology* (Vol. 15). Amsterdam: North-Holland, 1974.

Gastaut, H. & Gastaut, J.L. Computerized axial tomography in epilepsy. In J.K. Perry (Ed.). Epilepsy: The Eighth International Symposium. New York: Raven Press, 1977.

Gastaut, H., Gastaut, J.L., Gonçalves Silva, G.E. & Fernandez Sanchez, G.R. Relative frequency of different types of epilepsy: A study employing the classification of the international league against epilepsy. *Epilepsia*, 1975, *16*, 457–61.

Gates, M. Prognosis of febrile seizures. In M. Alter and W.A. Hauser (Eds.), *The Epidemiology of Epilepsy: A Workshop*. (NINDS Monograph #14; DHEW Pub. # [NIH] 73–390). U.S. DHEW Public Health Service, 1972, 123–28.

Gold, A.P. & Carter, S. Acute hemiplegia of infancy and childhood. *Pediatric Clinics of North America*, 1976, *23* (3), 413–33.

Gordon, N. Why does the medical treatment of epilepsy sometimes fail? In P. Harris & C. Mawdsley (Eds.), *Epilepsy: Proceedings of the Hans Berger Centenary Symposium*. Edinburgh: Churchill Livingstone, 1974, 187–91.

Gregoriades, A.D. A medical and social survey of 231 children with seizures. *Epilepsia*, 1972, *13*, 13–20.

Harrison, R.M. & Taylor, D.C. Childhood seizures: A 25-year follow-up of social and medical prognosis. *Lancet*, May 1, 1976, *1*, 948–51.

Holdsworth, L. & Whitmore, K. A study of children with epilepsy attending ordinary schools. Their seizure patterns, progress and behavior in school. *Developmental Medicine and Child Neurology*, 1974, *16*, 746–58.

Huttenlocher, P. Dendritic development in neocortex of children with mental defect and infantile spasms. *Neurology*, 1974, *24*, 203–10.

Jeavons, P.M., Bower, B.D. & Dimitrakoudi, M. Long-term prognosis of 150 cases of "West Syndrome." *Epilepsia*, 1973, *14*, 153–64.

Keith, H.M. *Convulsive Disorders in Children*. Boston: Little, Brown, 1963.

Krishnamoorthy, K.S., Fernandez, R.A., Momose, K.J., Delong, G.R., Moylan, F.M.B., Todres, I.D., & Shannon, D.C. Evaluation of neonatal intracranial hemorrhage by computerized tomography. *Pediatrics*, 1977, *59*, 165–72.

Lennox-Buchthal, M.A. Febrile convulsions. In P.J. Vinken & G.W. Bruyn (Eds.), *Handbook of Clinical Neurology* (Vol. 15). Amsterdam: North-Holland, 1974, 246–63.

Lewis, D.O. & Balla, D.A. *Delinquency and Psychopathology*. New York: Grune & Stratton, 1976.

Livingston, S. *Comprehensive Management of Epilepsy in Infancy, Childhood, and Adolescence*. Springfield, Illinois: Charles C Thomas, 1972.

Livingston, S. & Pauli, L.L. Ketogenic diet and epilepsy. *Developmental Medicine and Child Neurology*, 1975, *17*, 818–19.

Lombroso, C.T. Seizures in the newborn period. In P.J. Vinken & G.W. Bruyn (Eds.) Handbook of Clinical Neurology (Vol. 15). Amsterdam: North-Holland, 1974.

Lugaresi, E., Pazzaglia, P., Roger, J. & Tassinari, C.A. Evolution and prognosis in petit mal. In P. Harris & C. Mawdsley (Eds.), *Epilepsy: Proceedings of the*

Hans Berger Centenary Symposium. Edinburgh: Churchill Livingstone, 1974, 151–53.

Masland, R.L. The diagnosis and treatment of little seizures. *Hospital Medicine*, January 1976, 85–111.

Maynert, E.W. Marczynski, T.J. & Browning, R.A. The role of the neurotransmitters in the epilepsies. In W. J. Friedlander (Ed.), *Advances in Neurology* (Vol. 13). New York: Raven Press, 1975.

Menkes, J.H. Diagnosis and treatment of minor motor seizures. *Pediatric Clinics of North America*, 1976, *23* (3), 435–442.

Merlis, J.K. Proposal for an international classification of the epilepsies. *Epilepsia*, 1970, *11*, 114–19.

Metrakos, K. & Metrakos, J.D. Genetics of epilepsy. In P.J. Vinken & G. W. Bruyn (Eds.), *Handbook of Clinical Neurology* (Vol. 15). Amsterdam: North-Holland, 1974, 429–38.

Millichap, J.G. Drug treatment of convulsive disorders. *New England Journal of Medicine*, 1972, *286*, 464–69.

Milner, B. Psychological aspects of focal epilepsy and its neurosurgical management. In D.P. Purpura, J.K. Penry, & R.D. Walter (Eds.), *Advances in Neurology* (Vol. 8). New York: Raven Press, 1975, 299–321.

Nelson, K.B. & Ellenberg, J.H. Predictors of epilepsy in children who have experienced febrile seizures. *New England Journal of Medicine*, 1976, *295*, 1029–33.

Nelson, K.B. & Ellenberg, J.H. Prognosis in children with febrile seizures. Pediatrics, 1978, 61, 720–27.

O'Leary, J.L. & Goldring, S. *Science and Epilepsy. Neuroscience Gains in Epilepsy Research*. New York: Raven Press, 1976.

Olivares, L. Epilepsy in Mexico: A population study. In M. Alter & W.A. Hauser (Eds.), *The Epidemiology of Epilepsy: A Workshop*. (NINDS Monograph # 14, DHEW Pub # [NIH] 73–390). U.S. DHEW, Public Health Service, 1972, 55.

Ouellette, E.M. The child who convulses with fever. *Pediatric Clinics of North America*, 1974, *21* (2), 467–81.

Ounsted, C. Some aspects of seizure disorders. In D. Gairdner & D. Hull (Eds.), *Recent Advances in Paediatrics*. London: J. & A. Churchill, 1971, 363–400.

Penry, J.K. Absence seizures. In M. Alter & W. A. Hauser (Eds.), *The Epidemiology of Epilepsy: A Workshop*. (NINDS Monograph # 14; DHEW Pub. # [NIH] 73–390). U. S. DHEW Public Health Service, 1972, 133–35.

Penry, J.K., Porter, R.J. & Dreifuss, F.E. Simultaneous recording of absence seizures with video tape and electroencephalography. *Brain*, 1975, *98*, 427–40.

Purpura, D.P. Dendritic spine "dysgenesis" and mental retardation. *Science*, 1974, *186*, 1126–28.

Rasmussen, T. Seizures with local onset and elementary symptomatology. In P. J. Vinken & G.W. Bruyn (Eds.), *Handbook of Clinical Neurology* (Vol. 15). Amsterdam: North-Holland, 1974, 74–86.

Rasmussen, T. Cortical resection in the treatment of focal epilepsy. In D.P. Purpura, J.K. Penry & R.D. Walter (Eds.), *Advances in Neurology* (Vol. 8). New York: Raven Press, 1975, 139–54.

Rodin, E.A. *The Prognosis of Patients with Epilepsy.* Springfield, Illinois: Charles C Thomas, 1968.

Rodin, E.A. Race. In M. Alter and W.A. Hauser (Eds.), *The Epidemiology of Epilepsy: A Workshop.* (NINDS Monograph #14; DHEW Pub. #[NIH] 73–390). U. S. DHEW Public Health Service, 1972a.

Rodin, E.A. Comment after the presentation by A.E. Walker "Post-traumatic epilepsy." In M. Alter & W.A. Hauser (Eds.), *The Epidemiology of Epilepsy: A Workshop.* (NINDS Monograph #14; DHEW Pub. # [NIH] 73–390). U.S. DHEW Public Health Service, 1972b.

Rodin, E., Rennick, P., Dennerll, R. & Lin, Y. Vocational and educational problems of epileptic patients. *Epilepsia*, 1972, *13*, 149–60.

Rutter, M., Graham, P. & Yule, W. *A Neuropsychiatric Study in Childhood.* (Clinics in Developmental Medicine, Vol. 35/36). London: William Heinemann, 1970.

Speidel, B.D. & Meadow, S.R. Maternal epilepsy and abnormalities of the fetus and newborn. *Lancet*, 1972, *2*, 839–43.

Stores, G. Behavioral effects of anti-epileptic drugs. *Developmental Medicine and Child Neurology*, 1975a, *17*, 647–58.

Stores, G. Teaching medical students about epilepsy. *Developmental Medicine and Child Neurology*, 1975b, *17*, 518–19.

Stores, G. & Hart, J. Reading skills of children with generalized or focal epilepsy attending ordinary school. *Developmental Medicine and Child Neurology*, 1976, *18*, 705–16.

Swaiman, K.F. Seizures associated with centrencephalic discharges other than petit mal—Petit mal variant. In K.F. Swaiman and F.S. Wright (Eds.). *The Practice of Pediatric Neurology*, St. Louis: C.V. Mosby, 1975.

Swaiman, D.F. & Wright, F.S. *The Practice of Pediatric Neurology.* St. Louis: C.V. Mosby, 1975, 829–82.

Taylor, D.C. & Falconer, M.A. Clinical, socio-economic, and psychological changes after temporal lobectomy for epilepsy. *British Journal of Psychiatry*, 1968, *114*, 1247–61.

Temkin, O. *The Falling Sickness. A History of Epilepsy from the Greeks to the Beginnings of Modern Neurology*, 2nd ed. rev. Baltimore: Johns Hopkins University Press, 1971.

Tsuboi, T. Polygenic inheritance of epilepsy and febrile convulsions: Analysis based on a computational model. *British Journal of Psychiatry*, 129, 1976, 239–42.

Vaernet, K. The relationship of psychomotor epilepsy to pathological aggression. The effect of amygdalatomy. In P. Harris & C. Mawdsley (Eds.), *Epilepsy: Proceedings of the Hans Berger Centenary Symposium*. Edinburgh: Churchill Livingstone, 1974, 222–26.

van den Berg, B.J. Recurrence of febrile seizures in childhood. In M. Alter & W.A. Hauser (Eds.), *The Epidemiology of Epilepsy: A Workshop*. (NINDS Monograph #14; DHEW Pub. # [NIH] 73–390). U.S. DHEW Public Health Service, 1972, 119–22.

van der Lugt, P.J.M. Traffic accidents caused by epilepsy. *Epilepsia*, 1975, 16, 747–51.

Viani, F., Avanzini, B., Baruzzi, A. Bordo, B. et al. Long-term monitoring of antiepileptic drugs in patients with the Lennox-Gastaut syndrome. In J.K. Perry (Ed.), *Epilepsy: The Eighth International Symposium*. New York: Raven Press, 1977.

Voeller, K.K.S. Rothenberg, M.B. Psychosocial aspects of the mamagement of seizures in children. *Pediatrics*, 1973, 51, 1027–82.

Volpe, J. Neonatal seizures. *New England Journal of Medicine*, 1973, 289 (8), 413–16.

Walker, E.A. Post-traumatic epilepsy. In M. Alter & W.A. Hauser (Eds.), *The Epidemiology of Epilepsy: A Workshop*. (NINDS Monograph # 14; DHEW Pub. # [NIH] 73–390). U.S. Dept. HEW Public Health Service, 1972, 115–17.

Ward, A.A., Jr. Theoretical basis for surgical therapy of epilepsy. In D.P. Purpura, J.K. Penry, and R.D. Walter (Eds.), *Advances in Neurology* (Vol. 8). New York: Raven Press, 1975, 23–25.

Wasterlain, C.G. & Plum, F. The influence of seizures in infancy on brain development. An experimental study. In P. Harris and C. Mawdsley (Eds.), *Epilepsy. Proceedings of the Hans Berger Centenary Symposium*. Edinburgh: Churchill Livingstone, 1974, 127–39.

West, W.J. On a peculiar form of infantile convulsions. *Lancet*, 1840, 1, 724–25.

Whitehouse, D. Psychological and neurological correlates of seizure disorders. *Johns Hopkins Medical Journal*, 1971, 129, 36–42.

Wolf, S.M., Carr, A., Davis, D.C., Davidson, S. et al. The value of phenobarbital in the child who has had a single febrile seizure: A controlled prospective study. *Pediatrics*, 1977, 59, 378–85.

6

Disorders Associated with
Cerebral Dysfunction

In this chapter we will consider a number of behavior disorders that have been attributed—variously—and controversially to brain damage and/or dysfunction. More basically, we will consider a number of symptoms such as: hyperactivity, perceptual-motor impairments; distractibility; perseveration; impulsivity; reading, arithmetic, and spelling difficulties; general coordination difficulties; emotional lability; antisocial behavior; disorders of speech and hearing; and signs of immature neurological status and electroencephalographic irregularities, various combinations of which have been designated "syndromes." Although the term minimal brain dysfunction syndrome (MBD) is frequently used in a way that encompasses subgroups, including hyperactivity and learning disabilities, we will attempt to consider subgroup syndromes separately whenever possible. First, we will discuss the MBD and hyperactive child syndromes and, second, specific learning disability syndromes. Here we examine the conceptual development of these "syndromes," and the evidence for the syndrome as an entity in terms of clinical manifestations, etiology, and management. Third, we will study one specific learning disability—dyslexia—as representative of learning disabilities as a whole.

MINIMAL BRAIN DYSFUNCTION
AND HYPERACTIVE CHILD SYNDROME
DEFINITION AND HISTORY

The generally accepted definition of minimal brain dysfunction syndrome is that provided by Clements (1966, pp.9–10). "Children of near average, average, or above average general intelligence" who present with "certain learning or behavioral disabilities ranging from mild to severe, which are associated with deviations of function of the central nervous system" show the minimal brain dysfunction syndrome. "These deviations may manifest themselves by various combinations of impairment in perception, conceptualization, language, memory, and control of attention, impulse, or motor function."

Strother (1973) points out that there are several historical lines of interest that contributed to the development of the concept of minimal brain dysfunction. One such line was the interest in aphasia and dyslexia. Strother (1973) maintains that case descriptions can be found as early as 400 B.C. Although there is still disagreement, as we shall see, about definitions and diagnostic criteria, there is agreement that many children have difficulty in acquiring spoken and written language which cannot be accounted for on the basis of intelligence or sensory, motor, or emotional disorders or lack of environmental stimulation.

A second historical line comes from the investigations of behavioral signs and symptoms in children with known brain damage. The epidemic of encephalitis during the period of World War I and investigations of head trauma have helped to identify the sequelae of brain damage in the form of behavior disorders. These behavioral disorders included: hyperactivity, impulsivity, antisocial behavior, disturbances in motility, emotional lability, perceptual disorders, and developmental lag.

The next step is generally believed to have occurred with the work of Strauss (Strauss and Lehtinen, 1947; Strauss and Kephart, 1955) in extending these findings about the behavioral sequelae of demonstrable brain damage to children in whom no conclusive evidence of brain damage could be found. If the child exhibited some of these behavior disorders, minimal brain damage was inferred. This view persisted, although not without challenge, from the late 1940s to the 1960s.

In 1962, the Oxford International Study Group on Child Neurology came to two conclusions regarding the evidence at that point about the minimal brain damage syndrome. The first is that the term minimal brain damage should be replaced with minimal brain dysfunction. The consensus was that brain damage should never be inferred from behavioral signs alone. The second is that the classification of minimal brain dysfunction contains a number of heterogeneous groups that need to be classified into more specific and homogeneous categories.

During the last 10 years, some progress has been made, but there remains a significant lack of homogeneous grouping of symptoms and behaviors. Today, the interchangeable and synonymous uses of the terms "hyperactive child syndrome," "minimal brain dysfunction syndrome," and "learning disabilities" is characteristic (Cantwell, 1975). This interchangeability of terms is particularly prevalent with minimal brain dysfunction (MBD) and hyperactivity, although hyperactivity is generally recognized as one variant of the broad spectrum of behaviors linked together under the category of minimal brain dysfunction (Martin, 1975). The term hyperactive child refers to a child "who consistently exhibits a high level of activity in situations in which it is clearly inappropriate, is unable to inhibit his activity on command, often appears capable of only one speed of response, and is often characterized by other physiological, learning, and behavioral symptoms and problems" (Ross and Ross, 1976, p. 12). Ross and Ross (1976) point out that some of these behavioral symptoms are often concomitant with hyperactivity, such as impulsivity, while others may be a response to one's own feelings of inadequacy, such as self-esteem. The primary behavior essential for inclusion in this classification is hyperactivity. Thus, the hyperactive child syndrome is itself not homogenous but heterogeneous. However, this core symptom approach is an improvement upon the umbrella term minimal brain dysfunction.

While there is reason to believe that the hyperactive child syndrome is a subgroup of the umbrella category of MBD, the lack of uniformly employed classification criteria and the interchangeable use of hyperactivity and MBD characteristic of the literature necessitates lumping these two "syndromes" together when considering manifestations. Learning disabilities do lend themselves more easily to consideration as a subgroup.

MANIFESTATIONS

MBD is a syndrome that is defined by its manifestations. Wender (1971 p. 12) maintains that "MDB children manifest dysfunction in the following areas: motor activity and coordination; attention and cognitive function; impulse control; interpersonal relations, particularly dependence/independence and responsiveness to social influence; and emotionality." We will examine further these manifestations in terms of various areas of functioning.

Cognitive-Intellectual

While it would be unreasonable to expect a unique MBD pattern of psychological test performance because of the previously noted heterogeneity (Conners, 1973), there have been a number of studies comparing the intellectual functioning of MBD children and controls. Although studies have shown MBD and hyperactive children to have a significantly lower verbal than performance IQ (Kenny et al., 1971) and although other studies have shown that significantly lower verbal IQ scores are obtained with MBD and hyperactive children than controls, there is no consistent documentation for the belief that MBD and hyperactive children demonstrate a characteristic pattern of performance IQs being higher than verbal IQs (Wender, 1971). The pattern depends upon the particular makeup of the sample (i.e., the subgroups being evaluated). Some evidence suggests that a significantly lower verbal IQ than performance IQ is likely if the sample contains children with learning disabilities (Ackerman, Peters, and Dykman, 1971; Warrington, 1967).

Ross and Ross (1976) point out that one difficulty with IQ data, especially for the hyperactive child, is the confounding with educational difficulties. However, the studies tend to show not only consistently lower levels of functioning but also greater variability in performance (as reflected in WISC subtest scores) of hyperactive children as compared with controls. Interaction effects leading to downward spirals in functioning are reflected in Dykman, Peters, and Ackerman's finding (1973) that verbal IQ was significantly lower at initial evaluation at 8–11 years of age but both verbal and full-scale IQs were lower at followup age 14 for MBD subjects as compared with controls.

In a well-conceived study, Reitan and Boll (1973) compared 25 children with known brain damage with 25 controls and 25 MBD children with academic problems and 19 MBD children with behavioral problems. The diagnoses of the known brain damage group were as follows: left infantile hemiplegia (or hemiparesis), 6; right infantile hemiplegia (or hemiparesis), 4; brain damage resulting from encephalitis, 6; brain damage due to birth trauma, 2; accidental brain trauma, 6; cerebral palsy, 1; and frontal lobe cysts, 1. The MBD group as a whole was found to be more similar to controls than to the brain-damaged group on neuropsychological test data. The MBD group referred for academic difficulties were slightly more impaired intellectually, academically, and in motor and sensoriperceptual functioning than the MBD group referred for behavioral problems. The MBD academic group was significantly lower on verbal-, performance-, and full-scale WISC IQ than the controls, while the MBD behavior group was only significantly lower in verbal IQ.

In addition to intellectual manifestations, Wender (1971) refers to a number of other cognitive manifestations. These include shortness of attention span, poor concentration, and difficulty organizing hierarchically so that as much attention is directed toward the irrelevant and peripheral as to the relevant and essential aspects of an idea or event.

The work of Campbell (1973) and Douglas (1973) have suggested some differences in the hyperactive child's cognitive style. As contrasted with same-aged, equally intelligent controls, the hyperactive child's cognitive style is viewed as more impulsive, field dependent, with constricted control of attention and weaker automatization (rapid response to repetitive tasks) (Ross and Ross, 1976).

Neuromotor

Motor hyperactivity is a cardinal manifestation. Often it is noticed in the first days of life with parents reporting restless, colicky babies with sleeping problems (Wender, 1971). Impaired coordination is another frequent finding. Hyperactivity is qualitatively different from a high level of activity (Ross and Ross, 1976). The driven nature and forced responsiveness of the hyperactive child is the essential aspect. That is, the activity level of children differs qualitatively rather than quantitatively from normal activity. There is evidence that these qualitative differences are not apparent in free play situations but are evidenced in structured situations (Schleifer, 1975).

Physical

Waldrop, Pederson, and Bell (1968) have attempted to identify behaviors associated with congenital characteristics. Using 43 male and 41 female normal children 2 years 6 months old, they related a weighted score of physical anomaly with behavioral measures, derived from direct observations and from teachers' ratings. A significant correlation was found between the weighted anomaly score and a number of behavioral variables including inability to delay gratification, nomadic play, spilling and throwing, frenetic play, perseveration, opposing peers, and intractability.

Rapoport, Quinn, and Lamprecht (1974) used this system of weighted anomalies, presented in Table 6.1 to obtain stigmata scores. There was a

TABLE 6.1 Physical anomalies and scoring weights

Anomaly	Scoring weight
HEAD	
Head circumference	
More than 1.5 standard deviations	2
1 to 1.5 standard deviations	1
"Electric" hair	
Very fine hair that will not comb down	2
Fine hair that is soon awry after combing	1
Two or more whorls	0
EYES	
Epicanthus	
Where upper and lower lids join at the nose, point of union is:	
Deeply covered	2
Partly covered	1
Hypertelorism	
Approximate distance between tear ducts:	
>1.5 S.D.	2
1.25 to 1.5 S.D.	1
EARS	
Low-set	
Bottom of ears in line with:	
Mouth (or lower)	2
Area between mouth and nose	1
Adherent lobes	
Lower edges of ears extend:	
Upward and back toward crown of head	2
Straight back toward rear of neck	1
Malformed	1
Asymmetrical	1
Soft and pliable	0

Anomaly	Scoring weight
MOUTH	
High palate	
Roof of mouth:	
Flat and narrow at the top	1
Furrowed tongue	1
Smooth-rough spots on tongue	0
HANDS	
Fifth finger	
Markedly curved inward toward other fingers	2
Slightly curved inward toward other fingers	1
Single transverse palmer crease	1
Index finger longer than middle finger	0
FEET	
Third toe	
Definitely longer than second toe	2
Appears equal in length to second toe	1
Partial syndactyly of two middle toes	1
Gap between first and second toe (approximately ¼ inch)	1

positive association of stigmata present with scores on the hyperactivity ($r = .28$, $p < .01$) and conduct problems ($r = .35$, $p < .005$) dimensions of a teacher rating scale on 76 hyperactive boys. In addition, stigmata score was significantly associated with a history of obstetrical difficulties in the mother and with a history of childhood hyperactivity in the father.

Another area of physical manifestation in MBD and hyperactive children found on clinical examination are so-called soft neurological signs. These soft signs are slight, inconsistently present, findings not clearly associated with localized neuroanatomical lesions (Wender, 1971). Soft signs include a number of fine and gross motor deficits such as fine choreiform movements, jerky eye tracking and associative movements, and sensory impairment such as finger agnosia as well as difficulty with graphesthesia and stereognosis (Schain, 1972; Touwen and Prechtl, 1970). The value of soft signs has been questioned because they are transient and common under the age of seven; and often they are not reproducible and not well standardized. Schmitt (1975) maintains that soft signs are, at best, evidence for neurologic immaturity. Wender (1971) reports the prevalence of soft signs in approximately 50% of MBD children referred for psychiatric consultation. However, he also points out that the diagnostic usefulness of soft signs is limited because they occur in a moderate number of persons who are apparently normal.

The presence of abnormal electroencephalograms in MBD children is also inconsistent. Satterfield et al. (1973) reported a comparison of 31 MBD children with 21 normal controls matched for age and sex. The MBD children showed significantly lower amplitudes and longer latencies on evoked cortical potentials than did the normal controls. "The most common clinical EEG abnormality found was an excessive amount of slow wave activity" (p. 280). This finding is consistent with some of the soft sign data in suggesting delayed maturation of the nervous system. Although Cantwell (1975) also reports an increase in slow wave activity as the most common finding, he remarks: "There are no EEG abnormalities specific to the syndrome. There is even some question as to whether hyperactive children have a greater number of EEG abnormalities than carefully matched normal and non-hyperactive emotionally disturbed children" (p. 44).

Affective-Behavioral

Wender (1971) maintains that: "The emotionality of MBD children shows four major types of dysfunction: increased lability, altered reactivity, increased aggressiveness, and dysphoria" (p. 21). Frustration tolerance is notably poor with poor impulse control resulting in recklessness, poor judgment, and acting-out behavior. Schleifer (1975) found a group of 28 hyperactive children to be significantly poorer in reflectivity and more impulsive than a group of 26 controls matched on age, sex, IQ, and socioeconomic level. An extremely hyperactive subgroup was found to be significantly more impulsive motorically as measured by the Draw-A-Line Test. Wender (1971) portrays the typical MBD child as resisting social demands and controls by adults but as controlling with playmates who tend to be younger.

Because of the increased frustrations, negative feedback, and lack of academic and social success, the MBD and hyperactive child must be considered at risk for developing emotional, personality, and behavioral difficulties throughout the various stages of development. Cantwell (1975) reporting on followup studies maintains: "These data strongly suggest not only that the hyperactive child syndrome is a precursor to significant psychiatric and social pathology in adulthood but that alcoholism, sociopathy and hysteria are the likely psychiatric outcomes in adulthood" (p.59).

Sensoriperceptual

It is somewhat difficult to separate out manifestations that are primarily sensoriperceptual as opposed to cognitive-intellectual. For example, some of the cognitive manifestations, such as short attention and distractibility could be listed here. Reduced responsiveness to pain reported by Wender (1971) is a sensory manifestation. There has been some thought that MBD and hyperactive children manifest perceptual difficulties. However, there is little consistent support. In fact, analysis of WISC subtest data indicates that the so-called spatial factor, made up of scores on the picture arrangement, block design, and object assembly subtests, failed to differentiate between MBD and control subjects (Dykman et al., 1973).

Learning

Academic performance is a function of many factors including motivation, adequacy of teaching as well as emotional status, and integrity of the central and peripheral nervous system. It is not difficult to see that many children, exhibiting a sufficient number of the above-mentioned symptoms to be considered MBD or hyperactive, would have learning disabilities in school. Wender (1971) estimates that one-half to two-thirds of MBD children manifest learning difficulties. The type of learning problem is not specific and can range broadly from general academic delays to difficulties in reading and sloppy writing. A number of homogeneous learning problems have been identified and are considered specific learning disabilities such as dyslexia (reading difficulties), dysgraphia (writing difficulties), and dyscalcula (arithmetic difficulties). The first of these learning disabilities—dyslexia—will be considered in greater detail in a subsequent section of this chapter.

Keogh (1971) has proposed three hypothetical mechanisms to explain the learning problems of hyperactive children. One is that both the behavioral and cognitive manifestations are caused by some type of neurologic impairment. The second considers the motor activity of the hyperactive child as interfering with attention and thus disrupting acquisition. A third view attributes the learning problems to decision making so rapid that the child responds before he has enough information to respond accurately.

More research is needed in this area, especially in terms of identifying educational remediation approaches that are effective with specific homogenous subgroups. The three mechanisms proposed by Keogh (1971) are probably all operative; that is, each mechanism is operative with a particular subgroup. What is clear is that academic functioning is impaired in hyperactive children very early in their school career (Denhoff, 1972) and interacts with other factors such as failure and motivation problems throughout the child's school years to produce a downward spiral in school performance (Ross and Ross, 1976).

CHANGES IN MANIFESTATION OVER TIME

Not only are there changes in the manifestations of MBD and hyperactivity over time, but over time the view about these changes has changed. There have been an increasing number of investigations about the early life and later life of hyperactive children that have challenged previously held views. In the early 1960s, hyperactivity was seen as a brain damage syndrome "to be treated with stimulant drugs, minimal stimulation classrooms, and possibly psychotherapy," a syndrome accorded "a favorable prognosis for the adolescent years" (Ross and Ross, 1976, p.19). Typically, hyperactivity was considered as a problem of middle childhood that disappeared in adolescence. However, there is an increasing awareness of the duration of effect. "There is now evidence that hyperactivity may span the major developmental stages, often being apparent in the last trimester of pregnancy and continuing well into adulthood" (Ross and Ross, 1976, p.289). After reviewing a number of followup studies of hyperactive children, Cantwell (1975) paints the following picture of the hyperactive child in adolescence:

> Hyperactivity per se seems to diminish with age, but the children are still more restless, excitable, impulsive and distractible than their peers. Attentional and concentration difficulties remain major problems. Chronic, severe underachievement in almost all academic areas is a characteristic finding. Low self-esteem, poor self-image, depression and a sense of failure are common. Antisocial behavior occurs in up to one-quarter and a significant number have had police contact and court referral. (p.58)

The results of the followup study by Dykman et al. (1973) are similar in showing MBD cases to be improved over time on the neurological exam but still behind controls, who had also improved over time. In addition, the MBD cases were markedly behind in reading, spelling, and arithmetic. The school difficulties experienced by children with MBD and hyperactivity can be postulated as contributing to the pattern of secondary emotional problems that further interfere with the child's functioning. There are only a few studies of hyperactive children as adults, but Cantwell (1975) believes these are suggestive of as poor an adult outcome as has been found in adolescence.

Another recent advance has been to look for manifestations in infancy, and even in prenatal and neonatal factors, which would place a child at risk for the subsequent manifestations of MBD and hyperactivity later in childhood. The work of Thomas, Chess, and Birch (1960) has been instrumental in focusing attention on precursors of the hyperactive child in the temperament of infants. The infant characterized by high activity level, irregularity, nonadaptability, high intensity, and negative mood is considered to be at particular risk for behavioral and learning problems. Well-controlled longitudinal followup studies are needed to elucidate other manifestations in infancy and early childhood and their relationship to functioning in middle childhood, adolescence, and adulthood. Kalverboer, Touwen, and Prechtl (1973) followed up infants at risk for minor brain dysfunction. They attempted to relate obstetrical data and neonatal and preschool neurological data to detailed descriptions of behavior observed under different experimental conditions at preschool age (free field behavior with and without toys). They derived an optimality score, a global measure of the integrity of the nervous functions based on the number of nonoptimal items in neonatal and preschool neurological exams, for 147 children 4 to 5 years old. They found no significant correlation between the neonatal neurological optimality score and the optimality score at the age of 5 in the total group but a low correlation ($r = .28$, p. $= .03$) in the boys without complications in the interval between diagnostic assessment (N = 57). In comparing the free field behavior of optimal and nonoptimal boys, they found that the nonoptimal boys showed more inconsistency in motor activity and play behavior as a reaction to a lack of motivating objects (toys).

The retrospective study of birth records by Minde et al. (1968) with respect to 23 different prenatal and perinatal complications showed only limited support for the hypothesis that hyperactive children (N = 56) show a higher percentage of prenatal or perinatal abnormalities as compared with controls matched for sex and socioeconomic family status at birth (N = 56). More hyperactive than control children were born following an abnormally short or long labor, and there was a significantly higher incidence of hyperactive children who were born with the help of low forceps. The hyperactive group did not vary significantly in birth weight, fetal and neonatal distress, or type of resuscitation needed.

In a prospective study by Fitzhardinge and Steven (1972), 96 infants (39 boys and 57 girls), who were born at the Royal Victoria Hospital, Montreal, Canada, and who were singleton births with gestations of 38 weeks or more and birth weights at least 30% under the expected normal weight without obvious causes such as major congenital anomalies or prenatal infections, were followed for a minimum of five years. Also followed for five years were 36 siblings (14 boys and 22 girls) who had normal birth weights and birth histories and were paired by age and sex with test patients as a comparison group. The incidence of speech, hearing, and vision defects and major/minor neurological difficulties, including intellectual deficits and MBD, was determined. The diagnosis of MBD was based on the presence of hyperactivity, short attention span, learning problems particularly related to perceptual limitations, poor fine motor coordination, abnormal EEG tracing, and hyperreflexia in children at least 5 years of age. Of the 67 children over the age of 5 without major neurological difficulties, 22% of the boys (7/32) and 26% of the girls (9/35) had sufficient minor abnormalities to warrant the diagnosis of MBD. Only one girl of the 24 control siblings who were over the age of 5 (1/24) had such a diagnosis. There was no significant correlation, however, between the degree of growth stunting at birth and the incidence of major or minor cerebral abnormalities. In addition, there was also no significant correlation between degree of intrauterine growth retardation and subsequent intelligence scores. However, the need to assess total performance in determining incidence of difficulties was demonstrated by the findings with those children for whom adequate assessment of school performance was obtained. Poor school performance was demonstrated by 50% (11/22) of the boys and 36% (14/25) of the girls and one-third of the children with IQ scores over 100 were failing consistently at school.

Such work on the identification of clusters of symptoms and of obstetrical, prenatal, and neonatal factors that identify children at risk will en-

able not only early detection but also early initiation of intervention procedures to eliminate or reduce subsequent symptom development. With this
type of work, effort can truly be directed at prevention. Ross and Ross
(1976) have proposed a prevention strategy which consists of modifications
in caretaking and socialization routines so that family patterns are not
seriously disrupted and no impression of abnormality in the child is conveyed.

ETIOLOGY

Organic Factors

Although there is considerable diversity in the symptoms that comprise the MBD or hyperactive child syndrome, these basically constitute
behavioral disorders with neurological implications. The implication is "that
cerebral abnormality is the primary basis for the presenting behavioral
disturbance" (Benton, 1973, p.29). The implications of cerebral abnormality is arrived at by exclusion of other known causes for similar behavior,
such as environmental deprivation, primary emotional disturbance, peripheral nervous system damage, or central nervous system damage. Consequently, there is no firm evidence for organic etiology. The evidence is
inferential. The adoption of the adjective "minimal" adds nothing to the
clarity of the concept. This term even obfuscates any etiological analysis by
translating observed behavioral abnormalities, which are judged to be relatively "minor" as compared with mental deficiency or cerebral palsy, into a
hypothetical state of brain impairment that is, at worst, slight. But many
studies have shown that cerebral lesions in children must be extensive or
have specific disorganizing effects in order to result in significant behavioral
abnormalities (Benton, 1973). Consequently, the behavioral disorders constituting MBD and hyperactivity can hardly be considered to have resulted
from "minimal" cerebral dysfunction. Benton's (1973) remarks are worth
considering in full:

> These considerations lead to the conclusion that, if MBD is to be retained as a
> diagnostic category, it is reasonable to adopt the working hypothesis that it is
> caused by major (not minimal) cerebral abnormality. Presumably this conclu-
> sion is as true for a relatively discrete deficit such as developmental dyslexia as
> it is for a more pervasive disturbance such as hyperkinesis. It is also reason-

able to assume that the cerebral abnormalities underlying such contrasting behavioral deviation differ in nature and that no single type of neural dysfunction is likely to be identified as responsible for diverse manifestations of MBD. (p.31)

The fact that MBD children are a heterogeneous group in terms of behavior characteristics lends credence to the idea that they are likely to be etiologically heterogeneous also. Syndrome analysis is needed to find more homogeneous subgroups in terms of behavioral characteristics that can then be related to more specific etiological factors.

Wender (1973) has speculated about a possible biochemical basis for some MBD children. He postulates that primary psychological deficits can account for the observed behavioral abnormalities seen in MBD children. One postulated psychological deficit is an increase in arousal, which he views as contributing to a lessening of concentration, attention, and inhibition of responses to the irrelevant. This psychological deficit is seen as accounting for social noncompliance and academic difficulties. Another psychological deficit is diminished capacity for positive and negative affect, which results in subjectively diminished sensitivity to positive and negative reinforcement. This is seen as accounting for the child's greater difficulty in being socialized and greater readiness in being bored. These two primary psychological deficits are, in Wender's view, secondary to disorders of monoamine metabolism, which may occur on a genetic basis: "The major hypothesis I wish to advance is that the primary deficits can occur on a biochemical basis" (p.21).

Wender believes that the response of some of the MBD children to stimulants and antidepressants in terms of the dramatic quieting effect and improvement in complex psychological function, such as cognitive, social, and interpersonal behavior, suggests something about etiology. "Such responsiveness, if not documenting a restitution of a fundamental defect, does suggest an intervention close to the origin of the causal chain" (p.22). This belief is expressed with due recognition that the lack of a treatment agent is not the cause of disease, such that pneumonia does not result from an absence of penicillin. Stimulant and antidepressant drugs act variously to increase the functional activity of areas in the central nervous system in which serotonin, dopamine, and norepinephrine are neurotransmitters. It is known that serotonin acts to decrease motor activity while dopamine, and especially norepinephrine, increase activity and decrease sedation.

Wender points out that a subgroup of MBD children are apparently hypoaroused as evidenced by studies of heart rate, galvanic skin response (GSR), and EEG data. Stimulants such as amphetamines are seen as successful with this group in that they actively inhibit dopamine reuptake and diminish attentional and affective abnormalities. The improvement in these psychological deficits results in improvement in behavior.

Theoretical formulations similar to that of Wender, in conjunction with empirical investigations or syndrome analysis, are needed to specify homogeneous subgroups, with specific etiologies. These behaviorally and etiologically homogeneous subgroups could then be related to specific management approaches.

Environmental Factors

Although we have narrowed our etiological focus thus far to a consideration of organic factors, environmental contributions cannot be overlooked. As we have maintained previously, an individual's functioning always represents an interaction among organic and environmental factors.

A number of environmental factors have been postulated as having an etiological role in MBD. Traumatic events, such as severe illness, injury, and prenatal and perinatal problems, are environmental events that are seen as resulting in brain damage and hence in the MBD or hyperactive child. Although Wender (1971, p.38) contends that "there are well-documented associations between complications of pregnancy and birth and the later appearance of the MBD syndrome," others find the evidence less compelling (Ross and Ross, 1976, p.70).

Other damage-producing environmental agents postulated as having an etiological role in MBD and hyperactivity include food additives, lead poisoning, and radiation stress. These factors are in the preliminary stage of scientific investigation, and the interested reader is referred to the consideration of the current evidence by Ross and Ross (1976). Delayed maturation has also been postulated as a cause, and the hyperactive child or MBD child may be a function of developmental lag in a specific subgroup (Kinsbourne, 1973).

Additional environmental factors are the so-called psychogenic factors, such as learning and childrearing, which have been postulated as having an etiological role in MBD and hyperactivity. The traditional view has perceived the irritable, negative, nonadaptable child as resulting from inadequate parenting. The recent work on mother-child interactions, especially the recognition of the bidirectionality of these interactions. (Bell, 1968; Thompson and Linscheid, 1976) along with the work on infant temperament patterns (Thomas, Chess, and Birch, 1968; Buss and Plomin, 1975) and the effects these have on the caregiver (Lewis and Rosenblum, 1974) have provided fertile ground for investigation of the interaction of a number of etiological factors. The methodologies now exist to engage in longitudinal investigations of these causative factors—as well as risk factors based on organic damage or dysfunction—as they relate to subsequent behavior and learning disorders and to the effectiveness of early intervention efforts.

Psychogenic factors, in the form of emotional disturbance, while not viewed as having an etiological role in hyperactivity and MBD per se, may be the causative factor in some subgroups. Thompson and Schindler (1976) have postulated that some children viewed as hyperactive may in fact be exhibiting embryonic mania. The role of depression in the hyperkinetic syndrome has also been considered (Zrull, McDermott, and Pozanski, 1970).

Genetic Factors

In reviewing the evidence from family, adoption, and twin studies, Cantwell (1975) maintains that the data suggest an important role for genetic factors in the hyperactive child syndrome. Morrison and Stewart (1974) have suggested polygenic inheritance as the likely mode of transmission of this condition. In polygenic transmission, the phenotype is produced not by one gene but by the summation of a correct number or combination of genes. Although there is a suggestion of genetic transmission, there is as yet no proof, which requires the specification of the precise genetic mechanism involved. Cantwell (1975) points out that the only procedures that can precisely define a genetic mechanism are segregation studies and linkage studies that require the discovery of the "genetic marker" associated with the hyperactive child syndrome.

MBD AND HYPERACTIVITY AS SYNDROMES

Throughout our discussion of MBD and hyperactivity, we have consistently referred to these disorders as syndromes. However, whether these disorders warrant syndrome status is open to question. Now that we have considered the various manifestations and etiological factors, we can consider the appropriateness of assigning syndrome status to these disorders. Ross and Ross (1976, p. 9) point out that there are two critical requirements for syndrome status: "that the symptoms form an unitary cluster, and that they have a common cause or at least have major etiological factors in common."

Some studies have failed to find substantial clustering among the symptoms of MBD (Routh and Roberts, 1972), and there is little evidence that the symptoms have a common cause (Ross and Ross, 1976). Benton (1973) makes the following assessment:

> We call the several features of MBD a "syndrome," but there is in fact, no evidence that this congeries of diverse abnormalities—motor defects, impulsivity, distractibility and hyperactivity, specific failure in language development, personality deviation, and conduct disorder—warrant the designation either in the sense that the separate elements occur together or in the sense that they arise from a common, underlying functional abnormality. (p. 33)

Use of the term syndrome is inappropriate and adds little and may actually be counterproductive (Schmitt, 1975). Since the MBD and hyperactive groups are not homogeneous, it would be more productive to avoid these general umbrella terms and use the specific behavioral problems involved to refer to the difficulties of a child or a group of children. As we have repeatedly indicated, the more precisely defined the problems are behaviorally, the easier it will be to identify homogeneous subgroups that can then be investigated for common etiologies and effective management and prevention procedures.

MANAGEMENT

Most discussions of the management of the hyperactive or MBD child advocate multimodality treatment with three major modes: pharmacological, behavioral (including psychotherapeutic), and educational. We will consider each of these modes separately with recognition than an integrated treatment program is a necessity.

Pharmacological Treatment

Since 1937 when Bradley described the paradoxical effect of Benzedrine (amphetamine sulfate), a stimulating effect with adults but a calming effect on children, the "paradoxical response" of MBD children to the amphetamines has been repeatedly noted. The dramatic effectiveness of this medication in improving behavior has been a consistent finding with heterogeneous groups of children. In fact, Wender (1971, p.88) maintains: "It was the common responsiveness to amphetamines which constituted one of the reasons for grouping this seemingly heterogeneous group of children together under the cognomen 'minimal brain dysfunction.'"

The dramatic effectiveness of stimulant medication is reflected first in a general quieting, an increased attentiveness and persistence, a decreased distractibility, a decreased daydreaming, and an increased sensitivity to reward and punishment; then in more social controls and self-controls; and finally in increased introversion and better academic performance (Wender, 1971).

Before considering in more detail the response to stimulant drugs, we need to consider how amphetamine acts to produce such changes. Snyder and Meyerhoff (1973) present a concise description. Amphetamine is chemically similar to the catecholamines, dopamine and norepinephrine. Both methylphenidate hypochloride (Ritalin) and the tricyclic antidepressants seem to act in a way similar to amphetamine. Amphetamine increases the amount of norepinephrine or dopamine available at synapses for receptor stimulation. It can mimic catecholamines at their receptor sites, and it inhibits monomine oxidase, an enzyme that degrades the catecholamines. It impairs the reuptake inactivation of the catecholamines and can release catecholamines directly into the synaptic cleft. It has been found that _D_-amphetamine is considerably more potent than _L_-amphetamine in inhibition of reuptake inactivation and in synaptic release affecting norepinephrine neurons but similar in affecting dopamine neurons. This difference in potency is useful in determining which behaviors are mediated by which neurotransmitter. If _D_-amphetamine is more effective than _L_-amphetamine in eliciting a behavioral effect, norepinephrine may be responsible. If _D_-amphetamine and _L_-amphetamine have similar effects, dopamine would be the implicated neurotransmitter. Snyder and Meyerhoff (1973) point out that some results indicate that brain dopamine is involved in the effects of amphetamine upon symptoms of MBD and that dopamine tracts mediate MBD. But evidence also suggests that norepinephrine pathways mediate the alerting effects of amphetamine.

It has been pointed out (Fish, 1975; Ross and Ross, 1976) that there is not a true paradoxical effect in the response of MBD children to stimulant medication. The erroneous impression comes about by confusing the behavioral effect with the pharmacological. Furthermore, Satterfield (1975) hypothesizes that there is a subgroup of hyperactive children who have low CNS arousal and insufficient CNS inhibition. It is the insufficient inhibitory control over motor functions that is seen as resulting in excessive and inappropriate motor activity. Poor inhibitory control over sensory functions could result in distractibility as well as response to irrelevant and to relevant stimuli. Stimulant medication is hypothesized to increase arousal and inhibitory levels, which in turn enable the child to attend and inhibit motor and sensory overresponsiveness.

Having considered how stimulants work on the central nervous system and some possible mechanisms of effect, we can return to a consideration of the effects of stimulant medication upon the behavior of hyperactive and MBD children. Although Eisenberg and Conners (1971) acknowledge that the findings of a majority of the drug investigations are difficult to accept with any confidence because of the inadequacy of most study designs, they elaborate upon the previously reported dramatic effects:

> Effects on activity level and motor performance are generally in the direction of more controlled, skilled performances, particularly where goal directed striving is an important component of the task. Various perceptual, intellectual and performance tasks have been enhanced by the stimulants in children with a variety of behavioral disturbances, most notably in those with poor impulse control and impulsivity. These changes are most likely a function of enhanced attention to the tasks or control over response, or both. Effects on mood and personality are less well understood, though often the drugs appear to produce a sense of well being and a vigorous, zestful approach to the environment. (pp. 416–417)

Ross and Ross (1976) have attempted to evaluate what accounts for improvements in specific behaviors. The effect upon activity level of stimulant medication is seen as situation specific. That is, there is no pervasive general reduction of activity but a decrease in extraneous activity and task irrelevant behavior in demand situations. The improvement on an array of fine motor tasks is seen as resulting from the acquisition of more selective control of motor behavior. Drug studies on classroom behavior have not focused upon factors such as problem solving or academic achievement but instead have considered more repetitious routine tasks that require sustained attention and effort. Performance gains on standardized intelligence tests have been a consistent finding, but again, attention and motivation improvements are seen as the cause rather than any significant change in "intelligence." What needs to be demonstrated to support the assumption that stimulants make a child more amenable to remedial procedures is improvement in achievement and abilities scores.

Although we will not discuss them, a number of other medications have been used with varying success with hyperactive and MBD children. These include caffeine, Cylert, tricyclic antidepressants, Benadryl, and the phenothiazines, Thorazine and Mellaril. The interested reader is directed toward the reviews by Millichap (1973) and Eisenberg and Conners (1971).

SIDE EFFECTS   The most frequent side effects of amphetamine treatment are insomnia and anorexia (Wender, 1971); increased heart rate and delay in growth are seen as long-term side effects particularly at high-dose levels (Ross and Ross, 1976). It is important to be aware of the potential for interaction of amphetamine with other medications. For example, there is a report that therapeutic doses of seizure control medications, such as Dilantin and phenobarbital, can be raised to toxic levels by the inhibition effect of amphetamines on metabolizing enzymes of the liver (Ross and Ross, 1976).

PREDICTING GOOD RESPONDERS   The work of Satterfield (1973, 1975) is illustrative of efforts to identify constellations of findings which will predict good responses to medication. In an investigation of response to methylphenidate (1973), he found that MBD children with an abnormal EEG and an abnormal neurological examination responded significantly better (55% mean improvement) than the group with normal EEG and normal neurological examination (25% mean improvement). The group with abnormal EEG but normal neurological showed 35% mean improvement, and the group with normal EEG but abnormal neurological showed a mean improvement of 45%. The findings of both an abnormal EEG and an abnormal neurological would predict a good response to methylphenidate treatment (90% of these in Satterfield's study obtained 30% or greater improvement). However, the finding must be placed within the context of the good response of 70% of the 57 MBD children versus 21% made worse. Furthermore, 60% of those with both a normal EEG and a normal neurological also showed 30% or more improvement.

In other studies, Satterfield (1975) related good response to methylphenidate to laboratory measures such as low skin conductance level; high amplitude, low frequency resting EEG; large-evoked cortical response amplitudes; and excessive slow wave activity manifested in the clinical EEG, which is consistent with the hypothesis of low central nervous system arousal in good responder hyperactive children. The principle findings were as follows. There is an identifiable subgroup of good responders who have low CNS arousal. Pretreatment CNS arousal is negatively correlated with severity of the behavioral disturbance. Stimulant medications in these children with low CNS arousal increase CNS arousal level, and those with the greatest increase in CNS arousal obtained the best clinical response as measured by teacher rating scales.

Most of the studies on the effectiveness of stimulants with MBD and hyperactive children have been with elementary school-aged children. There is some indication that methylphenidate is ineffective with preschoolers (Schleifer, 1975).

Along with this varied picture of effectiveness of drug intervention, there is a growing concern about the uncritical use of stimulant medication in clinical situations with MBD and hyperactive children. Despite the fact that most practitioners recognize the necessity for a multidisciplinary approach to management, the only intervention is most frequently medication (Ross and Ross, 1976). Not only is medication alone inadequate, but drugs are very frequently initiated without proper prior assessment of the child and his environment. Many physicians initiate medication in order to use the child's response to diagnose hyperactivity (Ross and Ross, 1976). Even after initiating drug treatment, subsequent monitoring and followup are not adequately accomplished. Solomons (1973) found that 47% of a group of 97 hyperkinetic children were inadequately monitored. Adequate monitoring was defined as parents having contacted the physician concerning drug therapy, either by telephone or by visits, twice within six months or three times within 12 months after the child had been evaluated at a child development clinic and referred back to the physician. Solomons concluded that drugs for MBD children were not being properly employed by many physicians.

One cannot review this area without consternation over the variability of findings originating out of inadequate, poorly designed studies. The result is necessarily a lack of scientifically based, well-monitored, drug intervention practices. The crying need to alter the situation—beginning with basic clinical research—is stated with conviction by Ross and Ross (1976).

The lack of consensus concerning the extent to which drug intervention constitutes appropriate treatment for the hyperactive child has contributed to, and is
also a result of, inadequate and unsystematic research with conflicting results
due to methodological weaknesses. Since criteria for acceptable research procedures are well established, the presence of major methodological weaknesses in many drug studies can only be the result of indifference, ignorance,
or bias on the part of researchers. Whatever the reason, the effect is to render
the findings of these studies virtually worthless. One result is that many practitioners are prescribing drug intervention in the absence of a firm empirical
basis for their decision. (p.95)

Behavioral Management

Behavioral management is used here to refer to a variety of procedures
from psychotherapy to behavior therapy. Although the usefulness of, and
necessity for, psychotherapeutic intervention with MBD and hyperactive
children has been questioned (Wender, 1971), the array of disruptive behaviors characteristic of these disorders affect the stimulus value of the
child (Lewis and Rosenblum, 1974) and thus how significant others in the
environment will respond to him and his own self-evaluation. There are essential aspects of the child's functioning that must receive attention. While
drug therapy may enable greater motor control and attention, it is not
likely that the child's self-concept or his stimulus value to parents,
teachers, and peers will automatically change. In relation to these aspects
of overall functioning, there are three major roles for behavior management. The first is to assist the child and his family in understanding the
MBD or hyperactive child as an individual with unique strengths as well as
weaknesses and the reasonable expectancies of a comprehensive integrated
treatment plan derived from an interdisciplinary diagnostic evaluation. The
second is to assist the child and family in dealing with any secondary or
reactive emotional or behavioral problems that might exist. The third role
is to use behavioral management approaches to directly alter disruptive behavior such as overactivity, poor frustration tolerance, and temper outbursts and to increase appropriate behaviors such as impulse control and
attention.

Frequently, by the time a child is brought to a clinic for evaluation,
there has been a history of dissatisfaction and conflict within the home and
school. There tends to be a focusing upon the problem behaviors and areas
of dissatisfaction. The thorough interdisciplinary diagnostic evaluation is
necessary to reach a formulation that will present a holistic view of the

child's strengths and weaknesses, his or her assets and problems. A common problem for a family, but especially for a child, is overgeneralization of weakness and inadequacy. The child understands that he is different, has less success at many things, and gets more negative feedback than other children and overgeneralizes this to a pervasive feeling of inadequacy. A major role for behavioral management is to elucidate and delineate accurately different competencies and to provide appropriate remediation plans and expectancies accordingly. A particular area of concern involves drug therapy. The reason for prescribing a certain drug, the anticipated effects, including possible side effects, and the necessary monitoring, all need to be explained in detail to the child and his family. This is necessary to ensure accurate administration and reporting about behavioral change as well as compliance.

As a secondary or reactive component, emotional and behavioral problems occur in the MBD or hyperactive child. While not primary in terms of "causing" the MBD, these problems are often of equal importance in the functioning of the child and his family. The major problems include pervasive feeling of inadequacy and vulnerability, chronic anger and hostility (either repressed or expressed in acting-out behavior), and conflict-ridden interactions between parent and child. It is beyond the scope of this book to go into these problems and their treatment in detail. Suffice it to say, that when emotional and behavioral problems are identified, specific treatment approaches have to be included in the plan and instituted. The treatment approaches can be quite varied, ranging from traditional psychotherapy and play therapy through the newer, briefer therapies to behavior therapy along with corresponding therapy or child-management counseling with the parents. The critical aspect here is the specificity of treatment approach to problems. During the last decade, there has been a movement away from the almost random application of a heterogeneous array of psychotherapies to an equally heterogeneous array of problems. The need for matching specific treatment approaches to specific problems has been recognized (Di Loreto, 1971) and efforts are being made to determine what type of treatment is effective with particular problems in specific situations (Love, Kaswian and Bugental, 1972; Thompson, Palmer, and Linscheid, 1977). Research in this area should enable better matching of problems, therapists, and techniques and should increase the effectiveness of psychotherapeutic interventions over those customarily reported (Levitt, 1957, 1963, 1971).

Behavior therapy techniques, primarily operant conditioning and modeling, have been demonstrated to be effective in altering the inappropriate and disruptive behavior of hyperactive and MBD children (Patterson, 1965; Patterson et al., 1965). The process of behavior therapy is based upon learning principles and begins with a functional analysis of the problems. A functional analysis considers how the problem behaviors are related to other physical, emotional, cognitive, and social stimuli—and the "how" is stated in as an objective a manner as possible (Bijou and Peterson, 1971). A functional analysis, then, includes not only a consideration of the problem behavior but also the physical, emotional, cognitive, and social stimuli that elicit and maintain these behaviors. Using this approach, behaviors can be conceptualized as falling into three categories: behavioral excesses (e.g., hyperactivity); behavioral deficits (e.g., short attention span); and behavior under inappropriate stimulus control (e.g., out-of-seat in classroom). Behavior is viewed as being maintained by its consequences. Procedures such as extinction, shaping, differential reinforcement of other behaviors and modeling are utilized to eliminate undesirable behavior and to foster more appropriate behavior (Bandura, 1969).

Behavior therapy, other than operant conditioning and simple modeling, has also been utilized. Meichenbaum and Goodman (1971) have extended Luria's work (1961) on stages of the development of voluntary control over behavior. They developed a treatment program to help the child acquire voluntary control over behavior through internalization of self-control verbal commands that are modeled initially by an adult. Behavior therapy in the form of biofeedback is also beginning to be utilized (Braud, Lupin and Braud, 1975).

A cardinal feature of behavior therapy has been its rigorous utilization of experimental investigation with clinical problems through single-subject designs. This has enabled demonstration and verification of treatment responsibility for change (Birnbauer, Peterson, and Solnick 1974). Because of the precise objective specification of procedures and problems to which these are applied, replication is possible. In addition, there is a continuing effort to evaluate the behavior of the therapist so that it can be taught to other professionals and to parents (Berkowitz and Graziano, 1972; Thompson and Linscheid, 1976; Thompson et al., 1977).

Educational Management

There is little argument that children exhibiting MBD or hyperactivity present special educational needs and problems. There is a growing awareness that an overemphasis on the medical basis of hyperactivity and MBD is interfering with effective education of these children. The MBD classification and labels have provided sophisticated and respectable excuses for nonteaching and poor teaching (Bateman, 1973). Frequently, such children are perceived as "a patient and not as a learner who is ready to learn and profit from classroom instruction at least at some level" (Forness, 1975, p.159). Some consider etiology to be irrelevant to remedial education (Cohen, 1973) while others see little educational utility in the diagnosis of MBD or hyperactivity because of the heterogeneity of symptoms and behaviors included within these classifications (Forness, 1975; Bateman, 1973). The fact that a child is hyperactive does not necessarily preordain a specific educational approach. Furthermore, "so-called diagnostic-remedial matches or prescriptions rest on largely unsupported assumptions" (Bateman, 1973, p.246). Efforts to derive predictable aptitude-treatment interactions have been generally unsuccessful. For example, given poor visual memory, some educators advocate an approach based on remediating the weakness while others would advocate an approach using an intact modality (i.e., an auditory approach). Each approach may be successful with some children with visual memory problems and not with others. Thus, at present "there is no one definite school program for the hyperactive child any more than there is one kind of hyperactive child" (Ross and Ross, 1976, p.225). Educationally, what is needed is to meet the child at his or her particular level, to determine and specify behaviorally what a child needs to learn, to analyze these objectives into teachable units, and then to present concepts and skills along with opportunities for response and practice and subsequent reinforcement or correction (Bateman, 1973).

Diagnostic and etiologic classification may not yet enable specification of effective remediation procedures, but it is unwise to consider these factors as irrelevant to educational approaches. Such "labels" do convey an expectancy regarding the typical needs and behaviors of such children which will have to be met in educational endeavors. For example, Forness (1975) identifies three problems that need to be met with in helping a hyperactive child. First, there are attentional problems. Sometimes reducing distractions or reducing interference from motor behavior through medication has been useful. A second problem is motivation. It is necessary to decrease disruptive behavior and provide success experiences so that good behavior and performance can be reinforced. The third problem is impulse control. It is frequently necessary to teach a hyperactive child how to learn before trying to teach him content. For example, many hyperactive children have to learn to inhibit responding until they have sufficient information to answer a question or a problem.

Methods for handling these typical problems are also not yet specific and uniformly effective. The review by Ross and Ross (1976) of the research on minimal stimulation educational programs to deal with the problem of distractibility is a good example of the complexities involved in developing effective remediation procedures. The evidence is seen as supporting the belief that cubicles are helpful in increasing attention and volume of performance, but there seems to be little effect on test scores. Furthermore, there are indications that some hyperactive children need more, not less, stimulation.

Again, in educational management as well as in pharmacological and behavioral management, we are left with the hope that as more homogeneous subgroups of hyperactive and MBD children are identified, correspondingly effective management approaches will be delineated.

CONCLUDING REMARKS

It is hoped that this consideration of hyperactive and MBD children will convey the need for integrated, multifaceted diagnostic and management approaches to the complex problems presented by these children. Typically, diagnostic assessment will require interdisciplinary or multidisciplinary efforts, and management will include drug therapy, educational intervention, and behavioral intervention in varying combinations. Within each subpart and the whole, there is a need to carefully match specific intervention techniques with particular problems in order to improve the clinical management of these children as well as to increase our knowledge about these disorders. To do this, specific homogeneous subgroups must be delineated so that well-controlled drug intervention studies can be done and specific behavioral and educational remediation developed. This need has been recognized for the past 10 years, but in general, has been disregarded in one poorly designed study after another. Although the estimates of incidence vary with the diagnostic criteria, the reporting personnel, and the method of investigation used, the conservative estimates of from 4% to 10% of the children in the United States. (Ross and Ross, 1976) attests to the compelling need for scientifically based diagnostic and management procedures.

Recently, there have been some successes in delineating more homogeneous subgroups, for example, those who are hyperactive, those who have affective difficulties e.g., the depressed (Zrull et al., 1970), those who show embryonic mania (Thompson and Schindler, 1976), and those who are afflicted with allergy-based hyperactivity (Kittler, 1970). Typically, approaches to diagnostic classification have relied upon physical, neurological, and biochemical data to form subgroups. A different approach, which focuses upon behavior in the form of a pattern of scores on neuropsychological tests, offers considerable promise in arriving at more homogeneous subgrouping. Knights (1973) has developed a sophisticated computer-matching profile program that matches an individual's performance on 98 separate measures with those of 1,500 other individuals in the computer memory bank. Histories, and neurological data, and symptoms are also recorded for these children, and similarities in these areas are evaluated. A general finding to date has been that "the most similar characteristics among children are behavioral rather than etiological or neurological. This observation implies that for children classified as MBD, behavior may, in the long run, provide the best basis for establishing the criteria necessary for diagnosis" (p.131).

Conners (1973) also advocates the use of test data to classify subjects into homogeneous groups on the basis of behavior (pattern of responses). Then a more refined search for processes leading to a particular pattern, including genetic, neurophysiological, and environmental variables and their interactions, could be undertaken. In contrast to Knights' approach (1973), which is based on matching individual profile patterns, Conners used factor analysis of data on 267 children (aged 6–12) who were suspected of having MBD. Five factors were identified on the basis of psychological test scores (general IQ, achievement, rote learning, attentiveness, and impulse control) to arrive at six cluster types or homogeneous groups:

Group 1. Good impulse control, lower IQ, poor rote learning
Group 2. Low achievers, poor learner, somewhat inattentive
Group 3. Very poor impulse control, poor rote learner, moderate attentiveness
Group 4. Bright, high achievers, good impulse control, slightly inattentive
Group 5. Above average in most areas of functioning
Group 6. Low IQ, poor impulse control, good rote learning

Examples of group differences in response to drug therapy, motor development, and asymmetry of cortical evoked responses were given to show that the total sample of children originally diagnosed as MBD shows significant differences among the groups identified through psychological tests. (p. 300)

The utilization of individual patterns or group patterns based on measured behavior to form homogeneous subgroups will enable, it is hoped, a qualitative advance in the investigation of MBD and hyperactivity to follow the recent exponential increase in numbers of articles published on the topic (Ross and Ross, 1976). What is not needed is more "trash" in a "waste paper basket" category of MBD.

NEUROLOGICALLY BASED LEARNING DISABILITIES
INTRODUCTION

There can be little doubt that a person's ability to learn influences his adjustment in our society. Those who have difficulty in learning are indeed handicapped individuals, and, if this difficulty becomes chronic, they are indeed disabled. Learning difficulties can arise for numerous reasons such as blindness, deafness, mental retardation, and mental deficiency, all of which we have discussed previously.

Just as the concept of developmental disabilities gradually evolved from the field of mental subnormality, there has been an emerging recognition of the existence of children who do not learn normally but who are not subnormal intellectually. With the mentally subnormal, learning difficulties are intrinsic and the focus has been on developing special education techniques to develop the individual's learning to the full extent of his or her capacity. With those individuals not intellectually subnormal but still not learning normally, there has been an awareness of a discrepancy between learning performance and presumed capacity. These individuals seemed to have the integrities of the peripheral and central nervous systems and to have adequate opportunity necessary for learning, but they do not learn according to expectancy. From these gradually emerging recognitions and differentiations has come the concept of the child with a learning disability. There are numerous definitions of learning disability but a few representative samples will suffice.

Johnson and Myklebust (1967) term the condition psychoneurological learning disability, which reflects their belief that the disorder is behavioral and the causation is neurological. The criteria they utilize in effect serves as a definition: "In those having a psychoneurological learning disability, it is the fact of adequate motor ability, average to high intelligence, adequate hearing and vision, and adequate emotional adjustment together with a deficiency in learning that constitutes the basis for homogeneity" (p. 9).

Thus, the essentials of the definition are generalized integrity and a deficiency in learning. Benton (1975) maintains a similar view. In the broad sense, any learning failure for any reason is a learning disorder, but in the narrower sense it refers to "failure to learn a scholastic skill by a child whose general intelligence, maturational level, and cultural background appear to provide a fully adequate basis for such learning" (p. 2).

In the 1973 congressional hearing on the Developmental Disabilities Act, specific learning disabilities were defined as:

> A disorder in one or more of the basic psychological processes involved in understanding or in using language, spoken or written, which disorder may manifest itself in imperfect ability to listen, think, speak, read, write, spell, or do mathematical calculations, and such disorder may include such conditions as perceptual handicaps, brain injury, minimal brain dysfunction, dyslexia, or developmental aphasia, but such term does not include learning problems which are primarily the result of visual, hearing, or motor handicaps, or mental retardation, or emotional disturbance, or of environmental disadvantage.

These definitions are representative in indicating that the condition involves a deficiency in learning in spite of generalized integrity and adequate opportunity. Furthermore, Schain (1972, p.5) points out:

> It is important to recognize that the definitions of learning disability . . . tend to imply the presence of some type of selective central nervous system dysfunction that is responsible for suboptimal learning processes. However, the definitions do not require positive evidence of the presence of cerebral dysfunction; rather it is deduced from the absence of known causes of learning disorders, i.e., recognizable emotional disturbance, environmental disadvantage, sensory deficits or frank neurological disorders.

Thus we can see that the concept of learning disability has had an evolution similar to that of MBD. Learning disability is not one entity but includes various deficiencies in learning occurring in the presence of generalized integrity and adequate opportunity and attributed to cerebral dysfunction. The descriptive term, neurologically based learning disability, advocated by Silver (1975) is most appropriate.

Our consideration of this disorder must necessarily be different from those discussed previously because, by definition, the manifestations are primarily in one area—learning. However, because of the chronic confusion surrounding the interrelationship of learning and emotional problems, a fuller consideration of this area is needed.

LEARNING DISABILITIES AND EMOTIONAL PROBLEMS

Most people believe that there is a positive correlation between emotional problems and learning disorders. This view is held despite a paucity of sound research efforts to substantiate these beliefs (Connolly, 1971). Sound research is difficult to conduct in this area because emotional malfunctioning is a relative and subjective phenomenon. Furthermore, instruments to determine emotional malfunctioning are poorly developed because "man's emotional condition is largely an amorphous entity, constantly changing, developing, and being altered in an intangible fashion" (Connolly, 1971, p. 153). Thus, for many years there has existed a tacit assumption that learning disorders and emotional problems were related. This assumption influenced diagnostic and intervention thinking and procedures. Clements and Peters (1962, p. 185) report that for "many years, it has been the custom among child guidance workers to attribute the behavior and learning deviations seen in children almost exclusively to the rearing patterns and interpersonal relations experienced by such youngsters. In many clinics, it has become habitual to assume psychogenicity when no easily recognizable organic deviation can be found."

Perhaps the reliance upon psychogenic theories occurred because of their capacity to explain phenomena and assuage one's lack of knowledge and understanding. The traditional psychoanalytic view interprets learning problems as resulting from failure to identify with parents and teacher (Jampolsky, 1965; Connolly, 1971). Klein (1949) has stressed the importance of the need for the infant's gratification in the first year of life as a necessary preparation for learning, while Sylvester and Kunst (1943) have emphasized the significance of the thwarting of the child's early exploratory activities to later reading problems. Those children who have not resolved their Oedipal conflicts may be fearful of hostile and aggressive impulses and therefore be afraid to succeed or to be competitive and thereby demonstrate learning problems (Jampolsky, 1965). The role of anxiety, stemming from intrapersonal and interpersonal conflict, in inhibiting children from learning has also been acknowledged (Jampolsky, 1965). With marked impairment, the severely disturbed or schizophrenic child may be so involved in his own fantasy that he is unable to learn (Pearson, 1955; Jampolsky, 1965).

Although there has been a history of reliance upon psychogenic theories, "during recent years evidence has been accumulating that illustrates the gross inadequacy of conceptualizing learning disorders as simply a manifestation of an underlying emotional disturbance" (Connolly, 1971, p.154). Because of the evidence of the influence of neurological factors as well as psychological factors in learning problems, "The inaccuracies and limitations of the traditional psychiatric framework have become apparent" (Connolly, 1971, p.154).

What has resulted is a more considered view. Some children with learning problems do exhibit neurotic fears and traits previously described in the psychodynamic literature. But it is no longer assumed that all or most of the youngsters with learning problems fit into this conceptual framework. Some children fail to learn and exhibit behavior problems because of a primary emotional problem stemming from organic or environmental factors. For other children, the emotional problems are secondary and "the maladaptive behavior is best understood as a result of interplay of inadequately developed primary skill system and environmental stresses that interfere with psychosexual development, and adversely influence self-concept" (Rubin, 1971, p.182). The probability that a learning-disabled child will develop emotional or behavioral problems is related to many variables such as severity and chronicity of the problem, age, sex, subcultural group, socioeconomic level, and intelligence (Connolly, 1971). Many learning-disabled children do cope well. However, all encounter serious obstacles to adjustment, and emotional demands and stress exceed those encountered by most children.

Learning-disabled children have the same basic needs and drives as other children, such as need for acceptance, adequacy, competency, and mastery; but their handicap sometimes obstructs the satisfaction of these needs and drives. When this occurs, adjustment is threatened and emotional and behavior problems may develop. The expression of these problems is varied. "The literature is in almost unanimous agreement in stating that there is no single reaction pattern or syndrome of behavior common to the learning-disabled population" (Connolly, 1971, p.161).

However, there are some commonalities. Because of the cognitive-perceptual-motor difficulties, the child can be viewed as vulnerable (Rubin,

1971). This vulnerability can lead to learning and behavior problems that influence the reaction of environmental figures. Frequently, these significant environmental figures (parents and teachers) can respond with blame and criticism that in effect increases stress and consequently feelings of frustration and tension. Poor self-concept results from failures and from the feedback that the child receives from others. This poor self-concept and feelings of inadequacy are likely to prolong dependency and immaturity and the utilization of immature defense mechanisms, such as projection of blame and avoidance. This avoidance of tasks impairs motivation and causes a further deficit in skills because certain skills must be practiced to be learned. Thus, there is a lack of improvement, which perpetuates this vicious circle.

Recently, there has been a reliance upon categorizing models based upon an either/or theory of etiology. That is, conceptualizing school maladjustment either as a learning problem or as an emotional problem. This has resulted in some benefits such as classes for learning-disabled and for emotionally disturbed children. However, the underlying continuum has been obscured. "The absence of a theoretical construct that permits integration of personality deviations and learning disability means that many children with disturbed behavioral functioning are misunderstood and mishandled" (Rubin, 1971, p. 181).

What is needed for effective management is a model that integrates an understanding of personality variables with other functional impairments. The model of secondary emotional problems as outlined above with its focus upon environmental factors interacting with vulnerabilities is a step in the right direction.

With this introduction to the concept of learning disabilities, what it is and what it is not—and what is presumed responsible—we can now consider neurologically based learning disabilities in greater detail. A survey conducted by the U. S. Office of Education during the spring of 1970 revealed the numbers of pupils with specific learning disabilities in local public schools in the United States. The survey included 2,000 local public schools, which were representative of the 81,000 schools within school districts enrolling 300 or more pupils. It suggested that 2.6% of pupils (1,160,000) have specific learning disabilities, with 1.4% (648,000) receiving special instruction. Elementary schools reported a higher incidence (3.1%) than was reported by secondary schools (1.8%) (Silverman and Metz, 1973).

As previously noted, the disorder of neurologically based learning disabilities is a heterogeneous, umbrella category similar to that of MBD. Rather than consider each of the numerous specific learning disabilities, we will consider in detail a specific reading disability—dyslexia—as representative of the category as a whole and also of the movement toward greater specificity of homogeneous subgroups even within subgroups. The reader interested in a broader consideration of the area of learning disabilities is referred to several comprehensive sources (Hellmuth, 1968; Johnson and Myklebust, 1967; Myklebust, 1968, 1971, 1975).

DYSLEXIA
READING AS A PROCESS

Those of us who have learned to read with little difficulty take reading pretty much for granted. Reading is, however, a very complex cognitive-auditory-visuo-spatial process. It involves integration of several input, output, and mediating processes (Mattis, French, and Rapin, 1975) cross-modal integration, symbolization, and communication. It requires the development of cognitive clarity in terms of the necessary language concepts and the understanding of the purpose and mechanism of the reading act (Downing, 1973). Boder (1973, p.667) summarizes the necessary components: "Reading requires visual perception and discrimination, visual sequential memory and recall, and directional orientation (Benton 1962; Birch, 1962); it also requires cross-modal integration—including the translation of visual symbols into meaningful auditory equivalents (Bauza et al., 1962; Ingram, 1963; Birch and Belmont, 1964; Rabinovitch, 1968)."

And Benton (1975, p.6) elaborates upon the processing involved. "The act of reading involves many component processes of different degrees of complexity, ranging from the visual discrimination of graphemes and recognition of the phonemic value of single consonants and vowels, through the recognition of single words, to the apprehension of meaningful word sequences taken as units."

The two frequently utilized reading instruction methods are based on the visual and auditory processes underlying reading. The whole-word or look-say technique is based on the child's ability to experience the whole printed word as a visual gestalt. The phonics technique relies upon the child's analytic and synthesizing abilities in separating words into their phonetic components.

Any failure to learn or retardation in learning this complex reading process, can be considered as dyslexia. Reading retardation occurs whenever there is a significant discrepancy between the actual reading level of a child and the reading level expected according to mental age (Rabinovitch, 1968). The amount of discrepancy considered to be significant by most authors is between 1 and 2 years.

Meaningful estimates of prevalence of reading retardation are difficult to obtain and range in the area of 10% to 30% of the total grade school population. One reason for the difficulty in obtaining meaningful estimates is the tremendous variability of reading retardation from community to community. The incidence is significantly higher in areas of limited social opportunity and economic deprivation (Rabinovitch, 1968).

Along with the variability in incidence of reading retardation, it has long been recognized that there can be various factors contributing to or causing the reading disability. This recognition has resulted in efforts to derive a classification system for dyslexia. Blom and Jones (1971) reviewed 24 references on classification of dyslexia and found four methods of classification.

1. Functional—description of reading behavior
2. Etiological—classification according to cause
3. Theoretical—according to a theoretic model, e.g., a psychoanalytic ego model (Pearson, 1955); a structural model of the intellect (Guilford, 1967)
4. Nosological—a disease system.

Although there are four methods of classification, most of the efforts to date have focused on functional and etiological approaches. Those involved with remediation often turn to a functional approach, but for a comprehensive understanding of the condition, knowledge of cause and underlying pathology is necessary (Keeney, 1968). It is likely that remediation approaches will be much more successful if the technique is predicated not only upon the functional deficits but also the reasons for the deficit.

TYPES OF DYSLEXIA

Although we are presenting dyslexia as representative of specific learning disabilities, dyslexia is an umbrella term, similar to MBD and hyperactivity, and is used in reference to some reading disorders that constitute learning disabilities and others that do not. One etiological basis for classifying dyslexia has been on the presence or absence of evidence of brain damage. For example, Rabinovitch (1968, p.5–6) proposes two types of dyslexia. One is primary reading retardation or developmental dyslexia; the other is secondary or reactive reading retardation.

1. PRIMARY—Developmental dyslexia

   Capacity to learn to read is impaired without definite brain damage suggested in the history or on neurologic examination. The defect is in the ability to deal with letters and words as symbols, with resultant diminished ability to integrate the meaningfulness of written material. The problem appears to reflect a basic disturbed pattern of neurologic organization.

2. SECONDARY

   a. *Other encephalopathy*

      Capacity to learn to read is impaired by frank brain damage manifested by clear-cut neurologic deficits. The picture is similar to the early described adult dyslexic syndrome. Other definite aphasic difficulties are generally present. History usually reveals the cause of the brain injury, common agents being prenatal toxicity, birth trauma or anoxia, encephalitis, and head injury.

   b. *Other factors*

      Emotional, motivational, deprivation-opportunity. Capacity to learn to read is intact but is utilized insufficiently for the child to achieve a reading level appropriate to his mental age. This causative factor is exogenous, the child having a normal reading potential that has been impaired by negativism, anxiety, depression, emotional blocking, psychosis, limited schooling opportunity, or other external influence.

The most detailed and comprehensive classification of dyslexia (Table 6.2) has been developed by Keeney (1968).

It is recognized that classification systems are evolving and that it may not be possible to place every child with a reading disability into only one category; and no consensus has yet been reached on the number and nature of categories. However, researchers generally agree on the appropriateness of differentiating between dyslexia that is primary (developmental dyslexia) and dyslexia that is secondary to other pathology or environmental conditions. It is developmental dyslexia that constitutes a specific type of learning disability and as such will be considered in detail.

Developmental Dyslexia

The Research Group on Dyslexia and World Illiteracy of the World Federation of Neurologists, meeting in Dallas, Texas, in April 1968, de-

TABLE 6.2 Comprehensive classification of dyslexia

I. Specific (primary), developmental dyslexia (Strephosymbolia; dyssymbolia)
II. Secondary dyslexias (symptomatic; secondary reading retardation)
    A. Secondary to organic brain pathology
        1. Brain damage (cerebral dysfunction; other encephalopathy; cerebral palsy; mental retardation; low IQ; perceptual disorders; word blindness; visual agnosia, anomia, soft neurologic stigma)
            a. Genetic
            b. Posttraumatic
                (1) Prenatal
                (2) Natal
                (3) Postnatal
            c. Postinflammatory (intrauterine; extrauterine)
                (1) Encephalitic
                (2) Meningitic
            d. Asphyxic (hypoxic) (intrauterine; extrauterine)
                (1) Placenta previa
                (2) Cord strangulation
                (3) Maternal circulatory collapse
                (4) Excessive maternal narcosis; drugs
                (5) Circulatory collapse; cardiac arrest; cerebrovascular accidents
            e. Prematurity
            f. Other specific brain lesions (aneurysm; cyst; etc.)
    B. Secondary to slow maturation (late bloomer; developmental delay) (associated with impaired lateralization and dominance)
    C. Secondary to emotional disturbances
        1. Hyperactivity; short concentration span
        2. Depression
        3. Anxiety
    D. Secondary to uncontrolled seizure states
    E. Secondary to environmental disturbances
        1. Cultural deprivation
        2. Poor motivation (extrinsic or intrinsic)
        3. Poor instruction
III. Slow readers (handicapped without symbolic confusion), bradylexia
    A. Asthenopia; visual handicaps (hyperopia; heterophoria; astigmatism; binocular control abnormalities)
    B. Auditory impairments
    C. Hypothyroid states
IV. Acquired dyslexia (lesions of dominant hemisphere, angular gyrus, and splenium)
V. Mixed

SOURCE: Keeney, 1968

fined developmental dyslexia as: "A disorder manifested by difficulty in learning to read despite conventional instruction, adequate intelligence, and socio-cultural opportunity. It is dependent upon fundamental cognitive disabilities which are frequently of constitutional origin" (Naidoo, 1972, p. 10). Benton (1975) elaborates upon this basic definition by pointing out that (1) oral language development and sensory capacities (vision and hearing) appear to be adequate to enable the development of reading skills and (2) normal motivation to learn to read is present, at least at the beginning of schooling. Developmental dyslexia represents a specific learning disability because reading disability is present despite a general integrity of the central peripheral and nervous systems, adequate intelligence, opportunity, instruction, and motivation.

As with reading disorders in general, meaningful estimates of the numbers of persons who suffer developmental dyslexia are difficult to obtain, but dyslexics are seen as accounting for a relatively small proportion of disabled readers (Benton, 1975). Most of the evidence indicates a predominance of males exhibiting developmental dyslexia. However, Lovell, Shapton, and Warren (1964) provide data that show there is no substantial sex difference at low levels of intelligence (IQ <90), but there is impressive sex difference with average or above-average intelligence. Concerning the evidence regarding hereditary influences, Benton (1975) reports that "there is impressive evidence for the operation of a hereditary factor in developmental dyslexia" (p. 12).

Investigations of children with developmental dyslexia have endeavored to identify functional performance characteristics that accompany the condition. Attention has been directed to neurological status, speech, language, hearing functioning, visual memory, discrimination functioning, directionality, cerebral dominance, and intersensory integration capabilities of developmentally dyslexic children. These correlates of developmental dyslexia are important because they have a direct bearing on functional approaches to remediation and help to demonstrate the lack of homogeneity even within this apparently discrete category of developmental dyslexia.

Correlates of Developmental Dyslexia

NEUROLOGICAL ABNORMALITIES   A major difficulty in studies of this area has been in relating any abnormal findings to developmental dyslexia as opposed to other categories of reading retardation. Benton (1975) indicates that the data show a somewhat higher frequency of unfavorable perinatal events in histories of retarded readers as compared with those of the population at large, but all these factors are also associated with early brain damage. Also negative findings have been reported. Rutter, Tizard, and Whitmore (1970) compared the perinatal and prenatal histories of control, dyslexic, and intellectually retarded groups. They found no significant difference between the dyslexics and the controls with respect to eight factors, including complications during pregnancy, prematurity, and abnormal delivery.

The most frequently reported neurologic sign is clumsiness. Dyspraxia, hyperkinesis, motor impersistence, and choreiform movements are also reported (Benton, 1975). However, as with historical evidence of neurological abnormalities, neurologic signs cannot always be related specifically to developmental dyslexia as opposed to reading retardation or to some other condition. Benton (1975, p.30) reflects this lack of specificity. He reports that "the findings of Ingram et al. (1970) indicate that a generalized learning disability is far more likely to be associated with either minor or major neurologic abnormalities than is specific dyslexia." There continues to be little evidence of specific association between dyslexia and abnormal EEG tracings (Benton, 1975).

Also, inconsistency in findings is typical. Naidoo (1972) found no evidence that finger agnosia occurs with greater frequency among dyslexic boys than among controls but that there is a significant difference in right/left discrimination. Sparrow and Satz (1970) found dyslexics inferior to normals in finger recognition and right/left discrimination. Benton (1975) maintains that the evidence regarding finger recognition is inconsistent and that right/left confusion may be associated with reading failure in younger children but not in older children.

The role of cerebral dominance has also been focused upon (Belmont and Birch, 1965; Silver and Hagin, 1960) but it is not clearly associated with dyslexia. So-called mixed dominance has been observed in children who are adequate readers. Benton (1975, p.24) maintains that "for the most part, recent studies have reported no important differences between normal and retarded readers regarding the relative frequency of deviations from right-hand and right-eyed preferences."

Two neurological theories have been formulated concerning dyslexia. One postulates a focal maldevelopment of the brain in the parietal area. Another postulates a deficit in overall organization of cerebral function. Although these theories have some heuristic value and have not been dis-proved, they do lack substantial empirical support (Benton, 1975).

VISUOPERCEPTUAL DEFICIT   The findings concerning the association of visuoperceptual deficits, such as visual discrimination difficulties and trans-position of letters, are also inconsistent. Many investigations have found developmentally dyslexic children to be demonstrating visuoperceptual problems (Boder 1973; Johnson and Myklebust, 1967; Mason, 1967; Mattis et al., 1975; and Stanley, Kaplan, and Poole, 1975). However, Benton (1975) believes that only a relatively small portion of dyslexics are deficient in this area.

LANGUAGE AND AUDITORY DISABILITIES   Language is implicated as a logi-cal determinant of developmental dyslexia because of the evidence that poor linguistic development often predates the recognition of a reading dis-ability. Also significant delay in using sentences and greater incidence of articulatory deficits have been noted (Naidoo, 1972). Benton (1975, p.21) claims substantial evidence shows that "the majority of dyslexic children" do in fact have "some degree of oral language retardation in relation to level of general intelligence." Evidence that supports verbal weakness comes from examination of the relationship between Wechsler verbal and performance IQ scores. Many studies with dyslexic children show a signifi-cantly lower verbal than performance IQ (Ackerman et al., 1971; Belmont and Birch, 1966; Rutter et al., 1970; Warrington, 1967). There is consider-able variability reflected in the WISC subtest scores for dyslexic children, with relative weakness generally being exhibited in vocabulary, informa-tion, arithmetic, digit span, and coding.

Although Naidoo (1972) found no differences between dyslexic chil-dren and controls in auditory discrimination, he did find significant dif-ferences in sound blending. Dyslexics were also found inferior to controls in auditory sequential memory (Stanley et al., 1975). Additional support for language and auditory disorders in dyslexia comes from (Boder, 1973; John-son and Myklebust, 1967; and Mattis et al., 1975).

INTERSENSORY INTEGRATION   Reading has been described as a visual symbol system superimposed upon auditory language (Johnson and Mykle-bust, 1967). Since reading involves equating visual symbols with auditory sounds, cross-modal integration is required (Boder, 1973). Benton (1975) maintains that impairment in cross-modal matching has been empirically established in dyslexics, but questions still persist about the mechanisms involved, e.g., auditory memory, bisensory stimuli, or temporally sequential stimuli.

From this review of the correlates of developmental dyslexia, it can be readily seen that the findings are marked by inconsistency in almost all areas. This inconsistency led to the realization that considerable heterogeneity existed within the category of developmental dyslexia and more homogeneous subtypes would be necessary to determine antecedents and correlates and specific remediation techniques. Many of the efforts to delineate subtypes of developmental dyslexia were based on constellations of the above-enumerated correlates and functional deficits or performance patterns.

Subtypes of Developmental Dyslexia

Naidoo (1972) reports Ingram's (1964) proposal of three subcategories of developmental dyslexia based on the performance patterns exhibited.

1. *Visuospatial difficulties.* When reading, the child exhibits difficulty recognizing letters; reverses letters; transposes letters in syllables, syllables in words, and words in phrases. When writing, the child reverses letters; transposes letters, syllables, and word order; and cannot reproduce shapes.
2. *Speech-sound difficulties.* When reading, the child exhibits difficulties in synthesizing words (from component letter sounds) and in understanding words and sentences correctly read. When writing, the child has difficulties in breaking words into syllables and in constructing sentences.
3. *Correlation difficulties.* The child demonstrates difficulty in finding the appropriate speech sound for individual letters or groups of letters and has difficulty in recalling the visual form of sounds when writing.

This emphasis upon performance difficulties or symptomology also led Johnson and Myklebust (1967) to propose two subtypes similar to Ingram's. They subdivided dyslexia into visual dyslexia and auditory dyslexia. Boder (1973) utilized atypical reading and spelling patterns to directly derive three subcategories of developmental dyslexia.

GROUP I. *Dysphonetic dyslexia.* Children whose reading-spelling pattern reflects primary deficit in symbol-sound (grapheme-phoneme) integration, resulting in inability to develop phonetic word analysis-synthesis skills. (They have no gross deficit in gestalt function.)

GROUP II. *Dyseidetic dyslexia (Gestalt blind)*. Children whose reading-spelling pattern reflects primary deficit in the ability to perceive letters and whole words as configurations, or visual gestalts. (They have no gross deficit in analytic function.)

GROUP III. *Mixed dysphonetic-dyseidetic dyslexia (Alexia)*. Children whose reading-spelling pattern reflects primary deficit both in the ability to develop phonetic word analysis-synthesis skills and in the ability to perceive letters and whole words as visual gestalts.

Boder (1973) reports that of 107 dyslexic children, 67 fell into Group I, 10 into Group II, 23 into Group III, and 7 had to be placed in an undetermined group. The preponderance of Group I (dysphonetic dyslexia) is consistent with other studies showing audiophonic deficits as more frequent than visuo-spatial-perceptual deficits.

As with Johnson and Myklebust's categories of auditory and visual dyslexia (1967), Boder's system has remediation procedures specific to each subtype. For Group I, those who have auditory dyslexia, whole-word techniques are utilized. Phonetic skills will be difficult to learn, and should be used only after a large sight vocabulary is established. Effort should be made to convert the child from a dysphonetic to a phonetic speller. For Group II, those who have visual dyslexia, a remedial phonetic approach is needed because of their primary deficit in the visual channel. For Group III, those who have both visual and auditory deficits, a remedial approach utilizing a third channel—a tactile-kinesthetic approach—is necessary. "When able to recognize letter forms, remedial phonics reinforced by multisensory techniques can be introduced" (p.677). Boder reports that the prognosis for Group III is guarded. Group I begin to achieve normal proficiency in context reading as they acquire grade-level sight vocabulary. Word-analysis skills and spelling remain relatively poor. Group II remain slow and laborious readers and do not obtain a sight vocabulary commensurate with age-grade level and mental age.

Mattis et al. (1975) compared brain-damaged children who could read, brain-damaged children who were dyslexic, and those dyslexic children who had no brain damage. They derived three dyslexic syndromes based on multiple independent defects in higher cortical functioning.

1. *Language disorder syndrome*. Most often there is difficulty with speech-sound discrimination. Anomia is a critical factor. Verbal retrieval difficulties impede the acquisition of look-say vocabulary.

2. *Articulation and graphemotor dyscoordination syndrome*. These children

have intact visuo-spatial perception as well as language and constructional skills. Verbal IQ approximates performance IQ. Deficits are a buccal-lingual dyspraxia with resultant poor speech and graphemotor dyscoordination. There is difficulty with phonemes and graphemes.

3. *Visuo-perceptual disorder.* Perception, storage, and retrieval are so poor that visual stimuli and sequences cannot be associated with their sounds.

Approaches similar to those of Mattis et al. (1975) and Boder (1973) indicate the benefits of combining etiological and functional classification systems. It is clear that the same functional difficulty, such as poor phonetic skills, can have different causes. Combining etiological and functional systems provide a better rationale for the development of remediation techniques specific to the problem.

CONCLUDING REMARKS

In this chapter, we have considered the disorders associated with cerebral dysfunction. We have pointed out that the association of these disorders with cerebral dysfunction has been by inference, on the basis of the absence of known causes and of similarity to behavioral sequelae of brain damage. In addition to presenting what is known about the manifestations, etiology, and management of these disorders and about the evidence for syndrome status, we have stressed the necessity for delineation of more homogeneous subgroups instead of umbrella terms such as MBD, hyperactivity, and learning disability. Delineation needs to be on the basis of behavioral patterns, which also will provide the best opportunity for more homogeneous etiological subgrouping. The subsequent combination of homogeneous etiological and functional subgroups is a prerequisite for the development of correspondingly effective drug, behavioral, and educational remediation. The work on identifying obstetrical, prenatal, and neonatal risk factors offers exciting possibilities for early identification, remediation, and—ultimately—prevention.

References

Ackerman, P., Peters, J. & Dykman, R. Children with learning disabilities: WISC profiles. *Journal of Learning Disabilities*, 1971, *4*, 150–66.

Bandura, A. *Principles of Behavior Modification*. New York: Holt, Rinehart and Winston, 1969.

Bateman, B.D. Educational implications of minimal brain dysfunction. *Annals of the New York Academy of Sciences*, 1973, *205*, 245–50.

Bauza, C.A., deGrompone, M.A.C., Ecuder, E. & Drets, M.E. *La Dislexia de Evolución*. Montevideo: Garcia Morales-Merchant, 1962.

Belmont, L. & Birch, H.G. Lateral dominance, right-left awareness, and reading disability. *Child Development*, 1965, *36*, 257–71.

Belmont, L. & Birch, H.G. The intellectual profile of retarded readers. *Perceptual Motor Skills*, 1966, *22*, 787–816.

Bell. R.Q. A reinterpretation of the direction of effects in studies of socialization. *Psychological Review*, 1968, *75*, 81–95.

Benton, A.L. Dyslexia in relation to form perception and directional sense. In J. Money (Ed.), *Reading Disability: Progress and Research Needs in Dyslexia*. Baltimore: Johns Hopkins University Press, 1962.

Benton, A.L. Minimal brain dysfunction from a neuropsychological point of view. *Annals of the New York Academy of Sciences*, 1973, *205*, 29–37.

Benton, A.L. Developmental dyslexia: Neurological aspects. *Advances in Neurology*, 1975, *7*, 1–47.

Berkowitz, B.P. & Graziano, A.M. Training parents as behavior therapists: A review. *Behaviour Research and Therapy*, 1972, *10*, 297–317.

Bijou, S. & Peterson, R. Functional analysis in the assessment of children. In P. McReynolds (Ed.), *Advances in Psychological Assessment* (Vol. 2). Palo Alto, California: Science and Behavior Books, 1971.

Birch, H.G. Dyslexia and the maturation of visual function. In J. Money (Ed.), *Reading Disability: Progress and Research Needs in Dyslexia*. Baltimore: Johns Hopkins University Press, 1962.

Birch, H.G. & Belmont, L. Auditory-visual integration in normal and retarded readers. *American Journal of Orthopsychiatry*, 1964, *34*, 852–61.

Birnbrauer, J.S., Peterson, C.R. & Solnick, J.V. Design and interpretation of studies of single subjects. *American Journal of Mental Deficiency*, 1974, *79*, 191–203.

Blom, G.E. & Jones, A. Bases of classification of reading disorders. In E.O. Calkins (Ed.), *Reading forum: A Collection of Reference Papers Concerned with Reading Disability* (NINDS Monograph No. 11), 1971.

Boder, E. Developmental dyslexia: A diagnostic approach based on three atypical reading-spelling patterns. *Developmental Medicine and Child Neurology*, 1973, *15*, 663–87.

Bradley, C. The behavior of children receiving benzedrine. *American Journal of Psychiatry*, 1937, *94*, 577–85.

Braud, L.W., Lupin, M.N. & Braud, W.G. The use of electromyographic biofeedback in the control of hyperactivity. *Journal of Learning Disabilities*, 1975, *8*, 420–25.

Buss, A. & Plomin, R. *A Temperament Theory of Personality Development.* New York: John Wiley, 1975.

Campbell, S.B. Cognitive styles in reflective, impulsive, and hyperactive boys and their mothers. *Perceptual and Motor Skills*, 1973, *36*, 747–52.

Cantwell, D.P. (Ed.). *The Hyperactive Child: Diagnosis, Management, Current Research.* New York: Spectrum Publications, 1975.

Clements, S. & Peters, J. Minimal brain dysfunction in the school age child. *Archives of General Psychiatry*, 1962, *6*, 185–97.

Clements, S.D. *Minimal Brain Dysfunction in Children.* Washington, D.C.: U.S. Government Printing Office, 1966.

Cohen, S.A. Minimal brain dysfunction and practical matters such as teaching kids to read. *Annals of the New York Academy of Sciences*, 1973, *205*, 251–61.

Conners, C.K. The syndrome of minimal brain dysfunction: Psychological aspects. *Pediatric Clinics of North America*, 1967, *14*, 749–66.

Conners, C.K. Psychological assessment of children with minimal brain dysfunction. *Annals of the New York Academy of Sciences*, 1973, *205*, 283–302.

Connolly, C. Social and emotional factors in learning disabilities. In H.R.M. Myklebust (Ed.), *Progress in Learning Disabilities* (Vol. 2). New York: Grune & Stratton, 1971.

Denhoff, E., Hainsworth, P.K. & Hainsworth, M.L. The child at risk for learning disorder. *Clinical Pediatrics*, 1972, *11*, 164–70.

Di Loreto, L. *Comparative Psychotherapy: An Experimental Analysis.* New York: Aldine-Atherton, 1971.

Douglas, V. Stop, look, and listen: The problem of sustained attention and impulse control in hyperactive and normal children. *Canadian Journal of Behavioral Science*, 1972, *4*, 249–82.

Downing, J. Cognitive factors in dyslexia. *Child Psychiatry and Human Development*, 1973, *4*, 113–20.

Dykman, R.A., Peters, J.E. & Ackerman, P.T. Experimental approaches to the study of minimal brain dysfunction. *Annals of the New York Academy of Sciences*, 1973, *205*, 93–108.

Eisenberg, L. & Conners, C.K. Psychopharmacology in childhood. In N.B. Talbot, J. Kagan & L. Eisenberg (Eds.), *Behavioral Science in Pediatric Medicine.* Philadelphia: W.B. Saunders, 1971.

Fish, B. Stimulant drug treatment of hyperactive children. In D.P. Cantwell (Ed.), *The Hyperactive Child.* New York: Spectrum Publications, 1975.

Fitzhardinge, P.M. & Steven, E.M. The small-for-date infant. II Neurological and intellectual sequelae. *Pediatrics*, 1972, *50*, 50–57.

Forness, S. Educational approaches with hyperactive children. In D.P. Cantwell (Ed.), *The Hyperactive Child: Diagnosis, Management, Current Research.* New York: Spectrum Publications, 1975.

Guilford, J.P. *The Nature of Human Intelligence.* New York: McGraw-Hill, 1967.

Hellmuth, J. (Ed.). *Learning Disorders* (Vol. 3). Seattle, Washington: Special Child Publications, 1968.

Ingram, T.T. Delayed development of speech with special reference to dyslexia. *Proceedings of the Royal Society of Medicine,* 1963, *56,* 199.

Ingram, T.T. The dyslexic child. *Word Blind Bulletin,* 1964, 1.

Ingram, T.T., Mason, A.W. & Blackburn, I. A retrospective study of 82 children with reading disability. *Developmental Medicine and Child Neurology,* 1970, *12,* 271–81.

Jampolsky, G.G. Psychiatric considerations in reading disorders. In R.M. Flower, H.F. Gofman & L.I. Lawson, *Reading Disorders.* Philadelphia: F.A. Davis, 1965.

Johnson, D.J. & Myklebust, H.R. *Learning Disabilities: Educationl Principles and Practices.* New York: Grune & Stratton, 1967.

Kalverboer, A.F., Touwin, B.C.L. & Prechtl, H.F.R. Follow-up of infants at risk of minor brain dysfunction. *Annals of the New York Academy of Sciences,* 1973, *205,* 173–87.

Keeney, A.H. Comprehensive classification of the dyslexics. In A.H. Keeney & V.T. Keeney (Eds.), *Dyslexia: Diagnosis and Treatment of Reading Disorders.* St. Louis: C.V. Mosby, 1968.

Kenny, T.J. & Clemmens, R.L. Medical and psychological correlates in children with learning disabilities. *Journal of Pediatrics,* 1971, *78,* 273–77.

Kenny, T.J., Clemmens, R.L., Hudson, B.W., Lentz et al. Characteristics of children referred because of hyperactivity. *Journal of Pediatrics,* 1971, *79,* 618–22.

Keogh, B. Hyperactivity and learning disorders: Review and speculation. *Exceptional children,* 1971, *38,* 101–9.

Kinsbourne, M. Minimal brain dysfunction as a neurodevelopmental lag. *Annals of the New York Academy of Sciences,* 1973, *205,* 268–73.

Kittler, F.J. The role of allergic factors in the child with minimal brain dysfunction. *Annals of Allergy,* 1970, *28,* 203–6.

Klein, E. Psychoanalytic aspects of school problems. *Psychoanalytic Study of the Child,* 1949, *3,* 369–90.

Knights, R.M. Problems of criteria in diagnosis: A profile similarity approach. *Annals of the New York Academy of Sciences,* 1973, *205,* 124–31.

Levitt, E.E. The results of psychotherapy with children: An Evaluation. *Journal of Consulting Psychology,* 1957, *21,* 189–96.

Levitt, E.E. Psychotherapy with children: A further evaluation. *Behaviour Research and Therapy,* 1963, *1,* 45–51.

Levitt, E.E. Research on psychotherapy with children. In A.E. Berger & S.L. Garfield (Eds.), *Handbook of Psychotherapy and Behavior Change: An Empirical Analysis.* New York: Wiley, 1971, pp. 474–94.

Lewis, M. & Rosenblum, L.A. *The Effect of the Infant on Its Caregiver.* New York: John Wiley, 1974.

Love, L.R., Kaswan, J. & Bugental, D.E. Differential effectiveness of three clinical interventions for different socioeconomic groupings. *Journal of Consulting and Clinical Psychology,* 1972, *39,* 347–60.

Lovell, K., Shapton, D. & Warren, N.S. A study of some cognitive and other disabilities in backward readers of average intelligence as assessed by a nonverbal test. *British Journal of Educational Psychology,* 1964, *34,* 58–64.

Luria, A.R. *The Role of Speech in the Regulation of Normal and Abnormal Behavior.* New York: Liveright, 1961.

Luria, A.R. The role of speech in the formation of mental processes. In his *The Role of Speech in the Regulation of Normal and Abnormal Behavior.* U.S. DHEW Public Health Service, 1966.

Martin, G. In Winchell, C.A. (Ed.). *The Hyperactive Child. A Bibliography of Medical, Educational, and Behavioral Studies.* Westport, Connecticut: Greenwood Press, 1975, xi.

Mason, A.W. Specific (developmental) dyslexia. *Developmental Medicine and Child Neurology,* 1967, 9, 183–90.

Mattis, S., French, J.H. & Rapin, I. Dyslexia in children and young adults: Three independent neuropsychological syndromes. *Developmental Medicine and Child Neurology,* 1975, *17,* 150–63.

Meichenbaum, D.H. & Goodman, J. Training impulsive children to talk to themselves: A means of developing self-control. *Journal of Abnormal Psychology,* 171, 77, 115–26.

Millichap, J.G. Drugs in management of minimal brain dysfunction. *Annals of the New York Academy of Sciences,* 1973, *205,* 321–34.

Minde, K., Webb, G. & Sykes, D. Studies on the hyperactive child: II. Prenatal and paranatal factors associated with hyperactivity. *Developmental Medicine and Child Neurology,* 1968, *10,* 355–63.

Morrison, J. & Stewart, M. Bilateral inheritance as evidence for polygenicity in the hyperactive child syndrome. *Journal of Nervous and Mental Diseases,* 1974, *158,* 226–28.

Myklebust, H. *Progress in Learning Disabilities* (Vols. 1, 2, 3). New York: Grune & Stratton, 1968, 1971, 1975.

Naidoo, S. *Specific Dyslexia.* New York: Pitman, 1972.

Patterson, G.R. An application of conditioning technique to the control of a hyperactive child. In L.P. Ullman & L. Krasner (Eds.), *Case Studies in Behavior Modification.* New York: Holt, Rinehart and Winston, 1964.

Patterson, G.R., Jones, R., Whittier, J. & Wright, M.A. A behavior modification technique for the hyperactive child. *Behaviour Research and Therapy*, 1965, *2*, 217–26.

Pearson, G.H. *Psychoanalysis and the Education of the Child*. New York: W.W. Norton, 1954.

Pearson, G.H. A survey of learning difficulties in young children. *The Psychoanalytic Study of the Child*. New York: International University Press, 1955.

Quinn, P. & Rapoport, J. Minor physical anomalies and neurologic status in hyperactive boys. *Pediatrics*, 1974, *53*, 742–47.

Rabinovitch, R.D. Reading problems in children: Definitions and classifications. In A.H. Keeney and V.T. Keeney (Eds.), *Dyslexia*. St. Louis: C.V. Mosby, 1968.

Rapoport, J., Quinn, P. & Lamprecht, F. Minor physical anomalies and plasma dopamine. Beta-hydroxylase activity in hyperactive boys. *American Journal of Psychiatry*, 1974, *131*, 386–90.

Reitan, R. & Boll, T. Neuropsychological correlates of minimal brain dysfunction. *Annals of the New York Academy of Sciences*, 1973, *205*, 65–88.

Reitan, R.M. & Heineman, C. Interactions of neurological deficits and emotional disturbances in children with learning disorders. Methods for their differential assessment. In J. Hellmuth (Ed.), *Learning Disorders* (Vol. 3). Seattle, Washington: Special Child Publication, 1968, 93–135.

Ross, D.M. & Ross, S.A. *Hyperactivity: Research, Theory, and Action*. New York: John Wiley, 1976.

Routh, D. & Roberts, R. Minimal brain dysfunction in children: Failure to find evidence for a behavior syndrome. *Psychological Reports*, 1972, *31*, 307–14.

Rubin, E.Z. Cognitive dysfunction and emotional disorders. In H.R. Myklebust (Ed.), *Progress in Learning Disabilities* (Vol. 2). New York: Grune & Stratton, 1971.

Rutter, M.L., Tizard, J. & Whitmore, K. (Eds.). *Education, Health, and Behavior*. London: Longman, 1970.

Satterfield, J.H. Neurophysiologic studies with hyperactive children. In D.P. Cantwell (Ed.), *The Hyperactive Child: Diagnosis, Management, Current Research*. New York: Spectrum Publications, 1975.

Satterfield, J.H., Lesser, L.I., Saul, R.E. & Cantwell, D.P. EEG aspects in the diagnosis and treatment of minimal brain dysfunction. *Annals of the New York Academy of Sciences*, 1973, *205*, 274–82.

Schain, R.J. *Neurology of Childhood Learning Disorders*. Baltimore: Williams & Wilkins, 1972.

Schleifer, M., Weiss, G., Cohen, N., Elman, M. et al. Hyperactivity in preschoolers and the effect of methyphenidate. *American Journal of Orthopsychiatry*, 1975, *45*, 38–50.

Schmitt, B.D. The minimal brain dysfunction myth. *American Journal of Diseases of Children*, 1975, *129*, 1313–18.

Silver, A.A. & Hagin, R. Specific reading disability: Delineation of the syndrome and relationship to cerebral dominance. *Comprehensive Psychiatry*, 1960, *1*, 126–134.

Silver, L.B. Acceptable and controversial approaches to treating a child with learning disabilities. *Pediatrics*, 1975, *55*, 406–15.

Silverman, L.J. & Metz, A.S. Numbers of pupils with specific learning disabilities in local public schools in the United States: Spring 1970. *Annals of the New York Academy of Sciences*, 1973, *205*, 146–57.

Snyder, S.H. & Meyerhoff, J.L. How amphetamine acts in minimal brain dysfunction. *Annals of the New York Academy of Sciences*, 1973, *205*, 310–20.

Solomon, G. Drug therapy: Initiation and follow-up. *Annals of the New York Academy of Sciences*, 1973, *205*, 335–44.

Sparrow, S. & Satz, P. Dyslexia, laterality, and neuropsychological development. In D.J. Bakker & P. Satz (Eds.), *Specific Reading Disability: Advances in Theory and Method*. Rotterdam: University Press, 1970.

Stanley, G., Kaplan, I. & Poole, C. Cognitive and nonverbal perceptual processing in dyslexics. *Journal of General Psychology*, 1975, *93*, 67–72.

Strauss, A.A. & Kaphart, N.C. *Psychopathology and Education of the Brain-injured Child*. Progress in Theory and Clinic (Vol. 2). New York: Grune & Stratton, 1955.

Strauss, A.A. & Lehtinen, L.E. *Psychopathology and Education of the Brain-injured Child*. New York: Grune & Stratton, 1947.

Strother, C. Minimal cerebral dysfunction: A historical overview. *Annals of the New York Academy of Sciences*, 1973, *205*, 6–17.

Sylvester, E. & Kunst, M. Psychodynamic aspects of reading problems. *American Journal of Orthopsychiatry*, 1943, *13*, 69–76.

Thomas, A., Chess, S. & Birch, H.G. *Temperament and Behavior Disorders in Children*. New York: New York University Press, 1968.

Thompson, R.J., Jr., & Linscheid, T.R. Adult-child interaction analysis: Methodology and case application. *Child Psychiatry and Human Development*, 1976, *7*, 31–42.

Thompson, R.J., Jr., Palmer, S. & Linscheid, T.R. Single subject design and interaction analysis in the behavioral treatment of a child with a feeding problem. *Child Psychiatry and Human Development*, 1977, *8*, 43–53.

Thompson, R.J., Jr., & Schindler, F.H. Embryonic mania. *Child Psychiatry and Human Development*, 1976, *6*, 149–54.

Touwen, B.C.L. & Prechtl, H.F.R. *The Neurological Examination of the Child with Minor Nervous Dysfunction*. (Clinics in Developmental Medicine, No. 38). London: William Heinemann; Philadelphia: J.B. Lippincott, 1970.

Waldrop, M.F., Pedersen, F.A. & Bell, R.Q. Minor physical anomalies and behavior in preschool children. *Child Development*, 1968, *39*, 391–400.

Warrington, E.K. The incidence of verbal disability associated with reading retardation. *Neuropsychologia*, 1967, *5*, 175–79.

Wender, P. Minimal Brain Dysfunction in Children. New York: Wiley-Interscience, 1971.

Wender, P. Minimal brain dysfunction: Some recent advances. *Pediatric Annals*, 1973, *2*, 42–54.

Zrull, J., McDermott, J. & Pozanski, E. Hyperkinetic syndrome: The role of depression. *Child Psychiatry and Human Development*, 1970, *1*, 33–40.

7

Sensory Disorders

In Chapter 1 we presented the evolution of the concept of developmental disabilities and presented the current legislative definition. We also presented the Developmental Disabilities Cube and suggested that utilization of this conceptual schema enabled one to entertain a broader definition of developmental disabilities than the five specific conditions—mental retardation, early infantile autism, cerebral palsy, epilepsy, and dyslexia—that we have considered thus far. Any condition occurring during the developmental period that limits or potentially limits a person's physical, intellectual, emotional, or social development and that is expected to continue and constitute a substantial handicap to the individual can be considered a developmental disability. The sensory disorders—blindness and deafness—would seem to be particularly appropriate for inclusion.

Even though these inclusions would seem obvious, the blind and the deaf are frequently not recipients of services provided by centers for the developmentally disabled. Certainly disorders of the senses, which typically originate during the developmental period and continue throughout the individual's life, constitute substantial handicaps to the individual. In addition, the blind and the deaf would seem to have needs similar to those of other handicapped individuals and would require similar services. Also, many would have other handicaps that would also require attention. In short, the same points that led to including disabled persons with common needs but different diagnostic labels under one umbrella term would argue for including the blind and the deaf under the same umbrella term of developmental disability. Interdisciplinary team approaches would be particularly beneficial in that sensory disorders of any magnitude are likely to have implications for learning, concept development, affective-personality development, and general adaptive behavior necessitating integrated assessment, formulation, and treatment planning. We will utilize the schema of the Developmental Disabilities Cube to consider not only the etiologies and manifestations of sensory disorders but also their management.

DEFINITION

The sensory disorders that will be discussed are those of vision and hearing. The terms deafness and blindness imply the most severe form of impairment of hearing and impairment of vision, although less severe impairment may also result in disability. The impairment of function may be related to malfunction of any part of the auditory or visual mechanism. For example, in the case of hearing impairment, the problem may be conductive or sensorineural. The former involves mainly the lower frequencies and is related to any difficulty with the transmission of sound from the external ear canal, through the ossicular chain. Thus, tympanic membrane malfunction, fluid in the middle ear, or a problem in the ossicular chain may result in a "conductive component." Most of these problems are amenable to current modes of medical and surgical therapy. Sensorineural impairment is more noticeable at the higher frequencies, though it may be manifest by impairment of all frequencies. It implies a defect in function of the cochlea, eighth cranial nerve, or the auditory cortex, and is not amenable to current modes of medical and surgical therapy, although hearing aids may help.

In the case of visual impairment, the problem may be related to malfunction of the cornea (keratitis), anterior chamber (glaucoma), lens (cataract), uveal treact, retina, optic nerve, optic radiations, extraocular muscles, and/or visual cortex. As in the case of hearing impairment, some of these problems can be helped and/or prevented by current medical therapy, and some cannot.

The degree to which the functioning of an affected person is impaired depends upon several factors: (1) the severity of the disorder of special sense, (2) the etiology, and therefore the presence, of other disabilities, (3) the time period during which the disorder occurred and became manifest, (4) the reaction of the afflicted person and that of his or her family to the disability, and (5) the availability of appropriate resources to ameliorate the difficulty. The Developmental Disabilities Cube presents a good way to visualize the interaction of these variables.

Several systems of classification have emerged in an effort to document the numbers of affected individuals, and the severity of the disorder, and then ultimately to provide for appropriate resources. In the case of hearing impairment, two systems of classification are based on the severity of the disorder. Berg and Fletcher (1970, p. 8) present the following system suggested by the HEW Advisory Committee on the Education of the Deaf:

1. *The hard of hearing.* This group includes children with moderate hearing loss, those who are still able to understand fluent speech through hearing whether or not amplification is used. Educationally speaking, these are the children who, with some assistance, are able to attend classes with children who hear normally.
2. *The partially hearing.* This group includes those children whose loss of hearing is so severe that they require a special educational curriculum and program involving full-time auditory training along with vision for developing language and communication skills. Because of the severity of their loss of hearing, these children need the full-time services of a special teacher for their education. As a result of early identification of hearing loss and early auditory training, these children are able to progress academically at a somewhat more rapid rate than those classified as deaf since more efficient use can be made of their residual hearing.
3. *The deaf.* This group includes children whose principal source for learning language and communication skills is visual and whose loss of hearing, with or without amplifcation, is so great that it is of little or no practical value in training them to understand verbal communication auditorially. Their loss of hearing was acquired prelingually.

Some authors employ specific amounts of decibel (DB) loss to define deafness. For example, Knobloch and Pasamanick (1974) define deafness as a loss of 70 DB or more at all frequencies.

The other classification based on the severity of disorder was recently approved by the Executive Committee of the Conference of Executives of American Schools for the Deaf (Report of Ad Hoc Committee, 1975). It divides hearing impairment into four levels according to hearing threshold levels in the better ear as follows: Level I (26–53 DB), Level II (55–69 DB), Level III (70–89 DB), and Level IV (90 DB and above). The corresponding probable impact on communication and language development varies from mild to profound respectively, and the implication for educational settings, then, varies from functioning in a regular classroom setting, through needing resource help (partial integration), to needing a self-contained setting.

Another system of classification is based on the time of onset of the hearing impairment, i.e., prelingually, prevocationally (prior to 19 years of age), or late onset. This kind of information is useful in terms of prognosis. The earlier hearing is lost, the less likely the individual is to have normal speech and language development, the more likely he or she is to spend time in a residential school, and the less likely he or she is to do well in the job market (Schein and Delk, 1974).

In the case of visually impaired individuals, it has been difficult to define levels of visual impairment in spite of the obvious need to do so. According to Westat (1976), a modified version of the categories used by the Health Interview Survey is most meaningful. *Impaired vision* is the classification used for individuals who have any trouble seeing with one or both eyes, even when wearing glasses. *Severe visual impairment* is used for classifying those persons, 6 years of age or older, who are unable by their report to read ordinary newspaper print with glasses using both eyes or who, at any age, report "no useful vision" in either eye or "blindness" in both eyes. *Legal blindness* is defined as visual acuity for distant vision of 20/200 or less in the better eye with best correction, or the widest diameter of visual field subtending an angle $< 20°$.

INCIDENCE
HEARING IMPAIRMENT

In a recent survey of 42,000 households by the National Association of the Deaf conducted for the National Census of the Deaf Population of noninstitutionalized individuals, the prevalence rate for hearing impairment was 66 per 1,000, or 13.4 million people. The prevalence rate for significant bilateral hearing impairment was 32.4 per 1,000. The prevalence rate for deafness was 8.7 per 1,000, or 13% of the hearing-impaired population. The prevalence rate for prevocational deafness was two per 1,000 and of prelingual deafness was one per 1,000 (Schein and Delk, 1974). The survey concentrated on the prevocationally deaf population and noted that in 1971 there were almost a half million such individuals in the United States and that they constituted 3% of all the hearing-impaired population. The incidence of associated disabilities in the prevocationally deaf is noteworthy. According to the Annual Survey of Hearing Impaired Children and Youth quoted by Schein and Delk (1974), approximately 40% of children in schools for the hearing impaired had some other handicap, and 7% had two additional disabilities. Behavioral problems occurred in approximately 10%, mental retardation in 7%, severe visual problems in 5%, and cerebral palsy in 3%.

VISUAL IMPAIRMENT

The best information available about the prevalence of visual impairment in the general population has been compiled by Westat (1976) in a comprehensive study of existing data for the National Eye Institute. They reported that in 1972, more than 10.5 million individuals were estimated to have visual impairment. Approximately 1.5 million were deemed to be severely visually impaired, and approximately 500,000 were legally blind. Some information about the incidence of associated handicaps was presented by Gentile (1975) as part of the Health Interview Study wherein approximately 2.5 million people reported a combination of vision and hearing impairment and 5% of the severely visually impaired revealed that they wore a hearing aid. Cooper (1975) has indicated that 4,000 children in the United States have been identified as deaf-blind.

ETIOLOGY

The schema, utilized in previous chapters of considering hereditary and environmental factors operative in the prenatal, perinatal, and postnatal developmental periods, will be utilized to discuss the etiology of developmental disorders of special sense.

PRENATAL PERIOD

In the prenatal period, both genetic and environmental factors are important. We will discuss first the genetic etiologies of deafness and blindness and then the environmental. On the basis of a survey conducted from 1958 to 1967 of 2,330 children and 3,229 adults from the British Isles and South Australia regarding the causes of profound deafness in childhood, Fraser (1970) found that 40% to 60% were genetically determined. The types of genetic transmission were autosomal recessive (up to 6 types identified accounting for 20% to 40% of cases), autosomal dominant (10% to

30% of cases), and X-linked recessive (up to 2% of cases). Malformation syndromes accounted for approximately 1% of cases. Schein and Delk (1974) reported that 3% to 4% of hearing-impaired children have one or both parents who are hearing impaired. In the cases in which both parents are congenitally deaf, 17.4% of their children were deaf. This can be contrasted with the situation in which one parent has normal hearing and the other has acquired deafness, with the result that only 4.5% of the children were deaf. Clearly, the risk is nearly four times as great when both parents are congenitally deaf.

In a 1963 survey of the blind children who could attend school in England and Wales (25% of all blind children on the registry), Fraser and Friedman (1967) found that almost half (327) were visually impaired on the basis of a genetic etiology. The types of genetic transmission included autosomal dominant, autosomal recessive (including the inborn errors of metabolism), and X-linked. According to Fraser and Friedman (1967), "these preliminary estimates suggest that no less than nineteen autosomal dominant, thirty autosomal recessive, and ten sex-linked genetic entities play a part in the causation of childhood blindness" (p.137).

The environmental causes of visual and/or hearing disorders in the prenatal period may be related to any teratogen to which the mother may be exposed. The most common ones according to our current state of knowledge are the TORCH group of infectious agents. According to the survey reported by Fraser (1976), congenital infection with rubella was the most common "acquired" cause of profound deafness. Thus, 7% to 20% of profound deafness in childhood is related to prenatal environmental causes, and rubella was the specific agent found to be responsible in 7% to 15%. In the Annual Survey (1972–1973) of Hearing Impaired Children conducted through Gallaudet College (Jensema and Mullins, 1974), rubella was the cause of hearing impairment in 18% of the more than 40,000 children surveyed, while "pregnancy complications" were listed as the cause in 3%. The effect of the rubella epidemic in 1964–1965 is vividly demonstrated in that survey. The percentage of hearing impairment ascribed to rubella more than doubled and accounted for almost half of the total number of cases of hearing impairment in those years.

The associated handicaps encountered as a result of the 1964–1965 rubella epidemic included heart disorder in 8%, mental retardation in 7%, perceptual-motor dysfunction in 6%, emotional-behavioral disorder in 10%, and visual impairment in 15%. These figures were obtained from a population attending schools for the hearing impaired. Perhaps a comparison of the data reported by Cooper (1975) regarding the children followed by the Rubella Project (1964–1974) will serve to acquaint the reader with the severe impact of this infection on some children with more serious, multiorgan disease. Hearing loss was the most common manifestation and varied from mild to profound, unilateral to bilateral, but occurred in 87%. Cataract-glaucoma occurred in 33% of the patients, congenital heart disease in almost 50%, and mental retardation in 40%. By 10 years of age, only 19% of the children could get along in either regular school or with resource help. Thirty-six percent were in special education for single handicaps, 17% were in schools for the multiply handicapped, and 11% were in institutions. With the advent of the rubella vaccine capable of preventing rubella, these statistics will no doubt change.

Congenital infection with the cytomegalovirus (CMV) has recently been recognized as a more common cause of hearing impairment than had previously been appreciated. For example, Hanshaw et al. (1975) found that bilateral hearing loss was present in 12.5% (5/40) of children who were followed because of the presence of CMV-IgM antibody at birth in asymptomatic infants. The relative contribution of congenital CMV infection to the etiology of hearing impairment is thus not definitely known, but on the basis of the ubiquity of the organism and the relative frequency of infection, it is probably an extremely important etiology.

Chorioretinitis resulting in visual impairment is a relatively common concomitant of congenital toxoplasmosis infection (Alford, Stagno, and Reynolds, 1975) and of rubella. It can also occur with congenital CMV infection, but is not so common. Furthermore, rubella can also cause visual impairment on the basis of one or more of the following: glaucoma, cataract, and microphthalmos (Cooper, 1975). Congenital syphilis can result in interstitial keratitis and visual impairment on this basis (Curtis and Philpott, 1964). Fraser and Friedman (1967) found that only 6% (44) of the 776 blind children surveyed were so affected on the basis of prenatal environmental factors such as the TORCH group. However, they felt this group was probably underrepresented since the other manifestations of central nervous system dysfunction in this group of youngsters (mental retardation, hearing impairment) might have kept them out of the public school system. Another reason for the small percentage may well be that it has only been in recent years that we have become aware of the fact that congenital infection may be present but not diagnosed at birth because of its mild nature, only to become manifest in later years as visual impairment or hearing impairment. It is possible, for example, that some of the children included in the genetic etiology of choroidal-retinal degeneration had, in reality, congenital infection with toxoplasmosis, rubella, or cytomegalovirus.

PERINATAL PERIOD

Perinatal problems are responsible for 10% to 20% of the cases of hearing impairment in children (Fraser, 1976). Preterm infants are at greater risk, and they comprise 20% of the population in special schools for the hearing impaired. The specific reasons for hearing impairment are hypoxia–asphyxia, traumatic delivery, kernicterus, sepsis, and/or the toxic effects of some antibiotics (aminoglycosides), any or all of which may result in sensorineural hearing impairment.

Retrolental fibroplasia, resulting from generous oxygen administration to hypoxic preterm infants (also to some term), was the main cause of blindness in the perinatal period and occurred in 33% (258/776) of the children surveyed by Fraser and Friedman (1967). Recent changes in perinatal care have greatly reduced the frequency of occurrence of this entity (Ophthalmologic Staff of the Hospital for Sick Children, Toronto, 1967).

POSTNATAL PERIOD

The postnatal but prelingual causes for hearing impairment are usually conductive but may be sensorineural. The conductive component is most frequently related to recurrent otitis media and although treatable and reversible, children so affected often have intermittent hearing impairment of variable degree that may be detrimental to the development of language skills. This type of problem is particularly common in allergic children and in some with immune deficiency disease, although it can occur in children who are perfectly normal in all other respects. The causes of sensorineural hearing impairment are related to bacterial CNS infection (meningitis, encephalitis) and/or some of the medications used to eradicate such infections. According to Fraser (1976), postnatally acquired hearing impairment occurs in 20% to 30% of the hearing-impaired population.

Postnatal causes for blindness include trauma, some generalized connective tissue diseases, and some infectious diseases affecting the cornea.

Altogether, these postnatal etiologies accounted for only 11% of the total number of cases of blindness in the Fraser and Friedman study (1967).

MANIFESTATIONS

Through our discussion of the etiologies and primary manifestations of the sensory disorders, we have maintained that rarely is the functional impairment limited to just the sensory area. Frequently, the same factor that produces the blindness or deafness also produces additional CNS damage or dysfunction resulting in a multihandicapped person. If multiple handicaps are not present, then frequently there are secondary problems in learning and adjustment which are associated with the sensory disorder. The likelihood of multiple or associated manifestations, however, necessi-

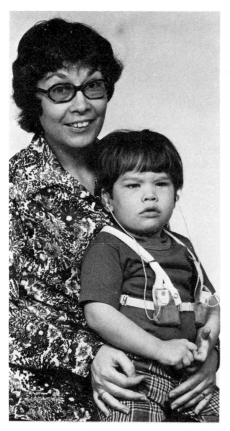
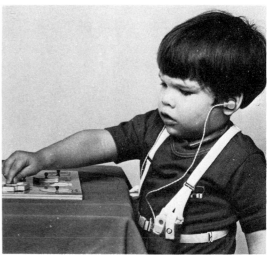

J.M., a 2-year 6-month-old youngster, had *Hemophilus influenzae* meningitis at 5 months of age and was subsequently noted to be delayed in language development. He was found to have a moderate bilateral sensorineural hearing impairment and is currently involved in an acoustic nursery. Of note is the excellent fine motor control which he demonstrates. The close and caring relationship with his parents has been helpful in his developmental progress.

tates an interdisciplinary approach to differential diagnosis so that management can be comprehensive and appropriately specific. In considering other manifestations associated with visual or hearing impairment, it is necessary to differentiate between those directly related to the sensory disorder, those related to underlying etiology, and those related to societal attitude and experiential factors. Three primary areas of associated manifestations are cognitive-intellectual functioning, personality-emotional functioning, and educational-learning capabilities. Each of these areas will be considered first for visual impairment and then for hearing impairment.

VISUAL IMPAIRMENT

With those exhibiting a sensory disorder, assessment of intelligence, personality, and educational capabilities is just as critical to adequate management as is assessment of the sensory disorder. However, even more so than in any of the other disorders we have discussed, sensory disorders make valid assessment difficult. The visually impaired demonstrate considerable variation in intellectual functioning. In general, as compared with sighted normative reference groups, there is a somewhat smaller percentage of the visually impaired in the average range of intelligence, a slightly higher percentage in the superior range, and a considerably larger percentage in the below average range (Lowenfeld, 1963). However, many investigators have questioned the validity of these findings generally obtained by using instruments that are based on the performance of sighted individuals, whose experiences are considerably different from those of the visually impaired. In addition, the etiology of the visual impairment must be considered in reference to the possibility of impairment of the CNS, which could be influencing intellectual functioning to a greater extent than the visual impairment. Consequently, the influence of visual impairment on intellectual functioning needs to be continually reassessed in light of advances in test development and of improvements in educational efforts at school and home. For, such advances and improvements can enhance learning style and cognitive capacity by purposeful intervention into the limited range of experiences of the visually impaired child.

There are other aspects of cognitive functioning that are affected by visual impairment. Those who are blind or who have lost their sight at a very early age must rely upon their remaining senses of touch (including kinesthesia), hearing, taste, and olfaction for gaining knowledge of the world.

The assumption of the presumed superiority of the visually impaired in sensory acuteness and memory is an appealing idea but one lacking in supportive evidence (Lowenfeld, 1963). The capacity of the visually impaired for form perception, space perception, and spatial orientation has been of considerable interest. The blind can perceive form through touch, and since they can also reproduce objects, Lowenfeld (1963) maintains that they must be able to unify separate perceptions into one. Jones (1975) maintains that the spatial senses (vision, hearing, touch) do not operate as distinct and independent modalities in the perception of space and that the sense of vision is not crucial to the development of spatial abilities. Furthermore, the blind do not suffer deficits in spatial perception in their remaining sense modalities as a consequence of loss of vision. While their abilities may lag developmentally or absolutely in performing spatial tasks away from the body, e.g., auditory localization, the blind may be equal to or superior to the sighted in performing spatial tasks within the body space, e.g., simple sensory discrimination, cutaneous and kinesthetic discrimination, and perception of movements of the body.

Worschel (1972) investigated the role of visualization in the ability of the blind to perceive and manipulate spatial relations tactually and to orient themselves spatially through a comparison of 33 totally blind and 33 sighted people matched on sex and chronological age. The results indicated that the sighted are superior to the blind in tactual form perception measured by verbal report and reproduction, in the imaginal manipulation of space relations, and in space orientation. The blind did as well as the sighted in the recognition of tactual form. It was determined that those accidentally blinded did better than those congenitally blind in tactual form perception, measured by verbal report and reproduction, and in spatial relations tests. In recognition of tactual form and in orientation in space, they equalled the congenitally blind. Thus, while these areas of cognitive functioning are undoubtedly influenced by the lack of sight, the visually impaired are capable of form perception, space perception, and spatial orientation. Jones (1975) maintains that well-controlled studies of the blind who have adequate experience demonstrate that they can function in space.

Lowenfeld (1963) points out that speech development can be affected by visual impairment because of the lack of visually aided imitation. The acquisition of word concepts is also affected, however, because the blind lack real experience with aspects of our world which are experienced visually (e.g., color, moon, soaring). Among blind children, a number of speech disorders have been reported, including lack of modulation, mild to severe oral inaccuracies, letter substitutions, and stuttering. In general, the lack of visual imitation capabilities have been offered as one reason, and psychological causes have also been postulated. However, Lowenfeld (1963) indicates that no evidence has been supplied to connect speech defects in the blind with any particular psychological reaction patterns.

For achievement test results, the same considerations regarding the validity of test measures apply as in our discussion of intelligence tests. The results in general indicate that blind pupils acquire approximately as much school information grade-by-grade as seeing children do, with the exception of arithmetic in which their scores are generally lower (Lowenfeld, 1963). In addition, it is important to note that in any given grade, blind pupils tend to be about 2 years older than the sighted children, which suggests a slower rate of acquisition of school information. This slower rate of acquisition can be anticipated when one considers, for example, that touch reading using Braille takes about three to four times as long as visual reading (Lowenfeld, 1963).

Mobility is another problem associated with visual impairment (Lowenfeld, 1963). The mobility of the visually impaired is obviously restricted, and the resulting limitation of experience has developmental consequences. There are two components of mobility: locomotion and mental orientation. The latter involves recognizing one's surroundings and the temporal and spatial relations to oneself. Because successful locomotion requires the avoidance of obstacles, the capability of some blind persons to perceive obstacles without bodily contact has been of considerable interest. Investigations have indicated that although no single condition is necessary for obstacle perception, auditory cues are the most reliable, most accurate, and most used; at the same time, cutaneous, olfactory, and thermal cues are also utilized (Lowenfeld, 1963). As noted above, the visually impaired are capable of spatial orientation and space perception and can utilize time sense and muscular memory to form "mental maps." Furthermore, mobility can be enhanced through training such as with the Hoover cane technique and through canine assistance. Thus, while the mobility of the visually impaired is restricted, they do possess capabilities that can be developed and trained to increase mobility and subsequent range of experience.

Personality assessment of the visually impaired, like their intellectual assessment, presents similar problems of establishing valid methods and in-struments. Also, it is difficult to differentiate the effect of visual impairment on personality and emotional functioning from the effects of societal atti-tudes toward the visually impaired person, especially if they are treated as helpless and dependent. It is generally recognized that the social and emo-tional effects of visual impairment are not specific in terms of personality factors. Lowenfeld (1963) presents the work of Cowen and his group (1961) as demonstrating no consistent or systematic differences in personality at-tributes or adjustment among three groups of adolescents matched on age, grade placement, intelligence, and socioeconomic status: a visually disabled day-school group of 71, a visually disabled residential school group of 56, and a sighted control group of 40. Kirtley (1975) maintains that the most important conclusion to be drawn from the study is that visual disability in and of itself does not predispose one to maladjustment.

Just as there is no common or unique personality characteristic of the visually impaired, so there is no single reaction pattern by the individual or by his or her family to the occurrence of this disability. The reaction pat-terns are within the range of those demonstrated in response to any disabil-ity such as the FAGS constellation (fear, anger, guilt, shame), discussed in relation to seizure disorders. Cull (1973) has examined the typical defense mechanisms as they are utilized by the visually impaired. However, it is not defenses but appropriate acceptance of the visual impairment by those involved that is crucial for adequate adjustment. The results presented by Keegan (1976) are consistent with other findings that earlier onset and younger age are correlated with better rehabilitation potential and out-come. Those who can be characterized as nonacceptors of their blindness are vulnerable to prolonged distress and possible maladjustment with sig-nificantly more psychological symptoms and poorer social adjustment than acceptors. Also, the acceptors exhibit less depression and dependency than the nonacceptors.

Some blind children develop habitual behaviors such as eye rubbing, waving of hands, rocking, and other mannerisms referred to as "blindisms." The consensus is that blindisms reflect self-stimulatory activity since they are also observed among sighted individuals and do not stem from blindness as such (Kirtley, 1975). These ritual behaviors are amenable to behavior modification approaches coupled with acquisition of more appro-priate methods of increasing levels of stimulation.

In addition to calling attention to the frequency of associated handi-

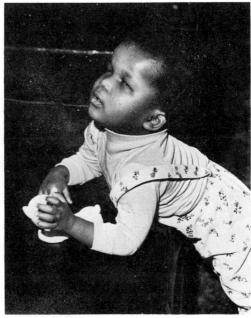

V.H. is a 2-year-old youngster who has severe visual impairment of unknown etiology. Note the delay in attainment of motor milestones (she is just beginning to pull herself up to stand) and typical posturing of the head.

caps, our consideration of visual impairment has attempted to present the associated manifestations and to differentiate those that are related directly to the visual impairment and those that may reflect a common etiological factor or societal attitude. An awareness of the limitations basic to visual impairment can serve as a basis for educational and remedial efforts. Lowenfeld (1963) has identified three direct effects of blindness: limitations in the range of variety of experiences, limitations in the ability to get about, and limitations in control of the environment and the self in relation to it. Intellectual impairment, psychopathology, particular personality pattern, or particular reaction pattern are not necessary consequences of visual impairment. The visually impaired are able to develop cognitive skills such as form perception, space perception, and spatial orientation, indicating that visualization is not essential for the skills to be developed. Thus, when difficulties do occur in these areas, they need to be seen as problems in their own right and effectively managed and not dismissed as characteristics that need to be tolerated.

HEARING IMPAIRMENT

Intellectual and personality assessment of the hearing impaired is difficult because the language deficiency of hearing-impaired children make many of the standard psychological assessment methods and instruments inappropriate. Vernon (1970) has presented an evaluation of the basic intellectual and personality assessment tests in terms of their usefulness with the hearing impaired. Well-controlled studies usually show that the hearing impaired score lower on intelligence tests than the nonhearing impaired but the difference is reduced or even eliminated if only appropriate nonverbal tests are utilized. It is clear that impaired intelligence is not a necessary result of hearing impairment.

The previously held view that language is necessary for thinking has gradually changed as increasing evidence indicates that thought precedes language development (Tomlinson-Keasey and Kelly, 1974). Furthermore, analysis of the developing thought process of hearing-impaired children suggests that they progress normally through the period of sensorimotor development, except in the area of vocal imitation (Best and Roberts, 1976). Hearing-impaired children are likely to have difficulty separating symbols from their images and in dealing with abstractions (Tomlinson-Keasey and Kelly, 1974) and to have a slower rate of concept development than hearing students (Austin, 1975). The excellent and comprehensive review of studies examining the relationship between linguistic deficiency and thinking in deaf subjects by Furth (1971) shows that the hearing impaired are deficient in linguistic capabilities. Linguistic capabilities are not necessary, however, to develop thinking up to and including the concrete operational stage. In the case of formal operational thinking, the data are not yet conclusive. There is evidence of a developmental lag in the thinking of the hearing impaired, but the later emergence of cognitive skills cannot be accounted for on the basis of increasing linguistic competency since the hearing impaired at the adult level—even after many years of schooling—are woefully lacking in linguistic competence. Furth (1971) maintains that a more parsimonious explanation for the developmental lag in cognitive skills is a lack of experience and training. Thus, because of the lack of adequate auditory input of language, the hearing-impaired child will have some language deficiencies, and his thought process may develop at a slower rate because of lack of experience and training. It is necessary to bear in mind that the language deficiency of the hard-of-hearing child "may be totally unrelated to his intelligence and may mime personality pathology that is not present" (Vernon, 1970, p.218).

Just as intellectual deficits are not a necessary condition of hearing impairment neither are personality nor emotional problems. In general, the major forms of psychotic disturbance are not more common in hearing-impaired children than in hearing children, but behavior problems and problems of impulse control are more common (Altshuler, 1974; Altshuler et al., 1976). The study by Freeman, Malkin, and Hastings (1975) of 120 prelingually deaf children compared with hearing controls matched on age, sex, and social class showed significant differences in number of hospitalizations, frequency of home moves, activities permitted by parents, amount of play, and parental expectations but showed no significant differences in frequency of divorce and separation of parents. It was concluded that deafness need not present psychiatric problems in the majority of cases. However, the behavioral problems of the hearing-impaired child, which include overaggressiveness, overactivity, impulsivity, and fearfulness, are not minor. They require prompt management to prevent these secondary problems from exacerbating functioning difficulties, or even from becoming primary handicaps.

There is a need for better definition of the nature and pattern of the behavioral problems of hearing-impaired children and a comparison with those of non-hearing-impaired children. Reivich and Rothrock's work (1972) using factor analysis is an advancement toward greater specificity. They found five factors in the ratings teachers used to assess the behavior problems of 327 students (ages 6–20) in a state school for the deaf. Three of these factors, immaturity, personality, and conduct, were similar to previous reports with normal and disturbed populations and two factors, isolation and communication problems, were not previously reported and may be specific to hearing-impaired children.

Schuldt and Schuldt (1972) reviewed personality research with deaf children for the last twenty years. They concluded that children with severe hearing losses do seem to manifest more abnormal personality characteristics and less adequate adjustment in comparison with either hearing controls or normative data on hearing children. They go on to point out that these findings do not necessarily indicate psychopathology resulting from deafness. The data can be interpreted as providing normative information on a minority group who—because of different educational and social environments and lack of linguistic and other requisite skills—do not develop personality characteristics or ways of adjusting similar to those developed by the majority of hearing children. Schuldt and Schuldt (1972) call for less descriptive and more experimental research and cite recent work in elucidating differences between subgroups of deaf children.

One approach to differentiation on the basis of subgroups was used by Meadow (1972), who found superior intellectual and social functioning of deaf children with deaf parents compared with deaf children with hearing parents. There were less clear-cut differences on communicative functioning. There were no differences in speechreading and speech but children with deaf parents had significantly higher ratings for facility with written language, receptive and expressive fingerspelling, and use of the language of signs.

Vernon (1969, 1972) has done extensive work on analysis of manifestations in subgroups of hearing-impaired children based on etiology. From 1953 to 1964 he examined the prevalence of five major etiologies of deafness in 1,468 children who entered, or applied for admission to, the California School for the Deaf at Riverside. The range of prevalence was 5.4% to 26.0% for genetic etiology, 8.8% to 9.5%, for maternal rubella, 8.1% to 8.7% for meningitis, 11.9% to 17.4% for prematurity, and 3.1% to 3.7% for kernicterus (Rh factor). He contrasted the prevalence of physical and psychological anomalies as a function of etiology and determined the prevalence of multiple handicaps or secondary problems. Among this sample the prevalence of cerebral palsy was 15 times greater (15.8% versus 0.1% to 0.7%) than in the general population. Mental retardation was six times as great (12.2% versus 2.2%), and aphasic disorders were present in about 25%. In terms of psychological adjustment, the premature and post-rubella children had a prevalence of psychosis of 5% to 7% and emotional disturbance of 25% to 30% while the postmeningitic group had slightly less prevalence and the Rh-factor group demonstrated 12% behavior disorder prevalence. In terms of educational achievement, the maternal rubella group scored the lowest, followed by the premature group, then the Rh group and the meningitic group, whose performance was characterized by marked variability. All these groups did more poorly than deaf children having a genetic etiology in which brain damage was not suspected. Over 66% of the premature group and the Rh group, over 50% of the rubella group, and over 33% of the meningitic group had at least one other major disability. However, among the genetically deaf group, there were only 6.5% who were multiply handicapped. Vernon contrasts the prevalence rates of the rubella, meningitic, Rh, and premature groups with those of the genetic group as a way of emphasizing his contention that a significant amount of the language disability, impulse disorders, psychosis, and general behavior disorders reported in hearing-impaired children are not due to deafness but have their basis in CNS dysfunction and are additional to the auditory impairment.

Vernon (1969, 1972) showed that the rubella group had significantly lower IQ scores and were lowest on written language and poorest in adjustment but were not significantly different in speech and speechreading. Furthermore, evidence from the rubella, premature, and meningitic groups suggest that the earlier in the development of the child the etiology occurs the more pervasive and permanent are the residua. These findings have implications for educational planning so that both expectancies and programs are related not just to degree of hearing impairment but also to the etiology of the impairment and likelihood of additional CNS manifestations. Furthermore, there is likely to be relatively less prevalence of genetic etiology and increased prevalence of rubella and meningitic etiologies in the school-age populations in the future owing to the rubella epidemic in 1962–1965 and the advances in infant and child care which result in more survivors from meningitis. The changing prevalence of etiologies will have to require commensurate changing of educational programs and expectancies.

There has been a long controversy regarding the education of hearing-impaired children in terms of academics and communication skills. The basic conflict has been over the method of teaching and communicating, with many advocating the traditional oral method and others the manual method (signs, fingerspelling). The oral method relies upon speechreading (i.e., reading speech by watching the lips and face of the speaker), written expressions, reading, and auditory training. It may also include the use of sound and gesture. Farwell (1976) maintains that the controversy has produced little quality research and finds no support for the major contention of proponents of the oral method that training in speechreading has long-term effects in enhancing language and lipreading abilities at later ages. Furthermore early exposure to the oral approach through preschool attendance does not seem to affect significantly later functioning in terms of academic achievement and of speech and language performance (Rodda, Godsane, and Stevens, 1974). A recent survey (Jordan, Gustason, and Rosen, 1976) indicates that there is a movement away from the oral method in favor of a total communication approach that utilizes all sensory and coding systems—visual, auditory, kinesthetic—available to the child. Out of 796 programs for the deaf who responded, 64% now use total communication and 43% have changed approaches—with 88% having changed from oral/aural and 97% having changed to total communication.

This controversy is basic to the management of the hearing impaired. The method of teaching is really a method of communicating with those who are handicapped in their ability to communicate by verbal language. Not only does the method used for teaching serve as the vehicle for learning about our world but it also becomes the method for interpersonal communication. The prevailing idea behind the traditional approach has been that the hearing-impaired child must function in the verbal-hearing world and thus needs the oral method to maximize adjustment and functioning. Now we are witnessing a movement to a total communications approach in which the prevailing idea is to help the individual use all methods at his or her disposal to maximize learning, communication, and functioning.

Berg (1970) points out that a new specialization has emerged to help meet the educational needs of hearing-impaired children. This new specialization is educational audiology which seeks for each hard-of-hearing child "to identify the educational and audiological parameters of hearing impairment, to isolate the psychological and educational deficiences arising from hearing loss, and to develop educational programs that will permit adjustment in a hearing world" (p.275).

Planning a comprehensive program requires assessment of the child's capacity for audition, auditory awareness, language development, speech skills, audio frequencies used, reading competencies, and written compositional competencies. Results of such a comprehensive assessment will permit individualized programs to be created with the appropriate combinations of auditory training, utilization of hearing aids, speechreading, and speech instruction as well as signs and fingerspelling.

Along with individualized educational planning, it is hoped that a corresponding change in research focus will occur. Existing research in this area has attempted to prove one system of communication as superior to the other, i.e., there has been a search for "the method" or for the mystical cure (Rodda et al., 1974). Because skills and techniques must be matched to the educational profile of an individual person, one can no longer maintain an absolute adherence to either the oral approach or to the manual approach. Research focus must hereafter attempt to delineate the conditions under which each approach—or some combination of each—promises to be the most effective.

The advent of individualized educational program planning will be limited unless the educational system as a whole is able to become more individualized. Lawrence and Kapfer (1970) point out that in most situations, two equally undesirable educational alternatives are all that is available to the hearing-impaired child. One is inclusion in the classroom for normal children, and the other is placement in a special school intended for the profoundly deaf. The actual implementation of individualized systems of instruction and learning is seen as the most important trend in education today, and effective public school education for the hard of hearing is seen as dependent upon individualized public school education for everyone.

In November 1975, the Congress of the United States passed Public Law 94–142, the Education for All Handicapped Children Act. This law requires formulation and implementation of individualized educational plans for all handicapped children. With the passage of this law, we are on the threshold of having the philosophy, legal mandate, and resources to foster the development of all children through appropriate individualized educational programming. It is now up to both professionals and consumers to actualize this potential.

References

Alford, C.A., Stagno, S. & Reynolds, D.W. Toxoplasmosis: Silent congenital infection. In S. Krugman and A. Gershon (Eds.), *Progress in Clinical and Biological Research* (Vol. 3). New York: Alan R. Liss, 1975.

Altshuler, K. The social and psychological development of the deaf child: Problems, their treatment and prevention. *American Annals of the Deaf*, 1974, *119*, 365–76.

Altshuler, K., Demeng, W., Vollenweider, J., Rainer, J. et al. Impulsivity and profound early deafness: A cross-cultural inquiry. *American Annals of the Deaf*, 1976, *121*, 331–45.

Austin, G. Knowledge of selected concepts obtained by an adolescent deaf population. *American Annals of the Deaf*, 1975, *120*, 360–70.

Berg, F. Educational audiology. In F. Berg & S. Fletcher (Eds.), *The Hard-of-Hearing Child: Clinical and Educational Management*. New York: Grune & Stratton, 1970.

Berg, F. & Fletcher S. (Eds.). *The Hard-of-Hearing Child: Clinical and Educational Management*. New York: Grune & Stratton, 1970.

Best, B. & Roberts, G. Early cognitive development in hearing-impaired children. *American Annals of the Deaf*, 1976, *121*, 560–64.

Cooper, L.Z. Congenital rubella in the United States. In S. Krugman & A. Gershon (Eds.), *Progress in Clinical and Biological Research* (Vol. 3). New York: Alan R. Liss, 1975.

Corven, E., Underberg, R., Verillo, R. & Benham, F. *Adjustment to Visual Disability in Adolescence.* New York: American Foundation for the Blind, 1961.

Cull, J. Psychological adjustment to blindness. In B. Cobb (Ed.). *Medical and Psychological Aspects of Disability*, Springfield, Illinois: Charles C Thomas, 1973.

Curtis, A.C. & Philpott, O.S. Prenatal syphilis. *The Medical Clinics of North America*, 1964, *48* (3), 707–19.

Farwell, R. Speech reading: A research review. *American Annals of the Deaf*, 1976, *121*, 19–27.

Fraser, G.R. *The Causes of Profound Deafness in Childhood.* Baltimore: Johns Hopkins University Press, 1976.

Fraser, G.R. & Friedman, A.I. *The Causes of Blindness in Childhood.* Baltimore: Johns Hopkins University Press, 1967.

Freeman, R., Malkin, S. & Hastings, J. Psychosocial problems of deaf children and their families: A comparative study. *American Annals of the Deaf*, 1975, *120*, 391–405.

Furth, H.C. Linguistic deficiency and thinking: Research with deaf subjects, 1964–1969. *Psychological Bulletin*, 1971, *76*, 58–76.

Gentile, A. Persons with impaired hearing, United States, 1971. *Vital and Health Statistics.* Data from the National Health Survey: Ser. 10, #101. (DHEW Pub. #[HRA] 76–1528). U.S. DHEW, 1975.

Hanshaw, J.B., Scheiner, A.P., Moxley, A.W., Gaer, L. et al. CNS sequelae of congenital cytomegalovirus infection. In S. Krugman & A. Gershon (Eds.), *Progress in Clinical and Biological Research* (Vol. 3). New York: Alan R. Liss, 1975.

Impaired Hearing, United States, 1971. Data from the National Health Survey, Ser. 10, #101. (DHEW Pub. #[HRA] 76–1528). U.S. DHEW, 1975.

Jensema, C. & Mullins, J. Onset, cause, and additional handicaps in hearing-impaired children. *American Annals of the Deaf*, 1974, 701–5.

Jones, B. Spatial perception in the blind. *British Journal of Psychology*, 1975, *66*, 461–72.

Jordan, I., Gustason, G. & Rosen, R. Current communication trends at programs for the deaf. *American Annals of the Deaf*, 1976, *121*, 527–32.

Keegan, D., Ash, D. & Greenough, T. Blindness: Some psychological and social implications. *Canadian Psychiatric Association Journal*, 1976, *21*, 333–40.

Kirtley, D. *The Psychology of Blindness.* Chicago, Illinois: Nelson-Hall, 1975.

Knobloch, H. & Pasamanick, B. (Eds.). *Gesell and Amatruda's Developmental Diagnosis*, 3rd ed. Hagerstown, Maryland: Harper & Row, 1974.

Lawrence, C. & Kapfer, M. The potential of current trends in public education for the hard-of-hearing child. In F. Berg & S. Fletcher (Eds.), *The Hard-of-Hearing Child: Clinical and Educational Management.* New York: Grune & Stratton, 1970.

Lowenfeld, B. Psychological problems of children with impaired vision. In W. Cruickshank (Ed.), *Psychology of Exceptional Children and Youth,* 2nd ed. Englewood Cliffs, New Jersey: Prentice-Hall, 1963.

Meadow, K. Early manual communication in relation to the deaf child's intellectual, social, and communicative functioning. In P.E. Trapp & P. Himelstein (Eds.), *Readings on the Exceptional Child: Research and Theory,* 2nd ed. New York: Appleton-Century-Crofts, 1972.

Ophthalmologic Staff of the Hospital for Sick Children, Toronto. *The Eye in Childhood.* Chicago, Illinois: Year Book Medical Publishers, 1967.

Reivich, R. & Rothrock, I. Behavior problems of deaf children and adolescents: A factor analytic study. *Journal of Speech and Hearing Research,* 1972, *15,* 93–104.

Report of the Ad Hoc Committee to Define Deaf and Hard of Hearing. *American Annals of the Deaf,* October, 1975, 509–512.

Rodda, M., Godsane, B. & Stevens, J. Some aspects of the development of young hearing-impaired children. *American Annals of the Deaf,* 1974, *119,* 729–35.

Schein, J.D. & Delk, M.T. *The Deaf Population of the United States.* Silver Spring, Maryland: National Association of the Deaf, 1974.

Schuldt, W.J. & Schuldt, D.A. A review of recent personality research on deaf children. In P.E. Trapp and P. Himelstein (Eds.), *Readings on the Exceptional Child,* 2nd ed. New York: Appleton-Century-Crofts, 1972.

Tomlinson-Keasey, C. & Kelly, R. The development of thought processes in deaf children. *American Annals of the Deaf,* 1974, *119,* 693–700.

Vernon, M. Multiply-handicapped deaf children: Medical, educational, and psychological considerations. Washington, D.C.: Council of Exceptional Children, 1969.

Vernon, M. The psychological examination. In F. Berg & S. Fletcher (Eds.), *The Hard-of-Hearing Child: Clinical and Educational Management.* New York: Grune & Stratton, 1970.

Westat, Inc. *Summary and Critique of Available Data on the Prevalence of Economic and Social Costs of Visual Disorders and Disabilities.* Public Health Service. National Institutes of Health. U.S. DHEW, 1976.

Worschel, P. Space perception and orientation in the blind. In P.E. Trapp and P. Himelstein (Eds.), *Readings on the Exceptional Child: Research and Theory.* 2nd ed. New York: Appleton-Century-Crofts, 1972.

8

Interdisciplinary Diagnostic and Treatment Approaches

Throughout this book, we have attempted to show how the thinking about various developmental disorders and the concept of developmental disabilities continue to evolve. There has also been a corresponding evolution in the procedures for assessing and treating these disorders and delays in development. Assessment and treatment approaches vary with conceptualization of the essential nature of man and of the beliefs about the training, skills, and qualifications necessary for the competency of practitioners.

From antiquity, the essential nature of man as composed of both mind and body, tangible and intangible, has been recognized. At times, monistic views of man prevailed, which emphasized either the mental and spiritual or the physical elements. At other times the doctrine of dualism, that man is composed of two distinct and different elements—the body and the mind—prevailed. The most influential proponent of dualism was Descartes (1596–1650) who viewed man as composed of two completely separate entities, each of a completely different nature.

The philosophy of dualism created the mind-body problem. The coexistence and the interrelationship, if any, of these two distinct components of human nature had to be accounted for. The most widely accepted view was the doctrine of psychophysical parallelism. This doctrine assumed the existence of two realms, one mental and one physical. No causal relationship was postulated between the two realms, but events in one realm were paralleled in the other realm. Very gradually, the inseparable interaction of the mental and physical components of man was recognized and the doctrine of psychophysical parallelism was replaced by an emphasis on the unity of man as an organism (Misiak, 1961).

Although the unified view of man emerged, it has not done so until relatively recently because of the pervasive grip of Cartesian dualism on not only philosophical, but also scientific thought for nearly three centuries. Misiak (1961) suggests that one reason for the longevity of the dualistic view was the convenient division of labors in the study of man which it afforded.

Even though the doctrine of psychophysical parallelism was replaced by a unified view, the mind-body problem has not disappeared. The holistic study of man still involves the relationship of the two classes of events, the intangible or not directly observable mental events, and the tangible or observable bodily events.

The conflict between the convenience of dualism and the necessity of a holistic view has been most evident in the applied areas of medicine and psychology. Within the broad realms of the mind and of the body, study was directed to sub areas of functioning and numerous fields of specialized knowledge and skill arose. However, increased specialization, although necessary, resulted in further increases in knowledge about circumscribed areas of functioning. This proliferation of specialisms has contributed to the view of the patient as an impersonal body and the passive carrier of a diseased organ. Gradually, the view of the patient as a thinking and feeling being who could influence, as well as be influenced by, his disease is emerging. This has led to the development of the new "specialty" of psychosomatic medicine to consider the interrelationship of mind and body in human clinical functioning. As noted by Levi (1967, p. 17), "in psychosomatic medicine as much consideration is paid to the psychological as to the somatic factors, to the mind as to the body, both when assessing the cause of the disease, establishing a diagnosis and selecting suitable treatment."

The development of comprehensive treatment procedures typically lags behind progressive philosophical and etiological concepts. Thus, until the holistic view was generally accepted, little emphasis was placed on integrating the array of specialized knowledge and findings in applied settings into holistic formulations of the patient as a person. Team approaches—first multidisciplinary and then interdisciplinary—evolved as practitioners recognized the necessity both for gathering specialized information and for integrating their findings.

THE MULTIDISCIPLINARY VERSUS
THE INTERDISCIPLINARY APPROACH IN PRINCIPLE

The competent treatment of many disorders now requires an array of knowledge and skills that no single practitioner, no matter how well trained, possesses. To provide the necessary specialized diagnostic and treatment input, multidisciplinary teams composed of specialists within a discipline and also members of various medical and nonmedical disciplines are assembled, usually by a managing physician. Typically, the requested input is given to the physician in the form of a verbal or written report to be used or not used, to be integrated or not integrated, in the diagnoses, recommendations, and treatments as he or she thinks best.

In this multidisciplinary team approach, the physician retains ultimate responsibility for the case and determines what information is needed to arrive at a diagnosis and treatment plan, what necessary information or treatment procedure is outside his or her area of expertise, and who should provide it.

The interdisciplinary team approach evolved out of the multidisciplinary approach as a better method of group process and comprehensive patient management. In an interdisciplinary approach, case managership rests neither with one person nor with one discipline, but instead rotates among team members or is determined on the basis of who seems best equipped for a particular problem at a particular time. For example, the speech pathologist might be the most appropriate case manager or case coordinator for a patient with a language problem, while the special educator might be most appropriate for a child with poor school performance. In contrast to the multidisciplinary approach, one person does not decide what disciplinary input is needed in a particular case. It is the responsibility of each disciplinary representative on the team to determine what their role in each case needs to be. Similarly, diagnosis, formulation, and treatment planning are the responsibilities of the entire team rather than of one individual. The formulation is a synthesis of the findings about manifestations and etiology into a comprehensive holistic picture which is crucial for treatment planning. Treatment is also the responsibility of team members and is carried out in recognition of the interaction among the various spheres of functioning so that, if necessary, priorities can be established. For example, a child exhibiting seizures as well as behavior, language, and motor difficulties subsequent to encephalitis may require an integrated treatment program involving the pediatrician, neurologist, speech pathologist, psychologist, physical therapist, and special educator. In a particular instance, establishing more appropriate behavior may be a prerequisite for the next stage of language and motor therapy.

The interdisciplinary approach is essential for problems and disorders that have multiple etiologies and multiple expressions. The need for an interdisciplinary approach with the developmentally disabled was recognized in the Developmental Disabilities Services and Facilities Construction Amendment of 1970 (Public Law 91–517), which specifically designated the funding of interdisciplinary training. With an interdisciplinary approach, team composition or makeup is essential if adequate comprehensiveness is to be obtained. The integrating schema of the Developmental Disabilities Cube presented in Chapter 1 indicates the interdependent systems of functioning that need to be assessed and the range of genetic and environmental etiologic factors potentially operative during various developmental periods about which some expertise is needed. However, given the skills and expertise typically associated with various disciplines, a representative interdisciplinary team might conceivably consist of a nurse, pediatrician, neurologist, physical therapist and/or occupational therapist, nutritionist, speech pathologist, audiologist, psychologist, psychiatrist, social worker, and special educator. The particular disciplinary composition of the team is not as important as assuring that the necessary expertise is represented.

Efficient organization and procedures can facilitate group process, maintain goal focus, and reduce conflict, all of which are essential for effective interdisciplinary team functioning (Thompson et al., 1976). The advent of the problem-oriented approach to patient management and recordkeeping is an excellent vehicle for such team organization (Hurst, 1971). In this system any complaints of the patient or any functional deficits that require management or diagnostic workup are considered as problems and are listed. This list is supplemented or changed as new problems emerge or as others are resolved; it serves as an index that reflects the patient's status. The foundation of the system is the compilation of a data base. The data base includes all relevant background and findings such as history, review of systems, complaints, and lab and disciplinary findings.

Use of the problem-oriented approach in a typical interdisciplinary process is as follows. The data base is initiated with an interdisciplinary intake interview conducted with the child's parents. There is a standard format to the interview which requires the interviewer to gather information

TABLE 8.1 Interdisciplinary case history interview outline

I. BIRTH HISTORY
  A. *Pregnancy:* length, condition of mother, unusual factors
  B. *Birth conditions:* mature or premature, duration of labor, weight, unusual circumstances
  C. *Conditions following birth*

II. PHYSICAL AND DEVELOPMENTAL DATA
  A. *Health history:* accidents, high fevers, other illnesses
  B. *Present health:* habits of eating and sleeping, energy and activity level, medications
  C. *Developmental history:* held head up, crawled, sat alone, walked, babbled, first words, first (2-word) sentences, language difficulties

III. SPEECH AND LANGUAGE
Parents' description of child's speech and language skills at the present time with regard to:
  A. *Sound production:* How easy is it to understand him?
  B. *Sentence construction*
    1. Sentence length
    2. Words in proper order
  C. *Grammar*
    1. Usage of pronouns
    2. Usage of plurals
    3. Usage of verb tenses
  D. *Voice quality*
    1. Nasality
    2. Hoarseness
    3. Breathiness
  E. *Rate and rhythm*
    1. Speaks too fast
    2. Speaks too slow
    3. "Stuttering" behavior
  F. *Language comprehension:* Does this child understand what is said to him?
    1. Does he follow instructions, with or without gestures?
    2. Can he answer questions appropriately?
    3. Does he relate verbally what has happened?
  G. Are the parents concerned about the child's speech and/or language skills?
  H. Are the child's speech and language skills as good as those of other children his age?
  I. What languages are spoken at home?

IV. MOTOR SKILLS
  A. Clumsiness, awkwardness, or lack of coordination and balance
  B. Ability to plan and execute skilled gross motor acts (ride a tricycle, put on clothing, etc.)

C. Abnormal types of movements, abnormal muscle tone, or orthopedic problems

D. Eye-hand coordination for fine motor tasks (using a pencil, cutting with a scissors, putting toys together, etc.)

V. NUTRITION

A. Does the child have any unusual food habits? E.g., pica, eating snacks only, eating no vegetables, etc.

B. Does the child have any difficulty in sucking, swallowing, chewing; or does he drool frequently?

C. Does the child suffer from any of the following conditions frequently: diarrhea, vomiting, constipation, colds, and fevers?

D. Is the child excessively over- or underweight, very pale? Does the child have rough, dry, or puffy skin?

VI. SOCIAL AND PERSONAL FACTORS

A. Friends

B. Sibling relationships

C. Hobbies, interests, recreational activities (toy and play activities)

D. Home and parent attitudes

E. Acceptance of responsibilities

F. Attitude toward learning problems

G. Self-care activities (degree of independence in dressing, feeding, toileting, etc.)

VII. EDUCATIONAL FACTORS

A. *Preschool education:* nursery school, kindergarten

B. *School experience:* skipped or repeated grades, moving, change of teachers

1. Teacher's report

2. Child's attitude toward school

C. *Special help*, if any, received previously

VIII. PERSONALITY CHARACTERISTICS—especially regarding

A. Anxieties

B. Fears

C. Dependence

D. Mood swings

E. Aggression tantrums

F. Reliability

G. Enuresis

IX. IMPRESSIONS

X. RECOMMENDATIONS

about history and current functioning in various areas. An example of the standard intake format is presented in Table 8.1. The intake interview can be conducted by any member of the team and can be augmented by brief developmental screening of the child such as the Denver Developmental Screening Test. The intake is designed to collect sufficient information in

271

various areas to enable the determination to be made upon presentation to the entire team of what specific problems exist.

After a comprehensive problem list is arrived at by consensus, the team decides in relation to each problem listed what additional information is necessary to arrive at a diagnosis, formulation, and treatment plan. What is needed is again arrived at by discussion and consensus. A common decision at this point is to increase the data base through specific assessment procedures such as an assessment of general intellectual functioning or expressive language skills and/or by requesting reports from the family physician, school, or hospital. Each person on the team is responsible for indicating for which particular problems and in what way their expertise is needed. A case coordinator or manager is then designated, usually on the basis of who is likely to be most involved with the child and family in light of their particular problems. If it does not appear that one particular team member will be more involved than others, a case coordinator is assigned on a rotating basis. The case coordinator's main responsibilities are to coordinate the gathering of data and the completion of the evaluations indicated by the team as necessary and to serve as the primary contact person for the family. Each team member utilizes assessment procedures commensurate with their training and specific to the problem being evaluated and writes a report of the findings that becomes part of the data base. Upon completion of the disciplinary evaluations, the team reconvenes, the findings are presented by the case coordinator and discussed by all team members. A diagnosis, formulation, and treatment plan that specifies goals and who is to be involved is arrived at by the team through consensus. Several members of the team, again usually based on who can best explain aspects of the findings and treatment plan, join the case coordinator for an interpretive session with the family.

The mechanics of the system have been discussed, but to be really effective the team members must function well as a group with mutual respect for each other. It is essential that team members have initially, or soon develop, an appreciation of the interrelationship of findings from their specialty with those of others and that they be able to integrate or synthesize findings into a meaningful whole. This requires personnel who have broad experience with the management and diagnosis of the particular disorder in question as well as a high degree of expertise within their own discipline. Furthermore, an understanding of, and respect for, the expertise and techniques of other professionals is necessary. Members must be open and flexible and have a good sense of their own personal and disciplinary identity and ability to contribute. Team functioning can be difficult because of the demands for information and explanation which can be placed on each other by team members. Furthermore, the common goal of arriving at an understanding, formulation, and treatment plan puts stress on team members over and above that occurring in a multidisciplinary approach.

If members are open, flexible, and have respect for each other, conflicts of opinion do not occur so frequently as one might anticipate, given the state of the art and science with most applied disciplines. Most often questions clearly fall within the domain of one team member. Conflicts can be anticipated if there is substantial overlapping of expertise or there are two members from the same discipline but with different theoretical orientations. Team functioning will not be disrupted, however, if team members can learn to disagree without being disagreeable and have sufficient ego strength to tolerate someone disagreeing with them. If an essential disagreement about diagnosis or treatment persists, it is usually possible to get an additional opinion or to agree upon a course of action to be monitored and altered if necessary.

The interdisciplinary approach is stimulating and challenging and will undoubtedly become increasingly recognized as necessary for competent management of many disorders. To be sure, many professionals of all disciplines are called upon to have a change of attitude and to rise above historical territorial battles with other disciplines. To provide competent patient management and service requires functioning collaboratively with other professionals in a group where authority and leadership varies and where several people will form relationships with a child and his or her family. Above all, it takes a degree of maturity, openness, and confidence in one's own competencies, which relates more to what they can do and contribute in a specific situation than to their disciplinary affiliations. Education and training programs within all the applied disciplines are likely to foster this attitude with their trainees of the future and to enable, it is hoped, the more widespread acceptance and utilization of the interdisciplinary approach.

THE INTERDISCIPLINARY APPROACH IN PRACTICE

In support of our proselytizing efforts, we would like to conclude by presenting in detail four cases that reflect the various disorders comprising the area of developmental disabilities and also the interdisciplinary approach to diagnosis and treatment.

CASE A.E.

The first case is that of a 6-year-5-month-old boy who was referred to the Duke Developmental Evaluation Center (DEC) by his teacher and parents. His teacher was concerned about his immaturity, short attention span, difficulties in learning to read and write, and clumsiness. The parents were primarily concerned about his behavior in that they had difficulty in getting him to respond to requests and to do things for himself. They believed that he was silly and "obnoxious to people." They managed his behavior by shouting at him a great deal, which in turn made them feel guilty. The following information was recorded during the intake process.

Parent Intake

BIRTH HISTORY   Mother was 19 years old at the time she became pregnant with A.E.; she and father married when she was 5 months pregnant. At 2 to 3 months into the pregnancy, mother became ill with the Hong Kong flu for about 2 to 3 weeks. Otherwise, the pregnancy was uneventful and full term. Labor lasted approximately 5 hours. At birth, A.E. was cyanotic and weighed 6 lb 4 oz. The parents were not sure how long it took to revive him. No additional complications occurred and both mother and child left hospital after a few days.

PHYSICAL AND DEVELOPMENTAL DATA   Parents unable to recall early developmental milestones. However, they believe the milestones were normal. Their only concern is that beginning at about 18 months of age, A.E. seemed more active than other children. Broke many toys; no respect for certain activities being off limits. They see him as more impulsive than other children, but as cognizant of danger. Parents wonder if perhaps they are not firm enough with him but also indicate they are unsure how firm they should be. They question whether he can understand what he is told to do and thus wonder what to expect of him. They described A.E.'s health as generally good, except for scarlet fever at 4 years 6 months of age.

SPEECH AND LANGUAGE   Again, parents unable to be specific about developmental milestones in this area. They think A.E. spoke his first words at about 18 months of age. Although they have perceived no problems with speech and language development, they reported that he has some immature speech sounds: substitutions such as *w* for *l*, and difficulties with the *th* sound. He is receiving speech therapy at school. Concerning his receptive language, the parents report that A.E. is able to follow simple directions, but not a string of directions.

MOTOR SKILLS   Although the teacher is concerned about A.E.'s coordination, the parents are not particularly concerned about this area of functioning. They reported he falls down more than other children and still stumbles a great deal. Until recently he was not able to tie his shoes or recognize which shoe he should put on each foot. Father believes this was a ruse so his parents would do it for him. One day, father became very angry, forcing A.E. to learn to tie his shoes in one session. Dressing still a major issue in the home because A.E. dresses very slowly and awkwardly.

SOCIAL AND PERSONAL FACTORS   The parents have always perceived A.E. as a behavioral problem. In addition to the difficulties centering around dressing, mealtimes have always been a struggle. As a young child, he was a picky eater; now he eats a great deal. He is perceived as disrupting the dinner hour by talking too much. A.E. has always been a restless sleeper and although he goes to bed at 7:30 P.M. and sleeps through the night, he still looks tired in the morning, with puffiness around his eyes. In terms of play, A.E. reportedly likes to climb, ride his bicycle, and play in the sand. He generally leads other children in play and reportedly fights too much with his 3-year-old sister. The parents did not spend much time playing with him when he was a young child. Now when father tries to engage him in games, A.E. becomes very nervous and anxious. In competitive activities, he tends to give up very easily. Shouting and spanking are the typical forms of discipline, and the parents feel guilty about the amount of shouting that goes on in the home. Mother is making a real effort to attempt to remain calm, but she is very frustrated about managing A.E.'s behavior. Reportedly, A.E. believes that his parents are angry with him too often and sometimes asks them: "Why don't you talk to me? Why are you angry all the time?" And he says, "Nobody even wants me around."

EDUCATIONAL FACTORS   A.E. first attended preschool when he was 3 years 6 months of age. When he entered kindergarten, his teacher believed that he was overactive and immature. The concerns of his first-grade teacher about the possibility of a learning disability prompted this referral.

FAMILY ASSESSMENT   Mother indicated that she was very depressed during her pregnancy with A.E. and that in general the first years of their marriage were very stressful. Mother perceives the marriage as having sufficient problems to warrant marriage counseling, but father believes their difficulties are typical of most marriages. Mother reports she would like to go to work in order to have a change of pace from the responsibilities at home. She blames father for not allowing her to do this and blames him for not understanding her problems with A.E. in the home. With a great deal of emotion, mother admits that both she and father have accused A.E. of being dumb and called him other derogatory names about which they feel a great deal of guilt. Both parents indicate they had difficulties themselves in school. Father had particular trouble with reading and grammar. He failed the third grade twice owing to illness and learning difficulties; failed the sixth grade once. He dropped out of high school at age 16 but is working at present as a researcher with an industrial firm.

Child Intake

BEHAVIORAL OBSERVATIONS   Throughout the session A.E. was immature, wiggly, and talkative. He exhibited both manipulative and impulsive behavior but responded well to ignoring and gentle physical restraint. At the beginning of the evaluation, he announced that he is "a dumb cluck"; at times he called the examiner names such as "goofy girl."

GROSS MOTOR SKILLS   No abnormalities of gait were noted. He jumped awkwardly and could not hop and refused to skip. He threw a ball with two hands, with poorly timed release; caught it with a body catch. He became so excited by the game of catch that his body trembled; he giggled and squealed like a much younger child.

FINE MOTOR SKILLS   A.E.'s pencil grasp is not good; he held it 2 to 3 inches back from the tip in his right hand with thumb and forefinger only. When asked how to hold a pencil, however, he approximated a dynamic tripod with correct finger placement on the pencil. He could not consistently identify left and right on himself and reported that sometimes he writes with his left hand.

VISUAL MOTOR INTEGRATION   On the Beery Test of Visual Motor Integration, A.E. achieved an age equivalency of 4 years 9 months, evidencing 1 year 6 months delay in this area. He disliked the task, drawing the figures quickly and carelessly. On the draw-a-man task, his drawing ranked in the 34th percentile for children his age. Based on the Harris Standards for Completeness of Detail, his drawing—undetailed and immature—approximate that expected of about a five-year-old. Yet he seemed to enjoy this task and drew in a fairly careful and controlled manner.

The session ended with administration of the Slosson Intelligence Scale on which A.E. obtained a mental age of 5 years 4 months, yielding an intelligence quotient of 83. Throughout the evaluation, he was noted to have difficulty with visual and auditory memory.

This intake information was presented at initial team staffing and the following list of problems and plans were derived:

Problems	*Plans*
1. Learning difficulties involving reading and math as well as visual motor integration and auditory and visual memory.	1. Increase data base (IDB) with special education and speech and language evaluations
2. Behavioral difficulties including immaturity, manipulativeness, high activity level, short attention span, and difficulty following directions	2. IDB with a psychological and pediatric evaluations
3. Low self-esteem	3. IDB with psychological evaluation
4. Fine and gross motor difficulties	4. IDB with a physical therapy evaluation
5. Conflict-ridden family interactions	5. IDB with a family assessment

The plans for increasing the data base were undertaken and summaries of the results are as follows:

SPECIAL EDUCATION EVALUATION   At the time of this evaluation, A.E. is three-fourths of the way through the first grade, yielding a grade equivalency of 1.7. His general fund of information is on the 2.2 grade level, with math being on the 1.3 grade level. His spelling grade level is 1.3, but his word identification is characterized by correct initial and final consonants and incorrect medial sounds, for example, *jap* for *jump*, *black* for *book*, *rate* for *rapid*. During the session, he made some errors owing to transpositions of sequences, reversals, and inversions; for example, *four* for *of*, *brown* for *down*. He also demonstrated poor auditory-blending skills and evidenced reversals, inversions, and transpositions in his visual discriminations and visual memory tasks. Throughout the evaluation his behavior was exceptionally active and distractible, with extremely short attention span. Although his overall educational skills are generally on an early first-grade level, he demonstrates substantial problems in sequencing, reversals, and inversions; poor fine motor control; poor auditory blending; and weak auditory and visual memory. He is strong in the area of auditory discrimination and general fund of information.

SPEECH AND LANGUAGE EVALUATION   This evaluation was scheduled primarily to learn more information about his difficulties in visual and auditory memory and reading. He was extremely distractible and manipulative throughout the evaluation, but the results suggest that he is not having primary language difficulties. However, the results also indicate substantial difficulties in auditory and visual memory and visual closure, and it is felt that these probably contribute significantly to A.E.'s problems in reading. In addition, he has a tendency to ramble off the subject and tends to lack coherency, which reduces his overall communicative effectiveness.

PSYCHOLOGICAL EVALUATION   A.E. was difficult to work with for a number of reasons. He was quite distractible and manipulative and demonstrated a severe lack of confidence in his own capabilities, along with a lack of persistence and poor frustration tolerance. He also engaged in some avoidance behaviors, and it was difficult to establish appropriate rapport, but he did remain pleasant and friendly. On the WISC–R, he obtained a verbal-scale IQ of 92, a performance-scale IQ of 81, and a full-scale IQ of 85. Verbally, he is functioning within the average range, and nonverbally and overall, within the dull normal range. These scores are likely to be an underestimation of his capabilities because of the influence of his behavior on the obtained scores. However, he shows considerable difficulty in performing perceptual motor tasks such as those requiring the synthesis of parts into meaningful wholes and the analysis of wholes into their subsequent parts. These tasks were difficult for him and he became noticeably frustrated with them. He demonstrates relative strength in comprehension and in visual discrimination tasks involving identification of essential missing parts and objects. Auditory rote memory is notably weak. An important theme of his projective stories is that of rejection. Additional themes in his stories are those of a search for nurturance and of a general sadness. He pointed out that people think he is stupid and that he feels this way at times. A.E. has marked difficulty with concepts and tends to miss the essential aspects of questions posed to him. He is immature in his response to frustration and seems to look toward external controls for his behavior. He has difficulty in forming abstractions and hierarchies and exhibits a pattern of difficulties essentially consistent with that of minimal brain dysfunction and hyperactivity. Additionally, he reveals a poor self-concept and feelings of inadequacy and is experiencing parental rejection. Throughout the session, he had a difficult time organizing his thoughts and controlling his behavior, but he remained a friendly youngster who was sensitive and exhibited unmet needs for nurturance.

PEDIATRIC EVALUATION   A.E. was cooperative during the evaluation. His height and weight are in the 60th percentile and blood pressure is 98/60. Sensory part of neurological exam was normal. On motor part, presence of choreiform and associative movements considered abnormal.

PHYSICAL THERAPY EVALUATION   A.E. was extremely active throughout the testing and was in constant motion even while sitting. Responded well to ignoring and to positive reinforcing. In spite of his difficulty in being evaluated, he is an extremely likeable child. His visual perception is age appropriate but he has difficulty in the area of fine motor control. These difficulties are especially discernible in spatial relations and directionality. In terms of gross motor functioning, he demonstrates considerable scatter, and thus it is difficult to assign an appropriate age level, but at most he is at approximately the 50-month level. It is believed that his difficulties of hyperactivity and poor fine motor and gross motor control are indicative of minimal brain dysfunction.

FAMILY ASSESSMENT   Both mother and father have experienced emotional deprivation in their childhood. Mother was raised in an orphanage, and father did not seem to have a very satisfying relationship with either of his parents. The home environment appears to be a very stressful one. During the interview, mother was depressed and very anxious; she views

A.E.'s problem as primarily a family problem. There is a considerable amount of open hostility between mother and father and also considerable anger directed toward A.E. When she is angry, mother tends to scream while father tends to withdraw. A.E.'s 3-year-old sister was described as more cooperative, obedient, and sensitive. The parents believe that she avoids difficulties because she has observed A.E.'s behavior and the resulting consequences. Both parents are motivated toward seeking help as evidenced by mother's plans to attend Parents Anonymous and father's acknowledgement that he is interested in working on changing the bad interactional patterns at home. Both perceive the relationship between their current behavioral patterns and that of their backgrounds, but they do not know how to break these patterns.

These findings were presented at a second team staffing and the following formulation was reached:

Formulation

A.E. is a 6-year-6-month-old white male of dull normal to normal intelligence who is evidencing signs of hyperactivity compounded by emotional disturbance. His emotional problems, which appear to be part of a pathological family situation, are characterized by depression, feelings of parental rejection, and low self-esteem. His academic skills are on an early first-grade level. Learning difficulties are characterized by poor fine motor control, weak auditory and visual memory, sequencing errors, difficulty with concept formation, and difficulty in forming abstractions and hierarchies. There is considerable marital conflict and parental difficulty in managing A.E.'s behavior adequately and appropriately.

Recommendations

Because of the consistent impression of hyperactivity, a trial of Ritalin is warranted for A.E. In addition, therapy for the parents and play therapy for A.E. to work on his feelings of rejection and inadequacy is recommended. Furthermore, educational programming for learning disabilities should be discussed with A.E.'s teacher.

Shortly after the interpretive session with the parents, A.E. was begun on 5 mg of Ritalin in the morning, and later this was increased to 10 mg every morning. A followup conference two weeks later indicated that within 7 to 10 days both the teacher at school and the parents at home noticed a marked improvement in his behavior in that A.E. was able to concentrate better and was less active at home. A reevaluation of the medication 6 months later indicated that he was continuing to do well. This evaluation was done after he had begun school the year subsequent to his initial evaluation, and he was doing better than he had done the previous year. In discussing his medication, A.E. said "I feel crazy without the medication," and "If I don't take it, I need help." His dosage was still 10 mg per day, and his physical examination was normal with height and weight in the 60th percentile. His blood pressure was 90/50. Thus, there were no difficulties with growth noted at this time, and in summary he was felt to be doing well on Ritalin. A.E. also responded well to the play therapy sessions and was able to begin to resolve some of his feelings of inadequacy and feelings of rejection. In addition, the parents made gains in marital therapy. After being separated for a while, they were able to respond to each other and to A.E. in a more appropriate and nurturing way.

One of the most striking aspects of this case is the unanimity with which the team members, representing various disciplines, arrived at the determination of the presence of a hyperactive behavior disorder. Also striking is the dramatic effect that instituting medication had on A.E.'s hyperactive behavior. This case is a good example of medication allowing a child to be more amenable to other types of intervention including educational programming and psychotherapy. Furthermore, because his behavior was altered somewhat by the medication, his parents were provided with an opportunity to begin to change their pattern of interacting with him. Previously, with family tension so high, there was little tolerance for the particular pattern of A.E.'s distractible and annoying behaviors. Consequently, he frequently was overtly rejected, criticized, and punished by his parents, and they felt particularly guilty about it. This led them to perceive A.E. as a particularly unrewarding child. The change in his behavior, or "stimulus value," was helpful because it provided an opportunity to elicit better, more appropriate behaviors from the parents. In addition, the marital therapy was helpful in resolving some of the family tension and conflicts, which contributed to their overall irritability and lack of tolerance. At this time, a full year after the initial evaluation, the therapy with A.E. and his parents continues as does the overall progress of the family.

CASE G.

This case is that of a 21-month-old youngster referred to the Duke DEC by her pediatrician for evaluation of developmental delay subsequent to pneumococcal meningitis, which she contacted at 4 months of age. The parents were particularly concerned that she was slow to walk. The following intake data were obtained.

Parent Intake

BIRTH HISTORY   G. was the product of a normal pregnancy and delivery with a birth weight of 8 lb 2.5 oz.

PHYSICAL AND DEVELOPMENTAL DATA   According to the mother, G. smiled at 2 months, was reaching and even sitting at 4 months. When she was 4.5 months old, she had a febrile illness that lasted several days and culminated in the development of right-sided seizures. The following information was obtained upon review of the hospital chart. A lumbar puncture was performed and revealed cloudy fluid with 150 white cells, 30% polymorphonuclear leukocytes, and 70% lymphocytes. Gram stain revealed gram positive diplococci (presumptive evidence for pneumococci), and she was begun on Ampicillin intravenously and Kanamycin intramuscularly. When the blood and spinal fluid cultures later grew out pneumococci, therapy was changed to high doseage intravenous penicillin. Her early hospital course was complicated by seizures and irritability alternating with dullness. She developed a right pareitotemporal subdural effusion as evidenced by transillumination, but her head circumference did not change and the effusion was not tapped. Her subsequent course was one of gradual improvement, and she was discharged on phenobarbital after two weeks of hospitalization. After discharge, mother noted G. seemed to have "forgotten the things she had been able to do," such as grasp, smile, and sit up. She began to reachieve these milestones between 5 to 6 months of age. Subsequently, her motor milestones (crawling and standing) were delayed, and she was just beginning to walk when she first visited the Duke DEC.

SPEECH AND LANGUAGE   Mother feels G.'s speech and language skills are age appropriate, though there is some concern that she may have suffered "brain damage" as a result of the meningitis.

MOTOR SKILLS   This is the area of development of most concern as the parents are very aware of her delay in standing alone and walking and of her walking on her tiptoes.

NUTRITION   No problem noted by the parents.

SOCIAL AND PERSONAL FACTORS   No problems noted by the parents.

EDUCATIONAL FACTORS   G. has been attending a day-care center since both parents work.

CHILD INTAKE   Results of the Denver Developmental Screening Test when G. was 21 months of age revealed three delays in the gross motor section—standing alone well, walking alone well, and stooping to recover. With the mother as informant, G. obtained a social maturity age of 20 months on the Vineland Social Maturity Scale.

The intake data were presented at the initial interdisciplinary team staffing and the following problems and plans were listed.

Problems	Plans
1. Sequelae of pneumococcal meningitis a. Seizure disorder b. Gross motor delay 2. Parents' understanding of current level of functioning	1. Increase data base (IDB) with pediatric, neurological, and physical therapy evaluations 2. IDB with audiology, speech and language, and psychological evaluations; parent interviews; and observation of parent-child interactions

The plans for increasing the data base were undertaken and summaries of the results are as follows:

PEDIATRIC EVALUATION   The examination was entirely normal except for the evidence of a right spastic hemiparesis. She remained alert and attentive, though a bit tired. She drags her right foot and circumducts the right leg when she walks; there is tightness of the right heel cord. The right hand is used primarily as a helping hand and is clumsy in fine motor tasks. Deep tendon reflexes are increased on the right.

NEUROLOGICAL EVALUATION   Head circumference 49 cm (within normal limits). The positive findings are an intermittent right lateral rectus palsy, increased tone in the right lower extremity, with the right foot held in mild equinus and internal rotation, and the right heel cord contracted, but not fixed. Mental status reveals an alert, curious, and active youngster. Sensory examination was intact for primary modalities. She has a wide-based unsteady gait with circumduction of the right foot.

PHYSICAL THERAPY EVALUATION   On the Bayley Gross Motor Test, G. scored in the 18 to 23 month range. She has difficulty in standing on her right leg. She wears straight last shoes because of metatarsus adductus. She goes up and down stairs by crawling. On her right hand, she has a lateral pincer, whereas, on the left a precise one. G. was able to stack seven blocks.

AUDIOLOGY EVALUATION   G.'s hearing in the left ear is within normal limits for speech frequency. G. appears to have loss in the right ear, but the degree could not be determined because she became fatigued and conditioning was lost before evaluation was completed. Further evaluation is necessary.

SPEECH AND LANGUAGE EVALUATION   G. demonstrated a scattering of age equivalents in the skills measured. In receptive language, she is able to decode one-step commands with 3 critical elements (23-month level) but cannot decode single-noun labels (12–15-month-level). She is attentive to voice inflection and gesture. Expressive language testing indicates that good spontaneous imitations cannot be elicited on command. Observation of her at play and in communication with her mother reveals that she does use single noun and noun-verb combinations to communicate. All these words are intelligible with contextual cues. She is also able to reproduce the inflection pattern in nursery rhyme songs. It was recommended that language stimulation at home be centered on noun-verb labels.

PSYCHOLOGICAL EVALUATION   G. was very pleasant, happy-appearing, and generally cooperative throughout the 30-minute evaluation. She was observed to use her left hand chiefly and to have a very awkward grasp. On the Bayley Mental Scale, she passed all items through the 17.6-month level and a scattering of items up to the 23-month level. Expressive language skills are her lowest area, though she reportedly talks more outside the testing situation. She imitates words well. Overall performance on the Bayley appears to be in the 18 to 20-month range, which is suggestive of borderline developmental delay. The home situation is quite stable, with father actively participating in childrearing responsibilities. Although father does not verbalize his feelings, he watches G.'s progress closely and demonstrates quiet concern, according to mother's report.

PARENT-CHILD INTERACTION AND PARENT INTERVIEWS AT HOME   During the parent-child interaction session, it was observed that mother initiated play and talked with G. G. appears to be an active and happy child and she enjoyed the loud noises she made by hitting the table with toys. Her attention span is short but she imitates and follows instruction well. The relationship between mother and G. is thought to be very good. However, some tendency toward overindulgence and some reluctance to discipline G. was noted.

At a staff meeting subsequent to the completion of all the evaluations, the above findings were reported and discussed and a formulation and recommendations were made.

Formulation

This 21-month-old youngster is demonstrating borderline developmental delay. Her seizure disorder is resolved, but mild right spastic hemiparesis involving the leg more than the arm is present with intermittent palsy of the right VI nerve. It is not possible to be conclusive about her hearing and further evaluations need to be conducted.

Recommendations

The following recommendations are made: (1) audiology evaluation; (2) stretching exercises of right heel cord as outlined to mother; (3) language stimulation; and (4) reevaluation in approximately 6 months. The following month the audiology evaluation was completed, and G. was found to be exhibiting a severe sensorineural loss in her right ear, with hearing in the left ear being within normal limits.

First Reevaluation

G. was reevaluated when she was 2 years 4 months of age (28 months). She obtained an overall mental age of approximately 2 years on the Stanford-Binet. However, on the Bayley Mental Scale, she passed nonverbal items at the 30-month level, indicating low average functioning, but passed verbal items only at the 20 to 31-month level, indicating borderline functioning. The physical therapy evaluation revealed improvement in overall motor development from the 18-month level at the last evaluation to the 23-month level at present. She demonstrated normal function on the right arm and no tightness of the right heel cord. The impression was that her hemiplegia was no longer noticeable. She had made some progress in expressive language but very little in receptive language. Recommendations were made to continue the language and motor stimulation programs at home. Discipline was apparently becoming a concern, and recommendations regarding consistency in this area were made.

Second Reevaluation

When she was 4 years 5 months of age, G. went through a screening evaluation prior to her entering into kindergarten. She obtained an overall general cognitive index of 68 on the McCarthy Scales of Children's Abilities, which was approximately 2 standard deviations below the mean. She continues to demonstrate both fine and gross motor difficulties. It was decided that another reevaluation at the Duke DEC would be useful in assisting her parents and teachers in planning appropriate activities for her.

An interview was scheduled with mother to discuss development and concerns since the time of her last evaluation, which occurred about 2 years before. Mother's current concerns are that G. is clumsy, falls frequently, engages in dangerous activities, and does not watch where she is going. A further maternal concern is that she is very active and indulges in a fair amount of fighting, yelling, and screaming with her five-year-old male cousin. Mother sees difficulty in the fact that it's hard to settle G. down and she is resistant to parental authority. Mother perceives these problems as affecting G.'s ability to learn in nursery school, which she had been attending for about one year. G. also has an imaginary friend on whom she blames the bad things that happen, a kind of response that mother described as "nerve wracking," at times.

In terms of her behavior, mother thinks that G. understands but insists on doing things her way anyway. Concerning bedtime, mother reports that G. will go to sleep about 8:30 P.M. and sleep until 1 A.M. and then get into bed with her parents, maintaining that she is afraid or cold. G. becomes quite agitated if someone leaves the house in the evening; thus they must prepare her all day if they are to go out in the evening. Reportedly, she is independent in dressing, but she puts things on backwards. She cannot tie her shoes. She enjoys watching TV, and watches all the educational TV programs until 7:00 P.M. without increased activity level. On shopping trips, she presents a particular problem to the mother because she likes to feel and touch everything, and she is quite loud. When mother tells her "no," she starts screaming, and mother prefers to avoid taking her shopping.

At school, mother thinks that G. gets along fine with the teacher and peers, and she appears happy and well adjusted. She is having trouble learning to write, which mother attributes to the fact that she's left-handed. Mother is very impressed by the child's "great memory" and claims that she is able to remember everyone's part in the Christmas play.

At the subsequent DEC staffing, the problem list and plans were updated.

Problems	*Plans*
1. Sequelae pneumococcal meningitis: right hemiplegia resolving; speech and language delays; profound hearing loss on the right	1. IDB with a pediatric, speech and language, audiology, and special education evaluations
2. Parents' assessment of the child-capabilities and judgment and their need for help with behavior management	2. IDB with a family assessment interview

The results in summary form of these additional evalutions were as follows:

PEDIATRIC EVALUATION   G.'s height is 107 cm (65th percentile) and her weight is 20.2 kg (80th percentile). Her vision on the right is 15/30 and on the left, 10/30. The examination was remarkable because of G.'s silence. She was cooperative but clumsy in dressing and undressing. The regular physical examination was within normal limits. She is left-handed. When walking on her toes, there is some posturing of the right upper extremity but this is not sustained. Her gait on close examination appears to be normal. There seems to be no increase in tone, no clonus, and no Babinski's reflex.

SPEECH AND LANGUAGE EVALUATION   The results suggest language disorder. There was a significant gap of over 1 year of measured functioning between tests results on verbally loaded tasks and on performance tasks (i.e., those that attempt to measure performance without using verbal instructions or requiring a verbal response). Receptive language skills are judged to be at the early 3-year level on verbal and at the 4-year level on nonverbal tasks. There is no real difference between receptive and expressive language levels, though expressively G.'s language is marked by formulation problems affecting the length, complexity, syntactic structure, and meaning of her productions.

SPECIAL EDUCATION EVALUATION   G. is currently attending preschool. Her fine motor skills are on a 3-year level, and her visual motor integration skills are on a 4-year-1-month level. G. displays average to above-average skills in the areas of visual discrimination and matching, motor planning and organizing (nonpaper diagonal pencil tasks), and visual memory. Auditory memory is weak. G. seems to have adequate academic readiness skills for kindergarten except in the area of prewriting. G. continues to demonstrate normal hearing on the left and a profound sensorineural hearing loss on the right.

FAMILY ASSESSMENT   Mother responds that she and her husband have difficulty knowing how to handle G.'s recently developed imaginary friend. Mother also acknowledges some guilt feelings regarding G.'s earlier medical problems and says that she does not want to be responsible for anything happening to G. She describes herself as a "nervous" mother and is concerned that she not "sabotage" G.'s growth. These feelings have led to overprotection and overindulgence of G., but mother believes she is improving in this area. Sleeping and expression of anger are additional problem areas. Until about a year ago, G. had been sleeping in her own room. Since the family moved into their present house, G. has been sleeping with mother and father. There is lack of agreement between mother and father about how to handle this problem. The parents are also having difficulty helping G. express her angry feelings appropriately.

Formulation

G. is a 4-year-5-month-old youngster who contacted pneumoccal meningitis at 4 months of age and has a resolving right hemiparesis. She continues to demonstrate a discrepancy between her verbal and nonverbal functioning. Nonverbally, she is functioning at an age-appropriate level but is almost 1 year 6 months behind age level on verbal tasks. Behavior problems are seen as a response to her language disorder. Although visual motor integration is at an age-appropriate level, there are indications of clumsiness in fine motor tasks and self-help skills.

Recommendations

The following recommendations were made: (1) language therapy and subsequent placement in a language-based classroom; (2) counseling for the parents in terms of their expectations and of ways to deal more appropriately with her behavior; (3) opportunities for G. to work on self-help both at home and at the day-care center (if G. continues to have difficulty in this area, consider a physical therapy and/or occupational therapy evaluation); (4) recommendations to the current nursery situation about programming.

This case demonstrates the changing manifestations of functioning over the course of three years. The initial primary sequelae of pneumoccal meningitis were a mild right spastic hemiparesis and severe hearing loss on the right side. Gradually the hemiparesis resolved, and the speech and language delays became evident. This continued to be demonstrated while her weaknesses in fine motor functioning and parental difficulties with behavior management emerged. The amount of attention she received was not only useful in remediating her motor problems but allowed for early intervention in her language and fine motor difficulties through specialized education programs and placement at the kindergarten level. It is likely that her progress will need to be monitored continually and her programs retuned in order to maximize her functioning. The parents play an essential role not only in the various remediation efforts but also in day-to-day behavior management in the context of their capabilities and their perceptions of difficulties presented by G.

CASE R.

The following case is that of a 7-year-11-month-old girl who was referred to the Duke DEC by her teacher because of a "drastic" change in her behavior. She had always been active, but about 2 months previously, she began going to school, pulling a hood over her head, and not doing anything all day long. The following data base was obtained during the intake interviews with mother and child and from a review of her medical record.

Parent Intake

BIRTH HISTORY   R. was the 3,200-gram product of a 42-week gestation in a 19-year-old mother. Breathing and crying times were immediate. There were no complications, and mother and baby left the hospital a few days later.

PHYSICAL AND DEVELOPMENTAL DATA   Mother reported that R. walked at less than 1 year of age. She is described as well coordinated but mother maintains that her writing is "terrible." R. was reportedly slow in talking and was 18 months of age before she said single words. Currently, the only perceived difficulty in this area is some reluctance to talk in groups. R.'s general health has been good apart from recurrent urinary tract infections since 5 years of age. She had been followed in the Urology Clinic and had been found to have an ectopic orifice of the left ureter, visicourethral reflux on the left, and a normal intravenous pyelogram. She underwent corrective surgery during the summer of 1977 and at the time of the intake was being maintained on Gantrisin.

SOCIAL AND PERSONAL FACTORS   Since R. was born, her father has rarely been at home. Parents were separated when R. was 2 years old; and mother, R., and her older sister and brother went to live with the maternal grandparents. Soon thereafter, the maternal grandfather was hospitalized and died. It was during this time that R. was very dependent upon mother and afraid to leave her. She was able to dress and feed herself. When R. was 4 years old, mother began working full time and R. attended nursery school. The initial separation difficulty gradually improved. When R. was 6 years old, her parents reunited.

Mother is currently concerned about her husband's bad temper and wonders if this is interfering with R.'s learning. In addition, mother reports being ill tempered recently because of financial problems and ceasing to smoke. She disciplines R. by sending her to bed early.

Mother reported that R. gets along fairly well with other children at school. However, this past year R. complained that children were calling her "stupid" and "dummy"; she was also being teased about wetting her pants owing to her urinary tract difficulties. At home, she is irresponsible about her household chores, refusing to do them unless someone stands over her. Mother wonders if some of her lack of performance in school may be related to this irresponsible attitude.

EDUCATIONAL FACTORS   When R. went to kindergarten, she was able to ride the bus back and forth without mother. However, mother indicates that she had to force R. to go until the end of the year when R. just resigned herself to attending school. In the first grade, she received some special reading help. This year in the second grade she sees the special reading teacher three times a week. Mother reports being told that R. has a learning disability but is coming to the DEC to find out the extent of this. R. attends a learning disabilities resource room twice a week and works on phonics. In the regular classroom, the teacher apparently makes no demands on her. Mother thinks they are too lenient with her and says, "If you give R. an inch, she'll take a mile." R. has difficulty distinguishing sounds and does not know the sounds of letters, except when they are at the beginning of the word. Mother is concerned about how to handle the schoolwork situation. Mother perceives R. as having a defeatist attitude at this point.

Child Intake

On the Beery Test of Visual Motor Integration, R. obtained an age equivalency of 6 years 7 months indicating a delay of 1 year and 4 months. On the Slosson Intelligence Test, R. obtained a mental age of 8 years and an IQ of 101, placing her in the average range. She exhibits difficulty with auditory rote memory, and there is some difficulty following her train of thought. She knows her ABCs and can write them without difficulty. She reverses the letter p and the numbers 7 and 9. She exhibits associative movements of her mouth while writing. R. is able to count by ones to 70 and does math fairly well unless borrowing or carrying is necessary. On the Dolche preprimer reading list, she missed at least half of the words.

At the initial team staffing, this data base was presented and the following problems and plans were identified:

Problems	*Plans*
1. Poor school performance, especially in reading	1. IDB with school visit and special education evaluation
2. Language difficulties involving organization of expressive language	2. IDB with speech, language, and audiology evaluations
3. Ectopic ureter on left with reflux	3. Followed by family physician
4. Stressful home with marital conflict and financial difficulties	4. IDB with a parent interview
5. Personality difficulties including passivity, poor motivation, and poor self-concept	5. IDB with psychological (intellectual and personality) evaluation

Summaries of the results of these evaluations, are as follows:

SPECIAL EDUCATION EVALUATION   R. was found to be grade appropriate in her general information (2.7 grade level) and arithmetic (2.6 grade level). However, her reading recognition grade level is 1.4, and her spelling grade level is 1.7. Her reading skills consist of knowing the alphabet, giving sounds for isolated consonants, and identifying a few preprimer words. Although visual-motor integration is an area of difficulty, she displays no gross difficulties with visual perception and no visual discrimination or short-term visual memory problems were noted.

SPEECH, LANGUAGE AND AUDIOLOGY EVALUATION   The results of the audiological evaluation indicated normal hearing with excellent speech discrimination ability bilaterally. To further evaluate the relationship between her linguistic, auditory, and visual skills and her learning problems, various auditory and visual skill tests were administered along with the Boder Diagnostic Test of Developmental Dyslexia. The results show that R. is not able to depend solely on vision or on audition for her reading strategy. She is severely impaired in her ability to use both the visual and auditory modalities and in integrating them into word attack skills. She scored below the 19th percentile in visual integration and obtained an age equivalency of 2 years 7 months on visual memory. R.'s sound-symbol association skills were extremely limited being at the 4-year-10-month age level. On sound memory tasks, she functions within the 13th percentile, with an age equivalency of 5 years 2 months. On sound recognition she scored in the 33rd percentile and in the 25th percentile for sound blending, having considerable difficulty with polysyllabic words.

PARENT INTERVIEW   The home situation is now described by mother as stable, and she denies any marital difficulties. She was reluctant to discuss much other than R.'s difficulties. Mother is strong in her belief that R. has a learning disability and sees signs of this at home with her distractibility and forgetfulness. She also wonders whether R. inherited these problems, since she thinks father has a learning disability as have other members of his family.

PSYCHOLOGICAL EVALUATION   R. is functioning within the average range of intelligence with a verbal-scale IQ of 98, a performance-scale IQ of 90, and a full-scale IQ of 93 on the WISC–R. Across the verbal and nonverbal subtests, she demonstrated considerable variability, which appears to be related to her style of work rather than to variability in intellectual abilities. Her functioning is characterized by inadequate concentration and attention and by low frustration tolerance. Personality evaluation shows that these difficulties are probably related to her high level of anxiety and depressed mood. She is struggling with her feelings about intense conflicts in her family. She reports being worried about her parents' bickering, and her present relationship with father and brother is conflict ridden and anxiety producing. She occasionally expresses regressive attitudes and exhibits regressive behaviors. Her projective test stories reveal feelings of sadness and she expresses self-attitudes that accentuate her feelings of being unable to control things in her environment and her feelings of being different from others and unliked.

After these evaluations were completed, the information in them was presented and discussed at a team conference. The following formulation and recommendations were made:

Formulation
This 7-year-11-month-old female with intellectual function within the average range is demonstrating poor school performance, especially in reading, which reflects a learning disability. She has both visual and auditory channel difficulties and would be classified as being dyseidetic and dysphonetic resulting in a severe reading handicap since she cannot read either by sight or by ear. She approaches being alexic or a nonreader. In addition, she is demonstrating anxiety and depression in response to a conflictual family situation. She is poorly motivated with poor self-concept and

feelings of inadequacy exacerbated with teasing and ridicule from peers because of urinary tract problems as well as poor school performance. This constellation renders prognosis guarded, even with intensive remedial attention.

Recommendations

It is thought that R.'s anxiety and poor self-concept will be alleviated with the reduction of familial conflict, the resolution of her urinary tract problems, and the enhancement of school functioning. The parents were encouraged to seek marital counseling. Specific educational recommendations were made regarding R.'s learning disabilities involving reading but also the corresponding spelling and written expression skills. The initial remedial approach should be tactile–kinesthetic in learning letters as well as whole words. When letter forms are consistently recognized, remedial phonics reinforced by multisensory techniques can be introduced. In spelling, it will be necessary to convert R. from a dysphonetic to a phonetic speller so that her spelling will be easier to interpret. Subsequently, sound-symbol association tasks should receive remedial attention. Finally, oral language and nonlanguage skill development should be fostered to help R. compensate for her deficits in the more academic language-oriented skills.

The case of R. demonstrates several points made in the section on neurologically based learning disabilities in Chapter 6, where we examined the disorders associated with cerebral dysfunction. She exhibits some of the correlates of developmental dyslexia such as visuoperceptual deficits, language and auditory disabilities, and difficulties with intersensory integration, but she does not exhibit many neurological abnormalities. Because of her severe auditory and visual channel difficulties, she is a good example of Boder's Group III subtype of dyslexia. (See pp. 234–35.) This classification into a subgroup allows for more specific remedial recommendation as well as some appreciation of the poor prognosis likely in remediation and of the probable carryover of problems into spelling and written expression. This enables an emphasis on developing compensatory skills in order to avoid undue frustration and to provide for alternative means of achievement. Finally, the likelihood of secondary emotional or personality problems developing in conjunction with learning problems can be seen to begin as R. confronts her own inadequacy and her peers' teasing.

CASE M.

The following case is that of a 3-year-old-black girl who was brought to the Duke DEC by her parents because they were primarily concerned about her lack of language development. When asked why they thought M was not talking, the parents stated that it was possibly because of a lack of interactions with other children or to overindulgence on their part or on that of the 75-year-old lady who keeps M. during the day. In addition, mother mentioned mental retardation and wondered about the relationship between mental retardation and delayed milestones. The parents also requested guidance in handling M.'s tantrum behavior.

The following data base was obtained during the intake interview with the parents and from review of medical records.

Parent Intake

BIRTH HISTORY   M. was the 2,980 gram product of a 40-week gestation in a 37-year-old mother. Breathing and crying times were immediate. Birth condition was good. Mother's blood type was A+, M.'s was 0+, and the direct antiglobulin (Coombs) test was 1+ postive. M. was discharged at 3 days of age with a bilirubin of 8.4. She was appropriate for gestational age in height, weight, and head circumference.

PHYSICAL AND DEVELOPMENTAL DATA   Parents remember no accidents, high fevers, or illnesses except for having the chicken pox last year. She does have recurrent ear infections, which are treated by her pediatrician but is at present on no medication.

Parents do not remember milestones exactly but report that most of M.'s milestones were slow; she did not walk until 17 months. The parents maintain that M. is toilet trained, but indicate she will not go to the bathroom alone.

SPEECH AND LANGUAGE   The parents reported that M's speech and language are not predictable. She says *dada* and *mama*, but may go for a week and not say anything. She babbles, talks to herself frequently, and likes to sing. However, the lyrics are replaced with a continuous *I, I, I*. Receptively, M. doesn't seem to understand what is said to her. She does not follow directions and frequently seems to ignore them by turning her head or walking away, as if she were "in a world of her own." She responds to loud noises and to the words, *no,* and *stop*. There is little eye contact, even though the parents have tried to get M. to watch their mouths when talking. However, M. merely looks beyond them and does not focus.

MOTOR SKILLS   M. tries to ride a bicycle, but the pedals are either "too low or too high." She pushes other mobile toys with her feet (tyke-bike). Parents thought when M. first started walking, that she was awkward. Now M. seems to be doing well. She is quite active and runs all the time. In the self-help area, M. is able to put on clothing when mother gets it started for her (e.g., putting it over her head so that M. can pull it down). She is able to undress herself. Although M. has to be highly encouraged to hold a pencil or crayon, last year she had a spot on the wall that she wrote on frequently. This ceased when the spot was painted. M. plays with small toys, many of which have press-down buttons, and she can handle these well. She also plays with popbeads, pulling them apart and putting them together.

NUTRITION   M. reportedly has no difficulty eating, chewing, or swallowing. Her favorite foods, however, are oatmeal, spaghetti, and rice. Parents reiterated a number of times her preference for starches.

SOCIAL AND PERSONAL FACTORS   M. has no neighborhood friends. Parents reported that she and her 5-year-old sister seldom play interactive games except at bedtime. M. likes all musical toys and balls. She can only attend to television for commercials, which she seems to enjoy. She most frequently plays by herself. Recently, she has enjoyed having books read to her. She will not name any pictures, however. M. takes few responsibilities. She is encouraged to pick up her toys, but never does this readily. She likes to help in the kitchen. She has a "play" broom with which she helps sweep the floor. She takes a sock and attempts to clean the counter, floor, and walls.

EDUCATIONAL FACTORS   Since M. was 9 months old, she has been cared for during work hours by a 75-year-old woman and her husband. Mother says they spoil M and overindulge her. There are no other children being cared for in that home. The parents are considering placement in preschool but are concerned that the present caretakers would be "crushed." M does attend a Sunday school nursery.

PERSONALITY CHARACTERISTICS   M.'s only reported fear is of doctors and medical facilities, and she reportedly cries everytime she goes to the pediatrician. Since 6 months of age, M. has frequently had temper tantrums during which she cries and throws things. Tantrums occur when her wants or intentions are blocked. The parents overlook these tantrums. Parents seldom spank, and if they do it, it is reported to be a "light pat." However, father reports that he recently threatened M. with a yardstick, which he says he wouldn't really use on her. The parents are surprised that upon seeing the yardstick, M. trembles all over and falls to her knees because they have never discplined her harshly.

This intake information was presented at the initial team staffing and the following problems and plans were identified:

Problems	Plans
1. Developmental delay in fine and gross motor functioning	1 & 2. IDB with psychological and pediatric evalutions
2. Receptive and expressive speech delay	3. IDB—audiology evalution
3. Hearing status uncertain with recurrent infections	4. IDB with observation of parent-child interaction and visits to day-care providers and to M.'s home.
4. Concerns about the amount of stimulation M received in the day-care home	

Summary of the various evaluations and visits called for in the plans are as follows:

PSYCHOLOGICAL EVALUATION   During the evaluation, M. mouthed the ring stack. When it was removed, she became angry, paced around the house, and refused all other attempts to be diverted or consoled. M. presented as a confused frantic child who cannot order her environment. She spoke to objects more than people and communicated with babbling, crying, and grunting. Her anger and crying lasted longer and was more intense than the situation called for. It is believed that M. will not be able to function sufficiently in a formal assessment situation.

PEDIATRIC EVLUATION   During the pediatric evaluation, M. appeared to be unhappy and worried. It was noted that she lacked interaction and warmth; she was difficult to examine. On examination of her ears, M. was found to have a right otitis media with perforation. Her ears are low set and rotated posteriorly. In addition, the impression gained was that M. is demonstrating a severe communication disorder such as autism.

AUDIOLOGY EVALUATION   Initially, the examiner was unable to get accurate measures of auditory thresholds. Overall, M.'s responses were that of a much younger child and were very subtle. On reevaluation, M. sat still and attended to tasks, and her hearing was determined to be grossly within normal limits.

By report of the mother, M. has recently started speaking several short sentences (e.g., "Leave it alone"; "Don't do that"). In addition, she has engaged in more eye contact, and understands *no, stop,* and *leave it alone*. If someone knocks on the door, she says "come in," and if the phone rings, she runs and picks it up.

PARENT-CHILD INTERACTION   A parent-child interaction situation was arranged to observe M.'s behavior. From the onset, M. was quite noticeably fearful in this situation, although she was with her mother and a number of attractive toys were present. She had a very pained, distressed look on her face and seemed to be attempting to get out of the room. It was very difficult for mother to console her, and M. was quite active and agitated in her perseverative pattern of walking back and forth between mother and the door. Frequently, M. would raise her arms up in the air to signal that she wanted to be picked up, but even though she was picked up by mother, she would only remain in that position for a few moments before desiring to get down on the floor and start walking again. After several minutes of this type of interaction, father was requested to join mother and M. Similar behavior was also evidenced with both parents present, although they were gradually able to calm M. to the point that she could direct some attention to the toys at hand. The parents thought M.'s distress was due to the fact that she does not like small rooms. They acknowledged her tendency toward perseverative behavior especially walking in repetitive patterns. They pointed out that since she has been coming to the clinic, there has been a spurt in language in that she now says not only some words but sentences also. Her language usage is, however, very unpredictable and inconsistent.

VISIT TO DAY-CARE PROVIDERS   A home visit was made to M.'s day-care situation to determine the amount of stimulation M. received and to determine the child's ability to interact with the caretakers. It was evident that M. receives good care but little stimulation. M. appeared much more relaxed than she was at the clinic; however, she also showed little affect or attentiveness to those around her, except to the television, which she attended to for long periods of time.

VISIT TO M.'S HOME   A visit was made to M.'s home to observe the mother and child interact and to evaluate M.'s intellectual functioning. The family resides in a clean modern home with a big yard. Many toys were available. M. did not initiate contact with others, except for pulling mother to indicate her wants. Initially, M. was happy but later became angry and started crying and grunting. She paced the room and walked in circles. She went twice to her mother for comfort but only long enough to touch base. Mother stated this is typical of M.'s behavior.

Upon completion of these evaluations, a team conference was held and the information presented and discussed. The following formulation and recommendations were made.

Formulation

This 3-year–3-month-old black female is exhibiting marked developmental delay with specific age levels not presently able to be determined. She is cared for daily by an elderly couple who give much love but little stimulation. Her parents work well with her despite her lack of warmth and interaction. M.'s behavior and functioning are strongly indicative of autism. Her communication patterns in the broad sense of the word—including verbal, nonverbal, and interpersonal communications—are markedly impaired. She exhibits difficulty tolerating any change in stimuli and has marked perseverative behavior. It is very difficult to console M., even though she appears to be quite distressed and fearful at times.

Recommendations

To continue the evaluation of her functioning and to initiate remediation efforts, a referral was made to a university-based program for autistic children.

The family accepted this referral and 4 months later an estimate of her overall functional level was achieved when she obtained a Mental Developmental Index of 34 on the Bayley Scales of Mental Development. During a followup visit 6 months after this, M. was 4 years 2 months old, it was possible to perform the Denver Developmental Screening evaluation.

She demonstrated a number of delays in each section with her overall performance falling within the 10-to-22-month range. Thus, the recognition of the presence of severe mental retardation in addition to autism was emerging. As we discussed in the chapter on autism (pp. 95–121) this diagnosis renders the prognosis as poor even with placement in a treatment program for autistic children.

CONCLUSION

We stated at the beginning of this chapter that just as there has been an evolution in the concept of developmental disabilities, there has also been an evolution in the philosophy of assessment and treatment and in the procedure utilized to implement the philosophy. We have discussed the emergence of the interdisciplinary team approach to health care and have considered the interdisciplinary process. Although there is little in the literature on the interdisciplinary process and method, implementation of the process into procedures can be done in a various ways. We have presented the procedures utilized at the Duke DEC as an example of one method of implementation that has been effective for our patients, team, and setting.

The evolution continues through the search for more effective and efficient methods of patient care and service. The interdisciplinary team approach is an expensive form of health care. It is not an economically feasible or professionally necessary service for every disorder or problem. It is most necessary for disorders such as developmental disabilities which are multiple in etiology, manifestations, and treatment needs. Even when the service is provided for only those for whom it is necessary, there would be very few families who could afford the cost of the professional and technical time involved. For example, in our center an average of 10 hours of professional time is provided to accomplish the intake and assessment procedures. This does not include time the entire team spends in staffing or the subsequent hours expended in treatment or in helping the family receive services elsewhere in the community. As we discussed in Chapter 1, most interdisciplinary programs for the developmentally disabled are supported by federal and/or state funds.

In addition to utilizing the interdisciplinary approach only with people manifesting complex disorders, other efforts at increasing effectiveness and efficiency have focused on procedures. Initially, many interdisciplinary teams were composed of autonomous disciplinary representatives who endeavored to work together. Typically, each patient was evaluated by every disciplinary representative on the team. This procedure was interdisciplinary but inefficient. The advent of the problem-oriented approach to patient record keeping enabled a more considered decision not only about the particular disciplinary evaluations that were needed, but also about the specific problem or aspect of functioning within the purview of that discipline that needed to be assessed. For example, in a case where only articulation difficulties were present, the speech and language clinician could focus his or her evaluation time on that particular problem. The change from routine assessment by everyone on the team to a more considered involvement on the basis of what the team decided was needed helped improve efficiency.

We have modified our own procedures several times to compile a data base of sufficient comprehensiveness to enable better determination of what additional information and evaluations are necessary. For example, the case of M. differs from the other case presented because there is no child intake information. At the time we evaluated M., gathering child intake data was not part of our procedure. The team gradually recognized that they could be more judicious in deciding what additional evaluations and procedures were necessary if there was a sample of the child's performance independent of, and supplemental to, that provided in the parent intake interview.

Judiciousness in allocating resources is important not only in terms of cost efficiency for each child, but also in terms of serving as many of those requiring the service as possible. As with most service programs, those requesting and needing the service exceed the service delivery capabilities of the program. Waiting lists are long and omnipresent. However, procedures can be adopted that assure that those waiting for service are truly appropriate. Team resources can be allocated so that intake interviews can be completed within several days after the initial request for service. Gathering an initial data base prior to an extended period of time on a waiting list enables the prompt redirection elsewhere of families needing different or less comprehensive services. This procedure does result in more cases being in the system than can be cared for immediately. This in turn causes a delay before the intake data can be considered, problems listed, and additional evaluations scheduled and completed. The total time from initial contact by the family to completion of the evaluation and formation of a treatment plan is approximately 3 months in our center.

The next step in the evolution of the interdisciplinary team approach to patient care is likely to be a further blurring of disciplinary emphasis and boundaries. Already the substantial overlap in functional areas of expertise among professionals from various disciplines is evident. Assessment procedures which yield standardized estimates of functioning levels meaningful to professionals from several disciplines will likely replace those of utility to a single discipline. Currently the interdisciplinary integration comes about by each disciplinary representative conducting their assessments individually and then coming together to discuss their findings. In the future there is likely to be integration at the level of the assessment process and data gathering as well as at the formulation and treatment planning levels. For example, the speech clinician and special educator could devise one procedure drawn from their respective disciplinary perspectives to jointly assess a learning problem such as dysphonic developmental dyslexia. When integration at this level occurs, we will have reached a stage of evolution in which the interdisciplinary team approach is an unique assessment process in its own right and not merely an interrelationship of assessment procedures specific to various disciplines. What will evolve thereafter remains to be forecasted and described by others more perceptive than we.

References

Hurst, J.W. How to implement the Weed system. *Archives of Internal Medicine*, 1971, *128*, 456–62.

Levi, L. *Stress: Sources, Management, and Prevention*. New York: Liveright, 1967.

Misiak, H. *The Philosophical Roots of Scientific Psychology*. New York: Fordham University Press, 1961.

Thompson, R.J., Jr., Garret, D.J., Striffler, N., Rutins, I.A. et al. A model interdisciplinary diagnostic and treatment nursery. *Child Psychiatry and Human Development*, 1976, *6*, 224–32.

Index